The One Year Book of Devotions for Girls
2

The ONE YEAR® BOOK OF
Devotions
for
Girls
2

Tyndale House Publishers, Wheaton, Illinois

Visit Tyndale's exciting Web site at www.tyndale.com

Copyright © 2002 by Children's Bible Hour. All rights reserved.

Edited by Annette LaPlaca and Erin Keeley

Designed by Jacqueline Noe

Stories written by Ruth Andrews, Linda C. Avallone, Esther M. Bailey, Melissa M. Bamburg, B. J. Bassett, Evelyn J. Behrens, Donna Bennett, Karen S. Birt, Rhonda L. Brunea, Teddie M. Bryant, Annette S. Bury, Robert Byers, Katherine Chapman, Michael R. Chapman, Teresa B. Chiano, Elaine Childs, Karen E. Cogan, Michelle Davidson, Brenda Decker, Susan Dillon, Jennifer Dorsey, M. Tanya Ferdinandusz, Gwen D. Foust, Rose Goble, Jorlyn A. Grasser, Darlene Griffin, Jonnye R. Griffin, Alicia H. Guevara, Jan L. Hansen, Christine P. Honey, Debbie Hophof, Bob Hostetler, Cindy Huff, Vera M. Hutchcroft, Mary M. Ihlenfeldt, Ruth I. Jay, Janice M. Jones, Nance E. Keys, Phyllis I. Klomparens, Daryl B. Knauer, Jackie Krutke, Sherry L. Kuyt, Rita Lackey, VaDonna J. Leaf, Joyce R. Lee, Suzanne M. Lima, Agnes G. Livezey, Karen R. Locklear, Richard S. Maffeo, Dawn E. Maloney, Hazel W. Marett, Lorna B. Marlowe, Diana M. Martin, Eunice C. Matchett, Pat A. McCarthy, Beverly McClain, Lynda G. McCracken, Nancy I. Merical, Melissa J. Montgomery, Mary Mosher, Valerae C. Murphy, Sara L. Nelson, Violet E. Nesdoly, Joy L. Newswanger, Sharyl Noelle, Miriam K. Nowak, Ellen C. Orr, Bernard Palmer, Mary Rose Pearson, Hazel M. Percy, Patricia A. Perry, Raelene E. Phillips, Nancy K. Potter, Linda A. Prince, Jessica C. Principe, Barbara Riegier, Phyllis M. Robinson, Deana L. Rogers, Lucinda J. Rollings, Catherine Runyon, Kelly M. Schaefer, A. J. Schut, Marilyn J. Senterfitt, Steve R. Smith, Deborah Stanton (DS1), Diane Strawbridge (DS2), Taire A. Street, Heather M. Tekavec, Betty J. Thomas, Gayle J. Thorn, Harry C. Trover, Robert Truesdale, Mary Ellen Uthlaut, Toni VandenAkker, Tom VandenBerg, Charles VanderMeer, Sandy K. Vaughn, Lyndel F. Walker, Mary F. Watkins, Janet Weaver (JW1), Linda M. Weddle, Jana Weed (JW2), Barbara J. Westberg, Sue C. Wheeler, Rosemary C. Wilson, Lois A. Witmer, Cameron Wroblewski, Carolyn E. Yost, Dawn Yrene, Rose R. Zediker. (The writer's initials appear at the end of each story.)

All stories are taken from issues of *Keys for Kids,* published bimonthly by the Children's Bible Hour, P.O. Box 1, Grand Rapids, Michigan 49501.

Unless otherwise indicated, all Scripture quotations are taken from the *Holy Bible,* New Living Translation, copyright © 1996. Used by permission of Tyndale House Publishers, Inc., Wheaton, Illinois 60189. All rights reserved.

Scripture quotations marked NIV are taken from the Holy Bible, New International Version®. NIV®. Copyright © 1973, 1978, 1984 by International Bible Society. Used by permission of Zondervan Publishing House. All rights reserved.

Scripture quotations marked KJV are taken from the Holy Bible, King James Version.

Scripture quotations marked NASB are taken from the New American Standard Bible, © 1960, 1962, 1963, 1968, 1971, 1972, 1973, 1975, 1977 by The Lockman Foundation. Used by permission.

Scripture quotations marked TLB are taken from The Living Bible, copyright © 1971. Used by permission of Tyndale House Publishers, Inc., Wheaton, Illinois 60189. All rights reserved.

Scripture quotations marked ICB are taken from the Holy Bible, International Children's Bible®, New Century Version®. Copyright © 1986, 1988, 1999 by Tommy Nelson™, a division of Thomas Nelson, Inc. All rights reserved.

Library of Congress Cataloging-in-Publication Data

One year book of devotions for girls.
    p. cm.
    Includes index.
    ISBN 0-8423-3619-2 (pbk.), 0-8423-6015-8 Vol. 2
    1. Girls—Prayer-books and devotions—English.   2. Devotional calendars—Juvenile literature. [1. Prayer books and devotions.   2. Devotional calendars.]   I. Title: Devotions for girls.   II. Tyndale House Publishers.
BV4860 .054 2000
242'.62—dc21   00-029915

Printed in the United States of America

07   06   05   04   03   02
6   5   4   3   2   1

Table of Contents

The Treasure Box

Read Malachi 3:16-18

A special note from Grandma . . . a ballet ticket stub . . . a fitness award patch . . . a birthstone ring . . . a Garfield book. Grace was looking over the contents of her treasure box. Before going to bed, she often held and inspected the items and then returned them to her box. The memories they brought gave her good, warm feelings.

One evening, Grace repeated her treasure box ritual as usual. When she finally fell asleep, she dreamed of a *huge* treasure box. The beautiful box was bigger than the sky and sparkled more than diamonds. But she couldn't see what was in it.

The next morning, Grace told her mother about the dream. "Who would own such a big box?" Grace asked. "A king? Or the president?" She snapped her fingers. "God!" she exclaimed. "I think God is the only one who might possibly own a box as big as the one in my dream. But if God had a treasure box, what would he put in it? Rainbows, maybe? Or oceans? Mountains? Gold?" No answer seemed right to her.

Mom smiled. "Let's think about it today," she suggested. "Let's see if we can come up with an answer."

"Okay," Grace agreed. But her day was busy, and she soon forgot her questions. She didn't think about her dream again until that evening when she pulled out her treasure box. She went to find Mom. "Did you figure out what God would put in his treasure box?" Grace asked.

"Go look up Deuteronomy 7:6," Mom suggested (see today's memory verse). "Maybe that will help you decide."

Grace took her Bible and looked up the verse. She saw the answer to her question. *People,* she thought. *God would put the people who love him in his treasure box!* Grace smiled. She knew she was God's treasure. *JLN*

HOW ABOUT YOU?

Whether or not you have a special box for treasures, you probably do have things that are "treasures" to you. God has treasures, too. His children—those who have trusted Jesus as Savior—are his treasures. Are you included in that group? Knowing that you're a treasure to him should give you joy, comfort, and peace.

God's People Are His Treasure

MEMORIZE:
"You are a holy people, who belong to the Lord your God. Of all the people on earth, the Lord your God has chosen you to be his own special treasure." Deuteronomy 7:6

January

2

To Tell the Truth (Part 1)

Read Ephesians 4:15-16

Lori looked glum as she came in the door. "Problems, honey?" Grandma asked.

"Oh, I just get tired of Marie bossing me around!" Lori complained. "Sometimes I wish I'd never tried to make friends with her!"

"Well," Grandma said, "I remember you said you were going to be friendly to her because she was new in school and you knew God would want you to do that. She seemed very pleased to be here the day you asked her over after school."

Lori scowled. "Yeah, and that's when she decided to become 'Director of the Playground.' She's been bossing everybody ever since," Lori complained. "At first the girls tried to be nice and play her games, but they're really getting fed up with her. Most of them won't even play with her anymore."

"But you still play with her?" Grandma asked.

"I did." Lori sighed. "But when she complained today about the other girls playing silly games instead of her games, I said I kind of felt like joining them. She got mad and told me I wasn't much of a friend. I guess I wasn't very nice about it. I wanted to help her, but all I could think of was telling her how horrible she was, so I didn't say anything more."

"Hmmmm," Grandma murmured. "Well, the Bible does say to tell the truth."

"You mean I should go ahead and tell her she's mean and selfish?" Lori gasped.

Grandma smiled. "Not exactly," she said, "but go look up Ephesians 4:15."

Lori found the verse in her Bible. "But speaking the truth in love . . ." she read slowly. "Oh, I see! We have to love the person we're telling the truth to." She paused, and Grandma nodded as Lori continued, "I can try to explain to Marie why she's losing all her friends. I can help her realize that everyone wants a turn at deciding what to do. But I have to show love when I do it . . . not be grouchy like I was today."

"I think you have the idea. It still won't be easy, but I'll be praying for you," Grandma promised.

Lori silently asked the Lord to help her know the right thing to say. *EC*

HOW ABOUT YOU?

Do you know someone who needs to be told the truth? Can you tell it in a loving way? Read 1 Corinthians 13 again to see what love is all about. Also, pray about the problem. Then if you're sure the Lord wants you to point out a fault to some person, do it lovingly. Be careful that you don't do it in a critical spirit, but rather to be helpful.

MEMORIZE:

"We will hold to the truth in love, becoming more and more in every way like Christ." Ephesians 4:15

Tell the Truth in Love

To Tell the Truth (Part 2)

Read Proverbs 1:1-5

Marie was sitting alone on the steps, watching the other girls, when Lori arrived at school. As Lori sat down next to her, Marie gave her a sideways glance. "Thought you were going to play that stupid game with the other girls. Well, go ahead," Marie growled. "I don't care if no one likes me. I don't like them, either! I can sit here alone."

Lori took a deep breath. "Why should you sit alone?" she asked. "The girls would be glad to have you join them."

"In that dumb game?" Marie snarled, feeling a little guilty for sounding so nasty. "I know one that's much more fun. But do the others want to listen? Oh, no!"

"You do know a lot of fun games," Lori agreed, "and you're fun to play with, too. I'm glad you came to our school. But don't you see? The girls sometimes like to choose their own games. They don't dislike you. They just dislike having you always telling them what to do. So come on—play this game with us now. We'll play yours again later."

Marie hesitated. "I don't know how to play that one," she said finally.

"That's totally fine! The girls can show *you* how to do something for a change. Come on," coaxed Lori as she stood up. "I'm going to go play."

Marie watched as Lori walked away. She tried to be mad at Lori for deserting her, but in her heart she knew Lori was right. Maybe she should join the others and learn to play their game—if they would still let her. She slowly approached the group. "Could you show me how to play that game?" she timidly asked Susan.

Susan smiled. "Sure, come on," she answered. She linked her arm through Marie's, and together they joined the game. Marie was surprised and sorry when the bell rang a short time later. "This game was really fun!" she announced with a grin. *EC*

HOW ABOUT YOU?

Has someone tried to tell you that you are bossy, selfish, lazy, or maybe stuck-up? Don't become angry when you receive criticism. Thank God for a friend who wants to help you. Think seriously about what is said. If it's true, ask God to help you change that area of your life.

Accept Criticism

January

4

The Feeder

Read Matthew 25:35-40

The cold winter wind bit at Gabrielle's nose and ears as she and her aunt Ellen were shopping downtown. "Can we stop at the pet store and get some birdseed?" Gabrielle asked. Aunt Ellen agreed, and they headed for the store.

As they crossed an alley, Gabrielle saw a man sleeping there, huddled against a wall. He was wrapped in a shabby coat, wore no gloves, and had worn-out shoes on his feet. Gabrielle frowned and glanced back over her shoulder. "Why is he dressed like that? And why is he sleeping on the street on such a cold day?" she asked.

"I suppose he's a homeless person," Aunt Ellen replied.

"At school we talked about homeless people," Gabrielle said as they entered a warm store, "but I didn't think we had any in a small town like ours."

After Gabrielle bought a bag of birdseed, she and her aunt started back home. As they passed the alley, Gabrielle noticed that the man was gone. Aunt Ellen looked sad. "I hope he's okay," she said. Gabrielle nodded.

When the two got home, Gabrielle filled the backyard feeder with birdseed. Then she came inside and rubbed the cold from her tingling fingers. "I like to feed the birds," she said as she and her aunt watched birds swoop down to the feeder. "It's so cold, and it's hard for them to find food. They might die without me." She paused, then added, "But you know what? My Sunday school teacher read some verses that say God sees every sparrow that falls."

Her aunt nodded. "God cares about the birds, but he says people are of more value than many sparrows," she said. "We found a way to help the birds through the cold winter; we could also find a way to help the homeless. Let's think of something together, shall we?" *DBK*

HOW ABOUT YOU?

Have you ever thought about what it would be like to be homeless? Really cold? Really hungry? Perhaps there's an organization in your town that needs money, food, or clothes in order to help homeless people. Would you be willing to do without something you want in order to help? Think about it.

MEMORIZE:

"You are more valuable to him than a whole flock of sparrows." Matthew 10:31

Help the Homeless

Open Wide

Read Joshua 24:14-16

"Want me to feed Josie today?" Tanya asked her mother.

"Sure. Thanks," Mom replied. "Here's her spoon and the jar of peas."

"Open wide," Tanya said, putting a spoonful of the mashed peas into Josie's mouth. Josie spit the green peas back out. "Hey! You're supposed to eat them!" Tanya scolded, scraping the peas off the baby's chin. When Tanya held up another spoonful, Josie clamped her lips shut and turned away.

Mom chuckled. "I guess she doesn't want them. You can keep offering them to her, but you can't make her eat them. Here, try some carrots instead," Mom suggested, handing Tanya the jar of baby food.

"Come on, Josie," Tanya coaxed, offering the carrots. "Try some of these." This time Josie opened her mouth and accepted a spoonful. After that she willingly took some more and ate hungrily. "See. They're good," Tanya said. "And they're good for you, too, aren't they, Mom?"

Mom smiled. "Babies don't realize that we know what's good for them, and they don't always want to accept what we offer."

Tanya turned to her mom. "At youth group, Mr. Simmons said we're something like that. He said God loves us and knows what's best for us, and he wants us to accept Jesus as Savior and to serve him. But God lets us choose whether or not we want to."

Mom nodded. "Just like Josie decided whether or not to accept the food you offered her, we decide whether or not to accept Jesus and receive the salvation God offers us. And after we do accept him, we have to decide whether to do things his way."

Tanya smiled and finished feeding her little sister. *GJT*

HOW ABOUT YOU?

Have you asked Jesus to be your Savior? Have you decided to do things his way? God loves you and knows it's best for you to not only have Jesus in your life, but also to spend your life serving him by showing his love to others. Why not "open wide" and do that today?

Decide to Love and Serve Jesus

MEMORIZE:
"Choose today whom you will serve."
Joshua 24:15

January
6

The Comforter

Read John 14:15-21

As Sheryl lay across the bed sobbing, she felt something silky shoved under her nose. "Sissy, you can have my blanket." A tiny hand patted Sheryl's head, and she looked up into the troubled eyes of her little sister, Cynthia, who added, "My blanket will make you feel all better."

Sheryl felt the bed move as her mother sat down beside her. "Missing Lindy?" Mom gently asked.

Sheryl looked up and nodded. "She was my best friend. I think about her all the time," she said. "Will I ever feel better? It's been three months since she died."

Mom handed her a tissue. "It's always hard to lose someone we love," she said, "especially someone as young as Lindy."

Sheryl took the tissue and blew her nose. Then she handed the blanket to Cynthia. "You can have your blanket back. Thanks."

With a contented sigh, Cynthia hugged her blanket to her. Mom pulled the little girl onto her lap. "That's your comforter, isn't it, honey?" she asked.

Cynthia looked puzzled. "No," she said. "It's my blanket."

Sheryl smiled and lifted the edge of the comforter that was spread across her bed. "See this, Cynthia?" she asked. "This is called a comforter."

Mom looked thoughtful as she spoke. "You know, Sheryl, the Holy Spirit is *my* Comforter—and yours, too."

Sheryl sat up. "Is that why I feel better after I pray?" she asked. "I know when I prayed this morning, God seemed to tell me to remember the good times. I did for a little bit, and then I felt better. I was still sad, but it was a . . . a warm and soft sadness."

"Warm and soft? Like my blanket?" Cynthia asked.

Mom smiled, then patted the bed. "For Christians, the Holy Spirit is our Comforter. He's always with us and reminds us of God's promises and care." *BJW*

HOW ABOUT YOU?

Do you feel sad because someone you love has died? Have you lost a pet? Or has a special friend moved away? If you know Jesus as Savior, you have the Holy Spirit. Ask him to help you feel his comfort.

MEMORIZE:
"I will not leave you comfortless: I will come to you." John 14:18, KJV

The Holy Spirit Gives Comfort

A Pretty Picture

Read Acts 9:36-39

"See my picture!" Little Emily proudly showed Donicka her page of scribbled lines. Red, blue, green, and yellow streaks crisscrossed the picture of balloons.

"Mom likes my coloring much better than yours," Donicka replied in a snooty tone. "You don't stay in the lines."

Emily's lips puckered, and big teardrops crept down her cheeks. "Mommy!" she wailed and ran to find her mother.

Donicka took an orange crayon from the box and began coloring a stained glass window in a picture of a church. "That looks too messy," she mumbled to herself after coloring for a while. She ripped the page out of the coloring book, crumpled it up, and dropped it on the floor. *I think I'll try this picture of a kitten,* she thought. She chose a yellow crayon to begin working on the calico cat. But after a few minutes, she looked at the picture critically. *This looks messy, too,* she decided. Again she ripped out the page and tossed it away.

Just then Mom walked into the room, holding Emily's hand. The little girl was still sniffling. "Donicka," Mom said, "do you think your words to Emily were very kind?"

"I guess not," Donicka mumbled.

Mom picked up some of the pages Donicka had tossed on the floor. "You know, Donicka, the outlines of the pictures in your coloring book are boundaries, and as you told Emily, a picture is prettier when you stay inside the lines. The boundaries of the pictures remind me that there are boundaries in life, too—God's boundaries, or rules. When we obey his rules—like 'Be kind to one another'—our lives are like a pretty picture. But when we go outside the boundaries, we don't look very pretty to others or to God." *LJR*

HOW ABOUT YOU?

How does your "life-picture" look? Today's Scripture tells about Dorcas, whose life was like a pretty picture. She was kind, she helped others, and she made clothes for the poor. People were sad when she died. Don't go outside God's boundaries by being unkind. If you love Jesus, your life should be a pretty picture so others can see what he is like. Let the beauty of Jesus' love be seen in you.

Follow God's Rules

MEMORIZE:
"Show mercy and kindness to one another." Zechariah 7:9

8

Wrinkles

Read Romans 8:26-28, 31

"This shirt is so wrinkled," Ashley complained.

Mom looked up and nodded. "Better get out the iron," she said. "I'll press the sleeves for you, and I think you can handle the rest."

When the shirt was pressed, Ashley held it up to admire it. "Wow," she said, "this looks much better now. The iron sure straightened out those wrinkles."

"Yes . . . like the Holy Spirit straightens out our 'wrinkly' prayers," Mom said thoughtfully.

"Wrinkly prayers?"

Mom smiled. "I was thinking of my lesson for Sunday school this week. I've just been going over it. It's about prayer."

"What have we said that would make you think of prayer?" Ashley asked as she unplugged the iron. "And what are wrinkly prayers?"

"Well, sometimes when we pray, we aren't sure what to say," Mom replied. "We may know only a part of someone's problems. And we may not be quite sure what we should ask for regarding those needs. So when we pray about those things, our prayers seem unclear and confused. Other times we actually ask for the wrong things because we don't know what the best solution for the problem would be." She folded up the ironing board.

"And so our prayers are kind of messy, like a wrinkled shirt?" Ashley asked.

"Exactly," Mom said, "but the Holy Spirit straightens out those prayers so that when they get to God the Father, they are all 'neat and smooth' and make perfect sense."

Ashley giggled. "That's good to know. But it's too bad the Holy Spirit doesn't iron shirts!" *GJT*

HOW ABOUT YOU?

Do you sometimes feel like you're not sure what to say when you pray? Don't worry if you are unsure what to tell God. He wants you to come to him with anything and everything that concerns you. The Holy Spirit knows exactly what you should pray. Trust him to "smooth out the wrinkles."

MEMORIZE:

"The Holy Spirit helps us in our distress. For we don't even know what we should pray for, nor how we should pray. But the Holy Spirit prays for us with groanings that cannot be expressed in words." Romans 8:26

Pray Freely to God

Camouflage Not Allowed

Read Matthew 5:13-16

The trip to Africa had been exciting so far, and the thing Kate had looked forward to most was traveling by car through the game reserve. Now the time had finally arrived, and she could view wild animals in their natural habitat. But Kate's excitement was rapidly fading and being replaced by frustration.

"There's a springbok!" their guide said, pointing out the window at the gazelle.

"And there's another one next to it!" Dad exclaimed.

"Where?" Kate wailed, straining to look. "I don't see them." She plopped back in her seat.

"It's just that they blend so well with the trees and grasses," Mom said.

Kate moaned. "If I had to depend on finding springbok for my meals, I think I'd starve to death." She managed a weak smile.

Dad grinned at her. "God gave wild animals effective camouflage, didn't he?" he asked. "That's just the opposite of the way he made us."

Kate rolled her eyes. "Please, Dad," she said with a laugh, "no riddles right now. My head is already hurting."

"I think Dad is talking about Christians," Mom suggested. "Right?"

"That's right," Dad answered. "God doesn't intend for Christians to lead camouflaged lives. He wants us to shine his light, his love, and his good news to the world. He wants others to *easily* see Jesus by the way we live and talk."

Kate stared into the distance, thinking of her friends and relatives who didn't know Jesus. She didn't want to camouflage her Christianity in any way. She truly wanted them to see Jesus in her.

Just then Kate saw a flicker of movement near a tree. "I see a giraffe—no, a whole bunch of giraffes—in those trees over there!" Kate beamed triumphantly. Looking at her dad, she added, "And I do hope people won't have as much trouble seeing Jesus when they look at me." *LCA*

HOW ABOUT YOU?

Do your actions, words, and attitudes make it easy for others to see Jesus living in you? Other people desperately need to see the light of God shining out from you. Ask God to use your life to show his love and light to those around you.

MEMORIZE:

"He created everything there is. Nothing exists that he didn't make. Life itself was in him, and this life gives light to everyone." John 1:3-4

Let Jesus Be Seen in You

The Best Computer

Read Job 38:4-7; 41:11

Lizzy stared thoughtfully at her dad's computer screen. "A boy in my class—Jared—says people don't need religion because we're smarter than God," she said. "He says if we can invent computers, we can do anything. I told him he's not as smart as he thinks he is. We'll always need God, won't we, Dad?"

"Yes, we will, but I'm afraid quite a few people think the way Jared does," Dad answered. He pointed to his computer. "This machine can give us a lot of information. Do you think it can give us the answer to the question you just asked?"

"Not unless somebody programmed it to answer that question," Lizzy replied. "Even then, the answer would depend on *who* programmed it. The computer can't think for itself."

Dad rubbed his chin. "So the computer can't be any smarter than the person who programs it, right?"

"Right," Lizzy agreed.

"Do you know when the first computer was built?" Dad asked. Lizzy shook her head, and Dad continued. "It happened thousands of years ago. It was built into a man named Adam, and that first 'computer' was called a brain. God programmed it."

Then he asked, "Do think the human brain could be smarter than the one who programmed it?"

"No," Lizzy said, "that isn't possible."

"No, it isn't. You know, Lizzy, when the mechanical computer was first invented, people called it an electronic brain. They were copying God's idea. God thought of it first, and he made it better than humans ever will. In fact, the human brain is still much more powerful than any electronic computer."

"Really?" Lizzy sighed. "It doesn't seem that way sometimes. I forget my locker number, but this computer remembers everything."

"That's because we use only a small percentage of our brain power," Dad told her.

"Why is that?"

Dad looked uncertain. "I don't know. Maybe God decided we weren't responsible enough to use it all," he suggested.

Lizzy grinned. "Yeah," she said. "If we did, maybe more people would get the idea that they were smarter than him." *HMT*

HOW ABOUT YOU?

Did you know that you own one of the most powerful computers in the world? Your brain is more wonderfully designed than anything man can create. Nothing has been done that God hasn't thought of first. People believe they can do anything with computers, but the truth is, they can't do anything without God. He always will be the all-powerful and all-knowing God.

MEMORIZE:

"Apart from me you can do nothing."
John 15:5

No One Can Outsmart God

Sniff

Read 2 Corinthians 2:14-17

"Oh, no!" Mom looked up when she heard the wail from upstairs.

"I bet Diane broke something," Tim said at once. "She's always dropping things!"

"Diane," Mom called. "What's the problem?" There was no reply, so Mom headed up the stairs with Tim galloping along behind. As they reached the top, Diane appeared at Mom's bedroom door.

"Phew!" Tim exclaimed, sniffing the air. "What's that smell?"

Diane's eyes filled with tears. "I was dusting your room like you asked me to do, Mom, and when I was moving things on the dresser, my hand slipped and knocked over your perfume—that bottle Aunt Carol gave you," she explained. "It didn't break, but I guess it wasn't shut tight, and some spilled out. I'm sorry, Mom. I didn't mean to do it."

"Never mind," Mom said gently. "It was an accident."

Tim held his nose. "Ugh! Perfume! You smell," he told Diane.

"I do not!" Diane replied indignantly.

"Sniff! Sniff! You do smell," her brother insisted. "Everything smells!"

Mom laughed. "Tim's right," she agreed.

"I guess so," Diane admitted, "but it's a nice smell—not a bad one."

"I hope both you kids will always spread a nice, pleasing fragrance," Mom said.

Tim looked horrified. "What? Me smell like this? No way!"

Mom laughed. "I'm not talking about the aroma of perfume, Tim," she said. "I'm talking about the aroma of Christ."

Diane and Tim looked puzzled, so Mom explained. "As Christians, we're called to fill our world with a sweet-smelling fragrance—not with designer-label perfumes, but with the love of Jesus."

The kids' eyes lit with understanding as they listened.

Mom continued patiently. "When we're helpful, kind to others, forgiving, loving—in other words, when we live the way Jesus wants us to—we become channels of his love; we become the 'fragrance' of Christ to those around us." *MTF*

HOW ABOUT YOU?

What kind of aroma are you spreading at home, in your school, at the mall, or on the play-ground? Are you spreading a sweet-smelling aroma by what you do and say? Although some people may criticize and turn away, to others you may be the fragrance that leads them to Christ.

MEMORIZE:

"We are to God the aroma of Christ among those who are being saved and those who are perishing."

2 Corinthians 2:15, NIV

Spread Jesus' Aroma

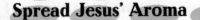

The Telltale Prints

Read Romans 16:19-20

Tara turned a page and showed the picture of Papa Bear to her little sister, Beth. Their brother, Jason, looked up as Tara continued to read the story to Beth. " 'Who's been eating my porridge?' Papa Bear growled."

Jason spoke up. "Papa Bear could have found out who ate it if he had lifted fingerprints from his spoon," he told them. "We learned in school that everybody has a different set of prints. No two are alike—ever. Match the prints and you've got the criminal."

"Yeah, well, that's nice, Jason. Now let us finish this story," Tara said.

But Jason grabbed his magnifying glass and held it above Tara's fingers. "See those ridges?" he asked. "They leave a mark on everything you touch. Investigators use special powders to dust for fingerprints, and then the print can be photographed and lifted with a print-lifting tape."

"Jason! We don't care about fingerprints right now. We just want to read the story," Tara said.

"All right, but just remember—I've been practicing with the Junior Detective kit I got for my birthday," Jason grumbled, "so you'd better keep your fingers off my stuff!" He scowled at his sisters.

"Don't be rude, Jason," Mom warned as she came into the room. "I hope you'll make sure the prints you're leaving on the lives of others are nice—not ugly."

"Prints on people's lives? What does that mean?" Tara asked.

"Well, the impressions we make on others are something like fingerprints," Mom explained. "People identify us by either the pleasant way we talk and act or by how rude we are. We develop a reputation for ourselves. And of course, it's especially important that our words and actions please God."

"Yeah, Jason," Tara said. "You better remember that, and . . ." She stopped when she saw her mother looking sternly in her direction. "And . . . and I'll remember it, too," she finished with a grin. *LJR*

HOW ABOUT YOU?

Do the prints—the impressions—you make on others please both them and God? Make sure the reputation you gain is that of helpfulness, friendliness, and patience.

MEMORIZE:

"Choose a good reputation over great riches, for being held in high esteem is better than having silver or gold."
Proverbs 22:1

Leave Good Impressions

The Nursery Lesson

Read 2 Timothy 3:13-17

Moments before the morning service began, Meredith walked down the church aisle and whispered in her mother's ear. "I'm going to the nursery, okay? They need my help again." Mom looked concerned, but nodded.

After the service, she was surprised to see her mother at the nursery door. The supervisor went to greet her while Meredith continued picking up toys.

"We appreciate your daughter's help," Meredith heard Mrs. Jones say.

"She likes to help," Mom responded, "but I'm hoping you'll be able to excuse her next week. She's missed so many services lately, and I'd like her to hear the missionary speaker next Sunday."

Mrs. Jones and Mom talked in low tones for a moment. When Meredith finished her work, she and her mother left together. "Meredith," Mom said as they walked down the hall, "you led me to believe that Mrs. Jones *asked* you to help in the nursery today. She says she didn't—neither today nor last week."

"Actually, I just said they *needed* my help," Meredith defended herself, "and they did. It was really busy." Meredith knew her argument was weak.

"How would you feel, Meredith," Mom questioned, "if Mrs. Jones said to you, 'I would like to pay you to take care of the babies every week'?"

"That would be great," Meredith said. "I'd earn some money."

"And what if you did the work, and she didn't pay you?" Mom asked.

"That wouldn't be fair," Meredith replied.

"But she didn't promise," Mom reminded her. "She only said she would *like to* pay you."

"It still wouldn't be fair," Meredith protested.

"No," agreed Mom, "but you did that to me today. You tricked me into believing something untrue so you could do what you wanted. Isn't that a kind of lie?"

"I . . . I'm sorry," Meredith mumbled. "I thought it was good to help."

Mom nodded. "Helping others is part of serving the Lord," she agreed, "but learning is important, too. The subject of today's sermon was honesty. I'll tell you about it on the drive home." *HMT*

HOW ABOUT YOU?

Have you deceived someone, or have you been deceived—tricked into believing something untrue? Lies take many forms. When you twist your words to make them sound like you're saying something you're not, it's a kind of lie—and it's sin. Ask God to help you be completely honest.

MEMORIZE:
"Do not steal. Do not cheat one another. Do not lie." Leviticus 19:11

Deceiving Is Lying

January

14

Clocks and People

Read Deuteronomy 4:1-8

(Note: This story may not be suitable for very young children.)

"Mom," Shawna said, as she stirred her cornflakes slowly, "you said abortion is wrong, but Mandy's big sister says it's legal in some states."

"Yes, it is *legal* in many states," Mom replied, "but sometimes people make up laws that go against God's laws. God says it's wrong."

As Mom was talking, Shawna's little brother, still in pajamas, appeared in the doorway. "Oh, Matt!" Shawna exclaimed. "You'd better hurry, or you'll be late for school!"

"No, I won't," Matt calmly replied. "The clock says it's only 7:00."

"But it's 7:30 already!" Shawna continued. "The clock is wrong!"

"I set the time back last night," Matt explained.

"You did?" Mom asked. "Why did you do that?"

"Because I didn't want to go to bed," Matt answered. He grinned happily and added, "So it's only 7:00, and I've got lots of time to get dressed."

Shawna stared at Matt, then burst out laughing. "That's silly!" she said. "It doesn't matter what the clock *says* if the *real* time is 7:30. You better hurry, little brother."

"That's right," Mom agreed, giving Matt a gentle push. "Off you go, young man. Hurry and get dressed." She turned to Shawna, who was looking at the clock and giggling. "Honey," she said, "Matt gave us a good example of what I was trying to explain about people making laws. He made the clock *say* the time he wanted it to be, but that didn't change the actual time. People may make a law that says abortion is all right, but God's law says it's wrong, so it *is* wrong—no matter what the law says."

Shawna nodded. "We need to live by what *God* says is right, and we can't always rely on what people say, can we?"

"Correct," Mom agreed. "Always consider what God says about things, no matter what anyone else tells you. And if other people tell you something different, don't pay attention to them." *MTF*

HOW ABOUT YOU?

Do your friends sometimes try to convince you that some wrong thing is right? Perhaps you've been told that cheating, lying, or disobeying your parents is sometimes okay. Even your country might have laws that go against God's Word. Christians need to know what God says—and then they need to obey him.

MEMORIZE:

"Do not add to or subtract from these commands I am giving you from the Lord your God. Just obey them."
Deuteronomy 4:2

Obey God's Laws

Sue Ellen's Choice

Read Joshua 24:16, 22-24

Sue Ellen wanted so badly to be part of Heather's group at school. *It will never happen unless Mom and Dad relax their rules a little and allow me to dress like Heather and her friends,* she thought. *I don't know why Mom and Dad have to be so old-fashioned!* So, on the way to school, Sue Ellen put on makeup and tied her blouse up in front to make it resemble a halter top. She knew her mother wouldn't like it, but she didn't care.

It worked! Heather's friends gave Sue Ellen friendly smiles and even invited her to a slumber party at Heather's house. Sue Ellen had never been so thrilled! *Mom won't approve, of course, but that's no big problem,* she thought. *I'll just pretend I'm going to stay with one of the girls from church. Then Mom will say it's okay.*

On Wednesday night, Sue Ellen's Bible study leader, Andrea, talked about the time Joshua challenged the children of Israel to choose the God they wanted to serve. "Sometimes kids have to choose whether they want to serve the god of popularity or the only true God," Andrea said. As Andrea continued speaking, Sue Ellen decided to ignore her guilty feelings.

Friday finally came—the big day of the slumber party. Sue Ellen was so excited! When she got to Heather's house, she was surprised to see boys there, too, and there didn't seem to be any adults around. *I wonder where Heather's folks are,* she thought. Wild music was playing, and the scene was pretty rowdy.

After a while, Heather came up to Sue Ellen. "Hi, Susie," she said. "My folks won't be home till late—isn't that great? I hope they'll never find out the guys were here." She giggled. "Here, have a cigarette," she urged.

"N-no, thanks," Sue Ellen stammered. She tried to enjoy herself, but she really wasn't comfortable. Before long she gave up, found a phone, and asked her mom to come get her.

When Mom picked her up, a very quiet, subdued Sue Ellen got into the car. "Mom, I'm sorry I lied," she said. "From now on, I'm going to serve God, not popularity." *REP*

HOW ABOUT YOU?

What god do you serve? Clothes? Good grades? Popularity? TV? (You name it.) Any of these can be a god to you if they become more important than pleasing the Lord. Like the children of Israel, you need to choose today whom you are going to serve.

MEMORIZE:
"Far be it from us to forsake the Lord to serve other gods." Joshua 24:16, NIV

Choose to Serve God

January

16

Unexpected Visit

Read Matthew 24:36-44

"Mom," Gina called, lowering the phone, "Sara and her folks are in town. She wants to know if she can stay with me for the weekend. Can she, Mom—please?"

Mom laughed. "Sure, honey," she said. "That will be fine."

Gina put the receiver to her mouth. "Mom says that's fine, Sara. How soon can you get here?" After the girls chatted a bit more, Gina hung up the phone. "Oh, Mom! I'm so excited!" she squealed. "Sara will be here in a couple of hours. It'll be the first time we've seen each other since they moved away. I'm so glad they're in town. Sara can stay until Monday."

"Great," Mom said with a smile, "but right now you'd better get out fresh sheets for the other bed in your room."

Gina dashed off. At the doorway of her room she stopped, dismayed. *How did my room get this messy?* she wondered. She quickly grabbed armloads of clothes from the chair and the floor. Dirty jeans went into the hamper . . . clean socks into a drawer . . . shoes into the closet. She walked past her desk, and papers fluttered away in all directions.

As Gina was picking up the fallen papers, she noticed last week's Sunday school handout among them. "Jesus is coming soon," she read as she opened a drawer to put the paper away. "We don't know when, but we need to be ready." Gina skimmed through the story that followed. Then she got back to cleaning, but the words she'd read echoed in her mind.

Would I be ready if Jesus suddenly arrived today? she asked herself. She knew he could come any time, but somehow it was easy to forget to think about that—just as easy as being careless about keeping her room clean. *I won't get a phone call to tell me Jesus is coming, and I won't have time to get ready for him.* She thought of Ramon at school, whom she was impatient with earlier that day. And she realized she often didn't think much about God throughout the week, until Sunday came. As Gina picked up the overflowing trash basket, she made up her mind to live every day ready to welcome Jesus at any moment. *DB*

HOW ABOUT YOU?

Would you need time to clean up your life if you knew Jesus were coming today? Should you apologize to someone? Is there a sin you need to confess to God and stop doing? Do you need to get to know him better through reading his Word? You won't be given advance notice of Jesus' coming. Live each day to please him.

MEMORIZE:

"You must be ready all the time, for the Son of Man will come when least expected." Luke 12:40

Be Ready for Jesus' Return

Hannah's Prayer

Read Psalm 40:8-10

When the waitress brought the food the Moore family had ordered, ten-year-old Hannah could hardly wait to eat. "Hannah," Dad said, "you seem eager to get started, so why don't you lead us in giving thanks?"

Hannah glanced around the busy restaurant. "Right now?" she asked. "What if the waitress comes back with the ketchup?"

"I'm sure she won't mind waiting," Dad replied. They all bowed their heads. Hannah glanced around again, then mumbled a quick prayer.

"I couldn't even understand what you said," Alex complained.

"Me, neither," Diana agreed. "You talked too fast."

"I wasn't praying to you," Hannah retorted. "God understood me, and he knows I'm thankful."

"That's enough, kids," Dad said. "Hannah's right. God does know what she prayed—but, honey, Alex and Diana are right, too."

Mom nodded. "Do you find it embarrassing to pray?" she asked.

"Not usually," Hannah said, "but everybody is watching us here."

"Who is?" Alex asked, looking at the other tables.

"Well . . . it *feels* like everybody is watching us when we all close our eyes," Hannah said. "Why can't we pray with our eyes open?"

"It isn't your eyes that God is concerned about," Dad said. "It's your heart. Since you're a Christian, Jesus is a part of your life just like you're part of our family's life. Wouldn't you feel bad if we left you at home because we didn't want to be seen talking to you?"

"I guess so," Hannah admitted.

"But we would never do that," Mom assured her, "because we love you and we're proud to be with you."

Hannah was quiet a moment. *I wonder how God feels if I'm ashamed to be seen talking to him,* she thought. Putting down her fork, she asked, "Could I pray again?" Mom and Dad smiled and nodded.

"Dear God," Hannah began, and from her heart she thanked God for the food. She finished with a hearty amen.

"Amen," another voice repeated beside the table. Hannah looked up and smiled as the waitress handed her the ketchup. *HMT*

HOW ABOUT YOU?

Is it hard to acknowledge God and show love for him when unbelievers are nearby? Do you wonder what they will think? When Jesus suffered and died for you, he didn't worry about what people would think. Never be ashamed of him!

Never Be Ashamed of Jesus

MEMORIZE:
"You must never be ashamed to tell others about our Lord." 2 Timothy 1:8

January

18

The Best Banana

Read 1 Peter 3:3-4, 8-9

"Mom, I don't like Renee," Teena announced one day. "Her hair is gross, and she's so fat."

Mom frowned. "Sit down, Teena," she said after a moment. "I want you to try some bananas."

"Bananas?" Teena asked. "How come?"

"I went shopping today with Maria Sutton, our church missionary to Panama," Mom replied. "She told me about four kinds of bananas they have in Panama—red crinkly ones, small yellow ones with big brown blotches, tiny green ones, and yellow ones like we buy at the grocery store. Then she took me to a health store where we could buy all four kinds, so I got some this afternoon."

"Are they good?" Teena asked, becoming interested.

Mom went to the kitchen and returned with four bananas, a knife, and a plate. "Let's try the pretty red one first," Teena suggested. Mom agreed, so Teena peeled it and popped a good-sized piece into her mouth. "Yuck! That's bad enough to choke a cow!" she sputtered.

Mom laughed. "Here," she said. "Try the brown, blotchy one."

But Teena shook her head. "No, it looks awful," she said. She tasted a piece of the small green one. "Nothing special," she decided, "but at least it's not as bad as the red one."

"How about the brown one?" her mother urged again.

Teena hesitated. "Well, all right," she agreed, "but it looks so horrible." Wrinkling up her nose, she gingerly peeled the banana. She tasted a tiny piece. "Ummm, good!" she exclaimed. She quickly finished the whole thing. "Let's get more of those," she said. "They look so bad, but they're so good!"

Mom nodded. "The outside isn't so important, is it?" she said. "It's the inside that counts. God's Word says something about that."

Teena looked ashamed. "You made me think about Renee," she said. "Renee has always been a good friend. And she's sweet to everyone. I'll be a better friend to Renee," said Teena, "just as God said to be." *MJS*

HOW ABOUT YOU?

Do you judge others by the way they look? Think hard now! Is there someone you've judged that way? God says inner beauty is much more important than outward looks. How beautiful are you on the inside? Ask God to help you recognize the value of everyone and to accept each one as he or she is.

MEMORIZE:

"You should be known for the beauty that comes from within, the unfading beauty of a gentle and quiet spirit, which is so precious to God." 1 Peter 3:4

Don't Judge by Appearance

Not a Snitch

Read Esther 4:6-16

Shannon stood still as her mother pinned up the hem of her costume. She was going to wear the brown, old-fashioned dress in a special colonial program at church. "Mom, do you remember Cathy Paige?" Shannon asked. "She doesn't go to Sunday school anymore. She says she's got better things to do than hang around church."

"Oh, I'm sorry to hear that," Mom replied. She eyed the hemline. "Okay. Your dress is ready for hemming."

"I saw Mrs. Paige today," Shannon said, slipping her costume off and putting her normal clothes back on. "We talked a while; she's really nice." She handed the dress to her mother and picked up a book. "Mom," she added hesitantly, "I'm sure Cathy's using drugs. In fact, I *know* she is. She as good as admitted it when I asked her about it the other day. But I don't believe Mrs. Paige suspects a thing."

"Oh, dear!" Mom looked concerned. "Don't you think we should tell her?"

"No way," Shannon said. "I'd get a reputation for snitching."

"Hmmm," Mom murmured as she began hemming the costume. Then she asked, "What part do you play in the program tomorrow night?"

"Paul Revere's wife—you know that," Shannon replied as she grinned. "My husband," she said, "is noted for having warned his fellow Americans that the British were coming. Thanks to him, they were prepared for the battle."

"Well, Mrs. Revere," Mom said, "you can get out the iron and get ready to press this dress." She smiled. "And tell me, wasn't your husband a snitch when he carried his message?"

"Some people said so," Shannon answered, "but his country was in danger, and he was being patriotic."

"So sometimes people *should* tell, right?" Mom continued.

Shannon was startled. "I . . . well . . . sometimes, I guess. But what in the world do I say to Mrs. Paige, Mom?"

"I'm not sure," Mom acknowledged. "Let's pray about this, and then let's get some advice from our pastor or from the Christian counseling service downtown. I'm not sure just how to handle it, but I do know that we must do something to help Cathy."

Shannon nodded. "Even if she does think I'm a snitch." *MM*

HOW ABOUT YOU?

Do you have a friend or relative who uses drugs? Is anybody doing anything about it? Do you know a caring adult who'd try to help? Ask God if it's time for you to speak up. Maybe, like Esther, you've been placed in your position in order to help someone. When such a serious problem is involved, telling is helping, not snitching.

Sometimes You Need to Tell

MEMORIZE:
"Who can say but that you have been elevated to the palace for just such a time as this?" Esther 4:14

January

20

Adopted by God

Read Galatians 4:3-7

Thuan remembered only small parts of living in the orphanage in the faraway country where she was born. She remembered bits and pieces of the war, including the sound of exploding grenades in the street outside. And Thuan remembered the day when she was adopted by a family in the United States. Though she was a stranger in a strange land, the Jeffersons, whom she now knew as "Mom and Dad," treated her with a gentle kindness that overcame her fears. They took her to church and Sunday school and taught her about Jesus.

"Mom," she said one day, "my Sunday school teacher says that when a sinner asks Jesus to forgive her, God adopts her into his family. Why would God want to do that?"

Mom looked thoughtfully at Thuan. "Let me tell you a story, honey," she said at last. "Many years ago, God gave us a son whom we named Michael, and we loved him very much. When Mike grew older, he went into the military and was sent to the country where you were born to fight in the war. He saved the lives of people like your birth parents and grandparents, and he even helped us adopt you." Mom paused as she went over to a desk and took out a picture. "This is Mike," she said.

Thuan studied the picture. Suddenly, she understood. "He was willing to save others, even though he ended up being killed in the war?"

Mom nodded and hugged her close. "We were so excited to adopt you. Now we get to raise you, just as we did with Michael. We consider you the most important person in the world, and we wanted you to be part of our family," she said. "Now we love you with all our hearts. It's the same way with God. His only Son died to save you from your sins, and now God wants to make you part of his family. He wants to take you to live with him in heaven someday. Would you like to become part of the family of God?"

With a tearful smile, Thuan nodded. *TVB*

HOW ABOUT YOU?

Are you a part of God's family? He loved you enough to send his Son, Jesus, to die for your sins. He wants to make you his child—to adopt you into his family. He'll do that when you admit your need for salvation and accept Jesus and what he has done for you.

MEMORIZE:
"You are all children of God through faith in Christ Jesus." Galatians 3:26

Be a Child of God

Tips from Tippy

Read Psalm 34:1-8

As Lindy packed the last few items into her suitcase, she looked worried. "What's wrong, honey?" her mother asked. "Aren't you excited about going to Grandma's?"

"Well, yes," Lindy replied slowly, "but it's such a long way. What if we have an accident?" She was thinking of a horrible car accident that she'd seen on the news.

Mom patted Lindy's arm. "Our lives are in God's hands," she said. "We realize that an accident could happen while we travel, but an accident could just as easily happen right here at home. We're trusting the Lord to take care of us." Lindy nodded, but she still felt uneasy.

Mom went to the kitchen to finish getting dinner, and Lindy followed. A fluffy little ball of puppy fur was curled up on an old rug in the corner. Just a few days ago, Dad had brought home the dripping-wet little animal. He had found it abandoned along the road. "Hi, Tippy," Lindy said softly. Tippy watched Lindy put some puppy chow into a bowl. "Come eat," Lindy coaxed, holding out her hand.

Tippy jerked up and shot under the corner shelves, trying to hide from Lindy's outstretched hands. "You poor little thing!" she murmured, gently gathering the shaking pup into her arms and stroking the soft fur. "You need to learn to trust me," Lindy said as she carried Tippy over to the bowl of food.

"Why should Tippy trust you?" Mom asked.

"Because I love him and will take good care of him," Lindy replied confidently. "I give him only what's good for him."

"Yes," Mom agreed, "and it will be good when Tippy learns that. It's always good when we learn to trust the One who cares for us."

Lindy smiled. "I get the point, Mom," she said. "You're saying that God loves me and knows what's best for me, so I can trust him on our trip to Grandma's." She nodded. "That's just what I'm going to do." *LGM*

HOW ABOUT YOU?

Are you afraid of what might happen to you in the future? When you see someone in a wheelchair, or when someone you know is hurt in a car accident, do you ever feel scared that the same thing might happen to you? Remember that God loves you and wants what is best for you. Ask him to take away your fears. Trust him.

Trust God to Take Care of You

MEMORIZE:
"When I am afraid, I put my trust in you." Psalm 56:3

January

22

The Right Path

Read Psalm 37:23-24, 31

"Are you reading your favorite story again?" Lauren asked Allie.

"Yep—Hansel and Gretel," Allie announced. "Wanna hear it?" She cleared her throat. " 'When Hansel and Gretel woke from their sleep, the woods were very dark.' " Allie began relating the story to Lauren without even looking at her book. " 'How will we find our way home?' Gretel asked. She began to cry. Hansel picked up a pebble lying on the pathway. 'Look, Gretel, here are the pebbles I dropped,' he said. 'We can follow them back home.' "

"I know the story," Lauren said, giving her little sister a big hug. "Have you memorized your Bible verses for Sunday already? You'll have to say them for Mom before she'll let us go to the zoo, you know."

"Those verses are too hard," Allie whined. "Besides, what good is learning a bunch of old verses anyway?"

"Don't let Mom hear you say that!" Lauren warned. "There are lots of reasons to memorize Bible verses. For one thing, God's Word helps us know right from wrong. It helps us make right choices." Allie continued to pout. "Think of it like this," Lauren explained. "When we've hidden verses from God's Word in our hearts, they're like the pebbles Hansel had hidden in his pocket and used to mark the path that would lead them home. The pebbles showed them the way to go, and having God's Word memorized will help us know the way to go, too. When we follow God's Word, we can always be sure we are on the right path in life."

"But it's too hard to memorize all those long words," Allie complained again.

"Didn't I just hear you reciting Hansel and Gretel? How did you learn it so well?" Lauren asked.

"I guess it's because I read it so much," Allie admitted.

"Well, if you'll read your Bible verses over and over again, I bet you'll remember them easily, too," Lauren suggested. "Try it."

So Allie took her Bible to the living room and curled up on the sofa. "Psalm 119:35," she began. " 'Make me walk along the path of your commands. . . .' "

When Mom came home, Allie jumped up, held her Bible behind her back, and said, "Listen, Mommy." Then she recited her verses perfectly. *LJR*

HOW ABOUT YOU?

Do you ever think that memorizing God's Word is too hard? Do you wonder why you even need to do it? Encouragement, comfort, and knowing the right things to do are only a few of the rewards God gives for studying his Word. Go ahead and put some extra effort in it today. You'll be glad you did!

MEMORIZE:

"Make me walk along the path of your commands, for that is where my happiness is found." Psalm 119:35

God's Word

Ashley and Oliver

23

Read Psalm 4:3-5

"Mom never has time for me anymore," Ashley complained in a low voice as she and her brother, Jeremy, cleared the table.

"Well, she's had to work long hours lately," Jeremy said.

"I know," Ashley admitted, "but it seems like she could spend a *little* more time with us."

"Have you told her how you feel?" Jeremy asked.

Ashley shook her head. "It seems to me that if she really loved me, she'd know without my having to spell it out." She scraped some leftover fish onto a plate and gave it to the cat.

Later that evening, Ashley noticed her cat making choking sounds and frantically pawing at its face. "Mom, come quick!" she called urgently. "Something's wrong with Oliver. Can we take him to the vet?" Her voice choked with tears.

Mom hurried to investigate. "Oh, my! Of course we'll take him," she agreed. Soon they were on their way.

They arrived back home about an hour later. The veterinarian had discovered that Oliver was choking on a fish bone. He was able to pull it out and said the cat would be fine. But Ashley was still upset. "It's my fault," she said. "I gave him the fish bones."

"It's okay, honey," Mom comforted. "It would have been nice if Oliver had a way to tell you he was having a problem, but he didn't. You had no way of knowing. I'm sure he knows you didn't hurt him on purpose, though. He knows you love him." She looked at her watch. "Now, I think you kids should get to bed. It's late, and you have school tomorrow. I'm going to work in the den for a while."

At the door of his room, Jeremy hesitated. "Ashley, remember how you said that if Mom really loved you, she'd automatically know how you felt?" he asked. "Well, you love Oliver and didn't mean to hurt him, but *you* couldn't tell how he felt without being told. Why is Mom any different from you?"

Ashley stood still. "Maybe you're right," she said thoughtfully. "Since I *can* tell Mom about my problem, I should." She turned toward the den. "Good night, Jeremy," she said. "I'm going to talk to Mom." *CW*

HOW ABOUT YOU?

Are you upset with someone? It's natural to get angry sometimes, and there are times when it may even be for good reason. But the Bible says you shouldn't sin by letting the sun set while you're angry. Don't hold a grudge—grudges generally get worse and often turn to bitterness or hate if you don't stop them. Follow God's command by talking about the problem and settling it before you go to sleep.

MEMORIZE:

" 'Don't sin by letting anger gain control over you.' Don't let the sun go down while you are still angry."

Ephesians 4:26

Don't Hold a Grudge

The New Desk

Read Proverbs 3:1-7

Jayne had a brand-new desk! "I'll always take good care of it," she exclaimed as her hand glided across the shiny top.

A few days later, Jayne slipped a box of matches out of the kitchen cabinet, took a candle, and headed for her room. *Dad will be mad if he catches me with this stuff,* she thought, *but after all, I'm old enough to do things like this and not start a fire.* After carefully locking her door, she lit the candle and placed it on her desk. *It's so pretty,* she thought as she picked up a book and began to read.

Suddenly, Dad was knocking on her door. "Jayne, what do I smell?" he called. With a fast-beating heart, Jayne grabbed for the candle, knocking it over and burning her fingers in the process. To her horror, a piece of paper on her desk caught fire! But it was a small piece, and the flame went out quickly. She sighed in relief, picked up the whole mess, and shut it in her closet. Fearfully, she let Dad into the room. She hoped her secret wouldn't be discovered, but in a moment, Dad exclaimed, "Jayne! What happened to your new desk?"

As Jayne turned around, she saw an ugly, black spot on the top of the desk. A few minutes later, Dad had the whole story. "Jayne, do you realize that you could have burned the house down?" he asked sternly.

"Oh, Dad," Jayne sobbed, "I just wanted to enjoy the candle a little while. I never thought it would hurt anything. I'm so sorry."

"Honey," Dad said, "sin often seems to be fun and exciting while you're doing it, but in the end someone gets hurt. You knew the rules about not playing with matches, and you disobeyed those rules. Now you'll have to pay the consequences. Do you see why it's so important to always obey?"

"Yes." Jayne nodded soberly. "If I ever forget, this spot on the top of my desk will remind me." *RL*

HOW ABOUT YOU?

Do the rules set by your parents sometimes seem silly or unimportant? Those rules, if kept, often protect you from harm. God's rules are like that too. When he says things like "Don't lie," "Be kind," and "Forgive," it's for your good. He wants you to obey him so you won't be hurt by the results of sin.

MEMORIZE:

"Fools think they need no advice, but the wise listen to others."
Proverbs 12:15

Obedience Protects You

God Says It

Read 1 Thessalonians 4:13-18

Alyssa wriggled uncomfortably when Pastor Burns gave an invitation for those who would like to be saved. He had talked about when Jesus would come and take Christians to heaven. Alyssa thought back to when she had accepted Christ. She had been so happy then. But now Alyssa was scared. *I know I still do wrong things sometimes. Maybe I didn't pray the right way, and Jesus will leave me behind when he comes back!* she thought. *Maybe I should ask him into my life again.* So she quietly told the Lord that she was sorry for her sin and she wanted him to control her life.

That afternoon, Alyssa took the dog for a walk. When they returned, the house was quiet. "Mom," she called, "where are you?" No answer. "Mom?" she called again. "Dad?" Still there was no answer. *Maybe Jesus came, and I'm the only one left at our house!* Alyssa thought as she hurried through the rooms and found no one. She ran outside. She breathed a sigh of relief when she saw her parents talking to the neighbors two doors over!

Alyssa was still nervous when Mom and Dad came home. Her mother noticed and asked what was wrong. "I was really sorry for my sins, and I really meant it when I asked Jesus to be my Savior," Alyssa replied. "But sometimes I still worry that I'm not really saved. How can I know for sure?"

Mom thought for a moment. "How do you know you're really my child?" she asked.

Alyssa was startled. "Why, I . . . ah . . . you told me so," she answered.

Mom nodded. "And you believe me, don't you?" she asked. "You trust me to tell you the truth about that. Well, you need to trust God, too, when he says that whoever honestly calls upon him is saved. Remember . . . it's *God* who says that, and his word is even better than mine!" She gave Alyssa a hug. "Why don't you learn a verse that you can quote whenever Satan causes you to doubt your salvation?" she suggested. "Romans 10:13 might be a good one for you." *LMW*

HOW ABOUT YOU?

Are you ever afraid the Lord is going to come back and you won't be ready? Won't you settle those fears by asking him into your life today? After you do that, memorize today's verse, and say it to yourself whenever you have doubts about your salvation. Rest on God's Word!

Trust in God and His Word

MEMORIZE:
"Anyone who calls on the name of the Lord will be saved." Romans 10:13

January
26

Try Again

Read Luke 11:5-13

Traci dialed, then listened to the buzz of the phone ringing. "Hello," a voice answered. "You're my third caller. Please hang up and try again." Traci did. "Hello, you're my seventh caller," the voice said this time. "Please hang up and try again." *One more time,* Traci thought. This time she heard, "You're my eleventh caller. Please hang up and try again." Traci groaned. "Oh well. Now it will be too late!" she said.

Traci's favorite Christian music group was coming to town, but all the tickets had been sold. Now the only way she could go was to win this radio contest. Whenever the station played a song by the group, the deejay gave two tickets to the twelfth caller. Traci had been trying for two days to win. Her older sister, Donna, had promised to take her to the concert if she won tickets. For an afternoon with her favorite band *and* her big sister, Traci just had to win! But every time someone else won, she felt a little more discouraged.

"Maybe I should pray that I'll win," Traci said when Donna asked how it was going. "God answers prayer if it's for good things, right? Why wouldn't he want us to spend time together at a concert that praises him?"

"Well, we *should* pray about it," Donna agreed, "but then we should trust God to work it out for the best and be content whether he lets you win or not." She smiled at her little sister. "Prayer can be like calling in to win a radio contest," Donna continued. "You can't win a radio contest if you don't try making calls, and you can't get answers to prayer unless you pray. But unlike a radio contest, you do *always* get through to God when you pray, even if it doesn't seem that way. God hears, and he's happy to have you bring your requests to him."

Traci listened quietly. She *had* given up on praying for some things when she hadn't gotten the answer she wanted.

"Hey, Traci, isn't this another one of their songs already?" Donna prompted.

"Oh, yes, it is!" Traci squealed. She ran to the phone to try once more. *SN*

HOW ABOUT YOU?

Do you sometimes wonder if God hears when you pray? Do you wonder if he's "taking other calls" at the same time you're praying? He is, but he's so powerful that he can take care of everyone at once and not make any mistakes. He knows what's best for all of his people—including you! Keep communicating with him. He wants to hear from you and show you his will by his answers.

MEMORIZE:

"The eyes of the Lord watch over those who do right; his ears are open to their cries for help." Psalm 34:15

Keep Praying

True Beauty

Read 1 Timothy 4:7-10

Rachel stumbled into her aunt's house and collapsed on the couch, sobbing. Aunt Karen knelt beside her. "What's the matter, honey?"

"I'm so fat and ugly," Rachel wailed. "The kids call me Tootsie Roll." She choked on the words.

Aunt Karen hugged Rachel close. "I know exactly how you feel, honey," she said solemnly. "The kids used to call me a tugboat."

Rachel stared at her lovely, slender aunt. "You? But Aunt Karen! You're beautiful."

Aunt Karen smiled. "When I was your age, I was a great deal overweight," she said. "Time and a well-balanced diet have made a lot of changes. But it didn't happen overnight."

Rachel sat up as Aunt Karen continued. "I often felt hurt when classmates teased me. Then one day I realized it isn't what's on the outside that matters the most. It's the inside that counts."

"You sound like Mom," Rachel said. "She always says, 'Pretty is as pretty does.'"

"That's right." Aunt Karen nodded. "I decided I would do my best to become pretty on the outside, but even if I didn't succeed, I was going to be beautiful inside."

"How did you do that?" Rachel asked.

"I prayed about it a lot, and God helped me," Aunt Karen answered. "He showed me that the ugliest thing inside me was selfishness. So I determined to quit thinking so much about myself. I decided to reach out to others with love and kindness. I did, and one day a friend said to me, 'Karen, you're different. You smile a lot more, and your eyes sparkle. You're getting prettier all the time.' I was so pleased." Aunt Karen stood up. "If you like, I'll help figure out a good diet and exercise program for you to follow. I know your mom will help, too. But if you want to be really beautiful, Rachel, you have to let Jesus' love shine through you. That's true beauty." *BJW*

HOW ABOUT YOU?

Are you unhappy about your appearance? Do your best to look your best, but then quit worrying about your weight or face. Ask God to help you get rid of any ugliness inside and to fill you with his joy. Think less about yourself and more about God and others. Soon the beauty of Jesus will shine through you!

MEMORIZE:

"Those who look to him for help will be radiant with joy; no shadow of shame will darken their faces."

Psalm 34:5

True Beauty Is Inside

January
28

Going with the Flow

Read Titus 2:11-15

"Look at those jellyfish!" Justin exclaimed. "They look like tiny parachutes!" He leaned forward, marveling at the shiny, silky-looking creatures floating in the fish tank.

Amy nudged her way closer to the tank. "Wow!" she cried. "Look at the colors—pink, white, blue, yellow, green, purple, and even striped!"

Dad was looking at the sign next to the popular attraction. "When out of the water," he read out loud, "jellyfish look like a glob of jelly dripping from your spoon. Jellyfish are invertebrates. They have no backbone and no central brain."

When Dad moved on, Amy continued to study the sign. "It says they float by opening and closing their bodies like an umbrella. They hardly move unless a current comes along."

That evening, the kids talked about the things they liked best at the aquarium. "Those jellyfish were so pretty," Amy declared. "They're kind of carefree, too—they just float along, going with the flow of the current."

"That's like some Christians I know," Dad commented.

"Really?" Amy asked. "Like who?"

"Well," replied Dad, "when Mariah and Sophie were over yesterday, they were mocking Leah's lisp, and I heard you laughing about it, too—just going along with whatever they said. I've been meaning to speak to you about it."

Amy bit her lip. "Mariah and Sophie are so popular at school," she explained, "and . . . well, they've just started acting friendly toward me, so I didn't want to . . ." Her voice trailed off.

"Jellyfish are beautiful, but they have no backbone," Dad said. "God didn't make you a jellyfish, Amy. He expects you to stand up for what is right. We sin when we just go along with others who are doing wrong things—no matter what the reason."

Amy sighed and nodded. "I guess I need to act more like I have a backbone, huh?" *LJR*

HOW ABOUT YOU?

How strongly do you stand up for what's right, especially when other kids don't agree with you? Don't just go with the flow like a jellyfish. It not only has no backbone, it also has no brain. God made you stronger than that! Ask him to fill you with his boldness to do what is right.

MEMORIZE:

"Say 'No' to ungodliness and worldly passions, and . . . live self-controlled, upright and godly lives in this present age." Titus 2:12, NIV

Stand Up for What's Right

Don't Run Away

Read Isaiah 40:28-31

Becky set her books on the table when she arrived home after school. "Can I stay home tomorrow?" she asked her mother.

Mom looked surprised. "Stay home?" she asked. "Are you sick?"

Becky shook her head. "No, but I . . . I have a problem," she replied. "See . . . Karina wants me to give her the answers on our test. Of course, I won't do it, but I don't want her to be mad at me. If I don't go to school, I won't have to worry about it."

Mom nodded. "So if you stay home tomorrow, you won't have to face the unpleasantness of telling her that you believe cheating is wrong?" Becky nodded, looking hopeful.

Just then, little Lydia awoke from her nap and began to cry. "Would you go get her, please?" Mom said.

Becky hurried to her baby sister and lifted her from the crib, gave her a hug, and carried her back into the kitchen. Becky had been helping Lydia learn to walk and decided to let her practice taking a step.

"Don't put her down," Mom said quickly. "She might fall and get hurt. From now on, let's hold her all the time."

Becky gave Mom a puzzled look. "She needs to practice walking, or she won't learn how!" Becky exclaimed.

"But walking is hard for her," Mom protested.

"Well, the more she practices, the easier it will get," Becky said. She frowned. "What are you really getting at?" she asked.

Mom smiled. "I'm just hoping you'll see that the way to overcome a problem—whether it's learning to walk or telling someone no—is to face that problem. Lydia won't learn to walk unless she keeps working at it, and you won't learn to stand for God and what's right by running away from the situation."

Becky was thoughtful. "You mean I should go to school tomorrow and tell Karina that cheating is wrong," she said.

Mom nodded. "Ask for God's help as you face her. You'll become stronger by standing up for what you believe." *KEC*

HOW ABOUT YOU?

Do you try to escape your problems, or do you ask God to help you meet them? Facing challenges takes faith and courage. Overcoming them builds strength and character. Ask God to help you deal with the difficulties in your life.

MEMORIZE:
"God has not given us a spirit of fear and timidity, but of power, love, and self-discipline." 2 Timothy 1:7

Face Your Problems

30

Those Dirty Socks

Read Exodus 16:4-5, 21-27

"Mom, I can't find any clean socks," Missy said as she entered the kitchen.

"Then you didn't put your dirty ones in the hamper like I told you to do," Mom said. "I washed everything yesterday."

"What am I going to do?" Missy wailed.

"You'll just have to wear the socks you wore yesterday," Mom said. "Find all the clothes that need washing and put them in the hamper. I'll wash again today."

Missy soon returned with an armload of rumpled clothes. She frowned grimly as she shoved them into the hamper. She started to stomp back to her room.

"Whoa," her mom said. She took a Bible from the kitchen shelf. "Wait a minute! You know, you remind me of the Israelites."

"Huh?" Missy stopped in surprise.

"Here. Read this." Her mom pointed to some verses on the page. "Read it aloud," she said.

Reluctantly, Missy took the Bible and began to read. "Some of the people went out anyway to gather food, even though it was the Sabbath day. But there was none to be found." Missy looked up from the page. "What's it talking about?" she asked.

"Picking up manna—the bread God sent them from heaven," Mom replied.

Missy still looked puzzled. "What has that got to do with me?"

"The Israelites were to gather only enough manna for each day," Mom explained, "except on the Sabbath."

"Oh, I remember!" Missy interrupted. "They were supposed to take double on the sixth day, but some didn't. When they looked for some on the Sabbath, there wasn't any." Missy shrugged. "I still don't see what that has to do with me."

"Well," Mom said, "when they didn't follow God's instructions on the sixth day, their plates were empty on the seventh day, so they went hungry. You didn't follow my instructions, so your sock drawer is empty. Whose fault is it?"

"Mine," Missy admitted. "I . . . I shouldn't have been angry at you. I'm sorry. I've followed your instructions now."

"So tomorrow you'll have clean socks!" Mom said, giving her a hug. *RG*

HOW ABOUT YOU?

Do you sometimes forget to do things—or perhaps do something wrong—and then become angry because of the results? Be careful not to blame others for things that are your own fault. Be careful not to blame God. Confess any complaining and receive God's forgiveness. Ask him to help you to accept your responsibilities without complaint.

MEMORIZE:

"In everything you do, stay away from complaining and arguing." Philippians 2:14

Don't Blame Others or God

It's Greek to Me

Read Revelation 22:12-21

Jamie sat at the kitchen table turning the pages of her Bible. "What are you doing?" her older sister, Beth, asked.

"Our Sunday school teacher gave us some homework," Jamie explained. "He's going to give a reward to the one who finds the most names or titles for God, but I can't find very many." Suddenly she brightened. "Hey, maybe you can help me. Don't you learn that kind of stuff in Bible college?" She looked hopefully at Beth as she added, "Mr. Benson doesn't care where we get our information, just so we learn."

Beth smiled. "How about Good Shepherd?" she asked. "Do you have that one? Remember the message Pastor Rader gave on Psalm 23 just a few weeks ago?"

Jamie eagerly wrote it down. "Can you think of any more?"

"Well," Beth said, "the book of John talks about Jesus being the True Vine and the Door."

"Oh, yeah! Thanks, Beth!" Jamie exclaimed. "I've already got some others from the book of John where Jesus says he is the Way, the Truth, and the Life."

"Don't forget Isaiah 9:6," Beth said. "In that verse God is called Wonderful, Counselor, the Mighty God, the Everlasting Father, and the Prince of Peace."

Jamie was writing the names down as fast as she could. "You're a big help," she said with a grin.

"Thanks." Beth nodded. "How about Alpha and Omega?"

"Alpha and Omega?" Jamie asked doubtfully. "That sounds like Greek to me!"

Beth laughed. "It is Greek, Jamie! *Alpha* and *omega* are the first and last letters in the Greek alphabet. It means that God is the beginning and the end of everything."

Jamie wrote "Alpha and Omega" on her paper. "That's kind of neat, isn't it, Beth?" she said thoughtfully.

Beth nodded. "That is neat!" she agreed. "Since God is the beginning and the end, it means he always was and always will be. He's everything that each name suggests." *LMW*

HOW ABOUT YOU?

Did you know that God has many names and titles? Why not see how many you can find? Write down what each title represents. For instance . . . Counselor? That's someone who can help you when you're faced with a difficult situation. Studying the names of God and what they mean is important, and it helps you realize how great he is.

MEMORIZE:
"Lord, there is no one like you! For you are great, and your name is full of power." Jeremiah 10:6

Learn Who God Is

True Power

Read Psalm 18:27-32

Aimee searched through her room one last time. She even pulled her pillows out of their cases to see if her half of the "best friend" broken-heart necklace could be hiding down inside one of them. But it was no use. She had lost the necklace she had bought together with Sandra. *Now Sandra and I can't be best friends anymore,* she thought sadly.

At breakfast, Aimee's mother noticed she had been crying and asked what was wrong. Aimee hesitated, but the story spilled out. Aimee was surprised to see her older brother, Rick, nodding sympathetically. "Aimee, do you remember when we had that big district track meet last year, and I discovered that you had eaten my last nutrition bar?" he asked. "I just about panicked! I thought I couldn't win my events—maybe not even finish the longer runs—unless I had one of those bars."

"Well, I sure won't ever take one again," Aimee said. "It tasted like . . . like cardboard."

Rick grinned. "I know," he said, "but our whole team eats them. It's kind of a sign that we're all in this together, so I thought I had to have one. But Coach Roberts convinced me that it's our hard work that helps us win, not those nutrition bars. He told me I could run, jump, and throw just as well on other wholesome foods."

"And you did—you won the long jump," Aimee said. "So what does that have to do with my lost necklace?"

"The nutrition bars weren't magic! They didn't make me win," Rick said. "And your necklace doesn't magically make you best friends with Sandra."

Mom nodded. "Maybe it's just as well that you lost it," she said, "because it's dangerous to regard anything as magic. If you want Sandra to be your best friend, ask God to help you be a real friend to her. That's the way true friendships are developed." *LBM*

HOW ABOUT YOU?

Do you remember that power comes from God, not from things? Don't cling too closely to something that reminds you of a person or perhaps a place. Resist any superstitious practices and thoughts. There's nothing wrong with keeping a visible reminder of a friend or a sport, but sin slips in if you start believing there is magic in such a sign or in any other material thing.

Power Comes from God

MEMORIZE:
"God arms me with strength; he has made my way safe." Psalm 18:32

February

2

Telling It Like It Is

Read 2 Corinthians 4:1-6

After shopping at the mall, Audrey and her mother decided to rest a while in the food court. As they munched on some fries, Audrey admired her new cross pendant. "Mom," she said, "at school today, Mackenzie asked me why I was wearing a cross."

"And what did you say?"

"Well, I told her that I thought it was pretty, and I liked it," Audrey replied. She frowned slightly and added, "I tried talking to her about Jesus and salvation, too, but she called me strict and narrow-minded. I feel really bad about that."

All of a sudden, a high-pitched voice startled Audrey. She looked up and saw an angry lady scolding the young man behind the hamburger counter. "What do you mean, my coupons have expired?" the lady demanded with a scowl. "Just close your eyes and bend the rules a bit!"

The young man answered her calmly. "I'm sorry, Ma'am, but I can't bend rules I didn't make. These coupons are no longer valid." The lady continued to complain loudly, but the clerk refused to honor the coupons. "I'm sorry, but I can't help you," he said firmly. "We were given stern warnings about accepting expired coupons."

When the lady finally left, Mom turned to Audrey. "That young man must seem pretty strict and narrow-minded to that lady," she said.

"I know," Audrey agreed, "but he's only telling it like it is."

Mom nodded. "That's right," she said. "I'm sure he's sorry she got angry, but he shouldn't feel bad about having done the right thing." Mom smiled at Audrey. "When you tell your friend about Jesus and she gives you a hard time, it's natural and right to be sorry that she doesn't understand. However, you shouldn't feel bad that you told her. Even though people don't like to accept it, they need to know that faith in Jesus is the only way to heaven."

"That is God's rule," Audrey agreed. "And even if Mackenzie thinks I'm narrow-minded, I have to tell her that—I have to tell it like it is." *SML*

HOW ABOUT YOU?

Has someone made you feel bad for speaking the truth about Jesus and salvation? Have you been called narrow-minded—or some other unpleasant name? The next time someone is hard on you for "telling it like it is," remind him that you're not giving your own opinion. Instead, you're simply speaking what God has already said.

MEMORIZE:

"We do not preach ourselves, but Jesus Christ as Lord." 2 Corinthians 4:5, NIV

Witness Boldly

Bearing Fruit

Read John 15:1-5, 8

Susan and Keri had enjoyed helping gather juicy, delicious oranges at their grandmother's home in Florida. "Grandma Bergen said she had a bumper crop this year," Susan said. "What does that mean?"

"It means the trees have lots and lots of oranges this year," Dad said.

"Grandma said she used a different kind of spray this year," Mom said. "And she put in a new irrigation system to water the trees. I think that's why the oranges are bigger and better than ever."

"Picking all this fruit reminds me of some Bible verses about the fruit of the Spirit," Dad said. "Didn't you kids learn those for Bible Club a few weeks ago?"

Keri nodded. "Yep. They're Galatians 5:22 and 23," she said, then quoted the verses.

"Good," Dad replied. "Having the fruit of the Spirit in our lives should be natural, just like it's natural for orange trees to have oranges. It's not something they have to struggle to do."

"I don't think it's all that easy to have the fruit of the Spirit," Keri said. "I think it's hard!"

Dad smiled. "Well, I have to agree with you," he said. "But when Grandma Bergen's orange trees didn't produce many oranges, she knew something was wrong, and when our lives don't show the fruit of the Spirit, perhaps there's something wrong, too. What do you think it might be?"

"Well . . . Grandma's oranges had worms last year, so the fruit wasn't so good. Maybe when our lives have sin in them, our fruit isn't so good either," Susan suggested after a moment.

"Excellent thought!" Dad exclaimed. "Anything else?"

Keri spoke quickly. "Just like orange trees need water, a Christian needs the Bible," she said.

Dad nodded. "Another good thought. God wants his children to live fruitful lives for him. And that's not just for adults. He wants kids to bring forth fruit too. Let's do all we can to make sure our lives show the fruit of the Spirit every day." *RB*

HOW ABOUT YOU?

Do you know what the "fruit of the Spirit" is? Think about the things listed in the verses below. Is the fruit of the Spirit evident in your life? It should be if you know Jesus as your Savior. Read your Bible daily and apply it to your life. Confess any sin to God. Let his fruit be seen in you.

MEMORIZE:

"When the Holy Spirit controls our lives, he will produce . . . love, joy, peace, patience, kindness, goodness, faithfulness, gentleness, and self-control." Galatians 5:22-23

Show the Fruit of the Spirit

February

4

Linnea Looks Back

Read Luke 9:57-62

Linnea was so homesick! Lately all she could think about was her life "before." When Dad had been a pastor, they'd lived in a lovely big parsonage. They'd visited Grandma and Grandpa nearly every week, and she often got to stay overnight. But that was "before"—before they had felt that God wanted them to be missionaries. Now she was halfway around the world, staying at a boarding school for missionary kids while Mom and Dad were away for six months at a time!

That evening, Linnea's house father led the junior-age girls in their devotions. He read the story of Lot's wife and how she turned into a pillar of salt when she looked back at the cities of sin (Genesis 19:17-26). "This story has a good lesson for Christians," he said. "Although it's good to look back to see the way God has led us, we shouldn't look back at what used to be and allow it to spoil us for service right now. We should look back to remember what great things God has done for us, not to see what we're missing now." He prayed for the girls, asking God to help them all to keep looking ahead.

Long after the other children were asleep, Linnea lay thinking of how God had led her family. She remembered the missionary conference a few years before when all of them (Mom, Dad, and—yes—Linnea, too!) had felt burdened for people who'd never heard of Jesus. She remembered how the Lord had called them to go, and how he had helped Mom and Dad finish their training. She remembered the commissioning service when the three of them had knelt as people laid hands on them and prayed God's blessing on their work. She had been eager to serve the Lord then.

Linnea knew she'd been looking back. *I'm sorry, Lord,* she prayed right there in her bed. *Please forgive me for grumbling and wishing we were back in the States. I really do want to serve you! Please show me what you want me to do with my life. REP*

HOW ABOUT YOU?

Are you guilty of looking back to the way things used to be—and making yourself miserable? Perhaps you've moved, and you won't allow yourself to like the new place because you long for the old. Or maybe there was a time when your family had more money than they do now. Don't be guilty of looking back and longing for a former way of life. Serve the Lord in the place he has put you now.

MEMORIZE:

"But Jesus told him, 'Anyone who puts a hand to the plow and then looks back is not fit for the Kingdom of God.' " Luke 9:62

Look Forward!

Choosing Obedience

Read Romans 6:11-15

Kathy ran upstairs to the room she shared with her sisters—actually, with just Holly, now that Mari was in college. Kathy wished there were still the three of them—it had been so much fun! "The Preston Girls," people called them. "Three of the sweetest Christians in church," they said.

Mari had been away on her own for a year, but Kathy missed her now just as much as she had when Mari first left.

"Holly," Kathy said, "what's going on? Grandma always looks like she's been crying. Mom does, too, and even Daddy looks miserable. What are you all hiding from me?"

"We're not hiding anything, Kathy—it's just that you're so young," Holly told her.

"I'm old enough!" Kathy protested. "It's something to do with Mari, isn't it?" Kathy's voice trembled. "Those gossipy girls at school said Mari was living with some guy, and they're not married. I didn't believe them, but it's true, isn't it?" Kathy burst into tears.

Holly sat beside her on the bed and put her arms around her little sister. "Why?" Kathy asked when she could speak again. "Why would Mari do that? It's so wrong. It's sin. And she's a—she's a Christian."

"Mari is a Christian who is living in disobedience to the Lord," Holly explained. "She says she's an adult and can do what she wants. She says she's responsible for herself. She just doesn't know how all of us who love her feel responsible, too—and sad and hurt. She doesn't realize that it hurts us because we know God will deal with her about this sin. She'll be hurt by what she's doing, too. Someday she'll have to listen to God."

"What can we do?" Kathy asked tearfully. "Can't we stop her?"

"Mom and Dad and Grandma and the church family are doing all they can," Holly replied, "but Mari wants her own way. We need to love her and pray for her. And I guess we can learn from Mari, too—we can learn how much it hurts others when someone is a disobedient Christian." *VJL*

HOW ABOUT YOU?

Is there someone in your family, or perhaps in your church family, who is a disobedient Christian, living in sin? If so, you know how much it hurts. It hurts God much more! But he will continue to work in the life of that person. You also must continue to love and pray for that person. Remember that when you sin, it hurts other people and God as well as you.

MEMORIZE:
"Give yourselves completely to God since you have been given new life. And use your whole body as a tool to do what is right for the glory of God."
Romans 6:13

Disobedience Hurts You and Others

6

Second Chance

Read Matthew 18:21-22

"Look what Joshua did to my tape!" Natalie's face was red with anger. "He's ruined it!" She turned to her little brother, who sat at the table eating ice cream. "Don't you ever touch my tape player or tapes again!"

"I'm sorry, Natalie," Joshua said sadly. "It just broke."

"Tapes don't just break!" Natalie argued. "You broke it." She shook her finger at him. "From now on you leave my tapes alone!" She stomped off to her room to study.

The next afternoon Mom came into Natalie's room. "More homework?" she asked.

"Another math test tomorrow," Natalie replied. "We had one today, but most of us messed up, so Miss Nelson is giving us another chance."

Mom smiled. "A second chance? That's nice of her. I know someone else who could use a second chance."

Natalie looked puzzled.

"What about Joshua?" her mother prompted. "He needs a second chance with you," she said. "Don't you think you were a little hard on him yesterday? He really enjoys listening to Bible stories on your tape player. You never seemed to mind before, and yesterday was the first time he ever hurt anything."

Joshua, who had been in the hall listening, came into the room. "I'll save my 'llowance and buy you another tape," he offered.

As Natalie hesitated, her glance fell on her math book. Remembering her second chance in math, she smiled. "You don't have to do that, Joshua," she said. "That was an old tape anyway. I've heard it a hundred times." She handed him another tape. "Here's a new one. Why don't you listen to it?" *BJW*

HOW ABOUT YOU?

Do you realize that God has often given you a second chance? How many times have you cheated, lied, or disobeyed? How many times have you failed him in one way or another? Yet when you confess your sin to God, he always forgives you. Are you holding a grudge against somebody? Don't you think that person deserves a second chance, too?

MEMORIZE:

"Make allowance for each other's faults and forgive the person who offends you. Remember, the Lord forgave you, so you must forgive others." Colossians 3:13

Be Forgiving

Mistaken

Read John 9:1-7

As Keiko and Nina started home, they met Justin—a school bully. "Hey, Nina, where'd you get this red hat?" asked Justin as he grabbed the cap from her head and tossed it down on the sidewalk. Nina stared, her mouth hanging open.

"Stop that!" commanded Keiko, darting toward the cap. She returned it to Nina. "You leave her alone," ordered Keiko, glaring at Justin.

"Thank you," said Nina, smiling happily as she placed the cap back on her head. Justin walked away, grinning broadly.

When Keiko reached her home, she hurried into the house. "What's up?" asked her mom when she saw Keiko's unhappy face.

"I'm just thinking about Nina Jarret," said Keiko glumly. She plopped down onto the couch. "She has learning problems, you know? She's just not smart, and some of the kids tease her." She sighed. "I don't understand why God lets people like her be born. Seems like a sad mistake for her."

"A mistake?" echoed Mom.

"Well, life couldn't be much fun for her," said Keiko. "She has to work so hard to learn to do even simple things."

"Yes, she does," agreed Mom, "and because of that, Nina's parents are extremely proud of all she can do. Nina is the joy of their lives."

"Yes, but . . ." Keiko paused. "Think of her," she added.

"I am," said Mom. "Nina's mom tells me how much Nina looks forward to going to school each day. She's so easily pleased and proudly shows her coloring papers to everyone. Nina is a happy girl who loves all the kids—and I'm pleased to tell you that she often talks about her friend Keiko." Mom smiled. "Remember, honey, God made each of us, and he has a purpose for all that he does. Even if we don't understand that purpose, we can be sure he knows what he's doing. This time, I'd say you're the one who was mistaken." *MD*

HOW ABOUT YOU?

Does it seem like God occasionally makes a mistake in what he allows to happen? He is all-knowing and all-powerful. He will do what is best, and he never makes mistakes.

MEMORIZE:

" 'Who makes mouths?' the Lord asked him. 'Who makes people so they can speak or not speak, hear or not hear, see or not see? Is it not I, the Lord?' " Exodus 4:11

God Has a Purpose for All

8

Whose Fault Is It?

Read 1 Corinthians 9:24-27; 10:31

Jenny walked into the dining room and plopped down on a chair. "What a rotten day!" she moaned. "I was the last one picked for the relay races in gym class. Then when it was my turn to run, I slipped and fell, and everyone laughed at me. Oh, why am I so fat?"

"I wouldn't call you fat, honey. You're just pleasingly plump," said Jenny's mother, who was also overweight, "but if it will make you feel better, I'll make a doctor's appointment for you. Maybe she can help."

"Okay," Jenny agreed as she opened a bag of potato chips. Perhaps the doctor would be able to explain why she kept gaining weight!

After Dr. Madison examined Jenny, she handed her some papers. "Here's a diet plan that will help you," she said. "Cut out snacks and eat well-balanced meals."

Jenny stayed on the diet for a few days, but then she gave up. "It'll never work. I'll always be fat," she said with a sigh. "I'm a Christian, so why doesn't God help me?" To make herself feel better, she ate two candy bars.

That week, Jenny's Sunday school lesson was on the fruit of the Spirit. "One of the characteristics God wants to see in us is temperance, or self-control," her teacher, Mrs. Graham, said. "That means being able to control our appetites and desires instead of letting them control us."

Jenny felt guilty, so after class, she talked to Mrs. Graham about her problem. "I felt like you were talking about me," she said. "But I just can't help eating so much—it's the way God made me."

"Jenny, as long as you try to find excuses for your actions, the Lord can't help you," Mrs. Graham explained kindly. "You need to be willing to take the responsibility instead of blaming him. Only when you admit that it's your own fault will you be able to claim God's power to overcome your weaknesses." *SLK*

HOW ABOUT YOU?

Do you let your appetites and desires control you? Do you tend to do things you know you shouldn't? Lack of self-control is not just a problem—it's sin. Take the blame for it yourself. Don't defend your sin. God will help you if you will commit to overcoming sin and depend on him.

MEMORIZE:

"Whatever you eat or drink or whatever you do, you must do all for the glory of God." 1 Corinthians 10:31

Control Your Appetites

Sharon's Decision

Read 1 Samuel 15:22; Colossians 3:20

"Mom! Dad!" Sharon called excitedly as she entered the house one Sunday afternoon. "I'm going to be baptized next week! Will you come to see me?"

Sharon's father scowled. "Look here, young lady," he said, "ever since you were 'saved,' as you call it, you've been bugging your mother and me to go to church with you. Now you want to be baptized! Forget that idea! You're fine the way you are. It's enough that I let you go to church!"

"But, Dad," Sharon began, "I have . . ."

"Not another word!" Dad commanded. "The subject is closed."

Sharon wondered what she should do. She believed the Bible taught that a person should be baptized after becoming a Christian. But the Bible also said, "Children, obey your parents." How could she do both? She decided to talk it over with Mrs. Burns, her Sunday school teacher.

"You're in a difficult position," Mrs. Burns agreed after hearing Sharon's problem. "Since your parents aren't Christians, we can't expect them to think as Christians do. However, they're still your mother and father, and you must obey them."

"But what about obeying God by being baptized?" Sharon wondered aloud.

"God knows your heart, Sharon. He knows you love him and want to obey him," Mrs. Burns said. "In your case, God knows that you would be baptized if you could. You won't always be a child. When you are old enough to make your own decision about it, it will be your responsibility to be baptized. Meanwhile, you should obey your parents as God commands. Perhaps as a result of your obedience, you will be able to win them to Jesus."

Sharon sighed. "Oh, I hope so. Thank you, Mrs. Burns. I will obey them and witness the best I can." *HCT*

HOW ABOUT YOU?

Do you obey your parents? Perhaps they're not Christians. God says to obey them. Or perhaps they are Christians, but you don't agree with them. God says to obey them. When you're older, you'll be responsible for many decisions. Right now, most of these decisions are made by your parents. Obey your parents, and trust that God knows your heart.

MEMORIZE:
"You children must always obey your parents, for this is what pleases the Lord." Colossians 3:20

Obey Your Parents

February

10

As Courtney nibbled at her breakfast, she thought about the big math test she would be taking later that day. Even though she had studied hard, it felt like there was a big knot in her stomach. Tests made her nervous!

"Not hungry this morning, honey?" Mom asked as she noticed Courtney's nearly full cereal bowl.

"I keep thinking about that horrible test," Courtney replied anxiously.

"You knew how to work all of the problems last night," Mom said.

"But it's different when I have to do them on a test," Courtney said with a sigh. "I'm comfortable when I'm at home with you and Daddy, but I get scared at school, and everything seems to get jumbled up in my mind."

Mom sat down next to Courtney and reached for her hands. "Daddy and I can't be with you at school, but your heavenly Father will be with you during your test," she said reassuringly. "He doesn't want you to worry. He tells us to give all of our worries and anxieties to him, because he cares for us so much."

"I know." Courtney sighed. "But I still get so nervous," she said.

"Why don't you tell God how you feel," Mom suggested, "and really give him your worries by believing he will help you. He wants to give you his peace in place of the worries that are there. Shall we pray about it together?"

Courtney nodded and bowed her head. Mom prayed first, and then Courtney prayed, too. "Dear heavenly Father," she said, "I'm really nervous about this test. Please give me your peace so I can think clearly on my test. If I start to worry today, remind me that you're with me. Thank you! In Jesus' name, Amen."

"Amen," Mom said. She gave Courtney a hug. "Now how about eating some breakfast? You can't do math problems on an empty stomach." *DLR*

HOW ABOUT YOU?

Is there something in particular that makes you nervous? Do you get butterflies in your stomach when you have to take a test or give an oral report? God wants you to give your worries to him. Let him give you his peace.

MEMORIZE:

"Give all your worries and cares to God, for he cares about what happens to you." 1 Peter 5:7

Give God Your Worries

The Heart Box (Part 1)

Read Matthew 19:16-22

"Dad!" The front door slammed as Cheri hurried in. "Look what Grandma gave me!" She held out a pretty, oval-shaped box with glittering red stones outlining the lid. "I'm going to keep special things in it," she said. Cheri took the box to her room and proudly set it on her dresser. Before long, she had placed quite a number of treasures in the box.

One day, Cheri's brother had a question. "Hey," he said, "my class is collecting money for the Jones family. They're the ones whose house burned down last week. Who wants to make a donation?"

"Not me!" Cheri answered. "I'm saving my money for a new Game Boy."

"I don't have much, either, but I can give a little," Cheri's older sister, Claudia, said. Turning to Cheri, she asked, "May I wear your red sweatshirt?"

"No! You'll spill something on it," Cheri grumbled. "You always wreck stuff." Dad frowned, but didn't say anything.

That afternoon, Cheri decided to look through her treasure box. As she lifted the lid, she puckered her face at a strange smell.

"Yuck!" she exclaimed. She ran to show it to her dad. "The rose petals I saved are all dried up," Cheri said, "but worst of all, my bird egg broke and made a smelly mess all over my box!" Big tears ran down her cheeks.

"Oh, honey, I'm sorry," Dad said. "Didn't you know it would spoil and smell if it broke? Better dump it out, and then let's see what we need to do to clean the box." Cheri got the wastebasket, and they began to sort through the things she had saved.

"You need to be careful about what you put into this box, Cheri," Dad said, "but it's even more important to be careful about what you put into your 'heart box.' I've heard some words that make me think you've been keeping selfishness in your heart. Sweatshirts will one day turn into rags, and money will be spent, but sharing will bring happiness that lasts forever." *LJR*

HOW ABOUT YOU?

Do you cheerfully share your money and your things? Do you offer to help your parents by doing extra chores from time to time? These are just a few ways to store real treasure—treasure in heaven.

MEMORIZE:

"Store your treasures in heaven, where they will never become moth-eaten or rusty and where they will be safe from thieves." Matthew 6:20

Don't Be Selfish

February

12

The Heart Box (Part 2)

Read Psalm 18:1-3

As Cheri cleaned out her special jeweled box, she turned to her sister. "Sorry for not sharing with you," Cheri apologized.

"That's okay," Claudia answered. "Can I help you clean out your box?"

Cheri handed her a small, glittering rock she had been keeping in the box. "It's mostly done," she said, "but you can wash this off and polish it if you like."

Claudia cleaned and polished the rock until it gleamed. She held it in the sunlight, and the reflected light bounced around the room. "Cool!" Cheri exclaimed. "Thanks, Claudia. I guess that's the best treasure I had in my box. Most of my other stuff needed to be dumped."

"You know," Mom said as she came in the room, "you needed to get rid of the bad stuff in your box, but you can keep that rock. You needed to get rid of the bad stuff—the sin—in the 'heart box,' of your life, too. But Jesus is like that rock. He is the treasure that will last forever."

Claudia looked puzzled. "I don't get it," she said.

"The Bible says everyone has done wrong things. We're all sinners," Mom explained. "That's like having bad things in our hearts—things that need to be removed. We can never go to heaven in our sinful condition; no sin is allowed there."

"Well, I've never done anything really terrible," Claudia said. "Just little stuff—like lying maybe. That's not really so bad, is it?"

"Because God is holy and just, *no* sin can enter heaven, Claudia," Mom said. "All sin has to be punished."

"That sounds scary," Claudia said.

"Yes," Mom agreed, "but God loves us very much—so much that he sent his Son, Jesus, to die on a cross and take the punishment we deserve. When we accept him into our lives, he removes the sin in our hearts and replaces it with real treasure—his Spirit—and he will always be with us. All we have to do is ask him." *LJR*

HOW ABOUT YOU?

Do you have Jesus in your heart and life? Have you asked him to forgive your sins and to be your Savior? You can do that right now.

MEMORIZE:

"For God so loved the world that he gave his only Son, so that everyone who believes in him will not perish but have eternal life." John 3:16

Invite Jesus into Your Life

Melissa's Valentines

Read Micah 6:6-8

Mom knocked gently and then opened the door to Melissa's room. School clothes were in a pile against one wall; pajamas were still on the unmade bed; several library books and old homework papers peeked out from under the bed. Melissa herself sat in the middle of the floor among red construction paper, doilies, scissors, glue, and colored marking pens.

Mom frowned. "The Weavers are coming over tonight," she said. "Please straighten up your room before they get here."

"Yes, Ma'am," Melissa agreed. The door closed, and Melissa returned to her project. "Let's see," she said aloud, "I need a valentine for Mom and one for Dad. Then I could make one for each of the Weavers. That's four more. Hmmm. I wonder if Bobby Weaver would mind a lacy doily on his?" She giggled. "Anyway, six valentines all together." She reached for her scissors and began carefully cutting out the first heart shape.

Melissa worked very hard. She lettered a special message for each person and glued a chocolate heart on each card. *It's good to show love,* she thought to herself. *I bet Mom and Dad and the Weavers will like these.*

When the doorbell rang, Melissa eagerly dashed out of her room, carrying all six valentines in her hand. In the hall, Mom stopped her. "Did you straighten up your room?" Mom asked.

"I didn't have time, but—" Melissa beamed a smile up at her mother. "Look what I made!"

Mom didn't even look at the valentines. "I'm sorry, Melissa," she said, shaking her head. "You'll have to go back and clean your room like I asked you to."

"But I want to give everyone these valentines," Melissa protested. "And I want to play with Bobby and Chrissie."

Mom shook her head. "That can wait," she said. "And after this, remember that the best way to show love is to obey." *MEU*

HOW ABOUT YOU?

Do you try to show love by doing things you think others should appreciate? Do you remember that obedience is the thing parents appreciate most? It's the thing God wants from you, too. He expects you to show your love to him by obeying his commands—and one of them is "Obey your parents."

Love Is Obedience

MEMORIZE:
"Obedience is far better than sacrifice." 1 Samuel 15:22

14

Valentines

Read 1 Corinthians 13:4-10

Jill and Valerie were looking for just the right valentine cards for their friends. "I give up! These are so corny," Jill complained. "Hey, Valerie, I have an idea! Let's make our cards."

"Good idea!" her friend agreed. "My mother did that one year for her Sunday school class—she used Bible verses about love. Should we do that, or would the kids think that's dumb?"

"Who cares?" Jill said after a moment. "Let's just do it."

That evening the girls busily prepared the cards.

"Nita Adams is first on the class list," Jill said. "What do you say to a girl who has everything?"

"Maybe she knows about everything but God's love. How about John 3:16 for her? 'For God so loved the world that he gave his only Son, so that everyone who believes in him will not perish but have eternal life.' "

"Good!" Valerie agreed. "Next is Sara Brown. She's so shy and afraid. First John 4:18 (NIV) might be good for her: 'There is no fear in love. But perfect love drives out fear.' And I know just the verse for Danny Dunbar. He's so smart and always uses big words. There's a verse with a big word that's sure to send him straight to the dictionary. 'This is love, not that we loved God, but that He loved us and sent His Son to be the propitiation for our sins.' "

"Wow!" Jill laughed. "What's that big word again?"

Valerie repeated it slowly. "Pro-pi-ti-a-tion. It means the act of regaining the good will of someone. The verse is saying Jesus paid the price for our sins to bring us back into the good will of God." She grinned. "I learned all that from my dad."

Soon the girls were down to the very last card . . . the hardest of all—their teacher's. They finally chose 1 Corinthians 13:4. "Love is patient and kind." They added a note saying, "Thank you for being so patient and kind."

After Valentine's Day, Jill's dad asked how everyone liked the cards. "Just great," Jill answered. She laughed as she added, "And Danny went straight for the dictionary, just like Valerie said." *BJW*

HOW ABOUT YOU?
Do you know that God loves you? There is no greater love and no greater gift! It can be yours. Accept it today.

MEMORIZE:
"This is love, not that we loved God, but that He loved us and sent His Son to be the propitiation for our sins."
1 John 4:10, NASB

God Loves You

Me First

Read Luke 14:7-11

"That's mine," Sasha said, taking the biggest piece of pie.

Her sister, Megan, scowled. "You always take the biggest piece for yourself," she grumbled.

Their brother, John, joined in. "Yeah. Can't you think of anyone but yourself?" he asked. "You just became a Christian, didn't you? You sure aren't acting like one!" Sasha just scowled at John and went out to play.

After dinner, some kids came over to play games in the yard. Sasha's voice could be heard over all the others. "Me first!" she shouted whenever a new game began. Megan and John were embarrassed and ashamed of their sister. "We've gotta do something about her!" Megan declared. So they thought up a plan.

The next day, after they had heard Sasha say "me first" several times, Megan and John put their plan into action. When Sasha came in from play, they were ready.

"Yum!" Sasha exclaimed when she saw three, shiny, red apples on a plate. She grabbed the biggest apple, and Megan and John quickly took the two smaller ones. Sasha started to put the big apple to her mouth, then pulled it away and looked at it suspiciously. She tested it with her teeth. "Hey!" she sputtered. "You tricked me! You served a plateful of wax apples."

"You tricked yourself," John said, biting into his apple. "Mmmmm . . . mine's sweet and juicy. How's yours, Megan?"

"Delicious!" Megan declared. She looked at Sasha. "If you hadn't been greedy and taken the biggest for yourself, you'd have been eating one of these apples."

With a very red face, Sasha admitted she had been wrong. "I got the message," she said. "I have been pretty selfish. Maybe you can help me remember to act more like Jesus. But no more wax apples!"

"It was pretty funny, though," said Megan, and they all had a good laugh as they shared the apples. *CEY*

HOW ABOUT YOU?

Are you willing to take turns being first? Do you let others sometimes have the biggest or best things? God warns against exalting yourself—putting yourself first. He teaches that the way to be first is to be a servant. If you want to be first, do it God's way.

MEMORIZE:

"Anyone who wants to be the first must take last place and be the servant of everyone else." Mark 9:35

Let Others Be First

February

16

Almost Isn't Enough

Read Acts 26:22-23, 27-29

"May I chop the zucchini?" Mallory asked. She was helping her mother make zucchini bread.

"Sure," Mom agreed. "Just be careful."

Mallory got out the food processor, put some of the zucchini in it, and turned it on. She waited, but it didn't run. "Mom, what's wrong with this thing?"

Mom looked at the appliance. "The container has to be placed in exactly the right spot or the machine won't work," she said. "You should hear it snap into place." She demonstrated.

Mallory finished the chopping and mixed the rest of the items. She brushed the pans with butter, and Mom poured the batter into them. Then they put the loaves in the oven and began to clean the kitchen.

"Picky old food processor," Mallory muttered as she washed the container. "It won't go unless it's just so." Then she laughed. "Hey! I'm a poet and don't know it."

Mom smiled. "That reminds me of the Bible story of the apostle Paul and King Agrippa."

"It does? Why?" Mallory asked.

"Do you remember it? Paul was talking to the king about believing in Jesus," Mom said. (See today's Scripture.) Mallory nodded. "Well, you had the food processor set up *almost* right—and when Paul witnessed to King Agrippa, the king was *almost* convinced to believe," Mom explained. "*Almost right* wasn't enough to make the food processor work, and *almost convinced* isn't enough for salvation." *DEM*

HOW ABOUT YOU?

Are you like people who admit that the Bible might be right—or that maybe Jesus is the way to heaven? It's not good enough to have something almost right. To be almost convinced to believe is to be lost. You need to be wholly convinced that Jesus is the only way to heaven. Accept him today.

MEMORIZE:

"Jesus answered, 'I am the way and the truth and the life. No one comes to the Father except through me.' " John 14:6, NIV

To Almost Believe Is to Be Lost

Family Photos

Read Psalm 51:5; 58:1-5

Several old albums and loose pictures were scattered over the living room floor, and Charissa and Joanna were helping their mother sort them out. "I'd like to rearrange our albums with captions above them," Mom said. "See what you can come up with."

"Lifeguard blows whistle at Joanna," Charissa suggested, picking up one of the pictures. "This was the time we were at the beach and the lifeguard yelled at Joanna, remember?"

"Forget that one!" Joanna exclaimed. "But just look at these pictures of Thanksgiving dinner. The food looks yummy!"

"The caption for that could say, 'Give thanks first; then eat,' " Charissa said promptly. "You were scolded for eating before we prayed." She picked up another photo. "Look at this one, Joanna. You're pouting in this snapshot," she said with a laugh.

"Will you quit bringing up all the bad things I've done?" Joanna protested angrily. "After all, you're not so perfect yourself."

"None of these pictures remind you of bad things about me," Charissa said smugly.

"Is that right?" Mom challenged. She picked up two photos. "In these I see not one, but two sinful little girls."

"Mom! Those are our baby pictures," Charissa objected. "You can't find anything bad about a baby."

Her mom smiled. "You *look* sweet enough," she agreed, "but you and your sister are the same when it comes to sin. Every single baby is born a sinner—no one is better than anyone else."

"So there!" Joanna exclaimed.

"Be quiet!" Charissa snapped back.

"There's no need to argue," Mom said. "The Bible clearly tells us that *all* have sinned and fallen short of the glory of God."

"Including you, Charissa," Joanna added, then blushed as she realized her sinful nature had done it again. *NEK*

HOW ABOUT YOU?

Do you ever think you aren't as sinful as someone else? Sin is sin, and it cannot enter heaven. But it can be forgiven through Jesus Christ. Have you asked for his forgiveness? Have you invited him into your life? Do it today.

Everyone Has Sinned

MEMORIZE:
"For all have sinned and fall short of the glory of God." Romans 3:23, NIV

February

18

The Onion

Read Hebrews 12:12-15

As Stephie opened her eyes one morning, she had a sick feeling in the pit of her stomach. She felt anger rise within her as it did so often lately. *Dad was so mad last night,* she remembered, *and he was yelling at Mom as usual.* Stephie reluctantly sat up in bed. "He makes me so mad," she muttered. "Why does he have to be so mean?" *Why can't I have parents who get along?* she thought with disgust as she went into the kitchen. She found her mother there, peeling vegetables.

"Good morning," Mom greeted her, smiling. "How'd you sleep?"

"Oh . . . fair, I guess," Stephie muttered. She shrugged, and her eyes filled with tears. "How do you stand it, Mom?" she blurted out angrily. "How can you stand the way Dad yells so much?"

Mom was quiet for a moment. "I used to be quite bitter about it, especially before I knew the Lord," she admitted, "but God is showing me that I need to forgive and deal with it one day at a time. It's working too, even if it's been a slow process. Your dad has never hit either one of us, and he seems to respond better when I remain calm, like Jesus wants me to." She picked up an onion. "Have you ever noticed that you sometimes get teary when you peel an onion? If you would peel one layer at a time off an onion, some tears would come with each layer, but eventually there would be no more onion," she said. "Dealing with bitterness is something like that. It takes daily prayer. It can take weeks, months, and sometimes years—but you will see victory. You need to deal with bitterness one day at a time. Some days will be better than others. You can't change your dad. But you can work on letting go of bitterness."

"So you're not really over it?" Stephie asked.

Mom pulled Stephie close in a warm hug. "God is helping me through the good days and the bad, honey. I have things I need to work on too—it's not just your dad's fault. My 'onion of bitterness' is gone, but I still need to keep working on it so it doesn't creep back into my life. Now, let's you and I pray for God to keep working in our family." *SLN*

HOW ABOUT YOU?

Are you angry about things that are happening to you that you cannot change? Does that anger keep growing and growing inside you? That's called bitterness. You need to ask God daily to help you overcome it. It will take time, but as you learn to trust him—accepting his forgiveness for you and granting forgiveness to others—you will have victory.

MEMORIZE:

"Get rid of all bitterness, rage, anger, harsh words, and slander, as well as all types of malicious behavior."
Ephesians 4:31

Overcome Bitterness

Love in Action

Read Ephesians 4:31–5:2

Kendra was distracted all during the Sunday school lesson. Mrs. Tracy, her teacher, noticed that her eyes were red and swollen as if she had been crying. After class, Mrs. Tracy approached her.

"Kendra, do you have a problem? Anything I can do to help?" she asked.

"Oh, Mrs. Tracy, my mom and dad have big problems," Kendra confided. "Dad packed his clothes and left last night. He said he was never coming back again! What can I do, Mrs. Tracy? I love my dad and want him to come home. Mom is so sad because she loves Dad, too!"

Mrs. Tracy hugged Kendra, and they talked about her problem. Together they prayed for Kendra's parents and also for wisdom for Kendra. "I think the most important thing you can do besides pray for your folks is to show through your actions that you love them," Mrs. Tracy said. "Put some 'feet on your love.' I know the situation hurts you, and one of the best ways to help yourself is to help others. You know your mother hurts, too. If you can stay a little longer, I'll give you some suggestions of how you can help her."

When Kendra went home, she had several ideas of what she could do. After dinner she cleared the table. She encouraged her younger brother to change from his Sunday clothes into play clothes. She helped her mother with the dishes.

Days turned into weeks, and weeks into months, and Kendra continued to put "feet on her love" as Mrs. Tracy had said. "Kendra, you've been such a help to me since your father left," her mother said one day. "You've made my life so much easier. Even though you're young, you've taken some of the burden of running this house off my shoulders."

As her mom gave Kendra a big hug, Kendra was thinking, *Mrs. Tracy was right. Helping Mom helped me most of all. It made me feel so much better, and it's really good to know that it pleased God, too.* AU

HOW ABOUT YOU?

When things get tough at your house, do you mope around and feel sorry for yourself? That only makes you and everyone else more miserable! Next time things go wrong at home, try putting "feet on your love." Help keep family peace and unity. You'll be happier as you follow God's command to walk in love. God will be pleased, too.

MEMORIZE:
"Live a life filled with love for others, following the example of Christ, who loved you and gave himself as a sacrifice to take away your sins."
Ephesians 5:2

Walk in Love

February
20

Snowcones and Eggs

Read Luke 19:1-10

Mercedes raced home from the corner store. She skipped and hopped and would have turned somersaults, but she didn't want to spill her snowcone. She had saved money all week for this triple tutti-frutti treat. What a day—to have a snowcone like this, and then to have the girl at the store give her too much change! Now she had enough money for another snowcone tomorrow!

She did feel a twinge in her conscience, but after all, it wasn't her fault she had been given too much money. She didn't steal it. She eased her conscience with that thought.

As her mom read the paper that afternoon, she gave an exclamation of surprise. "Mr. Hernandez died," she said.

"Who's that?" Mercedes asked.

Mom put the paper down. "He's someone I knew long before you were born," she said. "When I was a little girl, we raised chickens and sold eggs. One day a man came to buy eggs. After he left, I noticed he had given me a five-dollar bill instead of a one. I knew I should return his money, but I didn't do it. Well, the years went by, and from time to time the memory of the money I owed to that man came back to disturb me. Finally, I asked God to forgive me, and he did. In fact, he did even more than that. He allowed me to find that man and repay what I owed him."

"Was it Mr. Hernandez?" Mercedes asked when her mother paused.

Mom nodded. "After I repaid the money, I forgot all about it until just now. Believe me, Mercedes, if the Lord pricks your conscience about anything you've done, it will save you a lot of distress if you make it right immediately."

Mercedes had a huge lump in her throat and tears in her eyes. She knew what she must do. She would never be able to enjoy a snowcone tomorrow, knowing how she had gotten the money. *DS1*

HOW ABOUT YOU?

Have you told a lie, cheated, or disobeyed—and it seems like you got away with it? Do you feel guilty or uneasy every time you think about that? You should! God gave you a conscience to make you aware of wrong things in your life. And if you're a Christian, you have the Holy Spirit to guide you.

MEMORIZE:
"Confess your sins to each other and pray for each other." James 5:16

Make Wrong Things Right

Questions

Read Luke 2:41-52

"Mom, make Shawn leave me alone!" Bridget exclaimed as she pushed her little brother into the kitchen. "He follows me everywhere!"

Shawn's eyes clouded with tears. "I didn't do nothin'."

Mom hugged her son and turned to her daughter. "What's the problem?"

"He asks 'why' over and over and over," Bridget complained. "I get so tired of it."

Mom smiled. "I guess you can't remember all the questions you used to ask!"

"What questions?" Bridget asked in surprise.

"Oh, there were a lot of them," her mom told her. "Like, 'Why are puppies cute?' 'Why do birds sing?' 'Why do fingers have nails?' 'Why does Grandpa walk so slow?' 'Why are trees tall?' Now Shawn is learning by asking questions just like you did."

Bridget laughed. "Well, in that case I guess I better try to be a little more patient," she decided. "But I hope he learns fast. It does get annoying."

"I realize that," her mom sympathized. "You know, it just occurred to me that when Jesus was a boy, he asked questions, too. Get my Bible from the table." After Bridget brought the Bible, Mom turned several pages. Then she asked Bridget to read a verse.

"Three days later they finally discovered him," read Bridget. "He was in the temple, sitting among the religious teachers, discussing deep questions with them."

Mom took the Bible and closed it. "I've heard some preachers say that Jesus was teaching, but others have suggested that he was also learning," she said. "In any case, maybe it will help us have more patience if we remember that even Jesus asked questions."

Bridget held out her hand to her little brother. "Come on, Shawn. Let's go play in the living room."

Shawn went along happily. Mom smiled when she heard Shawn's voice begin, "Bridget, why . . . ?" *RG*

HOW ABOUT YOU?

Do you get impatient with someone who asks a lot of questions? Do you ask a lot of questions yourself? God is not annoyed by honest questions. It's a natural way of learning. Ask the Lord to help you to be patient when others ask you questions. When you don't know answers, be sure to ask questions yourself and learn from those teachers God has provided for you.

Learn by Asking Questions

MEMORIZE:
"Let the wise listen and add to their learning, and let the discerning get guidance." Proverbs 1:5, NIV

February

22

Serena's Shoes

Read Matthew 6:25-33

Serena put one foot on top of the other as she sat at her desk in school, hoping to hide the big hole in the toe of her shoe. Oh, how she wanted a new pair! Each week she hoped that at last there would be money left for shoes after buying groceries, but it hadn't happened yet.

Serena's dad had a steady job, but every Friday after work he'd stop at a bar. By the time he got home, long after Serena was in bed, there would be very little money left—just enough to buy a few groceries for the week. Serena knew this, because from her room she could hear her parents quarreling about it. *But maybe this week it will be different,* Serena thought. *Maybe tonight Dad will bring his check home, and there will be money for shoes for me.*

There was only a meager supper that evening. Serena ate it hungrily and then waited to see if her father would come home early. But when she went sadly to bed at nine o'clock, Dad still wasn't home. *He still could come home any minute,* she thought. Then she drifted off to sleep.

Serena woke suddenly, hearing loud voices from the kitchen. She knew from the angry tones that there would be no new shoes this week. A tear slid from her eye and dropped to her pillow. Her heart hurt with disappointment, and she felt no one cared for her.

As she lay in the dark, a thought came to her. She had been going to Sunday school with a friend, and last week the teacher had talked about God caring for people. The teacher had read it right from the Bible. How did it go? Something like: God takes care of the birds, lilies, and even the grass, so he surely will take care of you.

Even though she didn't have new shoes, Serena felt she must go back to this Sunday school. She wanted to know more about a God like that. Surely he cared for her! *CEY*

HOW ABOUT YOU?

Do you sometimes feel alone with your needs? God, who cares about the small things in nature, cares even more about you. Maybe he wants to use your needs to draw you to himself or to teach you something. Get to know him, and then take comfort in the knowledge that he'll supply all the things you really need.

MEMORIZE:

"Worry weighs a person down; an encouraging word cheers a person up." Proverbs 12:25

God Cares for You

No Results

Read 1 Corinthians 3:5-9

Sophie walked into the house more briskly than usual. "I've had it with her," she said, pulling up a kitchen chair.

"With whom?" her big sister, Yvette, asked.

"Jolene Andrews—that's who." Restlessly, Sophie pushed the chair back and fiddled with a strand of her hair. She bit her lower lip before starting to explain. "Do you remember what I gave her for her birthday?"

Yvette nodded. "Sure—you gave her a year's subscription to a Christian magazine. You used your baby-sitting money to get it."

"That's right," Sophie replied. There was still anger in her voice. "She was always reading my copy whenever she was over here, so I spent my own hard-earned money to get it for her. Well, I overheard her telling some girls that I was pushing religion on her and that she hasn't read either of the two issues that came to her house!"

"Wow—that's too bad," Yvette sympathized. "But you know, you shouldn't let her bad attitude keep you from staying friends with Jolene. After all, you gave her the subscription because you hoped the magazine would be a witness to her—that maybe it would help her come to know Christ."

"But she's not reading them!" Sophie complained. "And she's making accusations about me!"

"More proof that she really does need Jesus," Yvette insisted. "And you never know. It's possible that her reaction to your gift may be partly because she sees her need. Don't be angry. You've planted the seed, but when all is said and done, it's God who's going to work in her heart."

Both girls were quiet for a moment. Finally, Yvette reminded Sophie, "It's only the first two issues of her subscription. There are still ten more months of witness heading to her house. I'll pray with you that she'll read those and that God will work in her heart." *RIJ*

HOW ABOUT YOU?

Have you tried to witness and seen few results? Don't get discouraged or angry. Continue to show love and friendship. God asks you to be faithful in witnessing. He brings about the results.

MEMORIZE:
"Each of us did the work the Lord gave us. My job was to plant the seed in your hearts, and Apollos watered it, but it was God, not we, who made it grow." 1 Corinthians 3:5-6

Be a Faithful Witness

February

24

Something Beautiful

Read Psalm 37:18-23

Grandma worked on one side of a quilt while Ana helped on the other. They were tying knots on the corners of each square, and Ana could see that the quilt was going to be beautiful! Grandma nodded when Ana exclaimed over it. "The knots help hold the batting inside the quilt, so it will stay soft and comfortable," she said.

The quilt was a wedding gift for Ana's cousin, Elena. "Each square is cut from one of Elena's old shirts or dresses," Grandma said, smiling at Ana. "I plan to make a quilt for all of you children. Come, I'll show you something." She led Ana to the storage room and opened a box half full of cloth squares. Ana recognized the material of some of her favorite clothes—and she also saw squares made from some of her not-so-favorite ones. But lying all together in the box like that, they looked beautiful. Grandma had taken old, useless, outgrown clothes and was preparing to make something lovely from them.

Grandma spoke again. "You know, Ana, our lives are a lot like quilts. God sees all the pieces of our lives—the good and the bad. As we surrender ourselves to him, he cuts, shapes, and puts the pieces of our lives together to make something beautiful. He even takes the things we think are terrible and places them in the pattern of our lives to make the overall life more beautiful."

As Grandma was talking, Ana remembered some of the worst days of her life—the day her grandfather had died, the big fat zero she got in math one day even after she had studied hard, and the way her best friend had snubbed her just the day before. Only God could make something good out of those pieces of her life. She didn't understand how he would do it, but she would trust him with all of her days. *DS1*

HOW ABOUT YOU?

Does it seem that nothing good could come from some of the things in your life? Maybe you came in last at the track meet, or maybe one of your friends lied about you. Whatever it is, let Jesus take all of the bad, blend it in with the good, and use it to make your life beautiful. Trust him to do that.

MEMORIZE:
"Day by day the Lord takes care of the innocent, and they will receive a reward that lasts forever." Psalm 37:18

Trust God to Shape Your Life

Disappointment (Part 1)

Read Isaiah 46:9-11

"Won't Mom and Dad be surprised when they see the cake we've made to welcome them home!" Heidi exclaimed. She stirred the batter vigorously. "I can't wait! I've really missed them."

Grandma smiled. "While the cake's in the oven, you and I can hang up the 'Welcome Home' poster—with a few streamers, even if it isn't anyone's birthday!" They both laughed.

But just as Heidi popped the cake into the oven, the telephone rang. Grandma answered it, and Heidi could hear her soft voice speaking with someone. When Grandma returned to the kitchen with a sober look on her face, Heidi could guess what had happened.

"That was your father, honey," Grandma said. "Tonight's flight was overbooked, so they had to give up their seats. They'll be on the early morning flight."

"But, Grandma!" Heidi moaned. "That's not fair! It will spoil our surprise, and I miss them!" Tears filled her eyes.

Grandma held Heidi close. "I know you're disappointed, dear, but we still can have the cake when they get here. And remember, God orders all things, and all he does is right."

"Well, if he really cares which plane Mom and Dad take, I think he might have let them come home today as they had planned," Heidi stormed.

"Heidi, do you really think your plans for your mom and dad are better than the plans God has for them?" Grandma asked. "For reasons only God knows, he didn't allow them to come today, but his plan for us is best," Grandma said firmly. "It doesn't always seem that way to us, but the Bible says he knows the end from the beginning. We must trust him." *BD*

HOW ABOUT YOU?

Have you had some "unlucky breaks" lately? Has "fate" been unkind to you? Wait a minute! Fate and luck have no place in your life. Are you forgetting that God is in control? He knows all about what is happening in your life. He has a plan and a purpose for every single thing that takes place. Trust him with your disappointments.

God Is in Control

MEMORIZE:
"I have said I would do it, and I will."
Isaiah 46:11

February
26

Disappointment (Part 2)

Read Psalm 135:1-7

"Hooray! I'm so glad you're here!" Heidi exclaimed as her parents finally arrived home from their trip. "I was so disappointed when you didn't come last night." Heidi sighed. "It wasn't fair that you had to give up your seats on the plane!"

"Did you watch the news report last night?" Dad asked.

"No," Grandma replied. "We never turned on the TV—or the radio. Since you weren't coming home, we stayed up late playing board games. Then we slept in and didn't catch the news this morning, either. Why?"

"Last night's flight never reached its destination," Dad said. "Engines failed, and the pilots had to bring the plane down. They crash-landed, and a couple of passengers lost their lives."

Heidi gasped, her eyes wide.

"Many others were seriously injured," Mom added.

"Oh, God was good to us, wasn't he!" Heidi exclaimed.

"For a while yesterday you didn't think God was so good," Grandma reminded her.

"But I didn't know about the crash then," Heidi defended herself.

"God would have been just as good if we had lost our lives in that crash, Heidi," Dad said gently. "In this situation, we can see why he disappointed us. But God has a plan by which he rules the world, and everything he does is good, though sometimes we can't understand it. Right now there are families grieving over their loved ones who died on that plane. God is still in control of their lives as well."

Mom nodded. "God doesn't always reveal his reasons to us," she said. "We can be assured of one thing, though—all things work together for good to those who love him!"

Heidi smiled. "I'm glad God disappointed me this time," she said. "When I'm disappointed again, I'll try to remember that what God has planned is always good, whether I understand his reasons or not!" *BD*

HOW ABOUT YOU?

Are things going just the way you hoped? Or do things seem to be going all wrong for you? Then you have a choice to make. You can murmur and complain and be unhappy—or you can recognize that, although you cannot understand the reasons for what's happening, God is in control, and his plan is good. You can trust him to make it work for your best and "praise the Lord, for the Lord is good."

MEMORIZE:
"Praise the Lord, for the Lord is good." Psalm 135:3

God's Plan Is Always Good

Come

27

Read John 6:32-40

Andrea was the youngest member of the Taylor family. The rest of the family loved to swim, but Andrea was terrified of the water. "Get out there and get your feet wet," her brother, Mark, coaxed. "You'll never learn to swim if you don't get in and try." But Andrea could not make herself get into the water. And, for sure, no amount of prodding or teasing would make Andrea go out into the big ocean. She wished she could—she really wished she could—but she was afraid!

One day when the Taylors were on a winter vacation at the beach, Andrea's brother and sister joined Mom for a walk along the shore. Andrea and Dad stayed on the beach, building sand castles. "I wish I weren't afraid," Andrea confided to her father. "I'd really like to go out in the water and do what everyone else does. But I'm so scared!"

Dad was quiet for a moment, and then he stood up and waded out into the shallow water. He turned to face Andrea and held his outstretched hands toward his daughter. "Come, honey," he called. "Come to me."

Andrea hesitated. Then looking straight at her father, she left her spot and started toward him. Together they paddled in the water until Andrea felt comfortable. When the other members of her family returned, they were surprised to see Andrea wet from head to toe.

"What happened?!" they exclaimed.

Andrea laughed. "When Daddy said 'come' and held out his arms, I knew he would hold me. So I wasn't scared. I trusted him."

Andrea's dad smiled. "That seems just like a beautiful picture of salvation," he said. "Jesus invites everyone to come to him—to trust him and his death and resurrection for salvation." *RIJ*

HOW ABOUT YOU?

Have you "come to Jesus" to be saved from your sin? The Bible says, "all have sinned" (Romans 3:23), and that includes you. It says, "the wages of sin is death" (Romans 6:23). That's a fearful prospect! But Jesus says, "Come" (Matthew 11:28) and promises never to turn away from those who come to him (John 6:37). That's a wonderful promise. Come to Jesus today.

Come to Jesus and Trust Him

MEMORIZE:
"Those the Father has given me will come to me, and I will never reject them." John 6:37

February

28

It Hurts

Read 2 Corinthians 1:3-5

As Nicole walked around the corner of the school, she heard a strange sound. Someone was crying. Turning, she saw Amy hiding in a corner of the building. "Amy! What's wrong?" Nicole asked.

"Nothing," Amy said. "Just leave me alone!"

Nicole hesitated. She didn't know what to do. "I'll leave you alone if that's what you want," she said finally, "but I wish you'd tell me why you're crying."

Amy peered uncertainly at Nicole. Nicole did sound concerned, and Amy felt like she just had to talk to someone. "My dad left and doesn't live with us anymore, so some of the other kids make fun of me," she blurted between the tears. "They were calling me an orphan. Some of them asked why my dad left, and if he's going to marry someone else." She wiped her eyes. "I miss him so much!"

Nicole touched Amy's shoulder. "That's rough," she said. Nicole didn't really know what to say to Amy or how to help her. Suddenly she remembered her cousin, Julie, who had also been terribly hurt and confused when her dad had left their family. But Julie knew Jesus as her Savior and could rely on him for strength and help. *I've never heard Amy talk about Jesus,* she thought. *Maybe she doesn't know he can help her with her hurts. I wonder if she'll listen.* Fearfully at first, and then with more confidence, Nicole began to tell how Jesus helped her cousin and how he'd like to help Amy, too. She talked about how Jesus not only died for our sins, but also wants to carry our sorrows.

To Nicole's delight, Amy listened. It was a start. *DS1*

HOW ABOUT YOU?

Do you know someone who needs a friend? Someone without the security of a dad or the comfort of a mom? How do you treat that person? If you know someone in that situation, she may need a friend to listen and to help her not to feel so alone. But most of all, she needs Jesus as her very best friend. Jesus is always there to listen and help. Maybe you know of someone you could introduce to Jesus today.

MEMORIZE:
"One should be kind to a fainting friend." Job 6:14

Be a Friend to Those Who Hurt

Family Members

Read Galatians 4:1-7

"We had a new girl in our class today," Leilah said as she nibbled on cheese and crackers. "Her name is Anna. She's from an orphanage in Romania, and an American family—the Blackmans—adopted her."

"How wonderful for her!" Mom exclaimed.

"Deirdre says she feels sorry for Anna because she doesn't have any real family of her own," Leilah added.

Mom sat down at the table. "That's ridiculous," she declared. "Of course she has a family! The minute Anna was adopted, she became as much a part of the Blackman family as if she had been physically born into it." Mom smiled at Leilah. "I wonder if Deirdre realizes that you are also adopted."

Leilah's mouth dropped open, and she stared at her mother. "I didn't know I was adopted!" she exclaimed.

Still smiling, Mom said, "Well, you are. Not by your dad and me; we gave birth to you. But when you accepted Jesus as Savior last year, God immediately adopted you into his family. You're his child now, just like Anna is the Blackmans' child." Mom reached over and picked up her Bible from the counter. She opened it and handed it to Leilah. "Read Romans 8:16-17," she said.

Leilah read aloud. "His Holy Spirit speaks to us deep in our hearts and tells us that we are God's children. And since we are his children, we will share his treasures—for everything God gives to his Son, Christ, is ours, too."

Mom nodded. "You became a child of God and an heir to his heavenly riches," she said. "God accepts you as his own, and Anna's new parents accept her as their very own."

Leilah nodded. "I think Anna and I will get along well together," she said thoughtfully. "She'll be glad to learn that I've been adopted, too." After a moment she looked at her mother and grinned. "You know what, Mom? If Anna becomes a Christian, she'll have been adopted twice!" *JRG*

HOW ABOUT YOU?

Have you been adopted into God's family? If not, wouldn't you like to be? When you trust Jesus as Savior, you become a royal family member—you will even have an inheritance. Trust Jesus today.

Christians Are God's Children

2

The Picture Puzzle

Read Romans 12:3-8

Marissa, Natasha, and Darren decided to work on their new 500-piece picture puzzle. The cover showed a picture of three sailing boats out at sea. "Let's empty all the pieces onto the table and turn them up the right way first," Darren suggested as he munched on potato chips and carrot sticks.

"There sure are a lot of different colors in this puzzle," Marissa observed. "Some of the pieces are black or gray. I like the ones with the pretty, sunshiny yellow color."

"I like the reds and oranges, too," Natasha said. "I want to work with them. The ones with a lot of brown and dark blue and black are dull and ugly."

"Maybe so, but they're all part of the puzzle, and we need them all to finish the picture," Darren reminded her. He pointed to the cover of the box. "We couldn't make a picture like that if all the pieces were red and orange!"

"Like people," Aunt Sue murmured from nearby. All three of them looked at her curiously as she continued. "We're all so different—tall and short, thinner and heavier, quick and slow—but if we know the Lord, we're all part of his family," she explained. "We all look different and we all have different abilities, but we're all needed."

"Yeah. Imagine if everybody were preachers or teachers—who would there be to listen to them? And who would grow the food for us to eat?" Darren asked as he bit into another chip.

"Trust you to think about food!" Natasha teased. The kids laughed as they continued sorting the puzzle pieces.

Aunt Sue smiled with them. "As funny as it can be, think for a minute about how important it is that we're all different. Imagine what the world would be like with no doctors."

Marissa's eyes grew large. "That would be awful! Who would help sick people get better?"

"Or what if there were no garbage collectors?" Aunt Sue suggested.

Natasha wrinkled her nose. "Ick! The world would stink!"

"Yes," Aunt Sue agreed. "It's a very good thing that God is so creative!"

The kids grinned and kept sorting the many colors of the puzzle pieces. *MTF*

HOW ABOUT YOU?

What has God called you to be? You don't have to feel unimportant or inferior if he hasn't called you to be a preacher or teacher; nor should you think that only professions such as medicine or law are important. God calls different people to all different kinds of work. If you are faithfully carrying out the task he has given to you, then you are doing the most important work you can do!

MEMORIZE:

"Equip God's people to do his work and build up the church, the body of Christ." Ephesians 4:11-12

Christians Are Needed in All Occupations

Like Desert Plants (Part 1)

Read Psalm 37:30-31; Matthew 12:34-35

With her books scattered all around, Lynn hunched over the library table. "May I sit here?" asked her sister Monica. Lynn nodded and kept reading. "Isn't this rain yucky?" Monica whispered, looking out the window.

Lynn jumped as a clap of thunder startled her.

"Uh-huh," she muttered. "Now leave me alone."

"This rain will ruin our family reunion," Monica complained. "We'll be stuck inside listening to Uncle George's stupid jokes. We—"

"Will you shut up?" Lynn demanded loudly. The librarian gave her a stern look. "Can't you see I'm working?" continued Lynn, speaking softer, but with a threatening glare.

At the supper table that evening, Monica's complaining increased. She listed all the problems the rain caused her. "I wish it never rained!" she declared.

"Places where it never rains are called deserts," Lynn told her. "That's what my report is about. Deserts are so dry that hardly any plants can grow there. The mesquite tree sometimes sends its roots hundreds of feet into the ground to search for water. When it does rain, the barrel cactus swells with water and then shrinks again as it uses the water. And the—"

"Lynn told me to shut up at the library," tattled Monica, interrupting her sister. Lynn kicked her under the table.

"Lynn! You know better than to talk like that!" scolded Mom.

"Well, she's a pest," grumbled Lynn.

Mom frowned. "Watch your tongue, Lynn," she said. "I've noticed that you've been having trouble with it lately."

"Lynn, maybe you need to be more like that mesquite tree and barrel cactus you told us about—maybe you need to 'drink' more deeply from God's Word," suggested Dad. "In fact, we should all have a thirst for his Word. It would be nice if we were as motivated to read the Bible as those desert plants are to get water. If we were swelling up with God's Word, good words would be coming out of our mouths, and we'd have a desire to get along with one another." *LJR*

HOW ABOUT YOU?

What kind of words come from your mouth? Your words reflect what's in your heart. Read God's Word, think about it, and ask him to help you understand and obey it. As his Word fills your heart, good thoughts, words, and actions will come out.

Drink Deeply from God's Word

MEMORIZE:
"Whatever is in your heart determines what you say." Matthew 12:34

March

4

Like Desert Plants (Part 2)

Read Isaiah 55:8-11

Monica secretly gloated because her parents had pointedly reminded her sister, Lynn, of her need to control her tongue. "Lynn is always nasty to me," she complained aloud. She looked out the window. "She's almost as bad as the rain!" she added. "I hate rain! I wish—" Her words were interrupted by Dad's voice.

"As for you, Monica," Dad said, "you need to quit complaining so much. Remember what Lynn said? Places where there is little or no rain are deserts." The self-satisfied look disappeared from Monica's face. "Without rain, you wouldn't have enjoyed the mashed potatoes that we had for supper tonight," Dad added.

"Or the apple pie we're going to have for dessert," Mom said.

"But rain always ruins our plans," Monica whined.

"It doesn't ruin God's plans," said Dad.

Mom nodded. "It isn't always easy to accept what God has for us," she said, "but I think those desert plants have a lesson for you, too. Dad reminded us that we all need to 'drink' deeply from God's Word, remember? When we do that, it helps us to accept the 'rain' that falls in our lives, as well as the rain that falls outside."

"Rain in our lives?" asked Monica. "What do you mean?"

"I mean the disappointments and difficult circumstances that we all must face at one time or another," replied Mom. "We need to accept what God allows to happen to us and realize that he is working all things for our good."

"Someone put it this way, 'Every cloud has a silver lining,' " said Dad. "Paul said it even better. In Romans 8:28, he says, 'We know that God causes everything to work together for the good of those who love God.' Whenever it rains—whether it's literal rain coming from the sky or difficult times in our lives—we need to remember that God is in control and knows what is best. When we remember that God uses rain to bring good things, we can stop complaining." *LJR*

HOW ABOUT YOU?

Do your difficulties seem like "rain"? Do you complain and grumble? Let rain remind you that God truly does know what is best for you. God uses rain to bring good things.

MEMORIZE:

"[God]. . . provides rain for the earth, and makes the green grass grow in mountain pastures." Psalm 147:7-8

Don't Grumble— Trust God

Not Just a Game

Read Acts 16:16-19

Veronica felt a little uncomfortable as she listened to Dawn read aloud from a magazine article. "This says 'Power of the mind reveals your future and changes the course of your destiny.' " Dawn paused. "And here's a phone number we can call and get our fortunes told."

The girls were having a sleepover at Veronica's. Her parents had gone to bed when they were sure the girls were busy and behaving, but now Veronica wished they were still there. Just last week they had talked in Sunday school about fortune-tellers and the occult.

"Let's call the number," said Heather. She reached for the phone. "What is it?"

"Oops! It's a 900 number," answered Dawn. "It costs $3.50 a minute . . . and you have to be eighteen to call." Veronica breathed a sigh of relief. "But wait a minute," Dawn added. "Here's another number that doesn't say anything about age, and it costs only a dollar a minute."

"Good," said Heather reaching for her backpack. "We can use my phone card, and you can all . . ."

"Don't!" interrupted Veronica. "It's dangerous to play with fortune-telling and stuff like that."

The others stared at her. "Ah, it's just a game."

"No, it's not," Veronica argued. "It's of the devil, and it's dangerous."

"What's dangerous?" Veronica's older brother, Phil, came into the room. "Had a date and just got home. What's dangerous?"

"Phil," said Veronica, "will you explain why it's wrong to call a fortune-teller?"

"Oh, fortune-tellers!" said Phil. "You're right—they are dangerous. Satan uses them to get control over people's lives. For example, one guy was told by a fortune-teller that he'd live to be sixty-seven. Because he believed it, he took terrible risks. At age twenty-nine, he died while surfing in dangerous waters. When we trust the Lord, we don't have to worry about the future."

Dawn closed the magazine, and Heather put the phone card back in her backpack. Veronica sighed with relief. "Let's play charades," she said. *BJW*

HOW ABOUT YOU?

Are you concerned about the future? You don't have to know the future when you know God, nor do you have to be afraid. The God who holds the future holds your life in his hand. Trust him.

Trust God for Your Future

Getting Clean

Read Revelation 21:10, 22-27

Tanya sat at the table, while her mother mopped the floor. "Mom, how do you explain salvation to someone?" she asked. At that moment, the screen door flew open and Tanya's brother, Colin, stepped in.

"Stop!" Mom hollered. "Don't come in one more step with all that mud on you."

"But I'm thirsty," objected Colin. "I don't want to stay out any longer."

"I'm not asking you to stay out," Mom told him. "I'm asking you to leave all that mud at the door, and come in clean." She helped him pull off his dirty shoes and brushed the mud off the back of his jeans. Then she let him in, and Colin got a drink and headed to his room.

"What just happened here is an example of what happens in salvation," Mom told Tanya. "God loves us very much, and he wants to take us to heaven—but not covered in dirt."

"When you say 'dirt,' you mean sin, don't you?" asked Tanya.

"Exactly," agreed Mom. "To God, sin is dirt of the worst kind. When we admit that we're sinners and we ask Jesus to save us, he'll clean off the dirt—he'll wash away our sin—so that we can live with him in heaven someday."

"That's simple," said Tanya thoughtfully. "You'd think everyone would want to be saved."

"Yes," said Mom, "but look out the window." She pointed to Colin's friends, who were still climbing the dirt piles. "They're having a lot of fun out there, and they'll all complain when their mothers make them take a bath. Sometimes getting clean doesn't seem like as much fun as getting dirty."

"I get it," Tanya said. "I guess we have to help people understand how good it is to be clean—and especially how good it is to have God remove the dirt of sin. Right?"

"Right," agreed Mom. "Exactly right!" *HMT*

HOW ABOUT YOU?

Do you know the basics of the plan of salvation? The gospel message is simple. Sin is "dirt" and cannot be allowed in heaven. God wants to clean sin out of your life so that someday you can live with him in heaven. Do you have friends who need to know about that? Share the message with them.

MEMORIZE:
"Wash me clean from my guilt. Purify me from my sin." Psalm 51:2

Let God Cleanse You for Heaven

Brianna's Baby Book

Read Malachi 3:16-17, Colossians 3:23-24

"Why so quiet, Brianna?" Mom asked as she pulled a box of keepsakes from a closet.

Brianna shrugged. "I was just thinking about all the dumb things I did today," she said glumly. "I spilled my milk at lunch and splashed my teacher's new skirt. Then I misspelled 'broccoli' and caused my spelling team to lose. Everyone said I was dumb, and they were right."

Mom pulled a pink book from the box and sat down beside Brianna. "This is your baby book," said Mom. "Here's a lock of your downy infant hair—and look at your footprint."

Brianna grinned. "Wow!" she exclaimed. "It's really tiny, isn't it?"

Mom smiled. "This book says you walked and talked early. You took your first step at nine months. You said 'Dada' at five months—at least, Dad said you did—and you could sing the ABCs by your second birthday. You were a smart little cookie."

"Really?" asked Brianna. "Well, I'm not smart now."

"Yes, you are," Mom insisted. "You just dwell on your mistakes instead of what you do right. Why do you think I didn't write in your baby book, 'Brianna fell down fifteen times today trying to walk'?"

Brianna laughed. "That wouldn't sound nice."

"Falling down is part of learning to walk," said Mom. "The accomplishment is walking! I don't remember the times you fell down, but I remember the first step. I didn't record the times you cried for hours, but I recorded that you were a sweet baby. Mothers write good memories in baby books—and God has a book of remembrance, too. He records every good, kind thing you do."

"Really?" Brianna's eyes sparkled. "Does he write down only the good things— like mothers do?"

"I think so. After all, when we trust in Jesus as Savior, all of our sins—all the bad things we do—are forgiven," said Mom. "The Bible says they're washed away, and it also talks about God rewarding his servants." She smiled at Brianna. "Now tell me about something you did right today." *BJW*

HOW ABOUT YOU?

Aren't you glad that God remembers the good things you do? Don't dwell on your failures and mistakes. Confess them to God and ask him to help you do better. Thank him for what you can accomplish with his help.

MEMORIZE:

"God is not unfair. He will not forget how hard you have worked for him and how you have shown your love to him by caring for other Christians."

Hebrews 6:10

Remember the Good

8

Slug Bug

Read Numbers 13:25-33, 14:6-9

"Slug bug blue!" exclaimed Pete when he spied a new blue Volkswagen Beetle. He playfully slugged Terry's arm. The kids were in the car, on their way home from school, seeing who could spot the most Volkswagens first.

Carly shrugged. She pulled down the mirror on the sun visor. "My freckles look awful," she wailed. "I look like a monster."

"Slug bug yellow!" Terry yelled and slugged Pete as a yellow Volkswagen sped past them.

Carly frowned. "If I can't do something about these freckles, I think I'll go into hiding," she said mournfully.

"Now, Carly, you're being silly. Lots of people have freckles, and I think they make you look cute," Mom consoled her, as she turned onto their street.

"Slug bug black!" This time Pete got Terry. He laughed when Terry said he hit too hard. "That was a bus," Pete said. "The bigger the bug, the bigger the slug."

"That's not one of the rules!" Terry argued. "Mom?"

"Boys, if you can't play without arguing, forget the game," Mom ordered.

"Slug bug blue!" Both boys laughed as they spotted the car at the same time.

Carly turned around and glared at her little brothers. "I think you're making those up. I've never seen that many Volkswagens in my life, much less in one little trip home from school."

"You don't see them because you aren't looking for them," Terry said. "You only see what you look for."

Carly looked in the mirror again. *You only see what you look for,* she thought. This time she saw lovely long blonde hair and sparkling blue eyes. Suddenly the freckles didn't look so bad after all. As Mom braked for a red light, Carly repeated, "You only see what you look for."

"That's often true," Mom agreed. "Let's try to remember to look for good things, not only in appearance, but also in the actions of others." *BJW*

HOW ABOUT YOU?

What do you see—good things or bad? What you look for is what you will see. Ask God to help you watch for smiles and sunshine, friends and fun, love and laughter, and all the other wonderful blessings he has sent into your life.

MEMORIZE:

"Open my eyes to see the wonderful truths in your law." Psalm 119:18

Look for Good Things

Casts and Crutches

Read Philippians 4:10-13

Mira sat on a park bench watching some kids play ball and feeling sorry for herself. She frowned at the cast on her arm. After the first pain was gone, it hadn't seemed so bad to have a broken arm. Having all her friends autograph the cast was sort of fun—but only for a while. Now she could hardly wait for the doctor to take it off next week.

Suddenly Mira's eye caught the glint of the sun on a piece of metal. She saw a girl about her own age come hobbling along. The girl wore steel braces on her legs and helped herself along with crutches. Her progress was slow, but she had a smile on her face.

When she saw Mira, the girl said, "Hi! My name is Raquel. Do you mind if I sit and rest here a while?"

"Not at all," Mira said, moving to make room.

With effort, Raquel eased herself onto the bench, propping her crutches beside her, and soon the two were talking like old friends. "Isn't this a great park?" Raquel asked after a while. "Those kids seem to be having fun." She pointed to the ball game in progress.

"Yeah," Mira agreed, "but I wish I could play. Don't you?"

"Oh, it would be nice," Raquel said with a laugh, "but I'm just glad to be walking. A year ago I was in a wheelchair all the time. After three operations, I'm able to walk with braces and crutches. But I know I'm not going to have this body forever. I'm a Christian, so when I get to heaven, I'll get a brand new body that works perfectly." Carefully she pushed herself up. "I have to be going," she said cheerfully, putting a crutch under each arm.

Mira was thoughtful as she walked home. She was a Christian, too. She decided what she would do with her cast when it was removed. She would keep it as a reminder to thank the Lord for all she had, instead of complaining about the things she didn't have. *CEY*

HOW ABOUT YOU?

Are you unhappy because of some physical problem? Being grouchy about it won't help. Look around you—you're sure to find someone worse off than you are. Someone has said, "I complained because I had no shoes, and then I saw someone who had no feet." Learn to accept the way you are, and remember—if you're a Christian, someday your body will be perfect.

MEMORIZE:
"I have learned how to get along happily whether I have much or little." Philippians 4:11

Be Content

Passing Grade

Read 1 John 1:5-9

Math had always been hard for Sasha, but she needed to pass tomorrow's test in order to stay on the track team. She studied hard that evening, but she was still terribly worried as she took the test. She was worried, that is, until she noticed that by leaning to the right just a little, she could see John's paper. Then she did something she had never done. She copied! She felt guilty, but she promised herself that she'd study extra hard in the coming days.

Sasha thought that would be the end of it, but when she read her Bible that night, she seemed to hear a voice saying to her, *Sasha, what have you done?* . . . *You know cheating is wrong.* Sasha knew the Holy Spirit was convicting her.

The next day, Sasha learned that she had gotten a good grade on the test. After school, she went to get her track uniform, but there was a lump in her throat as she put it on. As she stood before the mirror, her thoughts challenged her. *This uniform doesn't really belong to you!* she told herself. *You got it by cheating.* Suddenly she knew what she had to do.

Sasha ran down the hall to her math room. "Mr. Parks, c-could I speak to you a minute?" she stammered. "I . . . oh, I hate to tell you this, b-but I looked on John's paper. That's how I got such a good grade on the test yesterday."

Mr. Parks was surprised. "This is very serious," he said. "I didn't know you had copied. Why did you tell?"

"I-I'm a Christian," Sasha answered. "I knew, and God knew. Would you forgive me?"

Mr. Parks studied Sasha's face for a moment. Finally he said, "I think it's great that your faith means so much to you that you'd come to me and confess what you did. Of course I'll forgive you—but I'll have to give you a failing grade on that test."

Sasha sighed. "I know," she said, "but I feel so much better anyway—even if I can't be on the track team." *BP*

HOW ABOUT YOU?

Have you cheated in school? Or done some other thing you know is wrong? A Christian cannot knowingly sin and be comfortable about it because the Holy Spirit brings conviction of sin. If there is something that you need to make right with God, and with others, do it today.

MEMORIZE:

"If we claim to have fellowship with him yet walk in the darkness, we lie and do not live by the truth." 1 John 1:6, NIV

Don't Cheat

I Should Have Listened

Read Hebrews 1:1-2; 2:1-4

Thirteen-year-old Tara was excited about her trip to Florida during spring vacation. Her aunt had written about the sunshine, the beaches, and a lot of other things. "I won't even have to drag a coat along," she said, sitting on her suitcase to get it shut.

"Oh, I think you'll need one," Dad said as he took his daughter's coat out of the closet. "Aunt Bess tells me it can be quite cool there."

As soon as her dad left the room, Tara picked up the coat and put it back on a hanger in the closet. "I still don't think I need this," she murmured. "It's a warm day here, and everybody knows it's even warmer in Florida."

Tara was thrilled with the plane trip. It was her first time traveling by herself. She looked out eagerly as the huge plane taxied up to the gate after landing in Florida. "The temperature is thirty-nine degrees," a voice announced over the loudspeaker. Tara couldn't believe what she heard. That was colder than back home! And she had decided not to bring a coat!

Tara was shivering when she met Aunt Bess. "Oh, honey," her aunt said apologetically, "didn't I tell you to bring a coat? I meant to."

"You did, Aunt Bess. Dad did, too, but I was sure I wouldn't need it," Tara confessed. "To tell you the truth, I just didn't pay any attention to anybody's warning."

"Well, jump in the car," Aunt Bess invited. "I'll find you warmer clothes when we get home." Soon Tara was comfortable, but still somewhat embarrassed.

"You know what this reminds me of?" Aunt Bess asked. "It reminds me of people who refuse to listen to those who warn them of the need to prepare for eternity. It's sad, but someday they'll be sorry they didn't confess their sin and come to Christ for forgiveness. Your situation can be easily fixed. Even though God keeps working in their hearts, someday it will be too late for the unsaved. They need to come to Jesus now." *RIJ*

HOW ABOUT YOU?

Have you heard God's message—that you need to accept Jesus as Savior? Have you been putting off that decision? Then you're not prepared for eternity. Only those who make this decision during their lifetime will be ready for eternity with Jesus. Ask him to be your Savior right now.

Be Prepared to Meet God

MEMORIZE:
"Prepare to meet your God!"
Amos 4:12

March
12

God's Way, My Way (Part 1)

Read Matthew 5:38-44

Tears of disappointment welled up in Amelia's eyes as the principal announced the winners of the writing competition. She didn't even get honorable mention for her story, and she had worked so hard! Yet she was sincerely happy for her friend Julianna, whose story had won first place.

Amelia warmly congratulated Julianna, but the warmth she felt disappeared when she talked to Mrs. Engel, one of the teachers who had judged the contest. Mrs. Engel expressed great disappointment that Amelia had not entered the contest.

"But I did!" Amelia exclaimed. "Julianna turned in my story along with hers." Together they looked over the list of participants. Amelia's name was not there.

"It's not fair!" Amelia stormed as she told her parents about it. "Julianna must not have turned in my paper because she knows I'm a good writer. Just wait till I get my hands on her! She'll be sorry! I'll get even with her!"

"It's too bad that happened," Mom sympathized, "but slow down, honey. You don't know for certain that Julianna is guilty, do you? Suppose you accuse her, but then find out you're wrong?"

"Even if she did treat you badly, don't hold a grudge," Dad advised. "Remember that Jesus tells us to pray for those who mistreat us."

"That's easy to say," Amelia muttered, turning away. She was quiet and unhappy the rest of the evening.

The next morning, Amelia was her usual, cheerful self. "I was so mad at Julianna, but I knew you were right," she admitted to her parents. "I asked God to help me forgive her, even if she did it on purpose, and I prayed for her. I guess I still feel a little angry about it, but I'm going to keep on praying for her. I'm praying that God will help me react the right way to Julianna so that she'll see Jesus in me." *JLH*

HOW ABOUT YOU?

Has someone treated you badly? Have you prayed for that person? It's not easy to do, but try it—you'll be surprised how hard it is to remain angry with someone you are sincerely praying for. Remember how much God has forgiven you, and it will be easier for you to forgive others.

MEMORIZE:
"Love your enemies! Pray for those who persecute you!" Matthew 5:44

Don't Get Even— Pray Instead

God's Way, My Way (Part 2)

Read Genesis 50:14-21; Proverbs 16:24, 32

"I'm not so mad at Julianna anymore," Amelia stated a few days later, "but I still don't see why this had to happen."

"Commit it to God, and trust him," Dad encouraged.

As the weeks passed, Amelia continued to pray for Julianna. She also invited Julianna and another friend, Marcy, to join her in Sunday school, but neither girl came. In fact, Julianna seemed to be avoiding her.

One week when Julianna was away on vacation, Marcy came to Amelia's house for an afternoon. "Um . . . Amelia, I have a confession to make to you," Marcy said timidly. "I know Julianna cheated and didn't turn in your paper for the writing contest. After it was over, she was really worried because Mrs. Engel called and asked questions. When things quieted down, she told me about it, but she thinks you knew what happened. You did, too, didn't you?" As Amelia nodded, Marcy continued, "But you've never said anything bad about her. Why not?"

"Well, at first I really had to bite my tongue to keep from accusing her," Amelia answered thoughtfully, "but I might have been wrong. Besides, I know God wouldn't want me to hold a grudge—and I know he has a purpose in it."

"You mean it's your religion that makes you treat her so nicely?" Marcy asked. "I know I couldn't be that nice about it." Marcy paused, then shyly asked, "Is your invitation to go to church still open?"

That night, Amelia told her folks about the conversation. "Because of what happened, Marcy wants to come to church with me next Sunday," she said. "God does know what he's doing. And I'm going to pray harder than ever for Julianna." *JLH*

HOW ABOUT YOU?

Is it hard to understand why your best plans go astray and things don't turn out like you want them to? Remember that God is not limited to your circumstances. He can take things that look bad to you and make them work out for good.

God Does What Is Best

MEMORIZE:
"As far as I am concerned, God turned into good what you meant for evil."
Genesis 50:20

Locked Out

Read Psalm 119:57-64

Summer and Erika were locked out on the school roof. Summer had known it was wrong to go through that window, but she was so tired of being called a "goody-goody." She wanted to be popular, but being stuck on this roof just wasn't what she'd planned.

The girls had gone to the school swim meet. About halfway through, Erika had nudged Summer. "Let's do something exciting," Erika said. She led Summer up to the third floor where the balcony running track was located. At one side, a hinged window opened to the roof. Erika crawled through and dared Summer to follow. Too scared to refuse, Summer climbed out, too, but when the wind blew the window shut, she wished with all her heart that she hadn't come.

Cautiously, they felt their way over the dark gravelly surface hoping to find another entrance into the building, but there was none. Summer shivered in her light pink jacket. She prayed silently. *Dear God, I'm sorry. I shouldn't have listened to Erika, and I wish I'd been brave enough to do the right thing. Forgive me, and please help us find a way down.*

Just then she heard a hoarse whisper. "Hey, Summer! Over here! We can slide down this pole." Summer stumbled across the roof, dangerously close to the edge. She finally reached the corner where her friend was clinging to the downspout anchored there.

Erika first, and then Summer, slid slowly to the ground—right into the waiting grasp of Mr. Cooper, the custodian. He had caught a glimpse of them from the parking lot. *Thank you, Lord,* Summer silently breathed. She knew punishment awaited her, but that was as it should be. For now, she was thankful to be safe on the ground.

"I'm glad I got caught," Summer tearfully admitted when she finally reached home. "I'm going to stop worrying about being friends with the popular kids—and trying to be part of the 'in' crowd. I'm going to be bolder about doing the right things and being the kind of person Jesus wants me to be." *PIK*

HOW ABOUT YOU?

Do you ever do things you know are wrong just so you'll be accepted by certain kids? Jesus wants you to stand true for him. Don't turn your back on him. Having his approval is more important than having the approval of anyone else.

MEMORIZE:

"Be on guard. Stand true to what you believe. Be courageous. Be strong."
1 Corinthians 16:13

Live to Please God, Not Others

Seed Sowing

Read Matthew 13:3-8, 18-23

One weekend at a youth retreat, Catherine accepted Christ as her Savior. She was glad she was a Christian, but she had mixed feelings about returning to school. She dreaded facing her old friends, for she had been a leader in a rather wild group. "I know that some things my friends and I have been doing aren't right," Catherine told her mom before school on Monday morning. "I don't want to be that way anymore, but I don't know how to tell them that I'm a Christian."

"It won't be easy, I know," Mom agreed. "I'll be praying a lot for you today, asking God to give you courage to be a witness to your friends."

Catherine's group of friends was waiting on the playground. They had been talking about ways to disrupt the class, and they expected her to take part as usual. During the morning, Tina threw paper wads, Joanie shot a rubber band, and Lorie tripped a girl. Everyone laughed, but Catherine didn't join in. Several times she noticed her friends staring at her.

At lunchtime, when Catherine bowed her head to thank God for the food, Tina scowled. "What on earth has come over you?" she snarled.

"Well," Catherine began nervously as she prayed silently, "I'm a different person than I was before. I've become a Christian, and now I want to live the way Jesus wants me to live."

Most of the girls hooted, but Libby snapped, "Leave her alone! At least give her a chance to explain!"

An excited Catherine burst into the house after school. "Oh, Mom!" she exclaimed. "Guess what! The girls noticed I was different, even before I told them. And God gave me enough nerve to tell them what happened. Some of them made fun of me, but Libby, at least, seems interested."

"That's great, honey," Mom said with a smile. "You know, the Bible compares witnessing to seed sowing, and you've begun to sow seed in the lives of your friends. Perhaps some will fall on good soil. We'll pray together that it will bring fruit." *AU*

HOW ABOUT YOU?

Do your friends at school know you're a Christian? Does it worry you that they may tease you and make fun of you? Ask God for courage to sow the seed—his Word—in the lives of your friends.

Witness by Life and Word

MEMORIZE:
"Those who save lives are wise."
Proverbs 11:30

Stubborn Love

Read Luke 6:27-36

As Jorie slammed the door and threw her heavy backpack on the floor, Grandma entered the kitchen with a basket of laundry. "Bad day at school, Jorie?" she asked.

"I'm sick of Ellie!" Jorie exclaimed. "She's talking behind my back again."

"Are you sure of that, honey?" Grandma questioned.

"And she's supposed to be a Christian!" Jorie muttered as she trudged toward her room to change clothes. Later, the fragrance of roast beef and potatoes drew Jorie from her homework. "Gram, would you like me to help with anything?"

"Yes, please," Grandma replied. "You can open this jar of applesauce and put some in a bowl for supper."

Grasping the jar, Jorie tried to loosen the lid, but it did not budge. "Ugggg," she groaned. Again, she twisted the lid, leaning her whole body into the effort.

Grandma noticed her struggle. "Looks like that's a stubborn one," she said. "You can loosen the seal by holding the jar under hot running water."

Jorie leaned against the counter as she waited for the water to get hot enough. "Grandma, do you think Ellie really knows Jesus?" she asked. "You've said that just because people attend church, it doesn't mean they have a personal relationship with Christ."

"That's true, Jorie," the older woman agreed. "Being a Christian is about a relationship with God, not just going to a church building every week."

The water steamed as Jorie held the jar under it for a few minutes. "I don't know how I'll bear any more backstabbing," she said as she turned off the faucet and tried the lid again. Pop! "Whew, that was easier." Jorie spooned the applesauce into a bowl and set it on the table. "It seems like Ellie is just as stubborn as that lid!"

"You'll have to be just as stubborn too, Jorie," Grandma said, "but in a different way."

"Me? Be stubborn?" Jorie asked. "What do you mean?"

"When someone hurts you, your love has to be strong," Grandma explained. "Don't give up. Just like that hot water broke the stubborn seal, the Holy Spirit will work in your heart—to open it and let God's love flow out to others." *KC*

HOW ABOUT YOU?

Has another Christian hurt you? Has someone said something behind your back that was untrue? Respond with love—God's love flowing through you.

Love Others, Even When It Hurts

Happily Ever After

Read Revelation 21:1-5

"And they lived happily ever after," Zora read. Then she closed the storybook.

"Read it again!" her little sister, Ida, begged. *"Cinderella* is my favorite book."

"You've got to go to sleep now," Zora said, tucking the blankets around Ida and giving her a quick kiss. "Kristen and I will be in the living room."

As Zora and her friend settled down on the living room floor with some popcorn, Kristen said, "Life isn't really lived happily ever after. We have all these neat wedding pictures of Mom and Dad . . ." Kristen choked up as tears began rolling down her cheeks, "and . . . and now they're get—getting d-divorced," she sobbed.

Zora put her arms around Kristen. "I'm sorry," she said, and she began to cry with her friend.

Just then Zora's mom entered the room. "What's going on?" she asked, and Zora told her the news.

"That 'happily ever after' stuff is a lie," Kristen cried.

"You're right, girls—'happily ever after' is not always the case here on earth," Mom agreed. "God doesn't promise that life on earth will be perfect. He created the earth perfect, but because of sin we now have war, murder, kidnapping, hunger, and divorce. People don't want to live according to God's laws. But God has prepared a 'happily ever after' place in heaven for all those who believe in him."

Zora's mom handed Kristen a tissue, and the tears slowed to a trickle. Kristen listened thoughtfully as Mom said, "God will wipe away all tears in heaven."

"How can I go there?" Kristen asked. "And can my mom and dad go there, too?"

Zora's mom took her Bible from the end table, turned a few pages, and showed Kristen that Jesus died for her sins, was buried, and rose again the third day—and that by believing in him, she would have everlasting life.

After Kristen prayed, Zora grabbed her hand. "We'll live happily ever after together!" she said excitedly, as both girls traded their tears for smiles. *LJR*

HOW ABOUT YOU?

Are you sad or disappointed because of some things happening in your life? Trust God. Talk to him, and ask for his help. "Happily ever after" times are coming for Christians.

MEMORIZE:
"He will remove all of their sorrows, and there will be no more death or sorrow or crying or pain. For the old world and its evils are gone forever."
Revelation 21:4

Live Happily Ever After with Jesus

March
18

Missing

Read Matthew 18:10-14

As Caroline poured milk into her cereal bowl, a photo on the carton's side caught her attention. The words "Have you seen this child?" were printed under the picture. "You know what?" said Caroline. "I'd love to find one of these missing kids. It must be awful to be kidnapped—or even just to be lost. And the parents of these kids must be so worried!"

"I'm sure they are," Mom agreed.

"I remember when I went home with Madelyn after school one day, and I forgot to call you," said Caroline. "You were so worried that you called all around trying to find me."

"I was very worried," recalled Mom, "and I was relieved when I finally located you."

"So relieved that you grounded me," laughed Caroline. "But that taught me to check with you if I wanted to do something before coming home. Anyway, I'd like to find a real missing kid and stop other parents from worrying."

Caroline pictured herself patrolling the park on the lookout for scared-looking tots. *I'd need lots of change for phone calls,* she thought, *and I'd bring some books so the kids would have something to do till their parents came. Or should I deliver the kids to their homes? Oh, well. I can decide later. First, I have to actually find a missing kid, and there's not much chance of that ever happening!* "You know, Mom," she said, "I'm sure I'll never find one, though."

"Well," Mom said, "I was just thinking that we probably know some 'missing kids' already."

Caroline's spoon clanged into her bowl. "Know some?" she asked. She looked at the faces on the milk carton. "You haven't seen this kid—Joshua Odell Lander—have you, Mom?"

Mom shook her head. "Actually, I'm thinking of kids who are 'missing' because they don't belong to God's family," she explained. "We know lots of kids, but many of them don't know Jesus. We need to tell them about him and let them know that he wants them to 'come home'—to become a part of the family of God." *SN*

HOW ABOUT YOU?

Are you aware that kids who don't know Jesus are lost in sin? You can't rescue them—only Jesus can do that—but you can tell them about him. You can invite them to places where they'll hear about his love. Do what you can to bring them to the place where they'll be found by Jesus.

MEMORIZE:

"I, the Son of Man, have come to seek and save those like him who are lost."
Luke 19:10

Tell Kids about God's Family

Never Too Busy

Read Philippians 2:3-5

"Mom!" Mindy called, "Mrs. Berg is on the phone." As Mom came to take the call, Mindy added loudly, "Again!"

Mom quickly took the phone. After talking with Mrs. Berg a little while, she hung up and turned to her daughter. "Mindy," she said sternly, "you should be ashamed of yourself. I'm sure Mrs. Berg could tell that you were annoyed with her. You hurt her feelings."

"But, Mom, she calls all the time," protested Mindy. "Why can't we just let the answering machine get her calls?"

"Because Mrs. Berg is lonesome," Mom replied, "and she's worried about her husband in the hospital. Besides, she isn't well herself, and I never know when her call might be an emergency."

"Well, she always talks to me forever before she asks for you," grumbled Mindy. "It's so boring! She always asks if I like school and what my favorite subject is. As if she cares! She just wants to talk about her problems."

"Oh, honey, I'm sure she's interested in what you have to say, too," Mom said. After a short pause, she added, "Actually, you've been acting a lot like Mrs. Berg."

Mindy frowned, "I act like Mrs. Berg?"

Mom nodded. "I'm thinking of a prayer request you've had for quite a while," Mom said. "I know you've been asking God to help you understand the things you've been studying in science."

"Why is that like Mrs. Berg's calls?" asked Mindy.

"Well, you've asked God so many times—you keep going to him again and again with your problems," Mom said. "Aren't you glad that he's never too busy to listen when you talk to him, and that he never loses patience with you or thinks you're boring?"

Mindy was silent a moment. "I see what you mean, Mom," she admitted.

"God doesn't give us a busy signal or put us on hold—or make us talk to an answering machine," Mom said. "He's always available to us, and we need to be available to others. Mrs. Berg is going through hard times and needs someone to listen to her." *NIM*

HOW ABOUT YOU?

Do you know people who seem boring? Do you ignore them—or are you willing to listen, knowing that it's one way you can follow God's example? Be interested in others. Often you can help them simply by being friendly and listening to them.

MEMORIZE:

"Follow God's example in everything you do, because you are his dear children." Ephesians 5:1

Follow God's Example—
Listen!

March
20

A Light to Share

Read John 1:1-5; Ephesians 1:18

"Come on, Dad. We're ready," called Leigh. She and her family were gathered for family night. It was storming outside, but in the den, they felt snug and cozy with plenty of games, popcorn, and soda.

"Coming," Dad called from the bedroom.

Just then the power went out. "Oh, no!" exclaimed Leigh. "No lights! Not on family night!"

"Honey," called Mom, "bring that big candle from the bedroom, please. There are matches in the drawer there, too."

"Okay," agreed Dad. "I hope I can find them in the dark—ouch! Stubbed my toe on the dresser!" A moment later they saw a glow in the bedroom as Dad lit a match, and he soon arrived in the den with the candle Mom kept just for times like this.

"I hope the power won't be off long," said Timothy. He was eager to play games and munch on popcorn.

"I like it with just candlelight," decided Leigh.

"It's interesting to see what a difference a small light makes, isn't it?" said Mom.

Leigh nodded. "It doesn't seem possible that such a tiny flame could give out so much light," she said. "It was kind of scary in the dark, but when you brought the candle, Dad, it lit up the whole room."

"A dark room may seem scary to us," said Dad, "but that's not as scary as the darkness of sin—the darkness in which people live when they don't know God. People in that kind of darkness have good reason to live in fear, and we need to share the light of God's love and truth with them."

Mom nodded. "If we don't, we're allowing them to go on stumbling in darkness," she said.

"Like Dad was doing in the bedroom?" asked Timothy with a grin.

"Like that," agreed Dad, "but with much more serious consequences. Let's always be faithful in sharing the light—God's truth." *RT*

HOW ABOUT YOU?

Are you sharing God's love and truth with those around you—at home, at school, and in your neighborhood? Don't hide his light because you're embarrassed about what others might think or say about you. Respond to God's call to share his much needed light.

MEMORIZE:
"Let your good deeds shine out for all to see." Matthew 5:16

Share the Light of God's Love

A Lesson in Names (Part 1)

Read 1 John 1:3-7

Carrie listened eagerly as her Sunday school teacher showed the class a book of names and what they mean. "We're going to learn the meaning of each of our names," Mrs. Wallace explained. "We'll also look at some Bible verses that go along with the meaning, and I think each of you will learn some things you can apply to daily living. Next Sunday we'll start with names beginning with the letter *A.*"

In just a few weeks, Carrie's name was at the top of the list. She learned that one meaning of her name was "the moon." "What is the purpose of the moon?" Mrs. Wallace asked.

After a moment, Nancy raised her hand. As Mrs. Wallace nodded, Nancy said, "It's to give light at night."

Mrs. Wallace nodded. "The moon gets its light from the sun," she said. "Carrie, read 1 John 1:5 to see the source of the Christian's light."

Quickly finding the verse, Carrie knew the answer as she read, " 'God is light; in him is no darkness at all.' "

"So you see," said Mrs. Wallace, "in order to be a light, you need to know God, who alone can give light. You have a pretty special name, Carrie."

Carrie agreed and thought more about her name later that day. She wondered how she could make sure she knew God better. Then she remembered something Mrs. Wallace had told the class a few weeks earlier. Before she went to bed that night, she got out her Bible and spent some time reading it and praying that God would help her know him so that she could be a light for the people in her life. *PMR*

HOW ABOUT YOU?

Are you able to be a "light" in the world today? You can be if you've accepted Jesus as your Savior, for then you know God, who is the source of light. If you've not done so before, accept him today.

God Is Light

A Lesson in Names (Part 2)

Read Philippians 2:14-16

So my name means "moon," and the moon gives light. Carrie continued to think about her name the whole week after her Sunday school class had discussed the meaning of names. She tried to think of ways she could give light. "I'll help Mom take care of Joey," she decided. Carrie had very good intentions, but when her little brother got into her jewelry box, a big frown crossed her face. Her temper took over, and she lost her patience.

On Monday evening, Carrie meant to do the dishes while her mother was at a meeting. But she hated washing dishes. *I'll do it later,* she decided. Before she knew it, it was bedtime, so when Mom came home the sink was still full.

On Tuesday, Carrie got up late and hurried off to school without taking out the trash.

At church on Wednesday night, Carrie saw her Sunday school teacher. "Hi, Miss Moon," Mrs. Wallace greeted her.

Carrie flinched. "Some light I've turned out to be," she confessed, as she told about her week so far. "I sure don't shed any light. They should've named me something else."

"Are you remembering that the moon has no light of its own?" Mrs. Wallace asked. "It reflects the sun. You have no light of your own either. You can be a light only by reflecting the Son—the Son of God. First of all, you need to belong to Jesus—have you accepted him into your life?" Carrie nodded. "Then ask him to help you reflect his love," Mrs. Wallace said.

The next day as Carrie walked home, she remembered her teacher's words just as she was about to throw her candy bar wrapper on Mrs. Grey's lawn. *Help me reflect you,* she prayed silently. Then she helped the elderly lady drag her garbage out to the curb.

When Mom insisted she do her homework before going out to play, Carrie was about to respond with some sassy words before she remembered. *Please help me, Lord,* she prayed again, and she actually hummed a tune while she got out her books. *Thank you, Jesus,* she prayed, *for letting me reflect your light. PMR*

HOW ABOUT YOU?

Can you think of ways your life could reflect Jesus? Can you help a younger brother or sister with homework? Read to your grandma? Set the table? Go to bed cheerfully? You may be just one young person, but if you reflect Jesus, others will see his love in you.

MEMORIZE:
"Shine like stars in the universe."
Philippians 2:15, NIV

Reflect the Son (Jesus)

For Your Own Good (Part 1)

Read Psalm 19:8-11

Bria just wouldn't listen to instructions. Several times she was warned about the danger of ignoring advice, but she went ahead anyway and did as she pleased.

At school, Bria was told that she had better study and do her homework, but she didn't listen. She goofed off and did failing work. "I'm sorry, Bria," her teacher said, "but you must stay in at recess and after school until all your homework is done right. I'm doing this for your own good. If you don't learn your lesson now, it will be much harder later on."

At home, Bria's parents warned her to stay off the lake because the ice was thawing. But one day Bria took a shortcut across the lake anyway. She fell in and got soaked. "Bria, you disobeyed me—you could have drowned," her mom said. "Now you must be punished. You're grounded for the next two weeks."

A few weeks later, Bria was riding her bike home from the playground. The red lights were flashing at the railroad crossing, but Bria figured she had plenty of time. As she raced across the tracks, her wheel hit the railroad tie and bent. Bria flew off the bike, and the next thing she knew, she was in the hospital with a broken leg.

"Thank goodness, you're alive, Bria. You could have been killed!" Dad exclaimed. "Didn't you see the train coming?"

"Yes, but I thought I could beat it," moaned Bria. "I should have stopped."

"The flashing red light was there for your own good. It was a warning to stop. Danger was ahead," Dad told her. "When we disobey warnings, we invite trouble into our lives."

"I sure invited trouble," Bria said. "I ache all over." *JLH*

HOW ABOUT YOU?

Do you obey God's warnings? He wants to keep you from the dangers of sin, so the Bible gives warnings about disobeying, lying, cheating, hating, stealing, and following friends who do wrong. God's warnings are for your own good.

MEMORIZE:
"I am not writing this to shame you, but to warn you, as my dear children." 1 Corinthians 4:14, NIV

Heed God's Warnings

24

For Your Own Good (Part 2)

Read Colossians 3:5-10

Bria was in the hospital for quite some time with her broken leg. She had to lie flat on her back, her leg up in the air with traction weights pulling on it. That was hard. Relatives and friends visited her, brought gifts, and played table games. Still, Bria was bored. "Please, Mom," she begged, "can't I get my leg out of this traction and go home?"

"It won't be much longer, dear," encouraged Mom. "The traction is hard for you, but it's for your good. If the bone doesn't heal properly, it might have to be reset. Just be patient."

Finally, Bria was able to go home—but that didn't turn out to be like she expected, either. It wasn't easy getting a pair of jeans over a cast. Then she had to learn how to walk on crutches.

As Bria was watching her friends play softball one day, she felt even more sorry for herself. "This cast is too heavy," she complained. "It's in my way. I hate having a broken leg. I don't know why God made it happen."

"God didn't make it happen, but he did allow it," her mom replied.

"But why?" Bria asked. "There's nothing good about it. I can't have any fun."

Mom searched for words. "Maybe God allowed it to get your attention—to let you know that if you keep ignoring warnings, you'll get into worse trouble. What do you think?"

"Well . . . maybe," Bria admitted.

"Your cast reminds me of sin in a Christian's life," Mom continued. "Sin weighs us down and keeps us from enjoying many good things God planned for our lives."

"Sin?" asked Bria. "Like . . . what kind of sin?"

"Any kind," Mom replied. "Impatience, for example. Disobedience. Doing things your own way."

Bria frowned. "And not listening to warnings, huh?" she said slowly.

Mom smiled at Bria. "I can see this is all working out for your good," she said with a smile. *JLH*

HOW ABOUT YOU?
Do you let sin keep you from being all God wants you to be? Have you gotten rid of all the things listed in today's Scripture reading? Don't let them weigh you down. Instead, let God have complete control of your life.

MEMORIZE:
"Let us throw off everything that hinders and the sin that so easily entangles." Hebrews 12:1, NIV

Turn from Sin

Back to Bethel

Read Genesis 28:11-21; 35:3

For the third week in a row, Renee came into Sunday school looking unhappy and paid little attention as Mrs. Puckett taught the lesson. After class, Mrs. Puckett talked with her. "Renee, can I help you in some way?"

Renee's eyes filled with tears. "I don't really know what's wrong," she said. "I just feel kinda down lately."

"That's too bad," her teacher sympathized. "I remember how happy you were when you came back from camp last summer and told me you had been saved."

Renee sighed. "I know. I felt good then—so close to God. But now . . ."

"It sounds like you need to go back to Bethel," Mrs. Puckett said.

Renee looked confused. She remembered hearing Mrs. Puckett mention a place called Bethel as she taught the Sunday school lesson. "Back to Bethel?" she asked.

"Our lesson was about how Jacob met God at Bethel. Bethel was a place where Jacob made a commitment to trust and follow God," Mrs. Puckett said. "But later, when he strayed far from God, God told him to go back to Bethel and remember how God had met him there. Sometimes we need to go back, too—back to the time when God seemed close."

"You mean I should go back to camp?" Renee asked.

"Well, you probably can't," Mrs. Puckett said. "But you don't need to go back to that actual spot. You just need to go back in your mind—to remember how God met you there. Ask him to help you get your heart and mind back into the same condition they were at that time."

Renee was thoughtful. "When I got home from camp, I thought a lot about knowing God better and pleasing him," she said, "but lately I seem to be busy with other things."

"Are you living to please him now?" Mrs. Puckett asked. Renee shook her head as the tears began to fall. "Then that's why you feel sad, Renee, and not close to God," Mrs. Puckett said. "Could I pray about it with you?" Renee nodded. Together they prayed, and, in her heart, Renee returned to her Bethel. *REP*

HOW ABOUT YOU?

Was there a time in your life when you felt much closer to God than you do today? If so, it's not God who moved away from you—you've moved from him. Have you become too interested in sports, clothes, your friends, or even your studies? Ask the Lord to help you to get back to your "Bethel." Then take whatever action is necessary to put God back in first place.

Give God First Place

MEMORIZE:
"Oh, return to me, for I have paid the price to set you free." Isaiah 44:22

March 26

Not Just on Sunday

Read Deuteronomy 6:5-9

"Leslie, I've never been around a family as religious as yours," Kelly told her friend. "Your mom is always saying 'Praise the Lord!'"

Leslie laughed. "I know," she said. "She means it, too. We don't use the word 'religious' very much, though. Christianity is more than just a religion."

Kelly was quiet a minute before she replied. "Yes, I guess you're right. Actually, my own family is pretty religious, but you're so different from us. Your family takes their Christianity seriously! You have plaques with Scripture verses on the walls, and your folks are always listening to Christian radio and CDs. It seems like your whole lives are filled with things about God. Don't you ever feel kind of funny about it?"

"Well . . . once in a while," Leslie admitted, remembering a time when she wanted to buy some music with questionable lyrics and thinking how she'd thought her folks were overdoing their Christian commitment. "But we believe God should be the center of our lives and that we should live every moment for him," she added.

The next week at Bible club, the teacher talked about the methods God said the Israelites were to use to teach their children about God. "They were to keep God constantly before them," Mrs. Kendall explained, "and we should do that, too. What are some ways we can remind ourselves of his goodness and his commandments every day of the week—not just on Sundays?"

Leslie was surprised when Kelly spoke up. "I know one family that does that," she said. "They have Scripture plaques around, and they listen to Christian music. I used to think it was weird, but now I see that they just do what the Bible says!" *REP*

HOW ABOUT YOU?

Have you ever thought your parents were too serious about God? Have you been just a little embarrassed and concerned about what your friends might think? God says to use daily reminders of his work and words. He wants you to talk about what he's done for you when "sitting, walking, lying down, and rising up." In other words, all the time—not just on Sunday!

MEMORIZE:

"Repeat [these commands] again and again to your children. Talk about them when you are at home and when you are away on a journey, when you are lying down and when you are getting up again."
Deuteronomy 6:7

Remember God All the Time

A Mistreated Child

Read Ephesians 6:1-3

Michaela was angry with her father. *He's just too strict!* she thought. *Every time I want to do something, he asks all kinds of questions. Why can't he just trust me?* She had asked if she could go on a retreat with some of the kids from school, but Dad's answer was a definite no! "I'm sorry, honey, but the young people going on that retreat aren't the type of kids I want you to be with," he had said. "Some have even been in trouble with the law. I can't approve of an overnight trip with that group." Michaela was so upset that she had walked out of the house without answering.

As Michaela settled down on the back steps, she saw Elsa sitting out on the steps of her home. Michaela jumped up and made her way next door, looking for sympathy. *I'll tell Elsa all about how unreasonable Dad is,* she thought. *She'll understand.* But as Michaela sat down next to her friend, she forgot all about her own problem. "What's wrong?" Michaela asked, staring at Elsa, whose eyes were red with tears.

Elsa covered her face with her hands and cried harder. "My . . . my father told me I couldn't visit him this weekend. He has to work again," she responded. "He's done this the last three times I was supposed to see him. My mom doesn't know yet because she's not home from work."

"Oh Elsa, I'm so sorry," Michaela comforted.

"I don't think he loves me," Elsa murmured. "Why doesn't he want to see me?" Michaela didn't know what to say, so she just hugged her friend.

Finally she spoke. "Do you hate him for it?" Michaela asked in wonder.

"No," Elsa replied. "He's my dad, and I love him." She swallowed hard. "I know he's busy. I just wish he were around more, that's all."

Guilt flooded through Michaela. Her father had done what he felt was right, and she was angry with him. Elsa's father didn't keep his promises to her, yet Elsa still wanted to spend time with him. She defended him! Michaela felt ashamed. Right there, she breathed a prayer of thanks for her parents. *RIJ*

HOW ABOUT YOU?

Do you willingly listen to the advice your parents offer? Do you humbly accept the discipline and correction they give you? Sometimes you may think they just don't understand your world. Sometimes perhaps they don't, but many times they understand better than you may think— they've been there. In any case, God has given them the responsibility of helping and guiding you, and he's given you the responsibility of honoring and obeying them.

MEMORIZE:

"Honor your father and mother. Then you will live a long, full life in the land the Lord your God will give you."

Exodus 20:12

Respect and Obey Your Parents

Two Masters

Read Romans 6:16-23

Lily was a new Christian when her parents got divorced. And less than a year later her father became a Christian, too. He loved to read and study God's Word and to tell everyone he could about God. He encouraged Lily to do so, too. On the weekends she was with her dad, it seemed so easy to live for God—but when she was with her mom, it was a different story! Her mom discouraged all her efforts to read her Bible or go to church.

"Dad, why didn't God give me a happy home with two Christian parents?" she asked one day.

Her father looked sad as he answered. "I can't tell you that, honey. I would be so happy if your mom would ask Jesus to be her Savior."

"But, Dad," Lily said, "God is powerful. Why can't he change her?"

"He can, Lily, and he will, if she'll let him," Dad replied. "You know, he can even use you to make a change in her life."

Lily was puzzled. "Use me? How?"

"You can be an example to her," Dad suggested. "Your life could convince her more than a thousand sermons ever could. The Bible is filled with examples of young people whom God used in the lives of other people. Samuel, David, Daniel . . ."

Lily sighed as she answered. "I know, but Mom wants me to forget all about God and the Bible. I feel like I have two masters—you and Mom."

"Your mom and I are not the two masters you're trying to serve," Dad replied. "They're God and Satan. The Bible says, 'Whatever you choose to obey becomes your master.' You can't live for Christ just when it's convenient . . . and then when it's tough, live for the devil. You need to yield yourself to God each day—when you're with Mom as well as when you're with me."

In the following weeks, Lily remembered her father's advice. She still found it difficult to live as a Christian when she was with her mom, but as she continued to allow God to be her master, she was much happier. *SLK*

HOW ABOUT YOU?

Are you living for God only when it's convenient? Do you serve him on Sunday, and then allow Satan to work in your life on the other days of the week? God wants your whole heart and life every day.

MEMORIZE:

"No one can serve two masters."
Matthew 6:24

Serve God, Not People

The Right Kind of Words

Read James 3:6-10

Amber barged through the front door, dumped her books in the overstuffed chair, and slumped down onto the sofa. "What's wrong?" her older sister, Autumn, asked. She stopped folding the mountain of clothes in the laundry basket at her feet.

"It's Todd Morgan—the bully at school. He . . . he . . ." Hot tears welled up in Amber's eyes and spilled onto her cheeks. She finally spurted out the words. "He called me ugly." She melted deeper into the couch.

Autumn sat down and put a comforting arm around Amber's shoulders. "I'm sorry, honey," she said softly.

Amber sniffled. "Why does Todd say mean things to everyone? He's fat, but I don't call him fat. I know it's wrong to say unkind things."

Autumn sighed. "Words can be wicked," she said. "I think Todd's words hurt you just as much as if he had hit you and given you a bloody nose." Amber wiped away her tears with the back of her hand as her sister continued. "I'm so proud of you for not answering with unkind words, Amber. Jesus taught us to be kind, even to our enemies." She handed Amber a tissue. "Out of the same mouth can come words that hurt or words that encourage. Everyone has a choice of what to say, and you've made the right choice."

"Thanks, Sis," Amber said. "I'm starting to feel a little better now."

Autumn dug into the laundry basket once again. "About Todd—he must not like himself very much if he says mean things to others. I'm going to pray for him."

There was silence. After a moment, Amber said, "I will too."

Autumn gave her a wink, and Amber squeezed her eyelids shut as she talked to God. When she opened them, she shared a smile with her sister as they folded clothes side by side. *BJB*

HOW ABOUT YOU?

Do your words help or hurt others? Ask God to help you say kind words. Make it a point to say something kind and encouraging to someone every day. Say only those things that are pleasing to God.

MEMORIZE:

"May the words of my mouth and the thoughts of my heart be pleasing to you, O Lord, my rock and my redeemer." Psalm 19:14

Always Speak Kindly

March

30

The Crispy Pops Winner

Read 1 John 3:16-18

"Boy, do I love this cereal," mumbled Madison, as she crunched a mouthful. "Crispy Pops are the greatest!"

"I've noticed! I'm lucky to get one bowl before the box is empty," complained her sister, Jenna. "You ought to enter the contest they're having." She pointed to the back of the box. "All you have to do is write and tell them why you like their cereal."

Madison decided it was a good idea, and she sent her letter right away.

Madison was a winner! She won a hundred boxes of Crispy Pops cereal! "Wow!" exclaimed Madison. "Now I can eat all the Crispy Pops I want, and there still will be plenty left for Jenna!"

There was, in fact, plenty left for everybody. They all ate the cereal, but the stack of boxes Madison had won didn't seem to be getting any smaller. Mother started making Crispy Pops cakes, Crispy Pops cookies, and even Crispy Pops meatloaf. Soon the whole family was absolutely sick of Crispy Pops!

One evening, Madison gazed sadly at the plate of roast chicken with Crispy Pops stuffing. "I never thought I'd say this," she said with a sigh, "but I hope I never see Crispy Pops again!"

"I know," agreed her mother. "But since God supplied us with all that good cereal, we can't just let it go to waste."

"Hey! I've got an idea," Dad said suddenly. "Nobody said we had to eat all of those Crispy Pops by ourselves. Wouldn't the Lord be pleased to have us share them? Why don't we call the city mission and see if they could use some?"

"That's a great idea," said Jenna. "And we could call the director of our church camp. They'd probably like some, too."

"I'm sure all those people will be happy to share our abundance," Mom agreed. "And maybe after we give away that cereal, Madison will learn to like Crispy Pops again."

"Maybe." Madison grinned. "But I doubt it!" *SLK*

HOW ABOUT YOU?

Is there something you can share—money, toys, food, time? Whatever it is, you'll be happier by sharing it than by keeping it all for yourself!

MEMORIZE:

"Your plenty will supply what they need." 2 Corinthians 8:14, NIV

Share with Others

The Beautiful Picture

Read Matthew 12:35-37; Philippians 4:8

Let's see . . . I know! I'll paint a sunset, Karena decided. *A sunset over a lake! That will make a pretty picture.* Soon she was engrossed in swirling various watercolors across the paper. After each stroke, she cleaned her brush in water, turning the water dark gray. Suddenly, Karena's elbow bumped the cup of dirty water, and some of it splashed across her picture. "Aunt Helen!" she wailed. "Look! My picture was turning out so good, and now it's ruined!"

"I'm sorry, honey," sympathized her aunt. "Why don't you get another piece of paper and start over?"

Karena sighed. "I think I'll do something else," she said. Gathering up the paints, she put them away and then went into her aunt's family room and turned on the TV. Karena watched evil-looking cartoon characters shoot and kill each other. She was so interested in the program that she didn't even notice her aunt enter the room.

"Karena, please turn that off," Aunt Helen instructed. "You know your parents don't allow you to watch that kind of program."

"Aunt Helen, it's just a cartoon," Karena whined. "It's not hurting me."

"I'm not so sure," Aunt Helen said. "It's full of violence. You should be thinking about good things instead of this kind of thing."

"Seeing something like this once in a while won't hurt anything," insisted Karena. "It's not as though I watch it every day."

"I certainly hope not!" agreed her aunt. "But it didn't take much ugly water to ruin your pretty picture this morning, did it?"

"No," Karena admitted reluctantly.

"Well, it doesn't take many ugly scenes to give you bad thoughts, either," said Aunt Helen. "On the flip side, when you see and hear good and beautiful things, they can help you think good thoughts."

"Okay," said Karena. "I guess I'll go find a book to read." She got up. "A good book," she added. "I promise." *KSB*

HOW ABOUT YOU?

What do you watch, read, and listen to? Don't allow Satan to fill your mind with ugly thoughts through violent TV shows, immoral books, or ungodly music. Philippians 4:8 tells you what kinds of things you should think about. Obey God and keep your mind pure.

Think on Good Things

MEMORIZE:
"I turned my thoughts once more to the Lord." Jonah 2:7

April Fool!

Read Ephesians 5:6-10

Jillian was late! She had overslept and had to hurry through breakfast. Then she saw that she was wearing socks that didn't match. Dashing back toward her room, she heard her brother say excitedly, "Guess what I just heard on the radio, Jillian!"

"Tell me fast," she answered. "I'm late."

"That's just it, Jillian," Kent went on quickly. "There was a water pipe break at school, so they've canceled school for the day." Jillian didn't see the twinkle in her brother's eye.

"Yippeee!" Jillian exclaimed. "That's the best news I've heard all morning! I'm going back to bed for a while, and then—"

"April Fool!" her brother interrupted gleefully.

Jillian grinned good-naturedly. "I'll get you back!"

Later that day, Jillian had her chance. "Hey, Kent," she called when she saw her brother in the hall between classes. "You know that trumpet solo you were hoping to get for the spring concert? Well, Mr. Rodriguez said he was going to ask you to do it!" This time it was Kent who missed the twinkling eyes.

"Wow! Really? Thank goodness. I thought for sure—" Kent stopped. "Jillian Bellamy! Are you paying me back for this morning's joke?"

"Yep!" Jillian said. "Caught you, too! April Fool!" They both laughed.

That night at the supper table, Jillian and Kent told their parents how easily each had been tricked by the other. Dad smiled. "So you both were easily tricked into believing something you really wanted to believe," he said. "Jillian wanted to believe there was no school, and Kent wanted to believe he had the trumpet solo for the band concert." He reached for the family Bible. "I know just the passage of Scripture we need to read for devotions tonight—Ephesians 5:6-10." After reading the verses, he added, "Satan is a great deceiver. The Bible warns us not to be fooled by him or by men who aren't Christians. What you did today was just a joke that you both enjoyed. But let it teach you to be careful to believe only the truth, not just what you want to believe." *CVM*

HOW ABOUT YOU?

Do you make sure that what you believe is true? Satan knows that it's very easy to believe what you want to believe. He often uses people to tell you things you like to hear—that you're really pretty good, or that you can earn your way to heaven, or maybe that it's not important to witness for Jesus. Don't be fooled. Check what you hear with what God has to say about it.

Don't Be Fooled by Satan

MEMORIZE:
"Don't be fooled by those who try to excuse these sins." Ephesians 5:6

April

2

The Mystery Seeds

Read Galatians 6:7-10

It was a sunny spring morning. Stacy and her brother, Benji, had received permission to plant a small vegetable garden. While Benji ran to his room to get the seeds, Stacy mapped out where she wanted everything planted.

"What's taking you so long?" Stacy asked as she entered Benji's room a little later. She frowned. "Your room's a mess," she said crossly. "I suppose you can't find the seeds."

"I know exactly where I put them," her brother replied. "I put them right here on my desk, but they're gone. Let's go ask Mom if she's seen them."

Stacy and Benji found Mom busily washing dirt off their little sister's face and arms. "How'd Jordan get so dirty?" Benji asked.

"Playing in the sandbox," Mom answered.

"No, I didn't," Jordan said. "I was planting the garden. I found the seeds on Benji's desk, so I planted 'em for you."

"You what?" Stacy's voice rose in frustration. "You don't know how to plant a garden!"

"Do, too," Jordan protested. "I dug a hole and dumped the seeds in it."

"Those were not your seeds! You're a thief!" Stacy yelled. "And everybody hates thieves!"

"That's enough, Stacy," Mom scolded.

"Well, they do!" Stacy exclaimed. "Including me!" She turned and ran to her room.

Mom followed a little later. "Stacy, do you remember what we read this morning from the Bible?"

"We . . . uh . . . it was something about reaping what we sow," Stacy mumbled.

"Yes," said Mom. "It was wrong of Jordan to plant those seeds, but what you planted was worse. You've planted a seed of hate in your sister's heart," Mom said. "I'm sure you don't want to reap hate from Jordan."

Stacy sighed. "I . . . I didn't mean what I said. I was just mad. I'm sorry, Mom, and I'll apologize to Jordan."

"Good for you," Mom said.

"Mom, can we go buy some more seeds?" Stacy asked. "Then I can teach Jordan how to plant them the right way."

"That's a great idea," Mom said. *"You'll* be learning how to plant seeds the right way, too—seeds of kindness." *TAS*

HOW ABOUT YOU?

When people do things you don't like, do you sow seeds of hate or seeds of kindness? The Bible says we are not to repay evil with evil, but with good. And remember that whatever it is you sow, that's what you'll eventually reap.

MEMORIZE:
"You will always reap what you sow!"
Galatians 6:7

You'll Reap What You Sow

The Human Race

Read Genesis 2:7, 21-23

"Our science teacher says all life began in the water that used to cover the earth," Jo informed her parents one evening. "He says that when dry land began to appear, some of the creatures grew legs and lungs so they could live on land. They kept on changing, and finally they became half animal and half human. Then they slowly developed into the intelligent beings we call humans, and that was the start of the human race."

"Mr. Broom called it evolution," added Jo's twin sister, Grace.

"And do you believe all that?" Dad asked.

Jo shook her head. "Not me," she declared. "It sounds dumb! We asked Mr. Broom about the Bible account of creation, and he says it's a myth. He says we have to learn what the science book teaches and . . ."

"Jo asked him if he really believed that stuff about evolution," interrupted Grace, "and he does. Just as the bell rang, Jo said, 'Well, I guess it's all right for you to believe your way as long as it's all right for us to believe the right way.' The whole class just howled!"

Jo grinned and added, "Mr. Brown was furious!"

The kids burst into laughter, but their parents didn't laugh. "It's never right to show disrespect for a teacher," said Dad, "even if you know he's wrong."

"But what can we do?" asked Grace. "We can't learn stuff we don't believe!"

"Mr. Broom says we'll fail the subject if we don't answer questions right on the tests," Jo added.

"Learn the material well, and when you write test answers with which you don't agree, you can add that the answer is according to the science book," suggested Dad. "Then at the end of the year, you can both go to Mr. Broom and tell him you still believe the Bible and that the human race began when God created Adam."

"Let's do it," Jo said thoughtfully. "Let's try to get the best grades in class, and then we'll let Mr. Broom know that we still don't agree with the science book."

"All right!" said Dad. "Mom and I will pray for you—and for him." *HCT*

HOW ABOUT YOU?

Do your teachers tell you that humans evolved from animals? The Bible says God made you. Be faithful to God. Let your teachers and classmates know you believe what God says, but be sure to show respect to your teachers so you can be a good testimony to them.

God Created Humans

MEMORIZE:
"God created people in his own image." Genesis 1:27

Undeserved Reward

Read Psalm 103:8-14

Moira was frightened. A fire had started in the woods near her home, and the sawmill where her dad worked had been damaged. *It's my fault!* Moira thought to herself. *I shouldn't have made that little fire to roast my marshmallows.* She sighed. *I sure hope nobody ever finds out! And I wonder if my eye operation will have to be postponed since Dad will be out of a job for a while now.* Moira felt awful!

Things got even worse when Mr. Simmons, the owner of the sawmill, stopped in. "A homeless man was picked up in the woods, and he's in jail. Of course, he claims he didn't do it, but even if he doesn't confess, I think we have enough evidence to prove him guilty."

"But . . . but . . ." stammered Moira. *What should I do?* she wondered. *An innocent person is in jail for something I did.* "It . . . it's my fault." The words came tumbling out, and she told Mr. Simmons and her parents about the fire. "I thought I put it out really well, but it must have started up again," she confessed. Fearfully, she awaited the reaction. Mr. Simmons was staring, open-mouthed. "Are . . . are you going to take me to jail now?" Moira asked with a shaking voice.

After what seemed a very long time, Mr. Simmons shook his head. "No," he said, "you're going to go for that operation on your eyes instead. You get the reward money I offered for turning in the guilty party!" Moira and her parents couldn't believe it, but Mr. Simmons insisted. "The crime was against me, and I have the right to pardon the offender if I choose," he said.

"I bet this is the first time somebody ever pardoned and rewarded the person who wronged him," said Moira in awe.

Mr. Simmons shook his head. "Not the first time," he said. "That's exactly what Jesus did for us. We sinned against him, and God had a right to demand that we pay for our sin. But God showed mercy, and Jesus paid the price for us. He gave his life on Calvary so we could be pardoned. If we confess our sin to him, he pardons us and then rewards us with eternal life." *HCT*

HOW ABOUT YOU?
Have you been pardoned and given eternal life? Have you come to God, confessing your sin and asking for his forgiveness? If not, why don't you do it today?

MEMORIZE:
"He has not punished us for all our sins, nor does he deal with us as we deserve." Psalm 103:10

Jesus Offers Pardon for Sin

The Rainy Day

Read Psalm 147:4-11

"Rain, rain, rain! Why does it have to rain today?" Tiffany complained. She stared out the window as drops splattered on the glass. Everything looked damp and soggy. The longer Tiffany sat at the window, the more grumpy she felt. All week she had planned to play at the nearby park on Saturday—but now that the day had arrived, her plans were ruined. She felt sorry for herself.

With a sigh, Tiffany went to her room and got out her stamp collection. For several weeks she had thrown any new stamps she got into a box, so there were many waiting to be put in the stamp book. She studied the pages, finding just the right place for each stamp. As she was putting the last one in place, her brother Bob called, "Hey, Tiffany, let's go to the park. It quit raining!"

Tiffany looked up in surprise. Quickly she put on her jacket and ran outside. A bird happily bathed in a puddle. He splashed water over himself and fluffed his feathers, then took a drink.

Drops of water sparkled on the bright, spring-green blades of grass. Over at the duck pond, three big ducks swam, wiggling their tails when they dived for food.

Tiffany took a deep breath and smelled the clean, refreshed air. "Oh, the rain made everything beautiful!" she exclaimed. Suddenly she realized that God knew what kind of weather the earth needed. After all, he was the one who made it. She felt a little guilty. *I shouldn't have grumbled,* she thought. *It didn't stop the rain. And once I started working on my stamp collection, I didn't even notice the weather.*

Silently Tiffany breathed a little prayer. *Dear Lord, I'm sorry I grumbled about the rain,* she prayed. *Thank you for sending it even though I thought I didn't want it. CEY*

HOW ABOUT YOU?

Do you grumble about bad weather? Or do you keep busy until you can go outdoors again? God is the maker and ruler of the earth. When you grumble about the weather, you're really grumbling against God. There are things to do on rainy days, too. So instead of grumbling, get busy. Soon the sun will shine again.

MEMORIZE:

"He covers the heavens with clouds, provides rain for the earth, and makes the green grass grow in mountain pastures." Psalm 147:8

Thank God for His Goodness in Nature

The Son Still Shines

Read Romans 8:35-39

Miranda zigzagged around mud puddles as she walked home, but her feet and her coat were completely wet from the rain. She knew she would be home alone for a little while, and it made her feel as gloomy as the dark clouds overhead.

When Miranda reached the back porch, she was surprised to see her sister, Kay. "I'm home from college for the weekend," Kay announced cheerfully. She grinned. "It's such a beautiful, sunshiny day, don't you think?" she teased.

"No, I don't!" Miranda exclaimed, wiping water off her face.

"But it really *is* a sunshiny day," Kay repeated, "even if it doesn't look like it."

"Well, today's sunshine is a little wet," Miranda protested. "I think you've been studying too hard, Kay, and your brain has gone to sleep."

"Just tell me this, Miranda," Kay said as she looked out into the rain. "Is the sun still up there? Has it moved? Did it go anywhere?"

"No, it didn't go anywhere," Miranda answered, "but it's sure hidden. I haven't seen it for days."

"Then think about it, Miranda," Kay continued. "We don't see the sun today, but that doesn't mean it isn't there. On the other side of those dark clouds, the sun still shines. We shouldn't trust only what we see right now; we should trust the truth." Kay smiled and added, "Just like Jesus."

Kay nodded in response to Miranda's look of confusion. "When things happen that upset us, we may feel all alone, but the truth is that we're not alone. Jesus is still with us, and his light shines in our hearts."

"So you're saying that clouds may keep us from seeing the sunshine, but it's still there," Miranda said, "and our problems may keep us from feeling like Jesus is with us, but he really is. Right?"

"Yes," Kay said. "God's love is always shining. Nothing can separate us from it; that's his promise in the Bible, and we should trust him."

Miranda grinned. "I guess it *is* a beautiful day. How about a walk in the rain?" *DS2*

HOW ABOUT YOU?

Have you invited Jesus to live in your heart and be part of your life? You may not always feel like he's there, but don't depend on your feelings. Trust the truth of God's Word, which says he will always be with his children. Nothing separates you from his love.

MEMORIZE:

"God has said, 'Never will I leave you; never will I forsake you.' " Hebrews 13:5, NIV

Trust God, Not Feelings

Always There

Read Joshua 1:5-9

"It's gone!" Josie exclaimed as she and her older sister walked to school one morning. "They just put it up, and now it's gone!" Josie was talking about a telescope the size of a skyscraper that had just been built on a mountain near their town. The girls usually saw it clearly as they walked to school.

Jenna laughed. "In this fog, lots of things are 'gone,'" she said. "I imagine we'll be able to see it by the time we walk home this afternoon."

Jenna was right. As they walked home, the telescope was again visible, but by then Josie had something else on her mind. "I don't want to go to school tomorrow," she confided to Jenna. "There's a girl who doesn't like me, and I'm scared of her. She's mean!"

"Maybe I can stay with you tomorrow till the bell rings," Jenna suggested.

"Yes, but then you'll have to go to your own class. You can't stay with me all day," Josie replied nervously.

Jenna thought for a minute. "No, I can't—but you know someone who can," she said.

"I do?" asked Josie. "Who?"

"Think about our Bible lesson last week," Jenna reminded her sister. "Mrs. Vargas talked about how Jesus is always with us. He—"

Josie interrupted her. "I know that, but I can't see Jesus," she said doubtfully.

Jenna was quiet for a minute. Then she pointed toward the big telescope on the mountain. "We couldn't see that telescope this morning, but it was there," she said. "And even though we can't see Jesus, he's there, too. He promised."

Josie sighed. "Okay. You stay with me till the bell, then I'll remember that Jesus is with me the rest of the time—even though I can't see him." Josie grinned. "I guess he can take better care of me than you can, anyway." *RRZ*

HOW ABOUT YOU?

Do you ever wish you could see Jesus? Even though you can't see him, he's right there with you! You can know that because the Bible says so. Jesus promised to be with you always, and he keeps his promises!

MEMORIZE:
"Be sure of this: I am with you always, even to the end of the age."
Matthew 28:20

April
8

Forgive Me My Sins

Read Psalm 32:1-2, 6

Paige and Bryan were eager to see Flash, Uncle Ted's new pony. "I have some pictures of him," Aunt Millie said as the children traveled with their uncle and aunt on their way to spend a weekend at the farm. She took an envelope from her purse. "Here they are."

"Let me see!" Paige said excitedly. "Wow! He's awesome!" Bryan wanted to see, too. He grabbed a picture, but Paige held on tight. Bryan hung on, too, and after a short tug of war and some angry words, Paige slapped him. "There!" she said. "That'll teach you!"

"Just a minute!" Uncle Ted interrupted. "Let Aunt Millie have the pictures, and you both just sit back in your corners for a bit. You both are to blame for what happened."

By the time they arrived at the farm, the fight was forgotten, and they enjoyed a delicious lunch after meeting Flash. As Paige helped wipe the dishes after lunch, one of the plates slipped from her hands and crashed to the floor. "Oh, Aunt Millie, I'm so sorry!" she exclaimed. "I broke your dish! I'll buy you a new one."

"That isn't necessary, Paige," Aunt Millie said kindly.

Just before bedtime, Uncle Ted read a chapter from the Bible, and each person prayed. Both Bryan and Paige ended their prayer with "Forgive my sins for Jesus' sake, Amen."

"What sins do you want God to forgive?" Uncle Ted asked.

Bryan looked surprised. "I . . . I . . . well, any wrong thing I did."

Uncle Ted nodded. "Anything specific that you should confess to God?" he asked.

"We quarreled in the car," Paige remembered. "I guess we should confess that."

"Paige, when you broke one of my dishes, you were sorry and told me about it right away," Aunt Millie said. "That was good—and when you sin against God, it's also good to immediately confess it to him and ask his forgiveness—like you did with me."

Uncle Ted nodded his agreement and added, "Okay, now who's up for riding Flash tomorrow?" Paige and Bryan grinned from ear to ear. *AGL*

HOW ABOUT YOU?
Have you told a lie? Talked back to your parents? Been unkind to someone? You need to confess to God the things you do wrong. Be specific. Ask God to help you not repeat those things that displease him.

MEMORIZE:
"If we confess our sins to him, he is faithful and just to forgive us and to cleanse us from every wrong."

1 John 1:9

Confess Your Sin to God

No Time Left

Read Luke 10:38-42

Now that spring had come, nine-year-old Jamie was often outside with her tennis racquet, practicing against the garage door. "Jamie, come inside for a bit, please," her mom called one day. "I want you to read a Bible story to your little brother while I make some bread. He's too little to help, and he keeps getting in the way."

Oh, brother, thought Jamie as she came in, *does it have to be a Bible story? I've got a really neat book about a tennis player that I'd rather read.* So she read her brother a tennis story.

Some time later Mom called again. "Jamie, I'd like you to take a loaf of bread over to Mrs. Rowan."

"Oh, why can't Charlie do it this time?" Jamie begged. "I've got to practice if I'm going to stay on the traveling tennis team." So her older brother took the bread to Mrs. Rowan.

After supper, Dad suggested that Jamie and Charlie study the verses they needed to learn for Sunday school. "Okay," Charlie agreed—but not Jamie. A tennis match was on TV. She decided to study after watching it.

And so her week went. Jamie didn't want to do anything but play tennis, watch tennis, and think tennis.

On Saturday afternoon, Jamie and Charlie went to their club meeting. "We have a surprise for you today," the group leader announced. "Special awards will be given to those in each age group who have learned the most Bible verses." Jamie watched as two boys and two girls in her group received gift certificates to use at a sports store. *Oops,* Jamie thought, feeling guilty. *I guess I haven't been thinking much about Jesus lately.* She had been so busy with tennis, that she hadn't learned even one verse! She had pushed Jesus aside all week long, and it took a tough lesson to remind her to focus on Jesus before anything else. *BMC*

HOW ABOUT YOU?

Do you sometimes leave Jesus for last? There's nothing wrong with sports, handicrafts, good books, or just having fun—unless those things take the place you should give to God. In today's Scripture reading, Mary chose to leave other things and listen to Jesus. He said that was wise. Give him first place in your life every day.

Put Jesus First

April

10

A Bored Friend

Read 1 Samuel 18:1-5

"Mom!" Samantha yelled. "Tell Michelle and Sean to get out of my room. I'm trying to do my homework, and they're throwing paper at me!" Mom went upstairs and again reminded Michelle and her friend to stay away from Samantha. So they decided to play outside.

"Michelle, whenever Sean is around, you two seem to get into trouble," Mom said that night. "You don't have that problem when Tina or Gabby are playing here."

"That's because Sean never wants to do anything I want to do," Michelle answered. "He doesn't like to play with my games or with my electronic set. Actually, there's nothing he likes to do."

"I think I know why the two of you often get into trouble," Michelle's dad added. "It's because you're bored, and when you are bored, trouble is easy to find. You know, Michelle, the Lord tells us that there's a solution to the problem of boredom."

"That's in the Bible?" Michelle was surprised.

Dad nodded. "It sure is. Proverbs 27:17 reads, 'As iron sharpens iron, a friend sharpens a friend.' That means that friends should help each other and encourage each other to become better people."

"A good example of doing what that verse says is the time you taught Tina to play Ping-Pong," Mom added. "As a friend, you helped her."

"I guess the only thing Sean and I help each other do is get into trouble," Michelle admitted. "I don't think we ever encourage each other. Usually we're cutting each other down." Michelle paused, then added thoughtfully, "Sean is a Christian, you know. I'm going to show that verse to him, and maybe together we can figure out an answer to our problem."

Dad smiled. "I think that would be a good idea, honey." *LMW*

HOW ABOUT YOU?

Do you sometimes get bored when a friend comes over to your house? Do you waste a lot of time watching TV or wondering what to do? Why not think of projects you can do together? Maybe your friend has a skill that he or she can teach you. Maybe you have a skill you can teach your friend. Work at making your friendships interesting.

MEMORIZE:
"As iron sharpens iron, a friend sharpens a friend." Proverbs 27:17

Work at Friendships

Why Can't I? (Part 1)

Read Luke 2:42-52

"I wish Aunt Dot was getting married here, instead of way off in another state," Josie complained. "I want to go with you to the wedding. Can't I, please?"

"I wish you could, Josie," Mom answered, "but the wedding is right at the time when you'll be having your final tests at school. You can't miss those."

"I could just cry!" Josie whined. "I want to go, too!"

"I know, but it can't be helped. You must accept it," Mom said firmly.

At bedtime that evening, Josie started her usual cry. "Why can't I stay up? Dan doesn't have to go to bed yet."

Mom sighed. "Josie, you were told to go to bed, and that should be enough."

"But why can't I stay up until ten o'clock like other kids?" she persisted. "Lexi stays up that late."

This time Dad answered. "We've been through all this before," he said, "You know your bedtime. Now go get ready, and not another word about it."

The next day, Josie's brother, Dan, left to go over to his friend's house. Josie wanted to go along, but Mom said no. "Why not?" Josie wailed. "You let Dan go."

"The boys are working on a project," Mom explained.

Josie pouted. "Well, you always let Dan do anything he wants! I suppose if I asked to go to Lexi's house, you'd say no to that, too."

"Right now I would, Josie," Mom replied sternly. "If you don't learn to accept the decisions of your parents and believe that they are best for you, I'm afraid you'll never accept *God's* will for you, either. You make such a fuss over the smallest disappointment. Making a fuss doesn't change or help anything—it just makes you feel worse, and it makes others not want to be around you. You need to learn to take no for an answer." *AGL*

HOW ABOUT YOU?

Do you often whine and complain about your parents' decisions? You need to learn to graciously accept what they decide. Jesus himself gave us an example of this by submitting to his parents. Practice remaining cheerful even when you don't get your way. This will make you a happier person.

Accept the Decisions of Your Parents

12

Why Can't I? (Part 2)

Read Job 1:1, 13-22

The day before Aunt Dot's wedding, Josie rushed into the house after school. She had to try once more. "Oh, can't you please take me along?" she begged.

"You know the answer to that," Mom replied, "but I'm afraid I'm not going, either. Dad called to say he swerved to miss a child on his way home, and he hit a tree. We need to get the car fixed, and he won't get home in time to take me into town to catch the bus."

By the time Dad arrived home, the last bus had gone. Mom could get to the wedding on time only if she would fly, but that was too expensive. "It's all right," Mom said. "I'm disappointed, of course, but I'm just glad no one was hurt."

Josie, who had been very quiet, now exclaimed, "But, Mom! You were all set to go! How can you bear it? If I were you, I'd be crying!"

"I am sad about this, Josie," Mom answered, "but there's nothing I can do about it. Besides, I know God's will is best, and I'm continually learning to accept whatever he sends."

Josie suddenly jumped up. "I've got it! I've got it!" she squealed. "Remember the money Aunt Dot gave me last year for my birthday and then again for Christmas? You said it was too much, but Aunt Dot said I was to keep it for something special. I want Mom to use some of it to fly to the wedding! Would you have enough then?"

Mom gasped. "Josie! A few days ago you were crying to go yourself!"

"I know I was," Josie agreed, "but you gave me a good example about accepting disappointments. Oh, please, Mom. I want to do it. It will be sort of a wedding gift from me to Aunt Dot, too."

"Let her do it," Dad advised with a smile. "Some good has come of this disappointment already. We've seen Josie do a little growing up today." *AGL*

HOW ABOUT YOU?

Do you find yourself overwhelmed with disappointment or sadness? Happiness doesn't depend so much on your circumstances as on how you react to those circumstances. You may shed some tears, but trust God to use all circumstances for your good.

MEMORIZE:
"Though he slay me, yet will I hope in him." Job 13:15, NIV

Accept Disappointments

Careless Kate

Read Proverbs 15:1-7

Kate had a problem, and it was a big one! Her problem was that she was care-less—so careless that she had earned the nickname "Careless Kate." Above all, she was careless with words—and it didn't really bother her if she said things that weren't exactly right. Family and friends were often upset with her after learning that something she said wasn't correct.

One day, Kate was given the opportunity to write an article for the school newspaper. She worked on it eagerly, and before long it was finished—all neatly typed on her mom's computer. Mom offered to check it, but Kate was in a hurry. "I'm sure it's okay," she said.

On the day the paper was published, Kate came home from school, quite upset. "Oh, Mom!" she cried. "I wrote an article about the bike obstacle races, and now Lucy's mad at me! It was all just an innocent mistake!"

"What was the innocent mistake?" Mom asked. Kate held out the paper, pointing to the end of her article. Mom read out loud, "Lucy Redford rounded the corner, narrowly kissing Blake Smith." Mom looked at Kate in surprise. "Why, honey, you shouldn't have put that in the article," she scolded gently.

"But I didn't," Kate protested. "I meant to say 'missing,' not 'kissing.' Now the kids are laughing and teasing Lucy and Blake, and they're both mad at me. They ought to know I didn't do it on purpose."

"Kate, careless words and actions always affect others," Mom said. "Can you see now how important just one word can be?" she asked. "Have you told Blake and Lucy what happened and that you're sorry?"

"Well . . . no," Kate admitted. "I guess I did avoid them. I'll apologize tomor-row. And I'm going to work at being more careful about everything I say or write from now on! Maybe they'll change my name to 'Careful Kate' then." *AGL*

HOW ABOUT YOU?

Are you careful about the words you use—in talking or in writing? Do you make sure you have all the facts straight when you talk about something? Words are important!

MEMORIZE:
"Wise people use knowledge when they speak. But fools speak only foolishness." Proverbs 15:2, ICB

Words Are Important

No Excuse

Read Proverbs 4:24; Ephesians 5:4

Marie and two of her friends were walking to school when Nolan, another class-mate, ran up to join them. "Go away! Walk with the boys, Nolan," Yvette ordered.

"Oh, don't be so mean," objected Marie. "He can walk with us." But the other girls ran on ahead, leaving Marie and Nolan to walk alone.

"Wanna hear a joke?" asked Nolan, and he proceeded to tell one.

Marie was shocked. "Nolan!" she exclaimed. "That's terrible! That's just dirty! I'm not going to walk with you, either."

Marie ran to catch up with her friends. "Oh," she fumed, "listen to what Nolan told me!" Then she told the dirty joke to them.

"That's disgusting!" Yvette exclaimed.

Sydney nodded. "The kids at school should be warned not to play with Nolan anymore," she said.

"Yeah! They should!" agreed Marie. "Since I'm the one he told the joke to, I'll warn them about it." So Marie repeated the story many times that week.

"I saw your teacher today, Marie," Mom said one evening. Marie frowned. Just that afternoon, her teacher had kept her in at recess to talk to her about the story she had been spreading. "Miss Cramer is concerned about you, and I am, too," Mom continued. "She said some of the other kids told her that you've been telling a dirty joke."

"But, Mom, you don't understand," protested Marie. "I was just telling the kids how Nolan talks—I was warning them so they wouldn't play with him. I tried to tell Miss Cramer that, but she doesn't understand, either!"

Mom shook her head. "I'm afraid you're the one who doesn't understand," she said. "First of all, you spread the story far more than Nolan did. Secondly, you were gossiping about Nolan. Are you proud of that?" Marie slowly shook her head. "You need to confess to God what you've been doing, Marie," Mom said, "and I think you should apologize to the kids you told the story to and also to Nolan." *AGL*

HOW ABOUT YOU?
Do you make excuses for spreading gossip or saying words you know you should not use? Is what you say acceptable and pleasing to God? Say only what is good, kind, and helpful.

MEMORIZE:
"Let everything you say be good and helpful, so that your words will be an encouragement to those who hear them." Ephesians 4:29

Use Words Acceptable to God

The Old Tin Can

Read Psalm 15:1-5

"Look!" Joy pointed to a tin can at the curb. "Somebody is a litterbug."

"Yeah," agreed Scott. "Let's kick that old can all the way home and then dump it." As he drew back his foot to give it a kick, he noticed something sticking out of the end of the can. "What's in here?" he wondered as he picked it up. He pulled the contents out of the can. "Money! There's money in here!" Sure enough—the can was stuffed full of money!

That evening, Scott and Joy eagerly discussed all the things they could do with the money they had found. "Hold on!" Dad said. "I'm sure someone will claim this money. It has to be returned, you know."

Joy and Scott looked at one another in dismay. They'd been afraid Dad would say that! "Let's pray about it," Joy suggested hopefully. "Maybe the Lord will show us that we should keep it." But they could see from the look on Dad's face that he didn't think much of the idea.

The newspaper that evening had an article about an old hermit who claimed to have lost a tin can containing his life savings. According to the article, no one believed his story. Even his relatives thought he was lying.

Joy and Scott looked at each other sadly. "Rats!" said Scott. "That crazy old guy is almost ready to die; he doesn't even need this money. We'd use it for good things and put some of it in the church offering."

Dad shook his head. "Look what that money is already doing to you," he said. "I've never heard you talk so selfishly and so heartlessly. You're Christians—and if a Christian is anything at all, he should be honest."

Joy and Scott looked at each other. "Yeah, I guess so," said Scott.

"We'd never be comfortable keeping it anyway," added Joy. When Scott nodded in agreement, Dad smiled. *HCT*

HOW ABOUT YOU?

When you find something that isn't yours—perhaps a pencil, a piece of candy, or money that someone dropped on the floor—do you try to find the owner? God wants his children to be honest, and he rewards those who do the right thing.

MEMORIZE:
"Do things in such a way that everyone can see you are honorable."
Romans 12:17

Be Honest

April

16

What's Inside

Read 1 Samuel 16:4-7

"I don't think I'm going to hang around with Paula anymore," Quinn said as she sat down at the kitchen table.

"Really? Why not?" Mom asked. "When you introduced me to her at the concert last month she seemed like a nice girl."

"Well . . ." Quinn hesitated. "She is pretty nice, but she dresses so weird. Her clothes never match!"

"Oh?" Mom stirred the sauce she was making. "That doesn't sound like a very good reason not to be friends with someone."

"Oh, Mom, you don't understand!" Quinn exclaimed. "Today she wore a fairly nice light pink shirt, but she wore it with ugly green and yellow pants! They looked awful together."

"Well, honey, you're especially good at coming up with creative outfits. Maybe you could help Paula," Mom suggested. "Maybe no one has ever taught her how to match her clothes. The next time she wears that outfit, maybe you could say to her, 'I like that shirt, Paula. I think it would really look nice with your white pants'—or whatever color you think would be good with it. But be sure to say it kindly." Mom put an arm around her daughter. "Remember, Quinn, you're a Christian, and God wants you to be kind to other people. I'm sure you know that God says it's not how a person looks on the outside that's most important, but what they're like inside."

Quinn considered her mother's suggestion. "I never thought of that, Mom," she said. "I guess it is kind of silly to judge a person on whether her clothes match or not. I'll see what I can do to help Paula, but even if she doesn't change, I'll still be her friend." *LMW*

HOW ABOUT YOU?

Do you decide whether or not people can be your friends by looking at the type of clothes they wear? Perhaps their families don't have much money. Or perhaps no one has taught them what looks nice with what! Is there somebody you could help? But be careful not to hurt your friend's feelings. Ask the Lord to show you how to help before you even try. And always remember that what's important is what is inside.

MEMORIZE:

"People judge by outward appearance, but the Lord looks at a person's thoughts and intentions." 1 Samuel 16:7

Don't Judge by Appearance

Creation and the Truth

Read John 17:17-19; 2 Timothy 3:14-17

"Are you ready for the test on evolution tomorrow?" asked Tara as she and her friend Dan walked home.

Dan sighed. "I guess so," he replied. "I can explain evolution the way Mr. Jackson did, but I don't believe it. I believe God created everything."

"Mr. Jackson says he believes the Bible, too, but he just doesn't think God really created everything," said Tara. She shrugged. "What's the big deal? What does it matter anyway?" As another girl rode by on a bike and waved, Tara scowled. "There goes Brenda Norris. That's one girl I'll never believe again!" she exclaimed. "You know what Brenda did? She promised me that when she got a new bike, I could buy her old one. After she finally got a new one, she told me she had sold the old one to Jenna for twice as much as she had asked me to pay."

"Well, you can't blame Brenda for wanting the extra money," said Dan.

"Maybe not, but I talked to Jenna last week, and she said she paid the same amount I was going to pay. Brenda's been bragging about her new bike—says her dad paid big bucks for it. But I heard her dad *gave* Brenda the bike for doing some work—and it's not new, either!" Tara frowned. "I'll never believe anything Brenda says. If she lies like that about one thing, she'll lie about other things, too."

"Wouldn't that be true about God and the Bible, too?" asked Dan.

"God?" asked Tara. "What do you mean?"

"Well, the Bible is God's Word, and the very first verse says, 'In the beginning God created the heavens and the earth,' " replied Dan. "There are lots of other verses in the Bible, too, that say God created everything. If these verses are lies, how can we believe anything in the Bible?"

Tara looked thoughtful. "So . . . if we're going to believe in the Bible and God at all, we've got to believe he created everything?" she asked.

"That's the way I see it," agreed Dan. "I think I'll put that somewhere on my test paper tomorrow, too." *VMH*

HOW ABOUT YOU?

Do you believe the Bible? All of it? Can you say, "I know God created everything"? To believe otherwise is to say that God does not always tell the truth—and that's wrong. God always tells the truth, for he is truth. All of his Word—the Bible—is true.

All of the Bible Is True

April
18

Why Am I Guilty?

Read Mark 7:20-23; Jeremiah 17:9-10

I've sure studied hard enough for my history test tomorrow, thought Calen, *but there are so many dates to remember! I hope I don't forget them.* As she closed her book, Calen remembered a trick her friend Eddie had told her about. *I'll try that,* she decided, so on a small piece of paper she wrote the dates that were hard to remember. The next morning, she slipped the paper up her long shirt sleeve. "I'll use this only if I have to," she muttered.

When Calen took the test, she found that studying had paid off. Much of it seemed easy. Still, all those dates were confusing. She looked over the finished test. Then she glanced at Miss Wilson. The teacher was busy at her desk, so Calen slipped the paper out of her sleeve and compared it to her test answers. *Oh good!* she thought. *I got 'em right.* As she slipped the paper back up her sleeve, she noticed someone standing beside her.

Miss Wilson reached down for her test. "I'm sorry, Calen. I'll have to give you a zero," she said as she tore the paper in half.

When her parents learned what had happened, Calen defended her actions. "It's not fair," she insisted. "Eddie cheated lots of times, and he never got caught. Besides, I didn't even do it—I didn't change a single answer! Miss Wilson could have just taken my paper and graded it. Since I didn't change any answers, how am I guilty?"

"God sees our hearts, Calen," Dad told her. "God knows you planned to change answers if they were wrong. The temptation to sin is not wrong. But when we want to sin—when we plan to sin—that is wrong."

Calen frowned. "But if it all begins with wanting to do something wrong, how do you get rid of the . . . the 'want to'?" she asked at last.

"Confess it to God and ask him for the victory," Dad told her. "Make Jesus the Lord of your life. Then whenever you want to do a wrong thing, turn that desire over to him. He'll take it away if you're willing to give it up." *AU*

HOW ABOUT YOU?

Do you desire to do what is right? Or do you wish you could get away with doing things you know are wrong? If you knew you wouldn't be caught, would you steal? Cheat? Disobey? If so, confess your sin to God. Ask him to control your mind and desires.

MEMORIZE:

"I, the Lord, search all hearts and examine secret motives." Jeremiah 17:10

Don't Plan to Sin

Dead, but Alive

Read 2 Corinthians 5:1, 6-9

Stretching sleepily, Mackenna wondered why she had that strange, empty feeling in the bottom of her stomach. Then it all came back to her. She glanced over at the other bed. Yes, it was empty. It really was true—her big sister, Maggie, was gone. Two weeks ago Maggie had left for school in the morning and had not come back. Tears rolled down Mackenna's cheeks as she remembered. There had been an accident, and Maggie had been killed. Mom said she had gone to heaven.

The door to Mackenna's room opened, and her mom came in. "Good morning! I see you're already awake," she said. Noticing Mackenna's tears, her mom sat beside her on the bed. "You're thinking of Maggie, aren't you, honey?" she asked. "Daddy and I miss her, too, but we try to remember how happy she is with Jesus."

"But, Mom, how do you know that?" asked Mackenna.

"I know because Maggie accepted Jesus as her Savior," Mom replied, "and the Bible says that when those who trust in Jesus leave this life, they go to be with him."

Mackenna nodded. "Yes, but I still don't understand," she said with a sob. "You always say Maggie's in heaven, but she was right there in the casket, and then she was put in the ground at the cemetery." Mackenna covered her face with her hands.

"Maggie's body is in the grave, but her soul, or her life—the real Maggie—is with Jesus," Mom explained.

"Your body is just a house in which the real you—your soul—lives. Your body may die, but your soul lives. Maggie's body died, and we buried it, but God took Maggie's life—her soul—to heaven. So when I think of Maggie, I think of her in heaven, not in the cemetery."

Mackenna sighed. "But I still wish I could see Maggie every day."

"I know," Mom answered, giving her a hug. "We all do. We can't see her again here on earth, but because we all know Jesus, we can look forward to seeing her in heaven forever!" *AU*

HOW ABOUT YOU?

Do you know that your life, or soul, lives forever—in either heaven or in hell? After death, a Christian's soul goes to be with Jesus. Be sure you have accepted the Savior so that you can know you're going to heaven.

MEMORIZE:

"We would rather be away from these bodies, for then we will be at home with the Lord." 2 Corinthians 5:8

Bodies Die; Souls Don't

Jesus, My Friend

Read John 15:12-15

"Robyn always spends more time with other kids than with me," Greta complained one afternoon. She sighed loudly. "They want to play tennis all the time. I like to play for a while, but then I get bored."

"I see," Mom said. "Maybe you should look for friends who enjoy the same things you do."

"I guess so," agreed Greta. Grinning, she reached into her book bag. "I got an A on my math test! Since I did so well, can I have an extra half hour of TV tonight? There's a quiz show that's fun to watch."

"Well . . . okay," Mom agreed, "but no TV until your homework is finished—and until you've finished your Bible reading, too. We've all agreed to read and think about a few verses each day, remember?"

"Okay! Thanks, Mom," said Greta as she hurried off. It wasn't long before she returned to the family room and turned on the TV.

"Is all your work done already?" Mom asked. "Bible reading, too?"

Greta frowned. "Well . . . um . . . " she stuttered. "I'll do that later."

Mom turned the TV off. "That wasn't the agreement."

"But, Mom," wailed Greta, "Bible reading is boring."

Mom sat on the couch beside Greta. "Were you happy when Robyn went off to play with others instead of spending time with you?" she asked.

"No," muttered Greta. "Of course not."

"Friends want to spend time together—they enjoy *fellowship* with one another," Mom said. "The Bible says we should have fellowship with Jesus, too. I think he feels bad when we don't have time for him."

"I guess so," Greta replied slowly as she stood up and moved toward the door. "But won't Jesus know I'm sort of bored?"

Mom smiled. "If Jesus were standing here and wanted to tell you something, would you want to hear it?" she asked. Greta nodded. "Well, he does have something to say to you, and he speaks through his Word," Mom said. "Try reading it with that in mind." *JD*

HOW ABOUT YOU?

Do you have time for TV, video games, playing with friends, and talking on the phone? Do you have time for Jesus? You'll be blessed as you give him time each day to learn about him and what he wants you to do.

MEMORIZE:

"Our fellowship is with the Father and with his Son, Jesus Christ." 1 John 1:3

Treat Jesus As a Friend

Someone to Trust

Read Deuteronomy 31:8; Psalm 91:1-4

"Look, Daddy!" exclaimed four-year-old Eric as he peered out the airplane window. "Look! There's snow down there!"

His older sister, Ariel, chuckled. "That's not snow," said Ariel. "Those are clouds."

Dad smiled and nodded. "The clouds look like snow, don't they?" he asked. "They look solid—as though you could walk right out on them."

Ariel grinned. "But they won't hold you up," she warned. "If you stepped out on them, it would be a giant first step down to earth."

"Maybe they're clouds of snow," suggested Eric.

Ariel shook her head. "No. Clouds are only water vapor," she said in her best big-sister tone. "I learned that in science class. They can't hold anything up."

"Oh-h-h-h," murmured Eric. Then he had another question. "Why does the plane stay up in the air?"

"The plane is built just right for flying," Dad answered, "and the pilot goes to school to learn how to make it stay up." Eric seemed satisfied with that explanation and turned back toward the window.

"Eric believes everything we tell him," observed Ariel, speaking softly.

"That's because he has faith in us and trusts us to tell him the truth," Dad said. "As we grow older, we find that there are some things and some people we can't trust, while many others are trustworthy—such as most doctors, firemen, police officers, preachers, and teachers. But even people we trust may sometimes disappoint us."

Ariel looked thoughtful. "Last week Pastor Mike said there was someone who would never fail us," she said. "He was talking about Jesus."

Dad smiled. "I'm glad you were listening," he said. "It's important to remember that God keeps every promise he makes. You can put your faith in him and trust him. He always does what he promises." *RA*

HOW ABOUT YOU?

Has someone you trusted let you down? If that happens, let it remind you to be a trustworthy person yourself—one who doesn't let others down. Most of all, let it remind you to put your faith and trust in God. He loves you and will never fail you.

**Trust God—He
Never Fails**

MEMORIZE:
"I come to you for protection, O Lord
my God." Psalm 7:1

April
22

It Won't Show

Read Psalm 32:3-6

Brittany took her friend Shannon into the dining room to show Shannon her mother's prized teacup collection. "Does your mother ever use them?" Shannon asked, being careful not to touch any of them.

"Sometimes when she has company; otherwise no one is supposed to handle them. But I'll show you my favorite one," Brittany replied, taking one of the cups in her hand. "When you hold it up to the light, you can see a picture in the bottom." She held it out to her friend, but Shannon backed away, shaking her head. Expecting her to take it, Brittany let go. The cup fell to the table below, and the handle broke off.

"I didn't do it," Shannon said quickly. "You took it off the cup rack."

Brittany looked at the break. "I think I can fix it," she said. "Dad has some strong glue. It fixes everything."

Later, several ladies from the church came for a committee meeting.

Brittany watched anxiously as her mother served her guests, using the special cups. Mrs. Clark offered to help. Brittany watched in horror as Mrs. Clark reached for the cup with the recently glued handle! As she picked it up, the handle came off in her hand. "Oh, what did I do?" Mrs. Clark exclaimed, upset. "I'm so sorry! I'll buy you a new teacup."

Now Brittany realized how wrong she had been not to tell her mother about the accident. "It isn't your fault, Mrs. Clark," Brittany said timidly. "I broke the cup." Then she explained how she had glued the handle only a short time ago. "I'm really sorry," Brittany said tearfully. "I shouldn't have tried to hide what I did." She looked at her mother. "I'm so sorry, Mom," she added. Brittany's mother gave her a tight hug, and Brittany knew she had been forgiven.

After the ladies left, Brittany and her mother talked about what had happened. "Remember, honey, that even if you could hide your sin from me, God knows all about it," Mom said. "You can't hide anything from him." *RIJ*

HOW ABOUT YOU?

Are you trying to hide or cover some sin in your life? God sees everything. There is no way you can cover sin from him. You need to confess it and be forgiven. Ask God to help you keep a clean, pure heart.

MEMORIZE:

"Create in me a clean heart, O God." Psalm 51:10

Sin Cannot Be Hidden

Too Much Work

Read Philippians 2:13-16

Jackie washed the last plate and cleaned the kitchen sink. "I'm getting tired of doing all this work," she grumbled as she finally hung up the dish towel.

"Doing all what work?" her brother Kevin asked. Opening the refrigerator door, he took out the milk carton.

"Dishes, making beds, straightening up the place, picking up newspapers . . ." Jackie paused to catch a breath.

"Well, hey," Kevin interjected, "you're not the only one who works around here. Dad and I made supper tonight—and, I might add, without griping about it, either."

"Well, I don't know why Mom thought it was so important to get a job," Jackie began, "and—"

Kevin broke in again. "Well, you oughta know," he said. "After all, you're one of the reasons Mom went to work."

"Me?" Jackie asked. "I didn't ask her to go out and find a job!"

"She's working for you, though," Kevin said emphatically, "and for me, too. You know how much sickness we've had around here lately, and with Dad laid off part of the time, money's been really tight. You know they've been praying about it, and when the chance came up for Mom to work for a few weeks, she felt she had to do it. The job will pay for things we need for school, and even for food. Mom's making all kinds of sacrifices for you. Can't you make a couple for her?" With that Kevin left the room.

Jackie thought about Kevin's words. Was she an ungrateful, spoiled child, grumbling just because she had to do a few more chores around the house? She really didn't mean to be, but she knew she was. She felt ashamed. She was a Christian, and she knew her attitude had hurt both God and her mother. She would have to ask them both to forgive her.

When the back door opened later, Jackie was there to meet her mother. She threw her arms around Mom's neck. "Thanks, Mom. I appreciate everything you're doing for me," she blurted. "I love you for it, and I'm not going to grumble anymore!" *RIJ*

HOW ABOUT YOU?

Do you complain if you have to do a few extra chores around the house? Remember that your parents work hard for you. Thank God for them and for the jobs he has given them. Cheerfully do your share to make things run smoothly at home.

**Appreciate Your
Parents' Work**

MEMORIZE:
"Stay away from complaining and arguing." Philippians 2:14

Look Out!

Read Proverbs 14:9-14

How Allison hated to take her report card home! *Maybe Mom will forget to ask about it,* she thought. No—her mother never forgot things like homework, report cards, and responsibilities. It was always, "Do your homework." "Hang up your clothes." And especially, "Do you think God is pleased with the way you're behaving?" Allison frowned. *And now she doesn't like my new friend. So what if Lana sometimes uses bad words and tells a few dirty jokes? No one's perfect.*

Allison was so busy with her thoughts that she almost walked past her house. Taking a deep breath, she opened the front door. A mini-tornado almost knocked her off her feet.

"Allison, Mommy said you could take me to the park. Will you, please?" four-year-old Jared begged.

Allison shrugged. "Okay." She'd do anything to delay the showdown.

At the park, Jared ran from the swings to the teeter-totter, to the merry-go-round, and then off to the slide. "Look out, Jared!" Allison called. "There's a puddle. . . ."

But Jared paid no attention. "Wheeeee! Look at me," he called as he came zooming down the slide with his hands in the air. He landed with a big splash in the mud puddle at the bottom.

"Just look at you!" Allison scolded. "What will Mom say? Why didn't you look where you were going? Let's go home."

After Jared was cleaned up, they sat at the table with a snack. "Allison," her mother said, looking at the report card in her hand, "you and Jared are a lot alike. He didn't look ahead as he went down the slide, and you're not looking ahead, either. You've been neglecting your homework, and this report card reflects that. I'm afraid your poor choices in friends and your sloppy work habits are also helping to push you faster and faster in the wrong direction."

"Yeah," Jared said solemnly. "I'm going to look out next time. Are you, Allison?" *BJW*

HOW ABOUT YOU?

Are bad habits and friends pushing you in the wrong direction? Are you neglecting important things like daily devotions, homework, and responsibilities? Now is the time to change directions. Look out! Don't wait until you fall on your face in the mud—until you fall into sin, get into trouble, or bring home a bad report card.

MEMORIZE:

"There is a path before each person that seems right, but it ends in death." Proverbs 16:25

Change Bad Habits

I Know I Can

Read 1 John 5:1-5

"It's not fair! You always win! You're a cheater! I'm not playing anymore!" Renata dumped the game board and playing pieces onto the floor and ran to her room, crying. She slammed the door and threw herself on the bed.

"There goes her temper again," Renata's cousin said with a sigh.

Renata was lying on her cousin's bed when Aunt Magda came to talk to her a short time later. "Renata," she said, "you made a mess, called your cousin a bad name, and slammed the door. Tell me about it. What happened?"

"I don't know what happened," Renata muttered. "I just never win!" She began to wail again. "I can't help it that it makes me mad. It's just the way I am. It's not my fault."

"A game can be fun whether you win or lose," Aunt Magda responded sternly. "Your actions were wrong—your temper tantrums are sin, and you certainly can help it."

Renata sniffled. "How?" she asked.

"When you accepted Jesus as your Savior last year, he gave you power over sin," Aunt Magda told her. "Our family read about that in our devotions just this morning. God gives us victory through Jesus. When we know Jesus, we have no right to say we can't help it. Keep that in mind, and the next time you feel like flying off the handle, ask God to help you. You always have a choice. When you feel that temper of yours start to flare up, you know what to do."

"Well . . . I still don't like to lose, but I . . . I'll try to remember to ask God to help me next time," Renata promised.

Aunt Magda smiled. "It's a little like a story we used to read to you kids," she said. "Remember *The Little Engine That Could*? Instead of saying, 'I think I can, I think I can,' you can say, 'With Jesus, I know I can!' Ask him for help. He'll never fail you." *DH*

HOW ABOUT YOU?

Do you give in to sin and say, "I can't help it"? Do you make excuses for behavior you know is wrong? Take responsibility for your actions. Ask the Lord to help you. You have power over sin when you have Jesus in your life. Let him have control, and you'll be a winner!

MEMORIZE:

"How we thank God, who gives us victory over sin and death through Jesus Christ our Lord!" 1 Corinthians 15:57

Don't Excuse Sin

April
26

Devotions As Usual

Read Romans 1:14-17

The family room of the Martin home was covered with sleeping bags, pillows, and giggling girls. Lindsay had waited eagerly for the night of her pajama party. Everyone was having fun, and the evening seemed perfect. As she served the second batch of popcorn, Mom beckoned to Lindsay from the door. "Lindsay, we'll be ready to have devotions at nine o'clock," Mom said.

"Oh, Mom, can't we skip it tonight? Some of the girls don't go to church—they'll be uncomfortable. Please, Mom," Lindsay begged. "Tonight's supposed to be fun."

Mom shook her head. "Lindsay, we have devotions every night," she said, "and tonight isn't any different. It's an opportunity to share our faith with your friends. We're not ashamed of being Christians."

Reluctantly, Lindsay gathered the girls together with her family. Mom read a story about an orphan boy who had been unloved all his life. Through a missionary, he discovered God's love for him. As Dad read some Scripture and prayed, Lindsay noticed that two of her friends seemed to be listening very closely. The girls seemed interested.

Oh, God, Lindsay prayed silently, *I'm sorry for being embarrassed to share you with my friends. Please help me to be a better witness for you.*

As the girls were leaving the next day, they thanked Lindsay for the fun time they'd had.

"I really enjoyed the party," Natalie said. "In fact, I think I liked your mom's story best of all."

"Well, hey," Lindsay said, "why don't you come to church with us on Sunday? In Sunday school we hear lots of good stories and learn lessons from the Bible."

"Okay," Natalie agreed. "I'll ask my mom if I can come." *DH*

HOW ABOUT YOU?

Do you find it hard to tell people about your faith? Are you afraid of what your friends will think? You might be surprised to find that they're interested. God wants to use you to help others find him! Without him, they cannot have eternal life.

MEMORIZE:

"For I am not ashamed of this Good News about Christ. It is the power of God at work, saving everyone who believes." Romans 1:16

Share Your Faith

New Glasses

Read Psalm 119:129-133

"What are you reading?" Dr. Trent asked as he entered the examination room and saw Isabel with a book opened on her lap.

Isabel blushed slightly. "It's . . . uh . . . the Bible."

"The Bible? Why are you reading that?" Dr. Trent asked. Before Isabel could answer, he continued. "I mean, with all the exciting stories out there, I should think you'd find an old book like that pretty boring."

"Oh, no," Isabel said. "It's not like that at all. My Sunday school teacher said we should read some stories about Daniel straight from the Bible—and they really are interesting. Besides, reading the Bible helps me . . . well, it's like . . . oh, I don't know." Isabel felt frustrated because she couldn't express what she was thinking.

Dr. Trent held up a new pair of glasses, and Isabel removed her old ones. The doctor placed the new pair on Isabel's face, checking behind her ears to see how they fit. "Wow!" Isabel said immediately. "What a difference!"

Dr. Trent smiled. "You didn't realize how much you were missing with your old glasses, did you?"

"No," said Isabel. "Everything is so sharp and clear now." Suddenly she had a thought and said, "That's why I read the Bible, Dr. Trent." The doctor raised his brows. Quickly Isabel added, "Reading the Bible is like getting a pair of glasses. It helps me see things more clearly—things like what is right and what is wrong. It encourages me to choose the right things to do."

"Reading the Bible really does that?" asked Dr. Trent.

Isabel nodded vigorously. "You ought to try it," she told him. "It tells the way to heaven, and how to worship God. And it teaches us to love others and be kind and honest. It teaches us how to live." *BH*

HOW ABOUT YOU?

Did you know that the Bible can help you make right choices? It gives instructions for living—how to be saved and how to find peace, comfort, help in trouble, and much more. Read it each day; think about it; obey it. You'll see life differently than before.

Read God's Word and Obey It

MEMORIZE:
"Guide my steps by your word."
Psalm 119:133

April
28

Lesson from Mickey (Part 1)

Read Hebrews 12:5-11

Olivia, who lived along the Amazon River as a missionary kid, had a unique variety of pets. She especially loved Mickey, her kitten-sized monkey, but he was a rascal. One day, he scampered to the bookcase and cautiously ran his hand across the tempting, paper-jacketed books. Then he began tearing off strips of paper and shredding them to bits.

"Mickey! What are you doing?" scolded Olivia as she entered the living room. She scooped him up and ruffled his fur. He swished his long bushy tail in aggravation. "Stop ripping the books, or you'll have to go outside," she threatened. Mickey calmed down; he didn't like to go outside. Olivia set him down and cleaned up the mess. Mickey turned and picked up his tail, combing his fingers through the silky, black fur while Olivia worked. But as soon as she disappeared into her room, Mickey hopped back to the bookcase and continued the shredding.

The sound of tearing paper came down the hall to Olivia. She reappeared and gently but firmly swatted him. "Naughty monkey! Do you want to go outside?" she sternly asked again. She shooed Mickey away from the books and returned to her room.

Mickey immediately scooted back to the bookcase. He was having a great time when he suddenly found himself lifted into the air. He whirled his tail furiously and chattered his disapproval, but he couldn't pull himself from Olivia's grip.

"I don't really want to put you outside, Mickey, but you have to learn to behave!" said Olivia sadly as she opened the door. Suddenly she thought of something. "Now I know how my parents feel when I disobey them," she murmured. She tossed Mickey lightly down onto the hot cement patio.

As Olivia went back into the house, she thought of something else. *When we sin, it must really hurt God to have to punish us, too, but he has to do it anyway. I guess I understand that a little better now. TBC*

HOW ABOUT YOU?

Do you try to get away with sin? Parents love you, and they must sometimes discipline you. God also disciplines his children because he loves them and wants to keep them from harm. When discipline comes, accept it and turn away from the wrong thing you've done.

MEMORIZE:

"As you endure this divine discipline, remember that God is treating you as his own children." Hebrews 12:7

God Disciplines His Children

Lesson from Mickey (Part 2)

Read Ephesians 2:4-10

From the window, Olivia watched Mickey, her pet monkey. He was not happy to be outside by himself. He sat on the step and unsuccessfully pulled at the edge of the door. Then he went behind the steps to the cool crawl space under the house. There he waited for his chance to get back into the house.

After a while, Olivia had to run an errand for her mother. From his hiding place, Mickey saw her leave, and he was ready and waiting when she returned.

When Olivia opened the door and went into the house, Mickey jumped out and ran in behind her. She didn't see him, and she let the heavy door snap shut. It closed on Mickey's tender tail.

Mickey turned around and grabbed his tail as though it were a rope. He chattered and cried in desperation. He pulled his hardest, but it was no use. His tail was stuck in the door.

"Poor Mickey!" Olivia gasped as she ran back to the door. With one hand she pushed the door open, and with the other she scooped Mickey into her arms. He swished his hurting tail and rubbed the spot where the door had slammed on it. "Oh, Mickey, your poor tail!" Olivia cried. "Why did you try to get in all by yourself?"

As Olivia cuddled him and tried to soothe away his hurt, she saw some of her friends outside. A thought struck her. "You're just like some of my friends who are trying to get into heaven on their own," she told Mickey. "You didn't make it into the house, and they won't make it into heaven by themselves." The little monkey snuggled into Olivia's arms. "There now," she soothed. "I rescued you, and you're safe and loved. Maybe if I use you as an example, my friends will understand about trusting the Lord instead of trying to work their way into heaven." *TBC*

HOW ABOUT YOU?

Are you trying to get into heaven all by yourself or by the things you do? Why not admit you're a sinner and let Jesus rescue you? He loves you and died for you. He is the only way to heaven.

Jesus Is the Way to Heaven

MEMORIZE:
"God saved you by his special favor when you believed. And you can't take credit for this; it is a gift from God." Ephesians 2:8

April

30

"Ouch!" Kimberly banged her foot hard against the floor. "I need new shoes! This one hurts my foot!"

"You probably have it on the wrong foot," said her big sister, Hope.

"I do not!" Kimberly argued. She scowled at Hope. "This shoe really hurts!" she repeated.

"You just don't know how to put shoes on right," insisted Hope. "You're just a baby!"

Kimberly frowned. "I'm six years old," she informed Hope. "I know which shoe goes on which foot."

"Let me see," Dad said, and Kimberly lifted her foot for him to check. "It's the tongue of the shoe, Kimberly," he said after untying it. "It's twisted and bunched up. We'll just straighten it out." Dad pulled hard on the tongue and retied the shoe. "How does it feel now?"

Kimberly jumped up. "Hey, that's a lot better! It's all fixed!"

"Did she have it on the wrong foot?" Hope asked.

"Be quiet!" said Kimberly. "You don't know anything."

"At least I know how to put my shoe on so it doesn't hurt!" said Hope. She grabbed her soccer ball and began bouncing it with her knee.

"Show off!" Kimberly shouted.

Dad caught the ball and held it up high. "It was the tongue in Kimberly's shoe that was causing a problem," he said. "Tell me something else that causes trouble when it's not used correctly."

"Ah . . . that ball?" guessed Hope. "If it's used wrong—like if we throw it around in the house—we could break a lamp or something."

"I was thinking of something smaller," Dad said. He made a silly face and pointed to his tongue.

"Our tongues?" asked Hope. "I guess you mean we need to talk nicer to each other."

"You shouldn't have called me a baby!" said Kimberly.

"Right, and you shouldn't have yelled at me," Hope replied.

Dad nodded. "God's Word says the tongue is small but can do enormous damage," he said. "Our words can hurt people a lot more than shoes can hurt our feet." *MFW*

HOW ABOUT YOU?

Have you listened to the words you say? Do you say encouraging things to others, or do your words make them feel bad? Ask God to help you use your tongue to help people, not hurt them!

MEMORIZE:

"I said to myself, 'I will watch what I do and not sin in what I say. I will curb my tongue.'" Psalm 39:1

Use Your Tongue Wisely

Without a Script

Read Exodus 4:10-12; Ephesians 6:18-20

As the curtain dropped at the end of her school play, Tara's parents made their way backstage. "You remembered every line perfectly," Dad said, giving her a hug.

"You were great!" Mom heartily agreed.

Tara smiled. "Before the curtain rose at the beginning, I was so scared that I couldn't remember anything," she confessed, "but when I had to start talking, the words just came back." Tara smiled at a girl walking by. "Good job, Emma," she said.

"Thanks," Emma murmured. "You did well, too."

As Tara and her parents drove home a little later, Tara spoke thoughtfully. "Remember Emma?" she asked. "I think she seems really unhappy lately, but I don't know why. I feel like I should talk to her, but I'm afraid I might say the wrong thing. I wish there were a script to memorize for this sort of thing."

"I can understand that," Dad said. "I think the apostle Paul from the Bible was sometimes a bit concerned about saying the wrong thing, too."

"You're kidding!" Tara exclaimed. She couldn't believe it. "Paul was one of the greatest preachers ever!"

"But he was human—just like you. He had a big responsibility—just like you," Dad said. "Do you know what he did about it?"

Tara shrugged. "Prayed?" she guessed.

"Yes," Dad answered, "and he also asked his Christian friends to pray that God would put the right words into his mouth."

"And God did? Sort of like the way the right words to the play popped into my head tonight?"

"Sort of," Dad agreed, "only the words he spoke came from God, not from a script. You may not know the right thing to say to Emma, but God knows exactly what you need to say—and what Emma needs to hear. He wants to help you say it. Ask God to do that, and Mom and I will pray for you, too." *HMT*

HOW ABOUT YOU?

Does the idea of speaking to others about the Lord or about how you can help them frighten you? Do you worry that you might say the wrong thing or not have anything to say at all? Ask God to help you speak the right words at the right time—just like he helped Paul and Moses. (See today's Scripture reading.) Trust God to give you the words you need when you need them.

MEMORIZE:

"Now go; I will help you speak and will teach you what to say." Exodus 4:12, NIV

Let God Help You Speak

That One's Mine

Read Psalm 139:1-6

"Mom, do you know how many people there are on earth?" Mary asked one afternoon.

"Oh, I've heard the number," Mom replied, "but I don't remember right now. Billions, I guess."

"God made so many people that you'd think he'd forget who's who," Mary said. "Take me, for example. There are lots of girls in the world with brown hair and brown eyes named Mary. There are even two in my class! So how does God know which one's me—the one who's hoping for a new bike for her birthday?"

Mom laughed. "Don't worry, honey," she said. "God can tell everyone apart. He knows you want that bike, and he knows whether or not it would be good for you to have it." She picked up her sweater. "My ceramics contest is today," she said, "and I'm ready to leave. Want to come along?" Mary nodded, and they were soon on their way to the school gym.

At the gym, Mary looked in amazement at several tables filled with identical clay vases, all resting on identical glass holders. "Why do they all look alike?" she asked.

"Actually, if you study each one, you'll notice they're all quite different. They're being judged based on the most minor things—smoothness, symmetry, and how closely they fit the measurement guidelines," Mom explained. "I'll show you which ones are mine." Her eyes searched each table. "Look!" Mom pointed to the table in a far corner. "That second one is mine. I finished it last week."

"How do you know?" Mary asked. "They all look the same to me."

"Not to me," Mom said. "I remember every little mark, every small variation in the clay." She smiled at Mary. "Remember what we were talking about at home? This reminds me that God made you, honey, and he recognizes you as a special person. There's not a chance that he'd mix you up with anyone else. You couldn't be more special than that!" *SML*

HOW ABOUT YOU?

Do you wonder if God knows you personally? You can be assured that he does! Even if everyone on earth had your name and face, God would still know you. The Bible says that he even knows the number of hairs on your head. Knowing that he cares about those little details should assure you that he cares about every part of your life.

MEMORIZE:

"O Lord, you have examined my heart and know everything about me."
Psalm 139:1

God Knows You

Crystal Clear

Read Psalm 62:1-2, 5-8

"Dad, can we go rock hunting tomorrow?" Jocelyn asked. "There's a really neat place about five miles from here. My new friend, Marti, goes there all the time."

"Just what you need—another rock," Dad teased. He had stretched out on the couch after a strenuous day of moving furniture and unpacking boxes in their new home. "As you can see, I'm worn out from carrying in all the boxes containing your rock collection," he added with a grin.

Jocelyn laughed. "You'll feel better tomorrow," she assured him, "so can we go then, please? Marti says these rocks are special. She's a rock hound like me, but she mostly collects crystals. This place is loaded with them."

"Well, I don't know about tomorrow, but we'll go soon," Dad promised.

When Dad took Jocelyn rock hunting several days later, Marti went along—and just as she had said, they found many interesting rocks. "Look at this one," Marti called. She rubbed dirt off a rock and held it up to the sunlight. "It's got a rainbow of colors. It's the best one I've found today."

"Cool!" Jocelyn exclaimed. "What are you going to do with it?"

"I'll probably give it to my Aunt Tami," Marti answered, still admiring the colors glittering off the rock. "She has a special shelf for crystals. They look so pretty surrounded by the candles she keeps lit there."

"Candles? Special shelf?" Jocelyn's dad asked. His face showed concern and doubt.

"Aunt Tami gets really stressed out from her job at the court, and she says crystals have healing power and give her strength," Marti explained. "I think crystals are just pretty rocks, myself."

"And you're right, Marti," Dad quickly agreed. "Crystals make sparkling pieces of jewelry, and they're even used in things like watches. But crystals were created by God—and God is the only Rock who can bring healing and give us strength. He's the one to depend on." *LJR*

HOW ABOUT YOU?

Do you know someone who is trusting in the wrong "rock"? Some people wear crystal jewelry as a good-luck charm. Some have a special altar-type place in their homes. But those are like idols—dead objects that people turn to for help. Don't let Satan fool you into thinking those things can help you. When you need help or strength or someone to turn to, it should be crystal clear that Jesus has the power to help.

**Trust Jesus—the
True Rock**

MEMORIZE:
"Who is God except the Lord? Who but our God is a solid rock?"
2 Samuel 22:32

4

Paid in Full

Read Isaiah 53:1-6

Megan coughed again. She was tired of being sick! Her throat ached, and her chest was sore. As she lay on the couch, she watched her parents whispering to each other in their tiny apartment kitchen. She knew they were worried about money. Yesterday's visit to the doctor, as well as her medicine, had been expensive.

A moment later, Dad came into the living room, with Mom close behind. He rested a gentle hand on Megan's forehead. "You still have a fever," he said to her. Megan could tell Mom was trying to hide a worried expression behind her smile.

"Don't worry, Mom," Megan said in a scratchy voice. "God will take care of us."

Mom's smile brightened. "You are absolutely right, Meggers," she said. "Thanks for the reminder, honey."

With the medicine's help, Megan soon felt much better. One evening a few days later, she offered to get the mail while her parents made supper.

After they ate, Dad flipped through the stack of mail. Suddenly his brow furrowed in confusion. "Hmm," he said, "here's an envelope with nothing written on it." His look changed to surprise as he read the letter.

"What does it say, dear?" Mom asked him.

Dad looked up at Mom and Megan. "The clinic bill was paid by an anonymous person who heard about Megan's illness. No other explanation but that. Look," he said, pointing to the stamped words "Paid in Full" on the bill. "I have no idea who did this."

Mom's eyes filled with tears, and Megan smiled. "See?" she told her parents. "God did provide, just like we knew he would!"

"I've heard of things like this happening, but it's something else to experience such a miracle," Dad said in a choked-up voice. He paused a moment, then cheered. "Hallelujah!"

Mom looked thoughtful. "You know, this is a great example of what Jesus did for us on the cross. He marked our 'sin bill' as 'Paid in Full.' This news calls for a celebration! Who wants dessert?" Mom added, grinning at Megan. *HCT*

HOW ABOUT YOU?

Have you ever experienced a miracle? Whether you realize it or not, God works miracles every day. One of his greatest was raising his Son, Jesus, from the dead. Through Jesus' death and resurrection, our "sin bill" has been marked "Paid in Full." He paid the price we owed for our sins. That is a miracle! Have you accepted his gift?

MEMORIZE:

"The punishment that brought us peace was upon him, and by his wounds we are healed." Isaiah 53:5, NIV

Salvation Is a Gift

Stolen Words

Read Proverbs 18:1-8

"Mother!" Cassidy shouted as she bounded in from school. "Did you hear the fire engines today? The fire was at a place close to our school, and we're pretty sure who started it."

"Really?" Mom asked in surprise.

"Yep—Danny Blaine," said Cassidy. "I told my teacher about him—you know—the things his mother told you about him liking fires and going to the firehouse so often. I overheard her when she was here the other day. Danny was called to the office, and he was crying when he came out."

"Cassidy!" Mom gasped. "When Mrs. Blaine came to ask me to pray for Danny, she didn't expect you to listen in and then talk about it! You had no right at all to that information. And you certainly had no right to tell it to anyone else. Why did you do such a thing?"

"I . . . I don't know," Cassidy stammered.

"Well, other than the few things you overheard, did you have any reason at all to believe Danny might have set that fire?" Mom asked. Cassidy shook her head, and Mom continued, "The Bible says you shouldn't steal, but you stole words right out of Mrs. Blaine's mouth. The sad part is that words can't be replaced. You can't totally undo the harm you've done. But I want you to go right now and apologize to Danny and his mother. I'll get my coat and go with you."

As Cassidy reluctantly started out with her mother, her friend, Marsha, came running up. "Did you hear?" she called. "A short circuit caused the fire today. It wasn't Danny after all." *AGL*

HOW ABOUT YOU?

Did you know that money and objects aren't the only things that can be stolen? Have you ever stolen words? Think about this the next time you're tempted to listen in on a conversation not meant for your ears. Think of it the next time you're tempted to repeat something that would hurt someone else. Ask yourself if God would be pleased with what you're about to do. If the answer is no, don't do it.

MEMORIZE:

"What dainty morsels rumors are—
but they sink deep into one's heart."

Proverbs 18:8

Don't Gossip

May 6

Ponies and Canopy Beds

Read 1 Timothy 6:6-12

One Friday evening Laura went to stay overnight with her new friend, Christi. She could hardly wait to get there, because Christi lived in the country and had a pony!

When Laura arrived, the girls ran straight to the corral. Calliope, the pony, was beautiful and so gentle that Laura wasn't afraid at all. They fed him sugar cubes and brushed his golden mane. Then they took turns riding him. "Christi, you're so lucky! I wish we could trade places," Laura shouted as Christi galloped by.

Laura thought Christi's home was amazing. It looked like something out of one of her mom's magazines. Christi's bedroom was exactly what Laura had always pictured a princess's room would be. And Christi had a canopy bed—something Laura had always wanted. "Wow, Christi! You must be rich!" Laura exclaimed as she plopped down on the soft, billowy comforter. "You have everything I've ever dreamed of. Your room is awesome!"

"I like it, too," Christi said. "We inherited this farm when my grandma died last year." Tears came to her eyes as she looked around her beautiful room. "I'd give it all up, though, if I could just have Grandma back again!"

Laura lay awake a long time that night, thinking of her own dear grandmother. She wouldn't give up her grandma for anything, either. She remembered a youth group lesson from a couple of months before. The leader spoke on coveting, or being jealous of the good things God had given to someone else. As a feeling of sadness pricked her conscious, Laura knew she needed to confess her feelings of envy to God. *Lord,* she prayed silently, *you know how I like nice things. Please give me right attitudes about them, though. Help me not to be jealous of the good things you've given to Christi. I still have my grandma. Thank you for her, God.*

As Laura finished her prayer, she breathed a sigh of contentment and fell into a deep and peaceful sleep. *REP*

HOW ABOUT YOU?

Do you have friends who seem to have everything you ever dreamed of having? Perhaps your friends wish they had something you have. God wants you to quit being jealous of things other people have and be content with what he has given you.

MEMORIZE:

"If we have enough food and clothing, let us be content." 1 Timothy 6:8

Be Content

Softballs and Speaking Truthfully

Read Romans 14:7-13

"Oh no!" Claire groaned as she and her sister, Sandi, waited for their dad outside the grocery store. "Here comes that old grouch!"

Sandi looked up and saw a neighbor, Mrs. Blake, approaching.

Mrs. Blake greeted the children pleasantly. "By the way, girls, I found a softball in my yard," she said. "Is it yours?" Sandi gasped when Claire said that it was.

After Mrs. Blake was gone, Sandi turned to Claire. "You know that ball's not yours," she scolded. "You don't even own a softball. How can you lie like that?"

"Aw, what's the difference? Mrs. Blake doesn't know whose it is, so I might as well have it," Claire argued. "Who is it hurting?"

When Dad heard the story, he told Claire that she could not have the ball, and he grounded her for lying.

That evening, Claire answered the door when Mrs. Blake came over. "Did you bring my ball?" she asked in a low tone, hoping Dad wouldn't hear.

"Right here it is," Mrs. Blake answered, handing a ball to Claire. "It landed on my prize rose bush and broke it off. I hope you'll be responsible enough to pay for it!"

Just then Dad appeared in the doorway and saw Claire with the ball in her hand. "Claire, you must tell the truth," he said sternly. "You know that ball is not yours."

"Well!" Mrs. Blake snorted. "The ball belongs to her until you find out it has done some damage. Then it isn't hers!" Claire and her dad tried to explain, but Mrs. Blake wouldn't believe them. "I'm simply amazed!" she declared. "And you claim to be Christians. Why, you're just hypocrites!" She stomped off.

Dad shook his head. "You thought you weren't hurting anyone, Claire, but now I'm being blamed because of what you did," he said. "And God's name has been hurt, too." He took the ball from Claire. "I don't know if it will help, but you will have to pay Mrs. Blake for the rose bush and return the ball," he told her. "And always remember that your actions do affect other people." *AGL*

HOW ABOUT YOU?

Are you aware that when you lie, cheat, disobey, or do other wrong things, those actions reflect on others? Your family and your friends may suffer because of it. God's name may be hurt, too. Remember that next time you're tempted to do wrong.

Your Sin Hurts Others

MEMORIZE:
"We do not live or die for ourselves."
Romans 14:7, ICB

The Buried Treasure

Read Matthew 6:19-21

As Elaine and Jerry were digging in the sand at the edge of the river, Elaine found something. "Hey, look!" she called. "Here's something gold. I bet it's buried treasure." She dug a little more, and a few minutes later she was holding a gold watch.

The children decided to take it to Mr. Poole's jewelry store to see if he knew how much it was worth. After Mr. Poole looked at the watch, he nodded. "Mrs. Rodriguez bought this watch for her husband shortly before she died," he told them. "Here—let me clean it before you take it to him."

"You know," Jerry said as he watched Mr. Poole, "we thought we had found some buried treasure."

"Mr. Rodriguez will think you did, too," Mr. Poole said with a smile. "Tell him hello for me—it's a long time since I've seen him. Mrs. Rodriguez was a Christian, and she attended our church. But her husband wouldn't have anything to do with Jesus and never even visits church anymore."

When Jerry and Elaine arrived at Mr. Rodriguez's house, he was very surprised to see his watch, and he was pleased that Mr. Poole had cleaned it. "Hmmm. Fine man, Mr. Poole," he said. "He goes to the same church where my Selena went."

"Oh, we go there, too!" the children exclaimed.

"You do, eh? Is that why you kids did an old man such a great favor?" Mr. Rodriguez wanted to know.

Elaine shrugged. "We're just doing what we know is right," she said.

When Mr. Rodriguez offered the children a reward for the return of his watch, they glanced at one another, then shook their heads. "No, thanks," Jerry said, "but I know what we would like—would you please be our visitor for church on Sunday?"

"How can I say no?" Mr. Rodriguez said with a smile. "You just don't know what a special treasure this watch is to me."

As the children headed home, Elaine sighed. "That felt great," she said. "If Mr. Rodriguez receives Jesus as Savior, *that* will be the real treasure." *DG*

HOW ABOUT YOU?

What do you think is the very best treasure you could find in this world? If you have Jesus, you have found the best treasure! Then, if you do what you can to help others know him, you are finding more treasure—treasure that will last for eternity.

MEMORIZE:

"Since we are his children, we will share his treasures—for everything God gives to his Son, Christ, is ours, too." Romans 8:17

Store Treasure in Heaven

What's Good about It?

Read Acts 16:22-34

Bethany was riding her bike down the street when suddenly a little girl ran right in front of her! As Bethany swerved, she hit the curb and toppled from her bike onto the hard pavement. The next thing she knew, she was in the hospital with a broken leg. "Now we won't be able to leave on our vacation tomorrow, will we?" she moaned to her dad. "I know you say everything is supposed to work out for good, but I sure don't see anything good about this!"

Two weeks later, Bethany was sitting on her front steps, drinking lemonade. She was surprised to see a big, expensive car stop in front of the house. An old man got out. "You must be Bethany," he said. "How is your leg?"

"All right, thank you," Bethany replied.

"Good," the man said. "I'm Mr. Benton. My granddaughter Darcy is the little girl responsible for your accident. I want to thank you for swerving as you did. Why, you might have been killed!"

"Oh, I don't think it was that risky," Bethany objected. Then she grinned as she added, "But at least I know that if I had died, I'd have gone to heaven." Bethany could hardly believe she had said that—it had just seemed to come out. She was even more surprised at Mr. Benton's reaction.

"You know," Mr. Benton said thoughtfully, "I'm a rich man, but I'd give up all my fortune to know for sure that I was going to heaven. Suppose you tell me more about it."

And so Bethany told the man about Jesus and how he died on the cross to pay for everyone's sins. Mr. Benton listened carefully and even asked if he could visit her church and learn more about it at a later time.

"Well, can you see that your accident worked out for good, after all?" Dad asked when Bethany told him about it. "What could be better than having Mr. Benton saved? And I'm sure he'll tell Darcy about Jesus too!" *AGL*

HOW ABOUT YOU?

When things don't work out like you plan, do you look for something good in what has happened? Paul and Silas probably didn't think being in jail was a good thing (see today's Scripture), but God used it to bring the jailer to Christ. Perhaps God has put a "detour" in your path, too, so that he can use you to meet another person's needs.

God's Ways Are Good

Courtesy Pays

Read Proverbs 17:1; 22:11

Kim bit into her pie as soon as her mother handed it to her. "Kimberly?" Mom's voice had a question in it.

Kim looked up. "Oh . . . thank you," she mumbled.

"You're welcome," Mom replied as she handed Matt his piece. He started to pick up his fork, then noticed his father frowning at him. "Thank you," he muttered.

"You're welcome, too." Mom sighed. "But you both should wait to eat till everyone is served," she added. "I do wish you children would remember your manners."

"I try," Kim grumbled, "but it's hard to always remember. Manners are a lot of trouble."

"But very important," Dad said. "God says to show love to one another, and showing love includes showing good manners."

After dinner Matt was swinging when Randy, who lived next door, ran up behind him and almost knocked him out of the swing. Matt scowled. He was just about to make an angry remark when Randy said, "Oh, excuse me. I'm sorry, Matt."

"That's okay," Matt replied. "Want to swing?"

"Sure," Randy agreed, and the boys were happily playing when Kim came out.

"I've got four pieces of candy," Kim said. "One for Matt, one for Randy, one for me, and one extra."

"Give me the extra one." Matt held out his hand.

"No!" Kim snapped. She gave Randy a piece and smiled when he thanked her. She handed a piece to her brother. "What do you say, Matt?" she asked importantly.

"I say you're selfish to keep two pieces for yourself," Matt complained.

"You should thank her for giving you a piece," Randy said. "She had four before she shared," Randy reminded him. Matt grudgingly admitted that this was true.

Kim handed Randy the extra piece of candy. "This is for you, Randy," she said. "I like you. You're polite."

"Why, thank you." Randy seemed surprised.

"My mother says it pays to be courteous," Kim said as she unwrapped her candy. "You'd get more if you had better manners, Matt."

"So would you." Matt replied. "But I guess Mom's right. Good manners saved Randy from a fight and got him a turn on the swing and two pieces of candy!" *BJW*

HOW ABOUT YOU?

Is God pleased with your manners? Do they show that you love others? A double benefit is that they often pay off with other people as well as with the Lord.

MEMORIZE:

"All of you should be of one mind, full of sympathy toward each other, loving one another with tender hearts and humble minds." 1 Peter 3:8

Practice Good Manners

Discordant Notes

Read Romans 6:1-7

"What if I forget which notes to play?" Cori cried on the day of her first piano recital. She laughed nervously and added, "My fingers are shaking so badly, they probably won't hit the right keys even if I do remember the notes."

"Calm down, Cori. I'm sure you'll do just fine," Mom reassured her.

Mom was right. After a few shaky notes near the beginning, Cori played beautifully.

Cori's friend Joyce played next. The music flowed from her fingertips with ease—that is, until the very end. Somehow her fingers tripped to the wrong keys, making a noticeable discord. She tried to correct her mistake, but she made another. She ended with three consecutive mistakes. Cori felt sorry for her.

On the way home, Cori's family pulled up alongside a car with annoying music blaring from the open windows. The teenage driver was smoking a cigarette. "That's Tim Prince," Cori said. "He used to be active in our church youth group, but now he never comes. I guess he's pretty wild now."

Mom nodded. "You know," she said, "Tim reminds me of Joyce's piano piece."

"How's that?" Cori asked in surprise.

"Tim started out so well in the Christian life, just like Joyce played so beautifully at the beginning of her piece," explained Mom. "The discordant notes at the end spoiled the effect of the song, and Tim's activities this past year have spoiled his testimony as a Christian."

"I see what you mean," Cori said soberly.

"Joyce's mistake will soon be forgotten," Mom added, "but I'm afraid Tim's mistakes will leave scars that only Jesus can heal." *JW1*

HOW ABOUT YOU?

Are there discordant notes in your life? Are there so-called "little" sins that will spoil your testimony? Perhaps you're getting careless about Sunday school attendance or Bible reading. Maybe you're starting to laugh at dirty jokes or to "just try" things like cigarettes or alcohol. Don't do it. Remember that the things you do now affect the rest of your life.

Don't Let Sin Ruin Your Testimony

MEMORIZE:
"You should consider yourselves dead to sin and able to live for the glory of God through Christ Jesus." Romans 6:11

May
12

A Sneaky Trap

Read 2 Corinthians 11:13-15

Ray Ann and her sister, Zoe, loved spending time with their grandfather. He knew all kinds of facts about so many things, and he'd often tell them stories about God's love.

One Saturday afternoon the sisters were helping their grandpa weed his flower garden when he pointed to a spider's web and the spider attached to it. "Which type of insect do you think would be most dangerous, a spider or a bee?" Grandpa asked.

Without pausing, both girls echoed, "A bee!"

"Last time I got stung by a bee, I thought the pain would never go away!" Ray Ann added.

Grandpa grinned as he dug another small hole in the flowerbed. "That's what I thought you'd say!" Then he paused, wiped his brow with the back of his hand, and sat back to rest. "But did you know that spiders are often dangerous for bees?"

The girls looked doubtful but waited for him to continue.

"It's true," the older man confirmed. "That spider's web is awfully dangerous for a bee to get caught in. Once it's stuck on the web, there's really no way for the bee to free itself."

"Wow," Zoe replied. "Who'd ever think a little old spider could scare a bumblebee? Spiders must be pretty sneaky creatures!"

Grandpa looked at the children and added one final thought. "Satan can be just as sneaky as the spider," he warned. "He can make sin look good and wants to trap you into things that do not honor God. It's very important to be watchful for ways he tries to trick us. Avoid his traps by reading and obeying what God commands in the Bible." *AHG*

HOW ABOUT YOU?

Do some things that are wrong look good to you? Is there a bad habit in your life that has stopped you from living God's way? Don't let Satan trap you. His traps often have dangerous consequences.

MEMORIZE:
"Resist the Devil, and he will flee from you." James 4:7

Avoid Satan's Traps

The Glassblower

Read Psalm 39:1-4

Kara's class was on a field trip to a restored historical town. The kids saw how things were done a hundred years ago, and they listened carefully as Mr. Seltzer, a glassblower, explained what he was doing. "The glass begins as potash and soda," Mr. Seltzer said. "We heat it to almost two thousand degrees Fahrenheit. Now watch as I get a glob of the molten material on the end of my blow-rod and then blow it into something. The only time I can blow into it and change its shape is when the glass is hot. After it cools down, it can't be molded or shaped anymore . . . unless it's reheated."

The children eagerly watched to see what Mr. Seltzer was making. They all agreed that the little vase he soon held up was beautiful, though one or two boys were heard to mumble that they would have liked a ship better!

That evening, Kara told her family all about the trip and the things the glassblower had said. "That sounds like Pastor Carr's sermon last Sunday," Dad reminded her. "He said Christians should keep their hearts warm so the Holy Spirit can mold them into what God wants them to be. Like the glass, if a Christian's heart grows cold, God can't shape that life."

Mom smiled and nodded. "Who can remember some of the things we can do to keep our hearts warm?" she asked.

Kara thought for a moment. "We can spend time talking with God and reading the Bible," she said. "And we need to decide that we'll do whatever he wants us to do."

Dad nodded. "I hope I'll always have a warm heart and spirit, so God can shape my life into whatever he wants me to be," he said, "don't you? In fact, it would be good to pray often for a warm heart!" *AU*

HOW ABOUT YOU?

Are you as "warm toward the Lord" as you used to be? The psalmist who wrote today's Scripture kept so close to God that he said his heart was "hot within him." This is how you need to be if you want God to shape you into something beautiful for his service. Learn the verse below; follow its advice; and then your heart will always stay warm enough for God to make you what he wants you to be.

MEMORIZE:
"Draw close to God, and God will draw close to you." James 4:8

Let God Mold You

Treat or Treasure?

Read Proverbs 11:24-28

"Are you allowed to use that for your homework?" asked Mom when she saw Cassandra punching numbers on her calculator.

"This isn't homework," said Cassandra. "I'm trying to figure out how I can afford to go on the mission trip."

"I thought that was settled," said Mom. "You earned half the money, and we're going to pay the rest."

"Yeah, but I wanted to see if I could get a jacket I saw and have enough for the trip, too," said Cassandra. "It won't work, so I'm not sure what I want to do."

"The mission trip has been really important to you," Mom reminded her.

"I know." Cassandra nodded. "The kids who went last year said it was really incredible! Hard work, but fun, too. Remember how they caught that monkey?"

Mom shook her head. "I don't think I heard about it."

Cassandra grinned. "There was this troublesome monkey in the churchyard. To catch him, the kids put treats in a big jar with a narrow opening and fastened it to a tree branch. The monkey stuck his paw in and grabbed the treats—but then his fist was so fat he couldn't get it out. The monkey was too stubborn to let go of the treats, so he was stuck. They took him to the animal shelter."

Mom smiled. "I know the young people put together a great Vacation Bible School," she said. "I know you'd enjoy the trip."

"Yeah," Cassandra agreed, "but I'd also love that jacket." She sighed. "How do I decide? Do I have to use my money for the mission trip, or can I get the jacket?"

Mom hesitated. "It's your money," she said at last, "but I hope you won't act like that monkey. He gave up his freedom for a small treat. That jacket you want is a small treat, while the mission trip would produce lasting treasure if it's truly done for the Lord. Will you give that up because you're too stubborn to let go of a treat?"

Cassandra shut off her calculator. "I guess the decision isn't so hard after all." *HMT*

HOW ABOUT YOU?

Do you find it hard to make choices? The choice of a fleeting pleasure may seem more attractive than something that brings lasting rewards. When you need to choose, don't hold on to the "treat" so tightly that you lose what really matters. Ask yourself, "WWJD—What would Jesus do?"

MEMORIZE:
"Store your treasures in heaven."
Matthew 6:20

Value Things That Really Matter

Rewards

Read Matthew 10:38-42

"Dad! Dad!" Jodi yelled. "Come quick! My lamb won't get up!"

Dad came over quickly and inspected the lamb. He frowned and said, "I'm afraid it's pneumonia, Jodi. I guess I'd better call the vet."

"Will Wooly die, Daddy?" Jodi asked.

"We'll do our best to see that he doesn't," her father answered. "You've worked hard to get Wooly ready to take to the fair, and we'll work hard to get him well again."

Jodi did work hard after the vet came—giving her lamb its medicine and keeping the stall clean so sores wouldn't develop on its body. But Wooly refused to eat for days and lost weight. Jodi couldn't walk her lamb, so its muscles didn't develop. When the day of the fair came, Jodi's lamb was well and looked good, but it was so underweight and poorly muscled, it didn't win any ribbons.

"I'm proud of you, Jodi," her dad told her. "You didn't give up on your lamb, and you worked so hard. We didn't see the result we hoped for, but I'm going to reward you for your efforts. Here's some extra money to spend at the fair."

"Jodi," Mom said, "all your efforts for Wooly remind me of your efforts to get Ruby interested in knowing Jesus."

"It does?" Jodi asked. "I don't see what Wooly has to do with me inviting Ruby to church. I keep asking her, but she hasn't accepted my invitation yet."

Mom smiled. "Your heavenly Father rewards you for your efforts, too—even if you don't get the results you want."

"That's right," Dad agreed. "It's up to us to be faithful. The results are in God's hands."

"Just keep inviting Ruby," Mom said. "Your faithfulness saved your lamb's life. Someday your faithfulness in witnessing to Ruby may result in her salvation. But God will reward you no matter what. He knows your heart." *NIM*

HOW ABOUT YOU?

Do you give up when your friends aren't interested in joining you at church or Sunday school— or do you continue to share your testimony? Jesus wants willing workers who are faithful, even when it seems everything they do is in vain. If you give up on your friends, who will tell them about God's salvation?

Be Faithful in Working for Jesus

MEMORIZE:
"I, the Son of Man, will come in the glory of my Father with his angels and will judge all people according to their deeds." Matthew 16:27

Ready on Time

Read Mark 13:32-37

Dad walked into the kitchen and poured himself a glass of milk. "Michaela, have you eaten breakfast?" he asked.

"No." Michaela shook her head and turned a page in the book she was reading.

"You'd better get a move on if you want me to give you a ride to school," Dad said as he left the kitchen.

Michaela glanced at the clock. 7:15. *I have time to finish this chapter,* she thought.

Just as Michaela finished the chapter and closed the book, Dad poked his head into the room. "Let's go," Dad said.

"Already?" asked Michaela. "It's awfully early."

"I told you last night that I can't run late today," Dad said. "I have an eight o'clock meeting."

Dad waited at the door as Michaela quickly dropped the book into her backpack, grabbed a juice box from the refrigerator, and picked up a cereal bar from the cupboard. Dad shook his head as Michaela held her breakfast in one hand and tried to zip the backpack with the other. "In the morning, you need to spend your time getting ready for school—not as recreation time," Dad said as they went to the car.

"Yeah, I guess so," replied Michaela. "I'm kinda hungry. I was going to have cereal for breakfast, but the time slipped away from me this morning." She nibbled the breakfast bar. "I didn't think it was time to go yet."

"At an hour when you think not . . ." murmured Dad.

"What are you talking about, Dad?" asked Michaela.

Dad smiled. "Your comment made me think of something Jesus said. He's coming back, you know, and we need to be ready. Unfortunately, a lot of Christians are more interested in having a good time than they are in preparing for Christ's return. It's easy to skip church and Bible reading in order to play games or read books or even just sleep. It's easy to think we have plenty of time to tell our friends about Jesus, but no one knows exactly when he will return. Each day we need to remember that he may come at any moment." *RRZ*

HOW ABOUT YOU?

If Jesus came back to earth today, would you be ready—or would you be caught off guard? Prepare to meet Jesus. Make sure you know him as Savior. Then spend time with God and his Word, and take advantage of opportunities to serve him.

MEMORIZE:

"You must be ready all the time, for the Son of Man will come when least expected." Luke 12:40

Be Ready to Meet Jesus

On Becoming Fossils

Read 2 Corinthians 4:7-16

Lane rushed into the house and dropped her books. "Look at this!" she said, holding out a fossilized bone. "My teacher said I could borrow it to show Grandpa Parks. Can I show it to him today?"

Mom smiled. "We'll go over there right after supper."

"Mrs. Patterson says only one out of millions of bones becomes a fossil," Lane told her mom. "They have to be buried in just the right minerals. As the bones decay, the minerals seep into the pores, and bit by bit they replace the bone until there's no bone left, just hard, strong rock mineral."

"Really? Grandpa will love to hear about that," Mom said. "I bet his neighbor, Mr. Wyatt, would like to see that fossil and hear about it, too."

"I doubt it," mumbled Lane. "He doesn't like anything—or anybody." Lane frowned. "He's too grumpy!" she added. "I know he's old, but Grandpa Parks isn't grumpy like that, and he's even older than Mr. Wyatt."

Mom thought for a moment. "Grandpa is a lot like that fossil," she said.

"He's not that old!" objected Lane.

Mom smiled. "That's true, but all through his life, Grandpa let God's Word and God's love seep into his heart. Like minerals filled and replaced the materials of the bones, God's goodness filled Grandpa with love, joy, and peace—all the right things. Now he's pretty old. He's growing weak and tired and is starting to forget things, but God's Spirit is evident in him."

"And it isn't in Mr. Wyatt, right?" asked Lane.

"It doesn't seem to be," Mom said. "As far as we know, Mr. Wyatt never let God into his life. He never let God's goodness replace his old self."

Lane looked at the fossil. "Maybe I should show this to Mr. Wyatt," she decided. She looked anxiously at Mom. "But will you tell him how God changes us like minerals change bones? Maybe it's not too late for him."

"Sure," Mom agreed, smiling, "and you can help me. God can still work a miracle in his life." *HMT*

HOW ABOUT YOU?

What things are seeping into you? Is God's goodness replacing your old self? Become like a strong fossil by being buried in the right "minerals" as you read your Bible, pray, enjoy Christian fellowship, and obey and serve God.

Let God Fill Your Life

MEMORIZE:
"Our spirits are being renewed every day." 2 Corinthians 4:16

Every Step Counts

Read Psalm 51:1-4, 10

"Dad!" called Nora as she hurried into the house. "David's brother is in jail!"

Dad sighed. Jon, the older brother of one of Nora's friends, had been in trouble before. "What did Jon do?" Dad asked.

"David said Jon and another kid broke into a house and stole some money," replied Nora.

Dad shook his head. "His parents must be very disappointed," he said.

"While I was there, David's mom was talking to Jon on the phone," said Nora. "She was crying. After she hung up, she told us that Jon said he was sorry, and he promised to go for counseling."

"We need to pray for them," Dad said. He stood up. "I was about to go running. Want to come along?"

"Sure!" agreed Nora, and soon they were running along the roadside.

When they came to the place where Dad usually turned to go back, Nora looked at him. "Let's go a little farther this time," suggested Nora.

"Farther?" asked Dad. "You sure?"

"Why not? Can't you hack it, Dad?" Nora teased him.

Dad grinned. "I've been training for weeks," he said. "Keep going. We'll see who can't hack it!"

As they went on, Nora's legs grew heavier. She soon felt as though her lungs would explode. Finally, Dad stopped. "Okay, that's enough," Dad said. "Let's head back."

"Yeah. This is . . . far enough," agreed Nora, panting heavily. "It'll take forever . . . to get back . . . from here."

"Well, that's the thing. For every step you go out, you have to take another one to go back," Dad said.

Nora was exhausted. "Let's just walk back. Why did I ever want to go so far?" she moaned.

"Jon's gone too far, too, hasn't he?" Dad asked as they started back. "It will take a lot of time and effort for him to make everything right again—with the law, with God, and with his folks. Always remember that for every step you go wrong, you have to take another one to go back. Every step in life has a consequence." *MKN*

HOW ABOUT YOU?

Have you done something that you wish you hadn't done? Remember that the more wrong steps you take, the more difficult it may be to make things right. Start back right now. Ask God to forgive you and to help you. Always remember that all actions have consequences.

MEMORIZE:

"Wash me clean from my guilt. Purify me from my sin." Psalm 51:2

All Actions Have Consequences

The Happy Home

Read Matthew 5:13-16

It seems like Mom is always mad at me, thought Sadie. *I'm always too early or too late, too busy or not busy enough, too noisy or too quiet.* She sighed. *After Bible club tomorrow, I'm going to ask Mrs. Davis about it. She always seems happy.* Mrs. Davis, who lived next door to Sadie and her mom, held a regular after-school Bible club in her home. Only a few weeks before, Sadie had talked with her about becoming a Christian, and she had asked Jesus to come into her life.

After the club meeting the next day, Sadie waited to speak with Mrs. Davis. "How can I have a happy home like yours?" she asked her hesitantly. "My mom . . . well, she seems unhappy most of the time."

"Oh, I'm sorry," said Mrs. Davis. "Well . . . a few weeks ago, you asked Jesus to come into your life and change you, right?" Sadie nodded. "Now that you're a Christian, you can pray for your mom," Mrs. Davis continued. "I'll pray, too, and ask God for an opportunity to talk with her. I think if your mom knew Jesus, it would make a real difference in her life." Mrs. Davis gave Sadie a hug. "Be sure to try hard to obey your mom. Do all the nice things you can for her, and whenever you get a chance, tell her about Jesus."

Sadie nodded. "I'll try," she said. And she did try. She was careful to listen to her mom, and she offered to help around the house.

"What's come over you, Sadie?" Mom asked one day. "You're so different lately." She looked thoughtful. "Did you say something about having let Jesus come into your heart?"

"Yes," answered Sadie. "And that's what makes me different."

"Quite a while ago, Mrs. Davis told me about Jesus," Mom said after a moment. "Do you suppose she would come and talk with me again?"

"Oh, I know she will, Mom," Sadie answered eagerly. "She wants to. She'll tell you how to be saved and how we can have a happy home in heaven—and down here, too." *AGL*

HOW ABOUT YOU?

Does Jesus make a difference in your life? When you do tasks willingly and cheerfully—even without being told—your attitude and actions are a witness to your family, and they help to make your home a happy place.

MEMORIZE:
"Those who become Christians become new persons. They are not the same anymore, for the old life is gone. A new life has begun!"
2 Corinthians 5:17

Witness at Home

The Lost Notebook

Read Matthew 5:43-48

"Randy—one of the kids at my school—is always picking on me," Blaire complained to her dad one night. "He always calls me 'midget' just because I'm the shortest one in our class." Blaire scowled. "I'm tired of being picked on," she added. "I . . . I hate Randy!"

"Whoa!" Dad said. "Remember those verses you learned for Bible club last week? Didn't they say Christians should do good even to those who don't treat them well?"

"You mean be nice to Randy, even after he has been so mean to me?" Blaire asked.

Dad nodded. "That's what Jesus said we should do," he replied. Blaire frowned.

On the way to school the next day, Blaire found a notebook. *Wow!* She thought. *Somebody lost a bunch of homework!* She looked at the name. *Randy! This is Randy's.* Blaire smiled to herself. *What if I hide it or tear it up? That will get Randy into plenty of trouble! I knew I'd get a chance to get even with him someday.* But when Blaire got to school and shoved the notebook under some papers in her desk, she remembered the talk with her dad about what Jesus had said she should do. It kept bothering her as she went back outside to play. When the bell rang, Blaire went in, took out the notebook, and gave it to Randy.

At recess, Randy found Blaire. "Thought you were real cool to turn my notebook in, huh? Now I'm supposed to thank you and be your pal, right?" he asked sarcastically.

"Not if you don't want to," said Blaire. "I was only doing what I thought I should do."

"Well, I don't want to be your pal," growled Randy.

"Don't be then," replied Blaire, "but I don't see what you're so mad about. All I did was help you. That might not make me your friend, but I just wanted to do what was right."

Randy was surprised! "You must be crazy," he said. He started walking away, then turned back. "Well . . . maybe you aren't so bad after all," he blurted. "You did keep me out of trouble. Thanks!" *JLH*

HOW ABOUT YOU?

Can you think of someone who has been mean to you? Will you do something nice for that person today? It's hard to do, but Jesus wants you to repay unkindness with kindness, and obeying Jesus always pays.

MEMORIZE:

"If your enemies are hungry, feed them. If they are thirsty, give them something to drink, and they will be ashamed of what they have done to you." Romans 12:20

Be Nice to Your Enemies

Up the Down Escalator

Read Titus 3:3-7

While Mom shopped on the first floor of a department store, Carmen and her sister, Ramona, rode the escalator up to the top floor and down again. Mom had said they could do it one time—as long as they didn't push, or run up and down, or bother other shoppers.

"That was okay, but you know what would be more fun?" Carmen said when they got back to the first floor.

"What's that?" Ramona wanted to know.

"Let's go up the 'down' escalator," Carmen challenged.

Ramona didn't think Mom would approve of that, but Carmen was determined to try it. Soon she was headed up the "down" escalator. She was really working hard. Her face got all red. The people riding down the escalator had red faces, too. They were annoyed with Carmen! But Carmen kept right on trying—until she bumped into the store manager.

With a few angry words, the manager took Carmen's arm and accompanied her back down.

Carmen knew she was in real trouble when she spotted Mom waiting at the foot of the escalator. She was right. Mom reprimanded her severely, and she had to apologize to the store manager.

That evening, Ramona made sure that Dad heard the whole story. "I told her not to do it," she said.

"You know, Carmen," Mom said, "you worked very hard to go up the 'down' escalator, but soon you were right back where you started. All you got for your efforts was punishment."

Dad nodded. "That's like people who think they can ride to heaven on their own good works," he said. "They try so hard to be good and work their way to heaven, but before they know it, they're right back where they started! And all they need to do to get to heaven is ask Jesus to be their Savior. That's what the Bible says." He paused, then added, "With enough effort, Carmen might have made it to the top, but no amount of effort will ever gain heaven for anybody. You'll get there only by trusting Jesus. You can never make it on your own." *CVM*

HOW ABOUT YOU?

Have you been trying to earn God's favor and get to heaven by doing good works? Good works are fine, but they will never get you to heaven. God wants you to trust his Son, the Lord Jesus Christ, as your Savior! Jesus is the only way to heaven.

MEMORIZE:
"He saved us, not because of the good things we did, but because of his mercy." Titus 3:5

Stop Trying; Trust Christ

Bonnie the Bookworm

Read 2 Peter 1:5-9

"Bonnie! Bonnie!" Trish called for the third time.

Bonnie wandered into the kitchen with a book in her hand. "Did you call me, Trish?" she asked.

Trish sighed; she had her hands full baby-sitting Bonnie and her brother every day after school. "Yes, I did. But you had your nose in that book and didn't hear me. Watch Joey for me while I go next door to Mrs. Murphy's. Make sure he doesn't try to climb the stairs."

"Oh, okay," Bonnie replied. After Trish left, Bonnie watched Joey stack his blocks for a while. Then she picked up the mystery novel she had been reading. *Maybe I can finish another chapter before Trish gets home,* she thought.

Bonnie was deep into her story when she heard a crash and a loud cry. Joey was lying at the bottom of the stairs! "Are you okay, Joey?" Bonnie cried as she cuddled her little brother, who seemed to be okay despite a few tears.

Just then Trish came back. "What happened?" she asked. "You didn't let Joey climb the stairs, did you?"

"I didn't mean to," Bonnie said. "I guess Joey climbed when I wasn't watching."

Trish noticed Bonnie's book lying at her side. "You were reading, weren't you?" she asked.

"I . . . I was only going to read for a minute," Bonnie stammered. "I didn't realize how much time went by."

Trish frowned. "Maybe we should call you 'Bonnie the Bookworm,' "she said. "A bookworm spends its whole life in libraries—it never knows what's going on in the world."

"But I like to read," Bonnie whined.

Trish shook her head. "I enjoy reading, too," she said. "But when reading takes the place of more important things, you have a problem. You need to keep a proper balance in your life."

Bonnie gave Joey another hug. "I'm really sorry about what happened, Trish," she said. "From now on, I'll try to control my reading habits."

Trish nodded. "All right," she said. "Right now you can run to the store and pick up this list of things your mom needs—I think you need the exercise!" *SLK*

HOW ABOUT YOU?

Do you like to read, work puzzles, or play games? These things can be good forms of entertainment, but don't let hobbies or pleasures control you. Don't let them keep you from doing a good job with your chores, reading and memorizing God's Word, or doing your homework. Live a balanced life for the glory of God.

MEMORIZE:

"Knowing God leads to self-control. Self-control leads to patient endurance, and patient endurance leads to godliness." 2 Peter 1:6

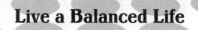

Live a Balanced Life

Bringing Firstfruits

Read Proverbs 3:9-10; Malachi 3:10

Ashley was earning money by selling stationery, and she had a goal—she wanted to make enough money to buy the bicycle on sale in the department store. She was excited when her neighbor Mrs. Grimaldi purchased three boxes of cards. As Ashley accepted the money, Mrs. Grimaldi began to reminisce. "I'll never forget the first money I earned," she said. "It was a thrill to bring my tithe to Sunday school for the offering. And the Lord blessed me just like he promised. I think a tenth is the least the Lord expects of us, don't you?" Ashley mumbled a reply and hurried away.

At last Ashley had enough money to buy the bike she wanted. Mom agreed to walk with her to the store to buy it. On the way, they passed Mrs. Grimaldi's house, and it made Ashley think about tithing. She told her mother what Mrs. Grimaldi had said. Mom nodded.

"We've talked about that before, haven't we?" Mom reminded her.

"But if I give a tenth of my money to God, I can't buy the bike," Ashley protested.

"Not right now anyway," Mom said.

"So what shall I do?" Ashley asked.

"I'll leave it up to you," Mom told her. "This is your money; you'll have to decide what to do with it."

When they arrived at the store, a struggle took place in Ashley's heart as she stared at the bike. Finally, she turned away. "I'll just wait for the bike a while longer—until I've sold more cards," she decided. She sighed as she trudged steadily toward home.

On the way home, Ashley and her mother noticed a "Garage Sale" sign, and they stopped to look around. As Ashley entered the garage, she saw a beautiful, bright blue, ten-speed bicycle! "Mom! Look!" she gasped. The bike was for sale—and even after giving her tithe, she'd have more than enough money left for it. With Mom's approval, she promptly bought it.

Mrs. Grimaldi is right, Ashley thought as she rode her new bike home. *When we obey God, he does bless us, just like he promised. REP*

HOW ABOUT YOU?

When you earn your own money, do you give some to the Lord? He wants you to give to him before doing anything else with the money. He promises blessings to those who are willing to do this. Sometimes he may provide even more money; sometimes he may cause your supplies to last longer; sometimes he may give a special peace and joy and an ability to get along with less. But he will always bless when you give to him first.

MEMORIZE:
"Honor the Lord with your wealth and with the best part of everything your land produces." Proverbs 3:9

Give to God First

Why? (Part 1)

Read Psalm 37:1-9

"Why, Mom? Why?" Tammy asked.

Mom sighed. She had heard that question often, for Tammy could never understand why unhappy things had to happen. Tammy was upset when a cat killed some baby birds, when a small boy was beaten up by a bigger boy, or when a little girl cried after being teased. Now she had come home from school rather late, almost in tears.

"The worst thing happened!" Tammy explained. "Roger got into the school-room early and wrote all kinds of bad words on the board. I came in just as he finished, but I walked back out before he saw me. Then he left, too. When Miss Harper came in, Sally was the only one in the room. Miss Harper accused her of writing those words. Sally said she didn't, but Miss Harper wouldn't believe her. When I said that I saw Roger writing them, he said he didn't and that I was just taking sides with my friend. So Sally and I were both kept after school!" Tammy paused, out of breath.

"Oh, that is too bad, Tammy," Mom sympathized. "I'm glad you stood up for Sally. I know it hurts now, but the truth will come out in time. If you want me to, I'll be happy to talk to Miss Harper. But first I want you to try handling this on your own."

"Thanks, Mom. I do want to handle it myself first. But, Mom, it just isn't fair!" Tammy cried. She stamped her foot. "Why does a bad kid like Roger get away with doing something bad while a good kid like Sally gets punished? It isn't fair! Why does God allow it?"

"It won't always be that way," Mom comforted. "It does sometimes look as though evil is winning, but remember that God is watching. In his own time, he will make everything right. God is just and fair. Trust him to take care of things. Try explaining things once more to Miss Harper tomorrow. Don't worry, honey. Your first job is to be an honest person. That will please God, and he knows the truth." *AGL*

HOW ABOUT YOU?

Is "That's not fair" a familiar cry to you? Do you trust God to work things out? He has a reason for all that he allows to happen, and he has lessons to teach through it. It may seem unfair to you, because you see only what is happening now. But God sees the future. He is just and will set everything right.

MEMORIZE:

"He is a faithful God who does no wrong; how just and upright he is!"
Deuteronomy 32:4

God Is Fair

Why? (Part 2)

Read Isaiah 61:1-3

For Tammy, who found it so difficult to accept things, the biggest blow was yet to come. Her grandfather was in a car accident, and he died a few days later. Her parents missed him greatly, but they accepted what happened as God's will. Tammy's own dad knew that his father was happy with Jesus. But Tammy seemed unable to get over it. "Does God know how bad we feel," she cried, "or how much we miss Grandpa?"

"Oh, yes, honey," Dad assured her. "He knew we would cry, but he promised to bring joy and comfort, too."

"But why did God take Grandpa away?" Tammy sobbed. "Why?"

"Why?" Dad repeated. "Well, that's one question I can't answer right now . . . and maybe I'll never be able to answer it. But even though we may not understand why God took your grandpa now, we know God's way is always best. Remember, too, that God doesn't ask us to suffer anything he, himself, has not suffered." This was a new thought to Tammy. She flicked away a tear as Dad continued, "You know, Tammy, God sent his only Son, Jesus, to earth. Even though Jesus loved the people, many of them hated him. They threw stones at him, spit on him, beat him, and crucified him. God allowed it to happen even though it hurt him very much."

"But *why* did God let them do that?" Tammy asked.

"He could have stopped them," Dad answered, "but he had a purpose in allowing it. He knew we needed a Savior, and Jesus was taking the punishment for our sins. God let it happen so that we could go to heaven."

Tammy sighed and nodded. "If he loved us that much, he wouldn't do anything to hurt us now, would he?" she asked slowly. "I'll try to remember that he does understand, and he does care."

"Absolutely," Dad replied. "And if you let him, he will help your heart heal from this hurt." *AGL*

HOW ABOUT YOU?

Are you hurting over something that has happened? God knows all about it, and he even understands how you feel. He cares. Let him comfort you. Leave the "why" to him, and trust him to use what has happened for his glory.

God Understands and Cares

MEMORIZE:
"He heals the brokenhearted, binding up their wounds." Psalm 147:3

Remember Me

Read Mark 14:3-9

The essay contest on great Americans was over. The winner had been chosen, and some of the kids were discussing it with their teacher, Mr. Nelson. "Boy, to think that Hank wrote the best essay." Sonja whistled. "Who else would think of an author as a great American?"

Mr. Nelson smiled. "You must admit that when Harriet Beecher Stowe wrote *Uncle Tom's Cabin,* her pen was a very effective weapon against slavery."

"Yeah," Tatiana agreed. "She helped people see we're all created equal. I wrote about George Washington Carver."

"You would think of him," Todd teased, "considering how much you like peanut butter. Imagine making three hundred products from peanuts! But who was really the greatest American, Mr. Nelson?"

Mr. Nelson smiled. "The person who is truly greatest might be someone we've never heard of. It could be a doctor, a missionary, a scientist, or even one of our neighbors." The kids appeared to consider this new idea silently for a few minutes.

Finally, Sonja got up and stretched. "Well, I gotta go home and mow the lawn and hit the books," she said with a grin. "Tell you what—I'll work hard, and a hundred years from now, your great-grandkids can write a 'Great American' essay about me."

The others laughed. "Do you think any of us will ever make the history books?" Tatiana wondered aloud.

"It's possible," Mr. Nelson said, "but whether you make history or not, remember that everybody is remembered by someone for something. It's up to you what it will be. Some people aren't known for good things. What do you want to be remembered for?" *AGL*

HOW ABOUT YOU?

How will you be remembered? Will people say you were a kind person? An honest one? A hard worker? A Christian? Or will they have to say the opposite? Being remembered as a true Christian who has done her best is more important than any other fame you might achieve. Live so today's verse may apply to you.

MEMORIZE:
"She has done what she could."
Mark 14:8

Do Your Best

Wishing, Praying, Working

Read James 5:16-18

"Oh, I wish I had a hundred dollars to put in the missionary offering tomorrow," Molly exclaimed. "The Durands are so eager to leave for the mission field."

"If you'll clean the basement for me this afternoon, I'll pay you—not a hundred dollars, but a little," Mom said. "Have you prayed about the money you'd like to give?"

"Prayed for a hundred dollars?" Molly asked. "No."

Mom smiled. "You should," she said. "God is able."

Molly was cleaning the basement when her friend Whitney came over. "I can play as soon as I finish cleaning this old cupboard," Molly told Whitney. "I wish it was done."

"Well, I'll help you," Whitney offered. "That'll do more good than wishing."

"Thanks," Molly replied. "I'm always wishing for things. Mom always tells me that wishing doesn't help; praying and working does. So guess what I'm praying for now? A hundred dollars for the missionary offering!" She got down on her hands and knees to pull out something that was stuck in a corner. "Look," she said, holding up an old penny. "This must be the start of the answer to my prayers." The girls laughed together.

The next morning, the only offering Molly had was her penny and the few dollars her mom had paid her. "Well, you're giving all you've got," Mom told her. "The Lord doesn't expect more."

That afternoon Whitney came over. She was all excited. "My dad helped count the offering this morning," she told them, "and he noticed an old penny. He says it's valuable, and he thinks the person who gave it should be told. I knew it was you, and he says you can have it back if you want." She stopped to catch her breath. "It might be worth a hundred dollars! Dad said so!"

Molly stared at her. "A hundred dollars! Mom!" she called. "I'm giving a hundred dollars to the missionary offering! Of course I don't want it back. I prayed for money to give, not to keep. I'm so glad!" *AGL*

HOW ABOUT YOU?

Are there things that you wish were different? Have you done what you can to accomplish your goals? Have you prayed about them? Prayer is so important. When you stop merely wishing and start praying and working, things happen. God works wonders when his people pray and work.

Don't Just Wish—Pray and Work

MEMORIZE:
"The earnest prayer of a righteous person has great power and wonderful results." James 5:16

May

28

Whose Rules?

Read Romans 14:13-18

"Chelsea!" called Mom. "Please turn off the television. Abby will be here any minute."

Chelsea did as she was told and went to the den, where her mother was working. "Can Abby and I watch that movie I was telling you about?" she asked. "It's on tonight."

"Didn't you say that Abby isn't allowed to watch TV?" Mom asked.

"Well, yes," admitted Chelsea, "but it's a really good kids' movie—no violence or swearing or anything."

"But that isn't the point," Mom said.

"What is the point?" asked Chelsea.

Mom thought for a moment. "I think I can explain it with the help of one of Britta's books. Do you want to get it from her room?"

Chelsea paused. "I don't think Britta would like it," she said. "At breakfast this morning, I promised her that I wouldn't take anything from her room without asking first. She'll be really mad if I do."

"Even if I say it's okay?" Mom asked. "You won't be going through her stuff; you'll just get that book."

Still Chelsea hesitated. "I think Britta might get really angry and never trust me again," she said.

"So you don't feel comfortable doing it, right?" Mom asked, and Chelsea nodded. Mom smiled and said, "I think you made the right choice."

"You do?" asked Chelsea. "Don't you want the book?"

"No," Mom said, "and I'd have stopped you if you had gone to get it. It was unfair to ask you to go against Britta's request and risk losing her trust. So do you think it would be fair to ask Abby to go against her parents' rules?"

"I guess not," admitted Chelsea. "It might make her uncomfortable, too."

"Not only that," Mom said, "but Abby could get into trouble and lose the trust of her parents. She has a responsibility to obey their rules, and we have a responsibility to help her do that." *HMT*

HOW ABOUT YOU?

Do your friends have rules that are different from yours? Christians don't always agree about everything, so be sure always to respect the rules and feelings of your parents and other people.

MEMORIZE:

"Live in such a way that you will not put an obstacle in another Christian's path." Romans 14:13

Help Others Do What Is Right

Mandy's Future

Read Romans 10:9-13

As Mandy entered the garage, her father looked up and smiled. "What are you doing, Dad?" she asked.

"I'm changing the oil in the car," Dad replied.

Mandy leaned against the car as she watched her father. "Why do you do that?"

"It keeps the engine running smoothly," Dad explained. "I'm getting the car ready for our camping trip this weekend."

There was silence as Mandy's father finished working on his car. "You know," Dad said at last, "I'm preparing for our trip, and I've been thinking—there's something you should prepare for, too."

Mandy looked up at him, a question in her eyes. "Like what?" she wanted to know.

"Like the future—eternity," Dad answered gently. "Your mother and I have both given our hearts to Jesus Christ and asked him to be our Savior, so we're prepared to spend eternity in heaven with him. But what about you, honey?"

Mandy was quiet. She had heard about heaven and eternity almost as long as she could remember. Her parents had talked about it, and so had her pastor and Sunday school teachers. But she had never done anything about it for herself. If she should die, would she go to heaven? Deep in her heart, she wasn't at all sure about that.

"Honey," Dad was saying, "how about preparing for eternity right now?"

Mandy nodded her head. "Will you help me, Daddy?" she asked.

Mandy's father smiled. "You bet I will," he answered. "Nothing would make me happier than to help you prepare for eternity with the Lord." Mandy and her dad prayed—right there in the garage! *RIJ*

HOW ABOUT YOU?

Have you heard about "eternity" for a long, long time? Are you prepared for it? You prepare for a test; you prepare for school games; be sure to prepare for eternity, too. God says you are a sinner (Romans 3:23). The penalty for sin is eternal death (Romans 6:23). But Jesus took the penalty upon himself when he died on the cross (1 Peter 2:24), and he offers the free gift of salvation (Romans 6:23). Accept that gift today. Ask Jesus to be your Savior.

MEMORIZE:
"Prepare to meet your God."
Amos 4:12

Prepare for Eternity

The Replacement

Read Joshua 1:5-9

The missionary speaker at Alyssa's church was very enthusiastic as she showed pictures and told about her work with children in Alaska. But as she finished her talk, there was a sad note in her voice. "I won't be going back to my mission work," she said. "I have an illness that will force me to stay in a warmer climate." Her voice broke, but she gave the audience a tearful smile. "I hope to get young people interested in our mission," she added. "Perhaps someone here will some-day go to Alaska—to help in the work that I won't be able to complete."

There was a hush over the audience. In the silence, Alyssa found herself wishing she could go. Just then a young lady stood to her feet. "I'll go," she said, her voice wavering. "Ever since I graduated from college last month, I've been asking God to show me his will. I believe this is what he wants me to do."

Both the audience and the missionary were deeply touched by this unexpected response.

When the pastor closed the meeting, he said, "Perhaps there is someone else who will stand to indicate a willingness to prepare for God's work—someone who wants to be ready to replace other missionaries in future years. Is there anyone who will accept this challenge?"

Alyssa had thought she might someday be a missionary, but she had not told anyone.

Suddenly she stood. *I'm willing,* her heart responded. She was glad to see that two of her friends were also standing.

As the service ended, the pastor asked those who stood to meet him at the front of the church. There was the missionary who could not return to her field. There was the college graduate who wanted to be her replacement. And there were Alyssa and the others who still had years of preparation ahead, but who were willing to serve God wherever he would lead them. *RIJ*

HOW ABOUT YOU?

Are you willing to serve God anywhere? He may want you here at home. Are you willing to stay? He may want you on the mission field. Are you willing to go? Say yes to whatever God asks of you.

MEMORIZE:

"I heard the Lord asking, 'Whom should I send as a messenger to my people? Who will go for us?' And I said, 'Lord, I'll go! Send me.' " Isaiah 6:8

Answer God's Call

A Special Memorial Day

Read Romans 5:1-5

Graciela ran out to the porch when she saw her uncle's car turn into the drive-way. "Hi!" she called. "Are you coming to the parade with us?"

"Parade? What parade?" Uncle Juan asked.

"The big Memorial Day parade," replied Graciela. "Dad's going to be driving the mayor's car, and Carlos is in the high school band."

"Uncle Juan is teasing you, Graciela." Aunt Ruth gave her a hug. "He knows all about the parade."

Half an hour later, the family stood together on the corner, watching the floats, the marching bands, and the mayor's car go by. When the parade was over, they walked to the cemetery for a special Memorial Day program.

"That speaker talked about how happy he was the day he knew the war was over," said Graciela when they were on their way home. "I guess everybody was happy about that."

Aunt Ruth nodded. "My parents sure were!" she said. "When I was born a few days later, they named me Ruth Victoria. Ruth means 'peace' and the Victoria part comes from 'victory.' "

"Really?" Graciela was impressed. Then she frowned. "But there have been a lot of wars since then," she said.

"That's true, Graciela," agreed Aunt Ruth, "but you know what? My name reminds me of something more than victory in that particular war. It also reminds me of my relationship with Jesus Christ."

"It does?" asked Graciela. "Why?"

"Even though the world doesn't have true peace or victory, I do!" explained Aunt Ruth. "Because Jesus took the punishment for my sins on the cross, I have peace with God, and I can have victory over the power of sin in my life. Through Christ we can have peace within, no matter what's going on in the world." *LMW*

HOW ABOUT YOU?

Do you wonder why there are so many wars? A country may fight to gain freedom because they want to control more land or to rebel against a bad ruler. In spite of all the unrest in the world, it's good to know that real peace and victory can be yours if you know Jesus.

True Peace Comes from God

MEMORIZE:
"We have peace with God because of what Jesus Christ our Lord has done for us." Romans 5:1

Heaven

Read 1 Corinthians 15:35-44

"Mom, I wish I could explain to Lindy about colors," Daisy said with a sigh. "This afternoon I mentioned that the sky was so blue, and she said she wished she could understand what that meant." Daisy sighed again. "I've tried and tried to explain it to her, but she just doesn't understand what I'm talking about."

"I know. Lindy misses a lot because she's blind," Mom said. "But have you noticed how her other senses seem to work better than ours? For one thing, she recognizes people by their footsteps or voice. We couldn't do that with very many people! Sometimes the best surprises are ones we can't see or even understand— like heaven, for instance. Daisy," Mom continued slowly, "remember how diffi- cult—even impossible—it is for Lindy to understand what colors are? In the same way, it's hard . . . and yes, impossible . . . for us to understand exactly what heaven is like. It's a completely different world, and we just can't totally know what it will be like."

"What if we don't like it?" Daisy asked, half jokingly but with a note of concern in her voice.

Mom smiled. "Do you think Lindy would like to be able to see?" she asked. "Do you think she'd hesitate if she had the chance to see?"

"Of course she wants to see," Daisy replied with a smile.

"But she doesn't understand what it's like to be able to see," Mom told her.

"No, but she knows that sight is something wonderful," Daisy argued, "even though she doesn't quite understand it. She can tell that from what we tell her about it."

"And we know that heaven is going to be wonderful because of the things *God* tells us about it," Mom replied. "All our descriptions and imaginings don't even come close to the glorious reality of heaven." *MTF*

HOW ABOUT YOU?

Do you ever wonder and question and argue—and even worry—about heaven and how life there will be different from your life here on earth? Although heaven will certainly be different, be assured that it will be wonderful and far better than life on earth.

Heaven Will Be Wonderful

MEMORIZE:
"Now we see things imperfectly as in a poor mirror, but then we will see everything with perfect clarity. All that I know now is partial and incomplete, but then I will know everything completely, just as God knows me now." 1 Corinthians 13:12

2

Julie's Light

Read Isaiah 60:1, 3; Ephesians 5:8-9

"Here's Mom now," Julie told her little brother as the blue van pulled up in front of the church. Julie opened the door, and she and Ben got in and fastened their seat belts.

"How was your first day at Bible school?" Mom asked.

"Great," Julie answered, "except that Mrs. Wilson asked me to play the piano for the Primary Department's song time the rest of the week."

Mom frowned. "You think that's bad?"

Julie nodded. "I'm not going to do it," she said. "I just can't. With all those little kids looking at me, I'd be so nervous that I'd mess up for sure." Just the thought of it made Julie's stomach feel funny.

Mom sighed. "I wish you'd try it," she said quietly.

Four-year-old Ben tugged at Julie's sleeve. "Listen to my song!" he said. Holding one chubby finger straight up before him he began to sing. "This little light of mine—I'm gonna let it shine. . . ."

When he had finished, Julie gave him a big hug. "Good job," she said. "When I was little like you, that was one of my favorite songs. Let's sing the 'hide it under a bushel' verse together, okay?"

"Maybe you shouldn't sing it if you don't mean it anymore," Mom suggested.

"Wha-a-t?" Julie turned toward her mother with a puzzled frown.

"Aren't you 'hiding your light under a bushel,' dear?" Mom asked. "I'm thinking of your refusal to play the piano."

"Oh, Mom," Julie grumbled as Ben began to sing again. But she didn't join him—not until the very last line, that is. When the song ended, she grinned at her mother. "Okay," she said. "I guess if God gave me the talent to play, he can give me the courage to do it in front of those kids. I'll try it." She turned to her brother. "My turn to sing a verse, Ben."

Julie smiled as she sang a new verse to the old familiar tune. "I'm gonna play for Jesus—let my light shine now!" *PAM*

HOW ABOUT YOU?

Are you ever afraid to use the talents God gave you? Do your knees shake, and does your throat get dry when you get up in front of others? Are you afraid you'll mess up? God gave you certain talents. Ask him for the courage to use them to help other people.

MEMORIZE:

"Let your light shine before men, that they may see your good deeds and praise your Father in heaven."
Matthew 5:16, NIV

Use Your Talents for God

Priority Baggage

Read Luke 10:38-42

Lena sighed as she dropped beach toys, snack food, games, and books into the car trunk.

"You don't seem very excited about going to Family Bible Camp this year," Dad said. "I thought you liked going there."

"I do, but I have to do so many things this summer," Lena said. "I have to help paint the new clubhouse and practice diving, and there are going to be sleepovers and . . ." Lena hesitated while she tried to cram the suitcases on top of all the other things. She finally set them on the ground. "I can't fit it all in," she complained.

"The luggage or your activities?" Dad asked.

"Both," Lena replied. "My summer's too full, and these suitcases are too big."

"Well, then let's make some choices," Dad suggested as he walked to the back of the car. "What's most important of all these items in here?"

Lena looked at the things in the trunk. "Our clothes," she decided. "We could leave the beach toys behind. The camp has lots of them—and lots of life jackets, too."

"Okay," Dad said. "Let's start over." So they emptied the trunk and then began refilling it—this time putting the luggage containing their clothes in first. Then Lena helped Dad fit the smaller things into the spaces around the suitcases. Soon everything was in, except the few items they felt they could do without.

"After we took care of the really important things, most of the little things fit into the empty spaces," Dad explained. "That principle will work for your summer schedule, too. What's your first priority in life this summer?"

Lena shrugged. "I don't know."

"Well," Dad continued, "since God created us to spend time with him, that should be our first priority. That's one reason we all go to camp for a week. If you fit in Bible camp first, you'll find that there will still be lots of empty spots left for other activities this summer. Sound good?"

Lena smiled and nodded. "Sounds like it might work!" *HMT*

HOW ABOUT YOU?

What is your first priority in life? Does God come before everything else? He never demands your time, but he longs for it, and he blesses you in many ways when you put him first.

MEMORIZE:

"He will give you all you need from day to day if you live for him and make the Kingdom of God your primary concern." Matthew 6:33

Put God First

4

Never Too Young

Read 1 Samuel 17:20-24, 41-50

As the Benson family enjoyed their supper, Mom and Dad told Payton and Lourdes about their new neighbors. "We helped them move in, and it was hard work," Dad said. "I sure am tired tonight. Your mom is, too." But the work was not yet done. Mom pushed back her chair and began to wash the dishes while Payton helped by wiping them. Then Payton went out to help Dad wash the car—even washing the windows!

When the work was finally finished, Dad read the paper and Mom relaxed in her favorite chair, reading a book. Payton was sitting at the table drawing a castle when Lourdes came in, needing her shoe tied. Quickly Payton jumped up to tie it for her. A little later, Lourdes wanted someone to read her favorite story to her. Noticing how tired Mom looked, Payton volunteered.

Shortly before going to bed, Lourdes wanted someone to play dolls. "Oh, no!" Payton groaned. "Not dolls!" But she went with Lourdes so that Mom could rest after the long, hard day.

After Lourdes was in bed, Payton got back to her drawing. She noticed Dad yawning. "It sure was nice of you two to help the neighbors move in," Payton told her parents. "When I grow up, I want to be helpful—just like you."

Dad smiled as he answered, "You don't have to wait until you're older. You've accepted Jesus as Savior, and he expects you to begin serving him right away. You already serve him by serving others."

"I do?" Payton asked.

"Sure," Mom said. "Tonight you helped me with the dishes."

"And you helped me wash the car," Dad chimed in. "I noticed you did an extra good job on the windows, too."

"You took care of Lourdes," Mom added. "You are very helpful, and Dad and I are pleased. I know the Lord is, too." *MMB*

HOW ABOUT YOU?

Do you think you're too young to help? You're not. God uses children as well as adults. Ask him to use you this year. Start serving him by serving at home—keeping your room clean, helping with the dishes, running errands, or watching your younger brother or sister. You're never too young to help!

MEMORIZE:

"Don't let anyone think less of you because you are young. Be an example to all believers." 1 Timothy 4:12

Be a Helper Now

Family Day

Read 1 Thessalonians 4:13-18

"I don't like camp! Don't go! Stay with me!" Four-year-old Joy sobbed, as she clung to her big sister.

"I'm not going to be gone forever," Gabrielle told her. "I'm just going for a couple of weeks."

"No! Stay and play with me," the little girl insisted. Gently, Mom pried Joy's hands loose from Gabrielle's leg and picked her up. "Next Saturday we're going to camp for Family Day. Gabrielle will do fun things with you there, and we'll have a picnic," she promised.

"Can we have marshmallows?" Joy asked.

Dad laughed. "Yes, we can have marshmallows," he said. "Get your tote bag, Gabrielle. It's time to go."

As the door closed behind them, Dad and Gabrielle heard Joy's voice: "How long is it till Family Day?"

On Saturday, Joy had a wonderful time at camp. "I like camp after all," she decided.

A couple of weeks after camp, Gabrielle's parents got the call they had been dreading. As Mom hung up, her eyes were wet with tears. "Poppy is gone," she said.

"Gone?" Gabrielle repeated. "Gone where?"

"Gone home to be with Jesus," Mom answered.

It took a minute for Gabrielle to grasp the fact that her grandfather had died. "But I asked Jesus to heal him," Gabrielle wailed. "I didn't want him to leave us."

Dad put his arms around Gabrielle and Mom. "We are never ready to give up our loved ones," said Dad, "but we know it's not forever."

"Not forever?" Gabrielle sobbed. "Death is forever."

"Oh, no!" Dad said. "Death is just a door leading into heaven. Someday we're going where Poppy is."

Joy tugged at her father's arm, wanting him to pick her up. "Don't worry, Gabby," she said. "We'll see Poppy when we go to Family Day in heaven. He can show you all the fun things, like you showed me at camp. We can have a picnic, too."

As she snuggled in her father's arms, she asked, "Do they have marshmallows in heaven?"

Through their tears, the family smiled together as they talked about memories of Poppy. *BJW*

HOW ABOUT YOU?
Has someone that you love gone to heaven? When you feel sad and lonely, remember that the separation is not forever. You can see your loved one again. What a wonderful Family Day that will be!

For the Christian, Death Is Not Forever

MEMORIZE:
"Do not . . . grieve like the rest of men, who have no hope."
1 Thessalonians 4:13, NIV

June

6

Wake Up

Read Matthew 25:1-13

It was three o'clock in the morning, and most of the campers were finally asleep. "Molly, what are you doing?" one of the girls murmured groggily when Molly woke her by sitting on her bunk.

Molly got up, turned, and walked toward another girl's bed. "Aaaah!" The girl screamed and jumped up when Molly sat down on her arm.

"What's all the noise?" Miss Ellen, their counselor, asked as she rubbed her eyes. Seeing Molly curled up on the other girl's bed, Miss Ellen got up to investigate. "Molly's walking in her sleep," she whispered, and soon she had Molly back in her own bed. The next morning, Molly didn't remember anything about her excursion.

During cabin devotions, Miss Ellen asked the girls to share some of the problems they faced as Christian kids in their schools. "We have to learn about mythology and Greek gods," one girl offered, "but we aren't allowed to talk about our God."

"In science class, my teacher talks about evolution," another girl said, "but she doesn't want to hear about God creating the world."

"Sometimes kids use God's name like a swear word," Molly added, "and if you say anything about it, they tell you to wake up and join the real world."

Miss Ellen nodded. "That makes me think of something," she said. "Remember how Molly walked in her sleep last night?" She paused as Molly and the girls laughed and nodded. "Molly's body was awake and walking around, but her mind—her consciousness—was asleep. She didn't know she was walking, and even now she doesn't remember anything about it. Well, in a way, your friends and teachers who don't know Jesus are walking in their sleep, too. Their hearts and souls are still sleeping. The sad thing is that they don't even know it. Ask God to help you show them that they're the ones who really need to wake up." *NEK*

HOW ABOUT YOU?

Is it hard to be patient and loving when classmates think your beliefs and ideas are odd or unreal? Realize that the devil is doing his best to keep their hearts asleep. Be willing for God to work through your example to awaken them.

MEMORIZE:

"So then, let us not be like others, who are asleep, but let us be alert and self-controlled." 1 Thessalonians 5:6, NIV

Help Those Who Are Spiritually Asleep

Sink or Swim

Read Romans 3:20-24, 28

Down under the water Roxy went! She came up sputtering. "What did I do wrong?" she asked Aunt Sue. She and her sister, Faith, were spending a week with their aunt at her lakeshore cottage, and Aunt Sue was teaching them to float. Roxy looked over at Faith. "She's just lying on the water!" Roxy exclaimed in surprise. "Why can't I do that?"

"You tried to help yourself float, so you sank," said Aunt Sue. "Try again— just relax and lie back on the water. Don't try to stay afloat." So Roxy took a deep breath and tried again, but once more . . . blub . . . gasp . . . she sank. "Relax," advised Aunt Sue.

After several tries, Roxy finally floated. "I'm not doing anything!" she exclaimed. "I'm just letting the water hold me up. This is great!"

That evening, Roxy was thoughtful. "Why so quiet, Roxy?" asked Aunt Sue.

"Well," said Roxy, "I was just thinking: As long as I tried to do something to make myself float, it didn't work. I had to quit trying to help myself."

"That's right," agreed Aunt Sue. "You had to simply trust the water to hold you up."

Roxy nodded. "It's kind of like what my teacher told us in Sunday school yesterday," she replied. "She said we can't do anything to help ourselves be saved— that we're saved by just trusting Jesus."

"That's what the Bible says, too," said Aunt Sue.

"I guess I always thought going to church and Sunday school helped—and obeying my parents and teachers. But that's not right, is it?" asked Roxy. "That doesn't help me be saved."

"No, it doesn't," said Aunt Sue. "You had to quit trying to float, and you have to quit trying to be saved by doing good things. You need to simply trust Jesus."

" 'Believe on the Lord Jesus Christ, and you will be saved,' " quoted Roxy. "That was my verse to learn." She smiled. "I do believe," she said. "I'll still go to church and obey Mom and Dad, but that won't save me. I'll just trust Jesus to save me!" *HCT*

HOW ABOUT YOU?
The only way to be saved is to trust Jesus to do it all. No amount of trying to save ourselves will work. Won't you trust Jesus today?

Trust Jesus to Save You from Sin

MEMORIZE:
"Believe on the Lord Jesus and you will be saved." Acts 16:31

June

8

The Gift

Read Mark 14:8-9; 1 Peter 4:10

"Mom, did you see the posters Jim drew for Vacation Bible School?" Gina asked as she helped her mother weed the flower beds. "They're really cool! And Tara's good at explaining things, so she's going to be a teacher's assistant in Aunt Renee's class. But me! I can't do anything except croak a bit for the song time and play dumb games with the kids."

"Singing and games are an important part of VBS," Mom said, "and you don't croak. You sing very well."

Gina sighed. "I bet God won't be impressed with what I have to offer," she said.

"Gina, that's just not true," Mom began. She was interrupted by a squeal from little Billy, who was hurrying across the lawn toward them.

"Me made present for Mommy!" Billy called. His soil-stained hands clutched a small pot half filled with sand. Billy had stuck a pink flower and a handful of leaves into the sand. Gina grinned.

Mom watched Billy run toward them with a huge smile on his face. She turned to Gina. "It's a stupid present, isn't it?" she asked solemnly. "That old pot he used is cracked and dirty. The flower is faded and those leaves are all withered. He should have brought me roses from the florist."

Gina looked horrified. "Mom!" she protested. "Where would he get them? He's only three, and he made that because he loves you so much!"

Mom smiled. "You're quite right," she agreed. "Actually, I love Billy's gift, even if it's not perfect. And honey, when we offer gifts to God with real love in our hearts, don't you think he accepts them in much the same way, even if they're not perfect?"

"You mean like my singing and playing with the kids?" Gina asked.

Mom nodded as she bent down and took the flower pot Billy offered. "Thank you, Billy Boy!" she cried. "I'll put this right in the middle of our dining room table!" She gave him a hug and then turned back to Gina. "I'm glad Billy did what he could. That's what God wants us to do, too." *MTF*

HOW ABOUT YOU?

Do you do what you can for God? Don't compare what you can do with what others do. Don't spend time wishing you had talents God gave to someone else. He wants you to serve him with the abilities he gave you. If your heart is filled with love for God and you're offering him your very best, he accepts your gifts with great joy.

MEMORIZE:

"God has given gifts to each of you from his great variety of spiritual gifts. Manage them well so that God's generosity can flow through you."
1 Peter 4:10

God Loves Your Gifts to Him

Part of the Family

Read Galatians 4:1-7

Brynn had always liked to hear how her parents fell in love with her when they first saw her at the adoption agency. But as she approached her twelfth birthday, the fact that she was adopted didn't seem so entertaining anymore. *I don't really belong to anybody,* she thought one day as she picked wild berries by herself. *Sure, my folks have taken care of me since I was six weeks old, but I'm not really part of their family.* She was feeling quite sorry for herself when a rather dirty, very skinny little dog timidly approached her. "Hi, little pup," Brynn said gently. "You look like you haven't had a bath or a meal for a long time. I'll bet someone dumped you along the road."

It didn't take much coaxing from Brynn to get the hungry puppy to follow her home. *I wonder if Mom will let me keep him,* she thought. *Nice word—* "mom." *Too bad it isn't true.*

When Brynn and the puppy reached home, Mom met them at the door. "Did you bring company for supper?" she asked, dropping to her knees and stroking the little puppy. "I wonder if he has a name. He doesn't look like he's got a home."

"Can I keep him?" Brynn asked eagerly. "I'll call him Sunshine."

It wasn't long before Brynn felt as though she'd had Sunshine all her life. "Well," Dad said one morning, "it looks as if your adopted dog is happy here with you, Brynn."

"Adopted!" Brynn exclaimed. "Dad, he's not adopted. He's my dog!"

"Of course he is," Dad replied. "He wasn't always your dog." A slow smile crossed Brynn's face as the truth sank in. *Hey!* she thought. *Sunshine and I really belong together, even if it wasn't always that way—and Mom and Dad and I belong together, too. Sunshine wouldn't want to be anyplace else in the world, and neither would I!*

"Being adopted isn't a bad thing, you know," Dad continued. "In fact, all of us who are Christians are adopted, too. We're adopted into God's family."

Brynn giggled and gave her dad a big hug. "We're one big happy family of 'adoptees'—even Sunshine," she said. *AU*

HOW ABOUT YOU?

Are you adopted? You are if you've been born again into God's family by accepting Jesus as Savior. If you haven't received him, do so today. God wants you to be a member of his family.

Christians Are Adopted into God's Family

MEMORIZE:

"God sent his Son . . . so that he could adopt us as his very own children." Galatians 4:4-5

June
10

A Little or a Lot

Read Luke 21:1-4

Trisha's Sunday school class was collecting money for a missionary in Africa, and the kids in her class had decided that all the money for the project had to be from their own allowances or money they had earned. "Next week will be the last opportunity to bring money for the special offering," the teacher reminded them one Sunday.

Trisha slid down in her seat. She didn't have one penny for the missionary offering. *What am I going to do?* she wondered. *I don't even get a regular allowance. And how can I earn money? I'm just a little kid.*

That evening Trisha told her parents about the missionary project and asked them if they had any jobs she could do to earn some money.

"You can help me weed the flower beds," Mom suggested. "I was going to hire one of the neighbor boys, but if you want the job, it's yours."

"And I was planning to run the car through the car wash tomorrow," Dad added. "If you'll wash it—and do a really good job—I'll pay you instead."

Besides the jobs her parents gave her to do, Trisha found another job—mowing a neighbor's lawn. Then she collected pop cans lying around at her neighborhood park and took them to the store for a refund. And when Mom gave her and her brother each some spending money for ice cream, she decided not to have any. She added the money to her missionary fund.

Trisha was surprised when she counted her money on Saturday night. *I didn't think I could give this much,* she thought. *I wish I had started on the project sooner so I'd have even more money to give to our missionary. TMB*

HOW ABOUT YOU?

Are you helping the missionaries your church supports? Maybe you feel you don't have anything to give or that the little you can give won't help much. God says that if you are willing to do what you can, he will accept and bless your gift.

MEMORIZE:

"If you are really eager to give, it isn't important how much you are able to give. God wants you to give what you have, not what you don't have."
2 Corinthians 8:12

Give to Missions

The Prize Cake

Read Ephesians 4:29-32

Rebecca was excited! Both she and Aunt Stephanie were going to enter a cake in the competition at the county fair—Rebecca in the "young bakers" division and her aunt in the adult division. Rebecca wanted her cake to be perfect, and she made so many practice cakes that the whole family was tired of them—except her brother, Warren. He declared they were getting better and better.

The day came for Rebecca to bake her cake for the fair. After carefully frosting it, she left it standing on the kitchen cupboard. Soon Warren came in, and he helped himself to a big piece. He was finishing the last bite when Rebecca came back into the kitchen. "Warren!" she hollered. "What are you doing? That's the cake for the fair! It turned out perfectly, and now you've ruined it!"

"Oh, Rebecca!" Warren cried. "I thought this was another cake for me to test. I'm really sorry. Will you forgive me?"

But Rebecca stalked away. "You ruin my prize cake and want me to forgive you? No way!" she wailed.

Later, as her aunt was working in the kitchen, Rebecca came in, slamming the door behind her. "Oh, Rebecca! My cake for the fair!" Aunt Stephanie gasped. "It's baking—and slamming the door could make it fall!" She peeked in the oven, and sure enough, the center of the cake had caved in. "My oven wasn't working, and three cakes didn't turn out at home because of it. This was my last hope for the competition," she said with a groan.

Rebecca felt terrible! "Oh, Aunt Stephanie," she cried, "I didn't know you had your cake in the oven. Please forgive me."

"Like you forgave Warren?" her aunt asked quietly. "He told me what happened, and I'm sorry. But you know, Rebecca, when someone asks forgiveness, we ought to forgive as God does. After all, we need forgiveness, too."

"I'm sorry," Rebecca repeated. "I guess I need to work on forgiveness even more than I need to work on baking cakes, huh?" *BP*

HOW ABOUT YOU?

Is there someone you need to forgive? Aren't you glad God doesn't hold grudges? As you realize how graciously he forgives your wrongdoing when you confess it, won't you also forgive other people who have wronged you? No one can expect forgiveness who isn't willing to offer it themselves.

MEMORIZE:
"Be kind to each other, tenderhearted, forgiving one another, just as God through Christ has forgiven you."
Ephesians 4:32

Forgive Others

June

12

Sara's Move

Read 2 Corinthians 12:7-10

"Oh, Jackie, it's just awful," Sara wrote to her best friend who still lived in the town from which Sara had recently moved. "I just hate it here! There isn't even one swimming pool in town, and that's the thing I do best. Our church here is so small that there are only four kids in the junior high department. Why did God have to make us move here? My brother and my folks like Minnesota, but I miss California. I wish I could come home. It makes me so mad that we came here."

And Sara acted mad, too. She grumbled about all her work. She argued with her brother. She refused to make new friends. She talked back to her parents. And she kept reminding herself—and everyone around her—that she would much rather be back in California.

After a few months, Sara's church held a Kids Krusade—a week of meetings especially for school-aged kids. Sara reluctantly admitted that she enjoyed the meetings. On Thursday, the lesson was from 2 Corinthians 12. "This Scripture indicates that Paul apparently had something wrong with him, which Paul called his 'thorn.' Three times he asked God to remove it," the speaker said. "But God's answer was, 'My grace is sufficient for you.' " Mrs. Johnson looked around the room. "Boys and girls," she said, "maybe you have a problem, too, that never goes away. It may be something physical or some other trouble. Are you holding a grudge against someone? Are you mad at your mom or dad? Maybe you're even mad at God! If so, you need this verse."

Sara wondered how this stranger knew so much about her. She knew she was so angry and bitter about moving that she hadn't even tried to like her new home. She bowed her head to ask God's forgiveness, and then she hurried home to ask her parents to forgive her, too.

Sara was surprised to find that after she gave up being angry, she really learned to like her new home pretty well. It was a great day when she wrote to share the news with Jackie in California. *REP*

HOW ABOUT YOU?

Is there something in your life that you find hard to bear? Are you mad at God? If you have a bad attitude or some other sin, confess it and be rid of it. If you're upset over a physical problem or a circumstance that you can't change, turn it over to God. He's still saying, "My grace is sufficient for you." In other words, he's here to go with you through your problems and to help you handle them.

MEMORIZE:
"My grace is sufficient for you."
2 Corinthians 12:9, NIV

God's Grace Is Enough

Cotton Clean-Up

Read James 4:7-10

Cara sighed impatiently as she stared out the car window. "Aren't we going to stop soon?" she whined.

"That's at least the tenth time you've asked, Cara," Dad finally scolded. "Now be patient."

"We could be having a nice time together," Mom added, "but you've been complaining the entire trip. It's becoming a bad habit." Mom pointed out the window. "It's interesting to see the fields of cotton, isn't it? I like to see how things grow."

But Cara didn't see anything interesting about the fluffy cotton plants. "Huh!" she scoffed. "Who cares about cotton, anyway?"

A few miles later, Dad turned off and stopped at a roadside stand near a cotton field. "We'll take a short break here," he said.

Cara began looking at the T-shirts on the racks. There were all kinds—some with pictures or words on them. One said, "Land of Cotton," but Cara threw it aside. "I'm sick of cotton," she grumbled.

The shopkeeper stood nearby. "Ho, Missy—tired of cotton, are you?" she asked. "Then I wouldn't buy any of these T-shirts if I were you." She pointed to the label in the neck of a shirt. "These are all made of cotton."

Cara was surprised. "These pretty shirts are made from that old cotton growing in the fields?" she asked.

"Sure thing," the shopkeeper assured her. "And that 'old cotton' hanging on the plants reminds me of myself. Natural cotton isn't much use until folks pick it, clean it, weave it, and sew it into useful clothing. God's doing that with me. My natural self isn't of much use to him, but I've accepted Jesus as my Savior. He's cleaning me up and making me into a useful person. Believe me, he's had to do some powerful cleaning up of bad habits." The shoplady chuckled.

Cara stared at the woman. Then she slowly picked up the shirt with "Land of Cotton" on the front. "Maybe I should take this one," she said, taking out her money. "I've been doing a lot of complaining. This shirt will remind me to ask God to clean the complaining habit out of my heart." *CEY*

HOW ABOUT YOU?

Do you have a habit, such as lying, complaining, or gossiping? God wants to help you clean up your bad habit so you can be useful for him. Ask him to continue his clean-up work.

**Let God Clean Out
Bad Habits**

MEMORIZE:
"Create in me a clean heart, O God."
Psalm 51:10

14

Welcome

Read John 14:1-3; 17:24

"All right!" exclaimed Catherine as they pulled into Grandma's driveway. "We're finally here!" Grandma Peck lived so far away that they had been traveling for two days to get there.

"Yeah," said Garret. "I'm glad we're here."

Dad grinned. "Me, too," he said. "I want to relax right now with a nice, tall glass of iced tea."

Garret laughed. "Well, I bet Grandma has a pitcher of it all ready so that you can have some right away." He pointed. "Look! There she is at the door to welcome us," he added, "and she's got a glass of something in her hand. It's probably your iced tea."

Garret was right. "I knew you'd want this right away," Grandma said. She had also been thinking of the others. She had baked Garret's favorite pie, made fudge for Catherine, and fixed a "nibble tray" with snacks that she knew Mom especially liked. In addition, the house had been scrubbed, clean sheets were on the beds, and a special meal was in the oven. There were new books for the kids to read and new games for them to play.

"Wow! You worked really hard to get ready for us to come," said Catherine when she realized all that Grandma had done.

"Oh, well, I loved preparing for you because I love you," Grandma said, giving Catherine a hug.

"Sounds like my Sunday school lesson all over," said Garret with a grin. "It was about how Jesus loves us and is preparing a place for those who love him."

"I'm so thankful to know that each one here loves Jesus and that we'll all enjoy heaven together," Grandma said. "What a wonderful place that will be!"

Dad nodded. "You've given us a great welcome here," he said, "but you're right. We can't even imagine how very special God's welcome will be!" *LMW*

HOW ABOUT YOU?

Have you helped prepare for company—getting everything just right for those who are coming to visit? If you're a Christian, the Lord Jesus is preparing a place in heaven for you. It's hard to imagine what a very special, wonderful place that will be—and it won't be just for a visit. It will be for all eternity!

MEMORIZE:
"I am going to prepare a place for you." John 14:2

Jesus Is Preparing a Place for Christians

Helpers Needed

Read Exodus 18:13-24

Denise ran down the library steps. "Hey, Leah!" she called. "Wait for me."

Leah stopped and turned. She was carrying two big sacks of groceries. Her shoulders were slumped, and she looked very tired.

"Where have you been all summer?" Denise asked. "I didn't even see you at the fair."

Leah shook her head. "Mom's been sick and missed a lot of work," she replied. "Since Dad's not around, it's up to me to take care of the little kids and everything."

Denise frowned. "I bet you've been doing the cooking and cleaning, too, right?" she asked. Leah nodded. "Why didn't you tell anyone?" asked Denise. She reached out for a grocery bag. "Come on. I'll carry one of those," she said. As they walked toward Leah's house, Denise asked. "Do you know who Moses was?"

Leah shrugged. "A guy in the Bible who got the Ten Commandments," she said. "I heard of the movie."

Denise nodded. "Moses was the leader of a very large and demanding bunch of people," she said. "They were stuck in the middle of the desert for forty years, and they whined a lot."

"Did you learn about him in church?" asked Leah.

"Yes," said Denise. "Anyway . . . Moses was trying to carry the whole load by himself. Then one day, his father-in-law came to him and said, 'Moses, you're going to kill yourself if you keep this up. How about getting some helpers?' So he did, and everything worked out fine." Denise stole a glance at her friend. "Moses needed help, and so do you," declared Denise.

Leah smiled slightly. "And I got help—thanks for carrying that, Denise," she said as she took the bag from her friend. She sighed as she turned to go up the driveway to her house.

"Wait! I . . . uh, I see you bought spaghetti," said Denise. "My mom's been teaching me to cook. Mind if I practice on you?"

Tears came to Leah's eyes. "Thanks," she whispered. *RB*

HOW ABOUT YOU?

Do you know someone in need of encouragement? Will you pray with—and for—that person? Try to think of practical ways to help, too. When God shows you someone who needs help or an encouraging word, be available.

**Encourage Someone
Today**

MEMORIZE:
"We should please others. If we do what helps them, we will build them up in the Lord." Romans 15:2

June

16

Bury That Seed

Read Mark 11:25; Luke 6:37

Gayle strolled toward the counter and picked up a container of dirt. She frowned as she looked at it. "I planted pumpkin seeds in here nearly three weeks ago, Mom. I wanted them to get a really early start, but the dumb things still haven't sprouted!" she complained.

There was a knock at the door, and Gayle went to see who was there. "Hi, Gayle," said Katie, who lived a few houses down the street. "Can you come out and play?"

"No, not today," replied Gayle. "Maybe another time." She shut the door abruptly and went back inside. "That was just Katie," said Gayle when she returned to the kitchen. "She can't get it through her head that I don't want to play with her anymore."

"Honey, I know Katie called you a bad name a couple of weeks ago," Mom said, "but she did apologize. Don't you think it's high time you forgave her?" Gayle shrugged as she again picked up the container of dirt. She poked around in it and pulled out a seed—just as she had done several times during the past weeks. "Gayle, if you want God to make those seeds grow, stop digging them up," Mom said.

"But I—" began Gayle. She sighed. "Okay," she said as she covered the seeds with dirt. "I'm not going to check these again; I'm just going to bury them and forget about them!"

"Good," Mom said. A minute later she added, "You need to do the same thing with your anger toward Katie—bury it and forget about it!"

"But she . . . she . . ." muttered Gayle as she thought about her mother's advice. Then she grinned. "If I bury my anger and forget about it, will God make it grow?" she asked mischievously.

"Gayle Johnson! You know better," scolded Mom, but she grinned, too. "Okay, I know my illustration isn't perfect, but you know what I mean. Forgetting your anger and forgiving Katie are important to your growth—your spiritual growth."

Gayle headed for the door. "I know," she admitted. "I'll go play with Katie for a while." *SRS*

HOW ABOUT YOU?

Are seeds of anger and seeds of unforgiveness keeping you from growing in Christ? Talk to God about them. Ask him to help you bury them and forget about them so that you can grow spiritually.

MEMORIZE:

"Forgive anyone you are holding a grudge against, so that your Father in heaven will forgive your sins, too."
Mark 11:25

Bury Your Anger and Forgive

Garage Sale

Read Colossians 3:12-15

Dina slammed the door. "I don't care if I never talk to Ginny again," she stormed. "She invited me over and then forgot I was coming and went to the mall."

"That's too bad," Grandma DiAngi said. "I'll bet it wasn't intentional. Can't you forgive her?"

"Why should I?" Dina asked indignantly.

"Because Jesus wants you to," was Grandma's answer. "Hasn't he forgiven you for worse things than that?"

"But Ginny's supposed to be my friend," whined Dina.

"You claim to be Jesus' friend, and he said his friends keep his commandments," Grandma reminded her. "One of them is to forgive others."

Dina went to her room and sat down on the bed. She looked around. The room was crowded with things—"wall-to-wall junk" her brother called it. She had an idea. "Grandma," she called, "may I have a garage sale?" Grandma thought it would be fine as long as Mom agreed, so they began sorting things.

When Ginny stopped in the next day, Dina's brother grinned at her. "Ginny, join the junk jamboree," invited Martin. Dina scowled, but noticing the look her grandmother gave her, she agreed that Ginny could bring things to sell, too.

The sale went well. "Nearly all my things sold, but Ginny had a lot of stuff left," Dina said with obvious satisfaction as she counted her money.

That evening, Dina didn't seem to be very happy in spite of her success. Grandma frowned. "Honey, you've cleaned your room, but what about your heart?" she asked gently. "I think you need to clean out some bad feelings. You apparently haven't forgiven Ginny yet. You can't be a truly happy Christian when your heart is cluttered with anger and grudges."

Martin looked up. "You should have cleaned them out and sold them at your garage sale," he joked.

Dina sighed. "They *are* pretty worthless," she said.

"So get rid of them," Grandma said. "Tell God you're sorry and ask him to help you forgive Ginny."

Dina smiled. "I will," she said. "And you know what? I feel better already."
AGL

HOW ABOUT YOU?

Do you forgive others when they treat you badly? Holding grudges brings unhappiness to you as well as to them. Ask God to help you forgive others as you remember how much he has forgiven you.

MEMORIZE:
"Make allowance for each other's faults and forgive the person who offends you." Colossians 3:13

Forgive Others

June

18

Phoebe and her brother, Ben, and their friends, Jeff and Wendy, were playing in the attic. "Hey, look!" called Phoebe, holding up an old dress she had pulled from a trunk.

"Yeah," agreed Jeff, pulling out an ancient tuxedo. "Look at this long coat!"

"These old lace curtains would make a good wedding veil and train," said Wendy. "Let's play wedding. I'll be the bride, Jeff can put on that tuxedo jacket and be the groom, and Ben can be the preacher."

"I'll be a bridesmaid," added Phoebe, slipping the old dress over her shirt and jeans. The boys protested, but finally agreed. The "wedding" was on.

"Raise your right hand," said Preacher Ben. "Do you solemnly swear to tell the truth, the whole truth—" He stopped as the others broke into peals of laughter.

"This isn't a murder trial!" Jeff said.

Just then Mom entered the room. She laughed when she heard how Ben was going to have them swear to tell the truth at a wedding. "The way so many marriages end up in divorce courts these days, that might not be a bad idea," she said.

"How old should you be when you get married, Mom?" asked Phoebe.

"That depends," Mom answered. "It varies with different people."

"I don't think a Christian should marry someone who isn't a Christian, do you?" asked Wendy.

"If you love somebody who isn't a Christian, shouldn't you pray about it?" asked Ben. "Maybe the Lord would tell you to marry her so you can win her to him. Couldn't that happen?"

"Many people have tried that, but no. This is a matter we don't need to pray about. We already have the answer in God's Word," Mom explained. "There are no exceptions to his rules. That's why it's so important that when you reach dating age, you choose to date Christians."

The children were thoughtful. Then Phoebe grinned at her brother. "Come on, Ben," she said. "We won't get married for real for years and years, but let's get on with this pretend wedding." *HCT*

HOW ABOUT YOU?
Do dating and marriage seem a long way off? When that time comes, remember that every person you date is a possible marriage partner. Don't take a chance on becoming interested in someone who is not a Christian. Listen to God in this matter.

MEMORIZE:
"Don't team up with those who are unbelievers." 2 Corinthians 6:14

Choose a Christian Partner

More Than Words

Read Matthew 25:14-17

"For he's a wonderful father, for he's a wonderful father, for he's a wonderful father, that nobody can outdo!" rang out the song after a good lunch on Father's Day. "Okay, Daddy! Open presents," said little Emma. "Open mine first. I made you a picture."

"Don't tell," said Melody, but everyone laughed as Emma insisted on helping her father open the package containing the picture she had drawn for him. Then they watched while he opened the rest of his gifts.

Mom had painted a small painting for Dad. Brian had spent hours making him a new tie rack. And Melody had taken every job she could find, saved the money, and bought her dad some fishing tackle he had been wanting. "These gifts are wonderful!" declared Dad. "I can hardly wait to use them. Thank you all very much!"

"You didn't open Carol's present," piped up Emma. "Where is it, Carol?"

Carol was embarrassed. Everyone was waiting to see what she had for Dad, and she had nothing. She had always found more interesting things to do than to work and make money so she could buy him something. She had thought about making something for him, but she never found time. "I . . . I intended to buy or make something, Dad, but I've been so busy," she explained lamely.

Dad was very gracious. "I know you have," he assured her, "and I have enough presents. Come on, let's have some ice cream, and some of that great-looking cake!"

That night Mom found Carol crying. "I sure didn't show Dad I love him," she sobbed.

"The lack of a present wasn't in itself so serious—presents are not really that important," Mom told her, "but it does seem as if you could have done something to show your love for your father. It's easy to say we love someone, but love is more than words. It's action. Our actions prove our love."

Carol nodded. "Tomorrow I'm going to get busy working on a gift," she declared. "I'll make another day Father's Day for Dad." *JLH*

HOW ABOUT YOU?

Do your actions prove your love for your parents? For God? When you stand before God some day, will you bow your head in shame and say, "I intended to serve you, but I was too busy"? Or will you hear the words, "Well done, good and faithful servant"?

Get Busy for Jesus

MEMORIZE:
"I will give to everyone according to what he has done." Revelation 22:12, NIV

June
20

What Is God Like?

Read Philippians 3:8-10

Tilly swayed back and forth on a park swing, deep in thought. "Hi, Tilly," said a voice. Looking up, Tilly saw Cindy Jones, a college student who lived in the neighborhood. "A penny for your thoughts," said Cindy.

Tilly grinned. "I was just wondering what God is like," she answered. "Cole thinks God is really strict—and maybe a little bossy. That's what Cole's dad is like. Reyna's dad is just the opposite, and Reyna thinks God is always loving and kind and wouldn't really punish anyone. I just don't know." She looked at Cindy. "Do you know what God is like, Cindy?" Tilly asked.

Cindy smiled. "As a matter of fact, I do," she replied, "because I know God." Tilly's eyes opened wide as Cindy continued, "We can know what God is like from studying the Bible. It tells us how great God is—that he made the world and everything in it. The Bible says God is holy—he can't do anything wrong. He's also perfect . . . and best of all, he loves us very much."

"Then Reyna's right. If God loves us, he would never be mean to us, would he?" asked Tilly.

"No," replied Cindy, "not mean—but God is righteous, and he can't stand sin. He punishes the wicked and rewards those who obey him. He's all-powerful, all-wise, and all-seeing—yet he cares about us."

"Wow!" exclaimed Tilly. "I'll have to tell Reyna and Cole."

"But, Tilly, it isn't enough to know what God is like," said Cindy. "You need to know him personally!"

"I can really know him?" asked Tilly.

"Yes, you can," Cindy assured her. "God loves you so much that he sent his Son, Jesus, to take the punishment for your sin. Jesus died on the cross so God could forgive your sin and not punish you."

"Oh," said Tilly thoughtfully, "I heard something about that before."

"Jesus not only died for you," continued Cindy. "He arose from the dead. That's what we celebrate on Easter. If you believe in Jesus and trust in him, God will forgive your sin and make you his child."

"I'd like that," said Tilly thoughtfully. "Tell me about it again." *AGL*

HOW ABOUT YOU?

Do you know a lot about God? That's good, but that doesn't make you a child of God—a Christian. You need to know him personally, and you can do that by receiving Jesus as your Savior."

MEMORIZE:

"I want to know Christ and the power of his resurrection." Philippians 3:10, NIV

You Can Know God

The Broken Train

Read Psalm 5:1-3

"My train is broken!" Nathan wailed.

"Oh, Nate, don't cry," comforted Mackenzie, giving him a hug. "Maybe Grandpa can fix it."

They took the train to Grandpa, who assured them that he could make it good as new. "Honest? Wow!" exclaimed Nathan. Grandpa took the train to his workshop, and Nathan hopped onto the table to watch, "Don't do that!" Nathan protested as Grandpa started bending a wheel. "You'll break it for good."

"Don't be silly, Nate!" Mackenzie scolded. "Grandpa's fixing your train, not breaking it. And he can't work properly when you get in his way."

Nathan pouted, but he wandered out into the yard. Soon he was back. "You're not doing it right," he informed Grandpa after watching for a few minutes. "That piece has to be fastened to the engine like this." He reached for the train.

"Nathan!" Mackenzie cried. "Stop trying to tell Grandpa what to do! Why don't you go play until Grandpa's done."

"That's a good idea," Grandpa said. "This is going to take some time, Nate."

"But I want my train now," Nathan complained. He suddenly grabbed the train and scooted out the door.

"Silly kid!" Mackenzie exclaimed scornfully. "He gave you his train to fix and then took it back without letting you fix it."

"We all do things like that sometimes," Grandpa said tolerantly.

Mackenzie shook her head firmly. "Not me!" she said.

Grandpa smiled. "You told me yesterday that you prayed about the problem you were having with those older girls at school and that you gave the problem to God, right?"

Mackenzie looked puzzled. "Yes . . . so?"

"But you were worrying about it again just this morning, Mackenzie," Grandpa reminded her, "so did you leave it with God, or did you take it back?"

"I . . . I guess I took it back," admitted Mackenzie. "I guess I acted as silly as Nathan!" *MTF*

HOW ABOUT YOU?

Do you bring your problems, worries, and needs to God in prayer? Having done that, do you start worrying all over again? Once you have given something to God, don't try to take it back. Handle the situation the way you believe he wants you to—without worrying. Trust him to work things out.

Wait Patiently for God to Answer Prayer

MEMORIZE:
"Be still in the presence of the Lord, and wait patiently for him to act."
Psalm 37:7

June

22

"Hey!" called Lynette as she ran into the backyard where her mom and dad were painting the new deck. "I got a job!"

"What kind of job?" Mom asked as she worked.

"I'm going to mow Mr. Radcliff's lawn every week," said Lynette, "and he's going to pay me!"

"That's great," Dad said, "but right now, why don't you help us paint?"

"Are you going to pay me?" asked Lynette.

"Sure we are," Mom said. "We'll give you a bed to sleep in and clothes to wear and food to eat and . . ."

"Aw, Mom," murmured Lynette, but she picked up a paintbrush. She dipped it into the bucket and began to paint, working quickly and carelessly.

"Lynette," Dad said, "I was hoping you would show me that you're ready for your first job outside the family. Instead, I'm seeing that you aren't mature enough to work for someone else."

"Sure I am," said Lynette. "I'll do much better when I'm getting paid."

"Why is that?" asked Dad. "Will the work you do for Mr. Radcliff be easier? Is he easier to work for? Is he more important to you than we are?"

"No," said Lynette sheepishly, "but it's just different. Like I said, I'll be getting paid."

"I thought Mom pointed out that payment can come in different forms," Dad said. "Actually, it shouldn't really matter who's in charge of a job you're doing or what the pay will be. What is important is that you have one boss who's always watching. He doesn't pay you in dollars and cents, but he will have a far greater reward for you if you do good work."

"Do you mean God?" asked Lynette.

"I sure do," Dad said. "That's who you're really working for, no matter who pays you—or who doesn't pay you." *HMT*

HOW ABOUT YOU?

Does your attitude toward work depend on the circumstances—on whether you're getting paid or who you're working for? Remember that God is the boss who really matters. His rewards are great.

MEMORIZE:

"No accounting was required . . . because they were honest and faithful workers." 2 Kings 12:15

Do Your Work for God's Approval

Arrowheads and Promises

Read Colossians 2:1-7

Rochelle, who was spending a couple of weeks with her grandfather, was helping Grandpa hoe the garden. *This ground sure is stony,* thought Rochelle as the hoe hit something hard. It glistened in the morning sun, and Rochelle picked it up. "Grandpa," she called, "come and look at this. I never saw a stone this shape before." She wiped the dirt from the pointed stone and handed it to her grandpa.

"Oh, ho!" Grandpa exclaimed. "This is interesting! You just dug up an arrow-head."

"Cool! We talked about arrowheads in history class," said Rochelle. "Native Americans used them to hunt game."

"Yes," Grandpa said, "and that was many years ago. Just think—this one was hidden in the ground for a long time—possibly a hundred years or even more."

"I'll show this to my history teacher," said Rochelle as Grandpa handed the arrowhead back to her.

As Rochelle continued hoeing, she was more interested in her task than she had been earlier. *Maybe I'll find another arrowhead,* she thought as her eyes carefully searched the ground. But there were no more to be found that day.

After supper, Grandpa reached for his Bible. "We'll read from Acts 17 tonight," he said, handing the Bible to Rochelle. "How about reading verses ten through fifteen aloud?" Rochelle found the verses and began reading. When she reached the eleventh verse, which says that the Bereans "searched the Scriptures day after day," Grandpa smiled. "That verse reminds me of the way we dug around in the garden today," he said.

"The garden?" asked Rochelle. "What does the garden have to do with the Bible?"

"Well, I've dug in that garden many times, but I've never found the arrow-head you dug up. Who knows? Maybe we'll find more another day. I've also 'dug' into God's Word many times. It contains valuable treasures. We can find many important instructions and promises and much wisdom as we search the Scrip-tures," Grandpa explained. "We'll miss a great deal if we don't keep searching." *LAW*

HOW ABOUT YOU?
Do you feel like you know all there is to learn from familiar Bible stories? You don't. Keep on "digging." Read the Bible for yourself, and listen when your pastor, Sunday school teacher, or parents talk about it. Get to know God better and see what treasures he has for you.

Find Treasure in God's Word

MEMORIZE:
"In him lie hidden all the treasures of wisdom and knowledge." Colossians 2:3

June

24

The Wallet (Part 1)

Read Luke 15:3-10

Tina looked everywhere for her pretty beaded wallet. She was sure it had been in her backpack just before she'd dropped everything to play softball with some friends on the school playground. She searched all around the ball diamond. No wallet. She looked indoors, where she and her friends kept their books. It wasn't there. She asked her friends if they had seen it. No one had. At home, she looked all over the house—including her own dresser drawers and closet and under the bed—even though she felt sure her wallet wouldn't be there. It wasn't.

The next day at school, Tina checked the lost-and-found box. "There it is!" she exclaimed in delight. She smiled and zipped it carefully into an inner pouch of her backpack.

Later, when Tina told Dad about her wallet, he smiled. "That lost-and-found story reminds me of a woman in the Bible who lost a coin and searched until she found it. She was so happy; she called her friends to let them know her coin was found."

Tina grinned. "We could celebrate that my wallet is found," she said. "How about some cake, Mom?"

Mom laughed, but she got out the cake and cut a slice for Tina. "Do you know who else is happy when something is found?" she asked. "The Bible says the angels rejoice when a lost sinner comes to Jesus."

"You mean when I accepted Jesus as my Savior, the angels knew about it and were happy?" Tina asked.

Dad nodded. "Yes, but I believe Jesus is the happiest of all when someone is saved," he said. "He loves us all so much." *JAG*

HOW ABOUT YOU?

Have you ever lost a book, toy, or wallet and searched for a long time before finding it? Jesus, too, has waited a long time for you to come to him. Believe that he died on the cross for your sin and receive his gift of eternal life. Even the angels in heaven will rejoice. Receive Jesus today.

MEMORIZE:

"There is joy in the presence of God's angels when even one sinner repents." Luke 15:10

Salvation Brings Joy

The Wallet (Part 2)

Read Psalm 13:5-6; 16:2, 5-6

Kim came into the room just as Tina took a bite of cake. "Have some, Kim," she said. "I'm celebrating—I found my wallet." She held it up.

Kim smiled. She knew that wallet well! She'd been so excited on the day of her school Christmas party the year before. During the gift exchange, she'd carefully studied the pile of brightly wrapped Christmas presents and chosen one that was long and flat—just the right shape for a wristwatch, necklace, or bracelet. Back at her seat, she quickly ripped through the ribbons and wrapping paper. A gasp of disappointment escaped her lips as she examined the contents of the package. "A wallet!" she whispered to herself. It wasn't nearly as nice as the one her aunt Helen had recently sent her—from Europe. She stuffed the wallet into her school bag and quickly tried to paste on a false smile. She wondered if the person who'd brought that gift was watching. She didn't want her own disappointment to make someone else feel hurt or embarrassed.

At home, Kim shared her disappointment with her mother. "So much for our Christmas party for me—a big zero, nothing," she moaned.

Mom stopped her dinner preparations to kiss her on the cheek. "I know it's disappointing, honey," she said, "but God can bring good out of anything—even out of disappointment. Let's pray about it." Kim obediently closed her eyes as her mother prayed. When they had finished, Mom was thoughtful for a few minutes.

"Kim, why don't you give the wallet to someone who will use it?" she suggested. "It's a pretty little wallet, even if it isn't as elegant as the one Aunt Helen sent you."

Kim had given it to Tina, who immediately stuffed it full of photos of her friends, her school I.D., and her few dollars of cash.

Now, as she took a piece of cake, Kim smiled over at her mother. "You were right," she said. "Good does come out of a disappointment when we ask God to help us." *JAG*

HOW ABOUT YOU?
We all face large and small disappointment at times. Tell God about it. He understands and can help you to see the good in every event.

MEMORIZE:
"Surely you have a future ahead of you; your hope will not be disappointed." Proverbs 23:18

Give Disappointments to God

June
26

Lauren's Visitor

Read Philippians 4:14-19

Lauren was annoyed. Her mother had invited Caryn Griffith, a missionary kid, to stay overnight. "What a bother," Lauren groaned. "Tonight's the talent show at school, and I'll have to drag her along. I just know I'll be embarrassed. After spending all that time in Africa, I bet she doesn't have the foggiest idea of what she should wear here. Besides, what will I talk about with a strange girl from a strange place?"

"Don't worry about it," Mom had said. "She's just an ordinary girl, like you." Lauren doubted it. Missionary kids would be, well, different, she was sure.

When Caryn arrived, Lauren had to admit that Caryn's outfit didn't look "different." In fact, it was cute! And she didn't act "different," either. When Mom explained that Lauren had a talent show at school and they'd be eating at a fast-food place, Caryn smiled. "That's my favorite. We have one of those near where we live in Nairobi," she said. "In some ways, our town is a lot like yours!"

While they ate, Mom and Dad asked Caryn lots of questions about her school and her life in Africa. Soon Lauren found herself eagerly joining in. It was fun to hear about a new place and another way of living. Lauren was surprised to find that Caryn's thoughts and reactions were much like her own. Mom was right when she said that Caryn was a girl "just like you."

"That was fun," Lauren said as she waved good-bye to Caryn the next day. "You know what, Mom? When Caryn goes back to Africa, she and I are going to be pen pals."

Mom smiled. "Great! Then the next time Caryn comes to our church, it won't be as a complete stranger, but as your friend." *LMW*

HOW ABOUT YOU?

Are you friendly to missionaries when they visit your church? If there are children your age, talk to them and become friends. Ask for their addresses so you can write to them when they go back to the mission field. Then you'll know better how to pray for them. They're interesting people. Thank the Lord for missionary friends.

MEMORIZE:

"Whenever we have the opportunity, we should do good to everyone, especially to our Christian brothers and sisters." Galatians 6:10

Be Friendly to Missionary Kids

With You Always (Part 1)

Read 1 Peter 4:12-16

Tina's parents were seldom home. They spent a lot of time at their club and didn't worry much about Tina's activities—but they were very displeased when they learned that she had joined a church youth group. They were even more unhappy when she told them she had been saved. "This child could become a religious freak!" her father stormed.

Her mother attempted to calm him. "I'm sure she's just going through a phase. She'll surely outgrow it." And so they decided to leave her alone.

When Tina arrived home from school one day, she found a note saying her parents had gone to a cocktail party, to be followed by dinner. So after fixing herself a bite to eat and doing her homework, Tina went to bed. She had been asleep for some time when her light suddenly flashed on. It was her parents, and she could tell that her father was angry. "Wake up!" he commanded. "Your mother and I were at the Afterglow Lounge on Main Street tonight. Gus, who owns the place, came up and told me that you and some other kids had been out in front of the building, handing out something about that church twice in the last two weeks! Is that true?"

"Yes, it is, Dad," Tina answered softly as she tried to swallow her fears.

Mom spoke up. "Tina, surely you can see how embarrassing this is for your father and me. With Dad's business connections and our social standing, we can't have you out on the street corners like the Salvation Army!"

"Tina, I want you to give me your word right now that you will forget all about this nonsense," Dad demanded. "Promise that you will never again pass out that stuff in public."

Tears streamed down Tina's face as she tried to keep her emotions under control. "I'll stop passing out tracts if you say I have to, Daddy, but I can't say I don't love Jesus," she sobbed. "He was killed because of my sin. I can't turn my back on him because I love him."

As her father angrily glared at her, Tina looked toward her mom, hoping to see understanding in her eyes. *HCT*

HOW ABOUT YOU?

Are you willing to endure suffering for the Lord if necessary? Do you love him enough to be true to him when it gets difficult? Remember that God promises to be with you always.

God Will Not Forsake You

MEMORIZE:
"Even if my father and mother abandon me, the Lord will hold me close." Psalm 27:10

June

28

With You Always (Part 2)

Read John 1:35-42

Tina's father stood at Tina's bedroom door, his look of rage gradually diminishing to one of confusion. His face was white, and perspiration stood on his forehead. After what seemed an eternity, he quietly said, "Tina, go back to bed." Then he turned and left the room.

Tina's mother turned out the light. She took Tina in her arms and kissed away her tears. "I don't understand your obsession with this Jesus stuff. I really don't. But I hope you think very hard about what it could cost you in your relationship with your dad."

Tina nodded her head against her mom's shoulder, and then her mother slipped from the room and closed the door. Tina didn't understand either. How could her parents not see their need for salvation? Why would they continue to reject Jesus' love?

As Tina dozed off, she whispered a quick prayer. "Lord, I don't know what to do for my parents anymore. It's all up to you."

The next morning Tina found her mother standing at the sliding door of the kitchen, just staring out at the trees and birds. When Tina pulled out a chair at the table, her mom turned around, and Tina saw tears filling her eyes. But something else was there as well. A new light. Maybe a look of peace?

Her mom spoke. "Honey, I'm not sure what's gotten into your father, but he was in the den all night. He's still there now. He's been reading your Bible."

Tina hardly knew what to think. But she didn't have long to wonder. A moment later her dad shuffled into the kitchen. His face looked tired, but his eyes were bright. He looked from his wife to Tina and slowly knelt down in front of his daughter. "I'm so sorry, sweetheart. I'm sorry for everything. I'll never be the same man again," he said quietly. "I want you to tell me more about Jesus. I don't know what happened to me since yesterday, but I'm ready to hear what you have to say."

They hugged and cried together. And then Tina shared all about Jesus, her Savior. *HCT*

HOW ABOUT YOU?

Do your parents know the Lord? If not, does it seem that they never will be saved? Don't be discouraged. Sometimes it takes a long time before they respond. Keep praying for them and witnessing to them. Be sure they can see Jesus in your life and actions. It may be many years before you see results, but be faithful, knowing that God will be faithful, too.

MEMORIZE:

"Be faithful, even to the point of death, and I will give you the crown of life." Revelation 2:10, NIV

Witness Faithfully

Mimosa Plants and Words

Read Psalm 19:12-14

"Hurry up, Meredith!" Emily skipped to her little sister's side. "Clean up your mess so we can have lunch!"

"Oh, be quiet," Meredith grumbled angrily as she carefully put a blue, heart-shaped bead onto the necklace string. "You're not my boss! I'm tired of you telling me what to do!" Emily's eyes filled with tears as she left the room.

That afternoon, Meredith went along with her mother to do some shopping while Emily played at a friend's house. When Mom stopped at a greenhouse to buy some roses, Meredith wandered around, looking at various types of plants. A greenhouse attendant noticed Meredith's restlessness. "Did you see our mimosa plants?" the attendant asked. "Come look at them." After getting permission from her mom, Meredith went over to see the spiky green plants. "Blow on one of the plants," invited the attendant with a grin.

Puzzled, Meredith blew. She was startled to see the plant's leaves curl up immediately. "I didn't hurt it, did I?" she asked.

"No—it will be fine," the worker told her. "These plants respond to possible injury by curling their leaves. That keeps them from being harmed by certain insects or by rain. It doesn't take much harsh treatment to cause them to curl up."

Meredith was fascinated by the plants. "Those mimosa plants are so cool!" she exclaimed as she and her mother drove home.

"They're interesting," Mom agreed, "and I think they must be a little like Emily."

"Like Emily?" asked Meredith. "How?"

"Well, when you blow on mimosa leaves, they curl up," Mom said, "and when you say harsh words to Emily, she 'curls up,' too. Oh, she doesn't actually curl into a ball, but unkind words hurt her deep inside, and she wilts—she withdraws from the conversation to avoid being hurt more. We've talked about this before."

"I'm sorry, Mom," Meredith said quietly. "I'll try to do better. I promise."

"Good," Mom said. "Make sure your words are helping people grow instead of causing them to wilt." *KSB*

HOW ABOUT YOU?

Do your words cause others to grow or to shrivel? God wants the things you say to build up others, not tear them down. Ask him to help you speak kindly.

Use Words to Help, Not Hurt

MEMORIZE:
"Be quick to listen, slow to speak, and slow to get angry." James 1:19

30

A Friend Like Me

Read John 15:10-15

Tasha came bounding into the house. "Grandma, you'll never guess what happened!" she said. "Samantha's aunt in England sent her some British money—five one-pound coins. Some of us stopped to see them after school, and Samantha let us pass them around. Janell left before the rest of us did—and you know what?" Tasha didn't wait for an answer, but hurried on. "When we left, one of the coins was missing!" she reported. "Everybody thinks Janell must have taken it!"

"Oh, I'm sure Janell wouldn't have done that!" exclaimed Grandma. "Did you see her take it? Did you ever see Janell take anything that didn't belong to her?"

Tasha shook her head.

"As her friend, you should have stood up for her and told Samantha that you don't believe Janell would do that."

"But who else could have taken it?" asked Tasha. She glanced at the clock. "Oh, no!" she groaned. "I told Janell I'd walk to the library with her in half an hour, but now I don't want to go. If the other kids see me with her, what will they think? I'll call and tell her mom I can't go."

"Listen to yourself!" Grandma scolded gently. "You have no good reason to think Janell has done anything wrong. You made a commitment, and you need to keep it."

At Grandma's insistence, Tasha met Janell as they had planned. As the girls walked along, Tasha saw Samantha approaching. "Wait up!" called Samantha. "I'll walk with you."

"Are you out to spend your five pounds?" asked Janell.

"No—I'm going to keep them!" Samantha laughed merrily. "You should have seen us this afternoon, Janell! We looked all over the house for one of the coins because I didn't know my mother had taken it to show our neighbor."

When Tasha returned home, she hesitantly told her grandmother what had happened to the money. "With a friend like me, who needs enemies?" she finished. "I'm so ashamed!"

Grandma nodded. "You've learned a lesson today," she said. "Proverbs 17:17 would be a good verse for you to learn—go look it up, okay?" *AGL*

HOW ABOUT YOU?

What kind of friend are you? Do you refuse to listen to gossip—or to spread gossip—about your friends? Are you "wishy-washy"—willing to play with someone on one day, but not the next? Be a friend that others can always depend on. Be the kind of friend God commends—one who loves, no matter what.

MEMORIZE:

"A friend is always loyal, and a brother is born to help in time of need." Proverbs 17:17

Be a True Friend

A Reward

Read Matthew 6:1-6

Even though the summer sunshine was bright, Candy's mood was not. As she sat sniffling on the back porch step, she heard Mom open and close the door behind her.

"What's wrong with my girl?" Mom asked sympathetically as she sat down next to Candy.

Candy's explanation tumbled out. "Last Sunday my teacher talked to us about being a helpful neighbor. I was excited about that, so Dad gave me permission to clean Mr. Thompson's yard. It was hot, Mom! And bugs kept landing on me. And then . . ." Candy's voice broke, and she impatiently brushed a tear off her cheek before continuing. "Mr. Thompson wasn't happy. He said I had pulled up some of his flowers. I didn't know, Mom! They looked like weeds!"

"Uh-oh!" Mom said. "What happened next?"

"I told him I was sorry, and then I ran home because I started to cry. He didn't even thank me for trying!"

"Hmm," Mom said thoughtfully. "It sounds like you chose the wrong person to please."

"I know!" Candy exclaimed. "Mr. Thompson's mean!"

"Well, sweetheart, he's not the one I meant," Mom replied.

Candy looked at her mother for an explanation.

"Whenever you give of your time and energy to someone—like you did to Mr. Thompson—instead of expecting gratitude from *that* person, do your best to please *God,*" Mom said. "It's nice to receive thanks from those we help, but we should help them in order to glorify God, not ourselves."

Candy thought about her mother's words. "That's hard to do," she said.

"Yes, it is," Mom agreed, "but when your goal is to simply serve others and glorify God, he sees that, and he will reward you. Sometimes he may give a happy, satisfied spirit. Sometimes he may give more. And sometimes your reward will be in heaven."

Candy breathed a satisfied sigh, then added, "I'm going to use my allowance to buy new flowers for Mr. Thompson. I'll leave them on his porch with a note of apology. And if he never thanks me, . . ." Candy shrugged. "I'll do my best not to worry about it." *LCA*

HOW ABOUT YOU?

When you do kind things, are you doing them to please God or to receive thanks and admiration for yourself? Remember that nothing you do escapes God's notice; he is always aware of the things you do for him. Make it your goal to please him instead of trying to win praise from people.

MEMORIZE:

"Work hard and cheerfully at whatever you do, as though you were working for the Lord rather than for people." Colossians 3:23

Work Only to Glorify God

July
2

Ocean of Love

Read Ephesians 3:14-19

It was a beautiful day for a picnic at the beach. The Parker family spread out a tablecloth and put up sun umbrellas in their favorite spot. When Ramie and Noah dashed for the water, Meg looked fearfully at the waves. "The waves are so big today," she murmured.

"Oh, come on in," Ramie called. "They're fun. Don't be so scared."

But Meg shook her head. She sat down on the beach and began to build a sand castle. "Dad," she began after a little while. She hesitated. Her voice trembled as she added, "I feel rotten inside. I think God has quit loving me."

"God has never quit loving you for a minute in your whole life," Dad assured her. "What makes you think he has?"

"Well, my Sunday school verse was, 'Keep yourselves in God's love.' I figure that means I have to keep God loving me, but I don't think I've done that," Meg replied, looking at the ground. "I . . . I lied to you and Mom the other day, so I just know I haven't kept God loving me."

"I remember," Dad said, "but you confessed that to us, and we forgave you."

"That's right," Mom added. "And when you confess your sin to God, he forgives you, too."

Dad nodded. "But through all that, God never stopped loving you," he said. He waved a hand toward the ocean and continued, "God's love is something like the ocean. Just think of how much water there is out there, and you're not enjoying any of it. Why not?"

"Because I'm afraid, so I'm not in it," Meg answered.

"Exactly," Dad agreed. "Your fear of the big waves keeps you from enjoying the water. And unconfessed sin has kept you from enjoying the love of God. But, his love for you is there, just as it's always been. The Bible doesn't say, 'Keep God loving you.' It says, 'Keep yourselves in God's love.' "

"But how do you do that?" Meg asked.

"To 'keep yourself in God's love' is to do the things God loves—to live the way he wants you to," Dad replied. "Then you can enjoy the love that's there for you." *MRP*

HOW ABOUT YOU?

Have you wondered if God still loves you? Perhaps you've disobeyed, been unkind, used bad language, or allowed some other sin to come into your life. Make things right with God and with others and enjoy the love that is there for you. God always loves you, but sin will keep you from enjoying his love.

MEMORIZE:

"Keep yourselves in God's love."

Jude 21, NIV

Enjoy God's Love

Dum Dum Douty

Read 1 John 3:16-18

Brynn walked proudly beside Lana, who had finally agreed to go to Bible club with her. Lana would be the seventh visitor she had brought! She was earning lots of points, and she was sure she'd win a prize!

"Look out, Lana! Here comes Dum Dum Douty and his little red wagon," Brynn warned. "Don't move to get out of his way—make *him* stop. His real name is Donny Douty, but I call him Dum Dum."

"Oh, Brynn, don't call him that," Lana protested as she stepped into the grass to make room for the little boy. But Brynn spread her feet out, put her hands on her hips, and did not move one inch.

When Donny tried to get past Brynn, his wagon tipped over, and he began to cry. Lana soothed him and helped him pick up the toys that spilled from the wagon. "Oh, Lana, hurry up. We'll be late," Brynn grumbled.

"What do you do at Bible club?" Lana asked when they were on their way again.

"Oh, we have Bible stories, and we learn verses," Brynn told her. "I've learned more than anybody. I'm going to win a prize for that and for bringing visitors, too—and for being on time every week."

"Oh," Lana murmured. Then she added, "Aren't you a Christian, Brynn?"

"Of course I am," Brynn answered with irritation. "How can you ask a thing like that?"

"Well, you just . . . you call Donny 'Dum Dum,' and you seem so interested in winning prizes," Lana replied. "If that's how you learn to act at your Bible club, I don't want to go." Lana stood still. "In fact, I'm not going. I'm going home."

Brynn stood speechless as Lana turned and walked away. Then, bursting into tears, she ran home. "Oh, Mom," she cried, as she entered the house, "maybe Lana will never be a Christian because of me!" Brynn poured out the story to her mother. "What should I do?" she sobbed.

"First of all, let's talk to God about these things," Mom suggested. "And then, if you're really sorry, I think you should go see Lana and Donny and apologize to them, too." *VJL*

HOW ABOUT YOU?

Do your actions, attitudes, and words show that you're a Christian? Can others see Christ's love in your life? It's important for Christians to live in such a way that others will want to know Jesus, too.

MEMORIZE:
"Let us stop just saying we love each other; let us really show it by our actions." 1 John 3:18

Love Is Action

July

4

The Law of Freedom

Read Romans 6:18-22

"Francesca, you know the rule," said Mom. "You do not go to sleepovers unless we know the adults who will be present. So, no, you can't go to Vicki's Friday night." Francesca recognized the "that's final" tone. Mom changed the subject. "Have you fed your fish?"

"I feed the fishes!" exclaimed little Jordan. He headed for the den.

"No!" Francesca ran after him. "You don't know how." As she got the fish food, Francesca scowled. "I thought this was a free country," she grumbled angrily, "but there's no freedom in this house! 'No, you can't go there.' 'Do this.' 'Don't do that.'"

"What's freedom?" asked Jordan.

"It's getting to do what you want to do when you want to do it," answered Francesca.

"I wanna feed the fishes," Jordan said. "Wanna feed 'em now."

"No!" Francesca snapped.

Jordan watched his big sister drop tiny grains of fish food into the water. The fish quickly swam to the top. "I like your fishes," the little boy said. He pressed his nose against the glass. "Fishes, do you wanna come out and play with me?"

"No, they don't," Francesca said crossly. "They're perfectly happy where they are." She put the fish food in the drawer, slammed it, and stomped from the room.

She was in her room, pouting, when Jordan came in. He held out his hand. "Fishy won't play," he said sadly. Francesca gasped. Jordan was holding a dead fish. "Fishy want outta bowl. Fishy want freedom. Now make him play, Frannie."

Anger rose in Francesca. "What a stupid—" she began. She stopped. *The fish was free only as long as he was in the aquarium,* she thought. *I guess I'm safe only when I'm in the right environment, too. That's why Mom and Dad make rules.* She took a small box from her desk drawer and handed it to Jordan. "He is dead, Jordan. Fish die when they get out of water. Put him in here. In a little while, we'll go bury him."

She sat at her computer and typed an e-mail: "Hi Vicki, I can't come to your sleepover. Thanks for inviting me." *BJW*

HOW ABOUT YOU?

Do the rules at your house seem to threaten your freedom? True freedom has boundaries, and rules and laws actually safeguard it. Thank God for parents who establish rules to help keep you safe.

MEMORIZE:

"I will walk in freedom, for I have devoted myself to your commandments." Psalm 119:45

Freedom Has Boundaries

Decision Made

Read Psalm 96:1-6,10

How Krista wished she could stop time and make Bible camp last forever! When she had agreed to go to camp with her friend Hailey she hadn't realized that there would be so much Bible reading and chapel attendance. It made her uncomfortable at first. Then she began to really listen, and on Wednesday night, she accepted Jesus as her Savior. She was so happy to be saved, and she hated to leave her Christian friends and go back home. She wasn't sure she could live like a Christian there.

Hailey's father, Pastor Randall, was the camp director. He spoke to the group around the campfire on their last evening at camp. "I've had a great week getting to know you kids," he told the campers. "I hate to see it come to an end. In fact, I don't know if I can adjust to going home. I might get kinda lonely sleeping without frogs and cracker crumbs . . . oh, yes—and water balloons." There was a great deal of laughter as the campers remembered some of the jokes they had played that week.

When the group was quiet again, Pastor Randall continued. "Many of you have made decisions this week—either to accept Jesus as Savior, or to serve him any way you can. When you get home, you may find it hard to live up to those decisions, but don't forget Jesus is living within you. He'll give you the needed strength to live for him at home as well as at camp. As you go home now, remember our verse of the week. Let's all say it together now, and be challenged by it."

With all the others, Krista quoted, "Psalm 96:2: 'Each day proclaim the good news that he saves.' "

"Good," Pastor Randall approved. "No matter what your decision was, that verse states your task. My prayers are with you. Let's stand for a closing song."

As Krista sang, she thought about her decision to accept Jesus as Savior. *No one in my family is a Christian,* she thought, *but I'm going to do my best to show them that I'm different.* JLH

HOW ABOUT YOU?

Have you made a decision—perhaps at camp, Bible club, or Sunday school—but now you wonder if you can carry it out? Decisions must be more than words. They must involve actions. Ask God to help you live for him. Begin right now to serve him by witnessing, helping, and using any talents he has given you.

MEMORIZE:
"Each day proclaim the good news that he saves." Psalm 96:2

Decisions Involve Actions

July 6

Sin Now, Pay Later

Read Galatians 6:7-10

After arguing with two friends, Jodi ran home. She spent a lonesome, quiet day and was glad when bedtime came. By that time, however, she wasn't quite so sure she had been right. "It all seems so silly now," she told her dad. "I was mean to Melissa and Nicki, and I'll apologize when I see them tomorrow."

Dad nodded. "That's a good idea," he agreed, "but don't forget that when you quarrel and say mean things, you displease the Lord, too."

"I know it," Jodi admitted. "I'll tell him I'm sorry."

The next morning, Jodi went to find Melissa and Nicki, but both girls were gone for the day. It was nearly eight o'clock that evening before they returned. "Hi, Jodi," they called. "Did we have fun!"

"Mom took us on a paddleboat trip down the river," Nicki explained. "I was going to invite you yesterday, but you got mad and went home before I could do it."

"Oh, I'm sorry I was mean," Jodi told them. "Can we play again tomorrow?"

But the girls shook their heads. "Tomorrow my mother is taking us to the zoo for the day," Melissa told her. "I wish you could come, too. We did have room for one more, but since you had left, I asked my cousin, Diane. Maybe we can play the next day."

With tears in her eyes, Jodi headed for home. "I'm missing out on lots of fun just because I got mad," she told Dad. "I'm paying for it now."

"That's too bad, honey," Dad comforted, "but there's an important lesson here. Remember that any wrong thing you do is sin, and sin brings sorrow. Even though you've been forgiven, the effects of your actions still go on. But be glad your friendships with those girls aren't over. Look forward to responding better the next time you're tempted to argue." *AGL*

HOW ABOUT YOU?

Aren't you glad that you can apologize and be forgiven when you've done something wrong? You are right to apologize. God, and often others, will forgive you. But even though you're sorry, the results of your sin may continue for a long time. One sin today can spoil a lot of tomorrows.

MEMORIZE:
"You will always reap what you sow!"
Galatians 6:7

Sin Brings Sorrow

A Prize Rose

Read 1 Peter 2:12

Ellen was walking down the street one day when her neighbor's dog, Daisy, dashed out of the yard and ran down the street. As Mrs. Kramer frantically called the dog, Ellen took off after Daisy. Soon she captured the little animal and returned it to her owner. "I guess she wanted some exercise," Ellen said. She smiled nervously at Mrs. Kramer, knowing the old lady often seemed unhappy with the neighborhood kids. "I'd be glad to come every day and walk her for you," she offered.

Mrs. Kramer, obviously surprised, agreed that it might be a good idea and muttered her thanks. So it was that Ellen found herself with a new job. Often after walking Daisy, she lingered to watch Mrs. Kramer work in her rose garden. In exchange for walking the dog, Mrs. Kramer taught Ellen about the proper care of the flowers and even let her help with her prize roses.

During the next months, Ellen began to like the grumpy older woman, and Mrs. Kramer seemed to look forward to Ellen's visits. As they worked and talked together, Ellen told Mrs. Kramer about verses she was learning for Sunday school and youth group. Mrs. Kramer occasionally asked Ellen to recite verses mentioning things like sowing seeds, pruning, and growing things.

One morning, Mrs. Kramer appeared at the door, apparently eager for Ellen to arrive. "I have something to tell you," she said. "I couldn't sleep last night, and all those verses you've been quoting kept coming back to me. Looking out my window, I could see my roses in the moonlight, and suddenly it was all clear to me. You're just like my prize rose."

Ellen was startled. "Like your prize rose? Me?" she asked.

"Yes, you," Mrs. Kramer said. "I think you've let Jesus prune you and water you . . . and with his care you've become a 'prize rose.' I realized I was only a thorn bush, more like that tree your verses talk about—the one that deserved to be cut down. Actually, I've been a Christian for a long time, but I've never really served the Lord. Now, even in my old age, I want others to see Jesus in me!" *CH*

HOW ABOUT YOU?
Are you like a prize rose? Do the things you do and say make others want to know Jesus? Or are you more like a thorn bush? Ask God to help you cut out the things that don't please him so that you can bear fruit for him.

Let Jesus Be Seen in Your Life

MEMORIZE:
"By their fruit you will recognize them." Matthew 7:20, NIV

July
8

Claire and Brendan and their mother had recently given their hearts to Jesus and had begun living for him. Now they were praying for Dad. Although Dad had noticed a difference in them, he hadn't accepted the change for his own life.

"Say, kids," Dad said one evening, "I borrowed Uncle Tony's tent for the weekend. Let's get up early tomorrow, and we can be settled at the Horn Lake campground before noon!"

"But Brendan and I have special parts in our youth group meeting on Sunday, Daddy," Claire said. "Will we be back by then?"

Dad shook his head. "You can miss for once!" he said.

As far as Dad was concerned, the conversation was over. But later, Brendan and Claire talked to their mother about it. "Mom, Dad planned this trip and doesn't care if Brendan and I miss church stuff on Sunday," Claire said. "Can we stay at Cindy's and Jimmy's instead of going on the campout?"

"I know your dad doesn't care about church, but he's eager for family activities," Mom told them. "I was thinking and praying about our family the other day, and I found eight places in the Bible where God says to honor and obey parents. If he said it that often, it must be important, don't you think?" Reluctantly the kids agreed. "I know you want to go to church—and that's good—but I think it's even more important to obey your father right now," their mom continued. "He's watching us, you know. If we have wrong attitudes towards him, it might make him even less interested in giving his life to God. Let's honor him and pray for him. And let's ask God to show us how to draw him to the Lord." *BJW*

HOW ABOUT YOU?
Are you obeying your parents? God gave them to you, and his Word says to obey them. Even if they are not followers of Christ, be obedient. God will honor you for doing that.

MEMORIZE:
"Children, obey your parents because you belong to the Lord, for this is the right thing to do." Ephesians 6:1

Obey Your Parents

Her Own Way

Read Romans 7:18-25

Just as Isobel was trying to mount Flame, a spirited horse on their Wyoming ranch, her brother Alejandro came along. "Don't try to ride him, Isobel," Alejandro called. "He'll probably throw you. Besides, you know Dad said never to try that."

Isobel laughed. "Pooh!" she snorted. "Mom and Dad have gone to town, so he'll never know." The horse reared up. "Whoa, boy! Easy there," she coaxed. "We'll show . . . oh, Flame! Easy there! Easy! Get out of the way, Alejandro!" Isobel screamed in panic as Flame snorted and bucked. He was just too much horse for Isobel to handle.

Alejandro dashed in close to the big horse, making a desperate grab for the bridle. Flame jerked away! Isobel screamed again, and Alejandro saw the slashing hooves poised above him. He scrambled to get out of the way, but it was too late. Flame sent him sprawling to the ground. Isobel slipped, unhurt, to the grass, and the riderless horse bolted down the lane, crashing into the barbed wire fence across the road.

An hour later, Isobel stood at her brother's bedside. "Alejandro, are you all right?" she sobbed.

"My shoulder's awfully sore," Alejandro moaned, "but I . . . I think I'm all right."

"Flame is hurt bad, Alejandro," Isobel said, "and it's all because I wanted to have my own way! Oh, what will Dad say when he gets home!"

As expected, Dad was very upset. At the same time, he was thankful that Alejandro and Isobel were all right. "As I've told you before, Isobel," Dad said sadly, "sin only brings trouble and heartache for everyone."

Isobel lifted a tearstained face. "I'm a Christian, and I don't want to do things that I shouldn't, but I do them anyway. What's wrong with me, Daddy?" she asked.

"Nothing the Lord can't cure," Dad answered. "Jesus wants to control your life and give you new desires. Don't you think you ought to allow him to do that for you?" Isobel nodded as Dad continued, "Let him have his way in your life. Don't insist on doing things your own way." *BP*

HOW ABOUT YOU?

Are you a Christian, but still trying to get your own way? You're not unusual. Today's Scripture lesson talks about how your old nature still tries to have control of your life. But through Jesus you can be delivered and have victory over yourself. Yield your life to him each day.

MEMORIZE:

"The power of the life-giving Spirit has freed you through Christ Jesus from the power of sin that leads to death." Romans 8:2

Make God's Way Your Way

July
10

Warning Sign

Read Psalm 107:17-21

"DANGER! SWIFT UNDERTOW! NO SWIMMING!"

The sign was posted in the water just off the pier at Sand Point. However, a number of teenage boys were surfing and jumping off the pier. Jane and Roxanne stood watching from the beach, wanting very much to join them. The water looked inviting, but the undertow sign made them nervous.

"I'm sure it's safe enough if we go in only up to our waists," Jane suggested after watching the boys for quite a while.

"Yeah," Roxanne agreed. "After all, no one seems to be bothered by the undertow."

The girls began jumping about in the waves. It was fun, and they didn't notice they were being pulled farther out into the water. Soon they were covered to the shoulders.

"Roxanne, something is pulling me," Jane gasped suddenly. "I can't stand up. Help!" Roxanne reached out for Jane, but she too was being pulled out by the undertow.

The girls' screams alerted a young man on a surfboard, and he quickly came to help them. When they were safely back on shore, they sat on their towels, trying to calm their racing hearts and shivering bodies.

Jane finally spoke. "Roxanne, what if we had died?" Her voice shook. "We probably would have if someone hadn't helped us!"

"I know." Roxanne nodded fearfully. "And it's all because we didn't obey the sign! Mom's always telling me that rules are made to protect us."

"Yeah," Jane agreed, "and my dad adds, 'Break a rule; pay the price of a fool.' I guess they're right." She sighed. "I was just thinking—we're both Christians, so at least we would have gone to heaven if we hadn't gotten help."

"That's true," Roxanne agreed, "but our bodies would have died just the same. From now on I'm going to obey the signs!" *PMR*

HOW ABOUT YOU?

Did you know that even though God is willing to forgive you for the wrong things you do, you often still have to suffer the consequences of your sin? Don't disregard rules and signs, thinking you can confess and be forgiven later. Yes, you can be forgiven, but there may still be a price to pay.

MEMORIZE:

"Some were fools in their rebellion; they suffered for their sins." Psalm 107:17

Be Obedient

Easy—but Wrong

Read Matthew 7:13-14, 21-23

Teresa and her family were going to spend a week vacationing at a friend's summer home in the mountains. "I hope we can reach the place before dark," Dad said after several hours on the road. "I'm sure the route we're taking will be shorter than the one the Greys suggested, but the road may not be marked as well."

Mom smiled. "I think we're all used to your shortcuts, dear." They all laughed.

The pavement ended as they neared the tiny village of Red Gap, and soon they came to a fork in the road. To the left, it branched off into a narrow, rough trail; to the right, the road was wide and packed smooth. "Oops!" Dad said. "This doesn't show on the map. But the road to the right is in better shape—it must be the one we need." He turned in that direction.

After driving for several miles Dad shook his head. "We should have been there by now," he said. Suddenly they saw a long, low building with several cars parked outside. There was loud music coming through the doorway, and a sign on the building read, "Devil's Inn."

"Dad," Teresa said in surprise, "that looks like a tavern!"

"That's what it is," her father replied, "and we're getting out of here!" He turned around, drove back to the fork in the road, and took the other trail. After a bumpy, but rather short ride, they reached their destination. Their friend's cottage was right next door to a small country church.

As they unpacked the van, Dad said, "Remember that wrong turn I took? I was certain that the wide, smooth road was the right one. But when I saw the tavern at the end of it, I realized that the reason it was so smooth was because of all the cars that drive there and back. Apparently not as many people take the twisting, narrow road to the church."

Mom nodded. "Just like Jesus said, right?" she asked. "He said that the road to hell is wide and easy, while the way to heaven is narrow and harder to find. The easy way is not always right!" *SLK*

HOW ABOUT YOU?

Do you think that going to church and doing your best is the way to heaven—that everyone will be okay as long as they're sincere? That's a popular idea, but don't be fooled. The Bible says you must believe on Jesus Christ and accept his sacrifice for your sins. It's the only way to heaven.

**Come to God
through Jesus**

MEMORIZE:
"Small is the gate and narrow the road
that leads to life." Matthew 7:14, NIV

July
12

Contented Heart

Read Philippians 4:9-13

"My friends have all gone 'horsey'!" Becka complained one summer afternoon. "Every time I see them, they're either riding or grooming their horses. They're no fun at all lately."

"And all my friends have scooters," Dan said. "It sort of makes me feel left out. I think I'll ask Dad if he'll teach me how to make a few things with some of those pieces of wood in the basement."

Becka was surprised. "Don't tell me you're planning to spend the summer in the basement, Dan!" she exclaimed.

"Not all of it," he answered, "but this is a chance to learn something worthwhile."

Mom spoke up. "Dan is right, Becka," she agreed. "You could find a project, too—like ceramics lessons. Mrs. Holt is going to have a class."

"No way! I want to have fun during summer vacation—not classes," Becka retorted. Then, with a long face, she sighed, "I just wish I had a horse."

In the following days, Dan was happy with his woodwork. His friends stopped in often, and they were very impressed with the things he made. Becka, on the other hand, trailed after her girlfriends. Occasionally they let her ride their horses, but more and more she was left standing as they rode away. She was quite unhappy!

Mom talked to Becka about it. "I'm afraid, honey, that you've forgotten to be content with what you have," she said. "You've let your desire for something you can't have make you very unhappy."

Thoughtfully Becka nodded. "You know, Mom, Dan's friends still like him," she said, "but my friends don't seem to want me around. I guess I chased them till they got tired of me. Maybe I'll ask the Lord to help me be happy with what he's given me. Is it too late to sign up for ceramics?" *AGL*

HOW ABOUT YOU?

If your friends won't play when you want to—or what you want to—do you ever pout and feel angry? When nothing seems to go right, do you sit around being miserable? You'll have disappointments in life, but you don't have to let them get you down. Instead of pouting, ask the Lord to help you find a worthwhile activity. Maybe you could read a good book, sew, build something, learn a Bible verse, or play with your pet.

MEMORIZE:

"Godliness with contentment is great gain." 1 Timothy 6:6, NIV

Be Content

Gone for Good

Read Isaiah 6:7; Jeremiah 31:34

With her sidewalk chalk, Tabitha colored in the flowers she had drawn along the edge of the driveway. Then she stood back and frowned as she looked at them. Dad came out of the house and smiled at Tabitha. "What lovely flowers!" he exclaimed. "The best part is that I won't ever have to water them."

"No—but I'm going to," said Tabitha. "I just decided I want them in a different color." She took the garden hose, aimed the stream of water at her artwork, and—*whoosh!* All trace of the chalk soon disappeared down the driveway and into a storm drain. Tabitha grinned at Dad. "Now I can start all over," she said. "Cool, huh?"

"Cool," Dad agreed. "It's a picture of what God does for us. He gives us a chance to start over when we confess our sin to him."

"Oh, no! I can already see that my chalk flowers are going to be used in a sermon illustration," teased Tabitha. Dad was a pastor, and Tabitha knew that he often used everyday happenings to illustrate what he was teaching.

Dad nodded. "Sometimes it's hard for us to forget the bad things we've done," he said, "and we wonder how God can forgive them. You just demonstrated what happens to them. Where are the flowers you drew?"

"Where are the flowers?" repeated Tabitha. "Well, they're . . . gone."

"Bring them back for a minute," Dad said.

"I can't!" said Tabitha, aware that Dad knew she couldn't get them back. "They washed down the drain; they don't exist anymore."

"No, they don't," Dad agreed. "They're gone, never to be seen again. That's what happens to our sins when we repent and confess them to God. The Bible says God forgives and forgets them." He smiled at Tabitha. "Another verse says they've been removed from us as far as the east is from the west—that's even farther than down the drain!" *HWM*

HOW ABOUT YOU?

Have you done something wrong—perhaps even without thinking? Does it make you feel bad? It should! If you're truly sorry, confess your sin to God, and believe him when he says he forgives you. Thank him for removing your sin.

MEMORIZE:
"I will forgive their wickedness and will never again remember their sins."
Jeremiah 31:34

God Forgives and Removes Sin

The Ant Trap

Read 1 Corinthians 6:19-20

Kai came into the kitchen, her cheeks flushed. "Whew! It's getting hot out there!" she exclaimed.

Mom looked up from the family computer. "You didn't stay long at Cara's," she said in surprise.

"Well, I would have stayed longer," said Kai, "but then—" She broke off and pointed to a tiny container on the floor near the door. There were a few ants on the floor, too. "What's that, Mom?" asked Kai. "I think an ant just went into one of the holes on the side of it."

"Good!" Mom said. "That's an ant trap. I'm trying to get rid of the ants."

"That thing might catch a few," said Kai, "but there must be a lot more where those came from."

Mom nodded. "Yes," she agreed, "but the idea is for the ants to eat some of the poison bait and then take it to their colony. When that happens, the whole colony can be wiped out."

"Really!" exclaimed Kai. "It looks like such a little thing, but it's pretty deadly." She sat down at the table. "Mom," she said, "the reason I came home so soon is because Cara's mom isn't home. Cara's older cousin Amy was there, and she took out some cigarettes and started to smoke. She tried to get us to try them, too. I wouldn't, though. I'm not sure they were regular cigarettes, either— they smelled different. I decided to come home."

"Were they marijuana?" Mom asked.

"Maybe," said Kai. "Amy tried hard to get us to try them, and I didn't like that."

"You know, Kai, drugs are like that ant bait," Mom said. "They harm the person who uses them—but even worse, that person often tries to get others to use them. In the end, many lives may be ruined because one person took the bait and then offered it to others."

"I'm glad I didn't take the bait from Amy," said Kai.

"I'm glad, too," Mom agreed. "God wants us to have healthy bodies and minds." *EJB*

HOW ABOUT YOU?

Has anyone offered you something that would harm your body? Cigarettes may look quite harmless, but they can be deadly. If you're a Christian, your body is God's temple. Honor God in the way you take care of it and use it.

MEMORIZE:
"Honor God with your body."
1 Corinthians 6:20

Honor God by Caring for Your Body

The Way You Sound

Read Philippians 2:1-11

Simone ran into the living room and flung herself onto the couch, sobbing. "Nobody, absolutely nobody, will do anything I want to do," she wailed.

Mom followed her into the room. "Simone, I know you've been unhappy all day," she said. "Why don't you record on a cassette tape all the things that made you unhappy. I'll be back as soon as I get my cookies out of the oven, and we'll listen to it." Sniffing, Simone agreed, and she went to get the tape player.

Before long, Mom and Simone were listening to the recording Simone had made. "Well, I wanted Mitch to go for a bike ride," came her voice from the tape, "but he wanted to shoot baskets and I didn't. Then I wanted Trini to go with me instead. She said no and asked me to rollerblade with her, but I didn't want to. Cookie came over, and I wanted to play jacks, but she wanted to play hopscotch, so I told her to find somebody else to play with. Sid was too bossy. I wanted Bonnie to come out and play jacks, but she was helping Mom. Then I wanted to go out, and Mom made me clean my room—"

Click! Simone stopped the tape. "Oh, Mom, this sounds awful," she cried.

"Yes," Mom agreed, "and this is how you sound to others—and to God. You weren't trying to please anybody except yourself this morning. The other kids wanted to have fun, but you didn't try to please them, so you didn't have a good time!"

"I guess I wasn't very nice," confessed Simone. "I . . . I'm going to do better—honest!"

Mom smiled. "You'll need God's help, honey," she said. "Ask God each day to keep you from being selfish." She gave Simone a hug as she added, "When you start to say something selfish, think of how it will sound to others. With God's help, don't say it. You'll be happier when you're willing to put others ahead of yourself." *AGL*

HOW ABOUT YOU?

Is "I want" too much a part of your vocabulary? Would a recording of what you say show that you are selfish and always want your own way? A selfish person is not generally a happy person. Each day ask Jesus to help you put others ahead of yourself.

Put Others before Yourself

MEMORIZE:
"Be humble, thinking of others as better than yourself." Philippians 2:3

July
16

The Bug Spray

Read 1 Timothy 6:6-10

When Antonia entered the kitchen, Mom was putting the finishing touches on her birthday cake. "Toni, the ants have decided to come to your party," Mom said without looking up.

"Aunt Rose and Aunt Linda?" asked Toni.

Mom laughed and pointed to the floor where several ants were scurrying around. "Get the bug spray out and take care of them, please," she said.

As Toni squirted the ants, she choked down a sob. Mom set the cake aside and put an arm around Toni. "What's wrong, honey?"

"Everything!" exclaimed Toni between sobs. "I hate this old h-house and—and Roseanne is getting a whole new outfit for my birthday, and I'm not." Roseanne was Toni's cousin.

Mom sighed as she gave Toni a hug. "I'm doing the best I can," she said softly.

Toni tried to stop her tears. "I know, Mom. But it's not fair. Roseanne has a daddy and a nice home, and her mom doesn't have to work. Sometimes I almost hate Roseanne." She blew her nose. "I don't like being jealous. It makes me feel ugly—and I want to be happy for my birthday party."

"I know," Mom replied. "But there will always be people with more and people with less. Do you know what kills jealousy?" Toni shook her head. "A thankful spirit does," Mom continued. "After your dad left us, I was bitter for a while. When I became thankful for what I did have—you, my church family, my health, my job—I was no longer jealous of those who had more. A thankful spirit kills jealousy like that spray kills ants."

Toni wiped her eyes. "I'm thankful for you, Mom," she said. She tried to smile as she looked around her. "And I'm thankful for that cake you made and for friends who are coming to my party and for—oh! There's another ant!" She grabbed the bug spray. As she pushed the button, she said, "Next time I feel jealous, I'll remember to give it a big shot of thankfulness. It works. I feel better already." *BJW*

HOW ABOUT YOU?

Are you jealous of someone who has more than you do? Isn't that a horrible feeling? Take out a pencil and paper and list the things you're thankful to God for. You'll feel better right away.

MEMORIZE:

"Let the peace of Christ rule in your hearts. . . . And be thankful."
Colossians 3:15, NIV

Be Thankful

Light for Life's Path

Read Psalm 119:33-40

"Come along, kids. We're going on a hike," Dad said.

Logan looked up in surprise. "Now?" he asked. "A hike at night! Cool!"

Whitney wasn't so sure it was a good idea. "It's awfully dark," she said. "I hope we don't get lost."

"We won't," Dad said. "We'll take flashlights so we can see the path."

"Okay," agreed Whitney. "Are you coming, Mom?"

"I sure am," Mom said, and with the help of flashlights, they were soon walking along the path in the dark. They enjoyed hearing the night sounds and watching for birds and animals that ventured out at night.

"Which way?" asked Logan when they came to a fork in the trail. "Where are we going?"

"I don't know," Mom said. "This hike is Dad's idea."

"We'll take the left path here," Dad said.

Whenever they had to decide which way to go, Dad made the decision. "We'll soon be back at our campsite," Dad said before long.

"We will?" asked Whitney, shining her flashlight all around. "Good thing you know where we're going. I have no idea where we are! Are you sure we're not lost, Dad?"

Dad chuckled. "Trust me," he said. As he predicted, they were soon back at their campsite.

"That was awesome!" declared Logan. "Let's go hiking every night."

"This night hike gives a good illustration of the meaning of a verse you kids memorized for Bible club last week," Mom said.

"I was thinking of it too," said Whitney. "God's Word is a lamp for our feet, right?"

Mom nodded. "The flashlights lit up a little of our path—just enough to see a few steps ahead," she explained, "and God's Word lights our path through life—a few steps at a time. It doesn't show us the whole path at once."

"Right," Dad agreed. "I knew where we were going tonight, but you didn't. You had to trust me, and we need to trust God as he uses his Word to light the way for us." *KMS*

HOW ABOUT YOU?

Are you using your "flashlight"—the Bible—as a guide through life? It gives many principles to show how you should live. Obey God's directions and trust him. He has a plan for your life and will show it to you, a little at a time, as you obey him.

God's Word Will Light Life's Path

MEMORIZE:
"Your word is a lamp for my feet and a light for my path." Psalm 119:105

Danger! Stay Away!

Read Psalm 1

"This is great, Uncle Mike!" exclaimed Kendra as she helped her uncle with the chores. "I'm glad Mom sent me to spend the summer with you here on the farm." She frowned. "Mom worries too much, though," added Kendra. "She doesn't like some of my friends back home—she thinks they're rough. Just because I hang around with them, it doesn't mean I'll do the stuff they do."

Uncle Mike frowned. "Yes, but friends of that kind will often tempt you to sin," he said. "Instead of seeing how far you can go along with the crowd without sinning, wouldn't it be smarter to keep clear of tempting situations?" Kendra just shrugged.

Uncle Mike cautiously opened the door to another room in the barn. It contained a heavily constructed stall in which there was a big, mean-looking bull with long horns. "This bull is the reason I don't let you play in this part of the barn," said Uncle Mike. "He's very dangerous. The man I bought him from told me he nearly gored a man to death with those horns."

"He did?" asked Kendra. "How did it happen?"

"Well, the man knew the animal could be mean, but he had raised this bull from the time it was a baby. He figured he knew it well and knew how to take care of himself. As he was putting clean straw in the bull's pen one day, he turned his back—just for a moment," explained Uncle Mike. "That was all it took. The bull rushed him and gored him." Uncle Mike shook his head. "If that man had stayed out of the bull's reach, he wouldn't have been hurt. Sin is like that. The only way to be safe is just to stay away from it. Choose friends who won't lead you into sin."

Kendra looked thoughtful. "But I have to be with the kids from school sometimes," she said.

"Right," agreed Uncle Mike, "but you don't have to be close friends with those who would encourage you to go along with wrong decisions. Dare to say no right from the start." *HCT*

HOW ABOUT YOU?

Do you think it won't hurt you to have close friends who like to do wrong things? Do you think you can take care of yourself? Satan is very clever. He likes you to think you can get close to sin and not be harmed. Don't let him fool you. Stay away from those who would tempt you.

MEMORIZE:

"Oh, the joys of those who do not follow the advice of the wicked, or stand around with sinners, or join in with scoffers." Psalm 1:1

Choose Friends Who Honor God

The Quiet Times

Read 1 Kings 19:9-12

Grandpa and Christine took their fishing gear and went to a nearby river. After sitting on the bank for a little while, Christine moved to another spot. Soon she got up and moved again. Before long, her excitement over fishing faded. "The fish aren't biting for me today," she said sadly. She looked at the fish her grandfather had caught. "Why are they biting for you and not me?" asked Christine.

"Well, you keep pulling in your line to check your bait, and that's the fourth fishing spot you've tried, Christine," Grandpa answered. "If you want to catch fish, try sitting still."

Christine sighed. "I don't like to sit still," she murmured.

"Well, unless you do, you'll miss out on a lot," Grandpa said. "Today you'll just miss a few fish, but someday you may miss more important things. For example, if you don't sit quietly and listen in school, you may fail a test. More importantly, if you don't take time to sit still and listen to God, you may fail to hear him."

Christine frowned. "You mean like Samuel heard him in the Bible?" she asked. "God doesn't talk to us like that anymore, does he?"

"Not like that," Grandpa said, "but if you set aside a special time to think about God, he may speak quietly to your heart. He may say he loves you, or he may make you aware of something he wants you to do."

"I pray every night," Christine told her grandfather.

"That's you talking again," Grandpa reminded her. "Let God talk to you."

"Can we be still and listen for God now?" asked Christine. Grandpa smiled and agreed. A few minutes later, Christine whispered, "I don't hear God, but I hear the water and the birds. It sounds like music!"

"God's music," agreed Grandpa. "It's the prettiest music in the world."

"I've got a bite!" Christine yelled suddenly. Soon she was taking a fish off her hook. "Look at that fish! It paid to sit still that time, didn't it?"

"It sure did," agreed Grandpa, "and it will pay off every time—in even better ways. Keep trying it!" *BJW*

HOW ABOUT YOU?

Do you take time to quietly wait for God to speak to your heart? Before reading the Bible, ask God to teach you through it. It's good to pause and wait for him to bring to your mind the lessons he wants you to learn.

Listen to God and Obey Him

MEMORIZE:
"Be still, and know that I am God."
Psalm 46:10, NIV

Follow the Rules

Read Proverbs 28:13; 29:15

Britta's friend, Nick, had a flat tire on his bike, so Britta ran home to see if she could use Dad's tire pump. She knew where her dad kept his tools, and usually Dad didn't mind if she borrowed his things. "Just follow my rules," Dad had said. "Get permission first, and put away what you borrow as soon as you're finished." But this time Dad wasn't home to ask. Britta shrugged and took the pump anyway. The kids fixed the tire and then went for a ride.

As Britta and Nick were returning home, it began to rain. "Don't bother to stop for your pump. I'll bring it over in the morning," Nick promised.

Britta hesitated. "Well . . . all right," she agreed. She felt a little guilty as she sped on home.

The next morning, Nick called Britta. "I can't find the pump anywhere," he said.

"Oh, no!" groaned Britta. "I have to get it back where it belongs before Dad notices."

"Look . . . just don't let on that you know anything about it," urged Nick. "If you don't say anything, no one will even know we used it."

At first that seemed like a good idea, but as the morning passed, Britta felt very uncomfortable about the whole thing. "I'm gonna have to tell," she muttered to herself. With a sigh, she went to her dad and told him the whole story.

Dad nodded. "Nick's dad called me just a few minutes ago," he said. "He found the pump last night and took it in out of the rain. He said it just occurred to him that it was mine, and he's sending Nick over with it now. As for you . . . consider yourself grounded."

"Aw, Dad . . . can't we just forget about it this one time?" pleaded Britta. "I did come and tell you about it."

"Yes, you did, and I appreciate that," Dad said. "Actually, I had intended to ground you for a week, but because you were honest about this, Britta, I'm going to ground you for only the rest of the day. And next time, follow the rules." *AGL*

HOW ABOUT YOU?

Do you follow the rules God gives in his Word? He expects you to obey them. If you disobey, confess your sin to him and experience his mercy. Then humbly accept any discipline he may send, and learn from it.

MEMORIZE:

"People who cover over their sins will not prosper. But if they confess and forsake them, they will receive mercy." Proverbs 28:13

Follow God's Rules

Fuel on the Fire

Read 2 Timothy 2:22-26

As Melinda and Daria were studying, their mom came to their room, holding her jewelry box. "I told you girls that if you look at my jewelry you must return the box to my room," Mom said sternly. "I found it sticking halfway out of your closet door."

"We're sorry, Mom," Daria said quickly. "We won't leave it out again, will we, Melinda?"

"No, you won't," Mom answered, "because you aren't allowed to play with it again!" Melinda began to protest that she was not to blame, but Mom didn't seem to hear as she turned and went out to the garage.

Melinda glared at Daria, "Why didn't you tell Mom I wasn't looking at her jewelry?" demanded Melinda, angrily. "You're the one who took the box and left it in our room."

Daria shrugged. "You play with Mom's jewelry as often as I do," she said. "Besides, you saw how angry she is! I'm not about to take the blame by myself."

As Melinda raised a hand to slap her sister, she vaguely remembered her youth leader kneeling down by a small fire at a recent campout. "What happens, kids, when I place wood on the fire?" Pastor Bill had asked.

"The fire gets bigger," someone had answered as the dry kindling started to burn, causing the fire to grow.

"That's right," agreed Pastor Bill. "What will happen if no more wood is added?"

"The fire will go out," came the quick response.

"Right." Pastor Bill nodded. "I want you to remember that Proverbs 26:20 compares a fire to an argument or a quarrel. Without wood a fire goes out, and without angry words or attitudes, a quarrel dies down. God doesn't want his children to quarrel. He commands us to be gentle and to love one another."

Melinda knew a big fight would erupt if she continued arguing with Daria— it had happened many times before. In fact, she could see that Daria was braced for an angry confrontation now. Melinda hesitated only a moment. Then she turned and walked away muttering quietly, "This time I'll do what God says I should." *GDF*

HOW ABOUT YOU?

If someone does or says something you dislike or that hurts your feelings, what do you do? If someone starts a quarrel with you, do you add fuel to the fire by saying something nasty in return? Obey God and be gentle, kind, and patient.

MEMORIZE:
"The Lord's servants must not quarrel but must be kind to everyone."
2 Timothy 2:24

Stop Quarrels

July
22

The Mime

Read Matthew 7:16-20

As Roberta and her mom got off the ferris wheel, Roberta pointed to a crowd of people. "Can we go see what's going on over there?" she asked. Mom nodded, and they walked over and joined the crowd.

Roberta was fascinated as she watched a man with a white painted face acting out various skits. The crowd laughed as the man pretended to be learning to ride a bike. "Mom, why doesn't he talk?" asked Roberta.

"Because he's a mime," Mom replied. "They never talk, but you can always tell what they're doing. Just watch—you'll see."

Next, the mime pretended to wash a window. He acted as though he bumped his head on the pretend ladder. Then he pretended he was eating an ice cream cone and the ice cream fell off. The crowd applauded as he acted out one scenario after another. The show ended with the mime making a sad face and waving good-bye.

Roberta turned to her mom. "Wow! He never said a thing, but I could follow the whole story."

"That goes to show you how loudly actions—even facial expressions—speak," Mom said. "It's good to remember that our actions really do speak louder than our words."

"Do my actions ever tell you anything?" asked Roberta.

"Sure they do," Mom said. "For instance, just yesterday I told you to clean your room. When you agreed and then rolled your eyes, I knew what you were saying."

"Oh, Mom!" protested Roberta. "I did clean my room!"

"Yes, you did," Mom agreed. "Your actions showed me two things. First of all, they told me that you didn't really want to clean your room. They also told me that you are an obedient daughter, because you cleaned it anyway." She smiled. "What I really want to point out is that as Christians, we should be especially careful how we act." *ASB*

HOW ABOUT YOU?
Are you aware that your actions speak loudly? Make sure they say good things—things that God wants to hear you saying. Show consideration, kindness, and God's love in actions as well as in words.

MEMORIZE:
"Even children are known by the way they act, whether their conduct is pure and right." Proverbs 20:11

Actions Are Important

Fence of Protection

Read Psalm 27:1-6

"Oh, Shari, can't we take Elm Street to Aunt Lizzie's?" Rachel pleaded as she walked along with her sister.

Shari shook her head. "That would make it too much farther," she answered, "and it's far enough already." Rounding the corner they could see the corner of Aunt Lizzie's street only three blocks away.

"Oh, I hope that big dog doesn't come out to chase us this time," Rachel said nervously as they approached a fenced yard.

"Did you forget the stuff we talked about yesterday?" Shari asked bravely. "We don't have to be afraid, 'cuz Jesus is with us, remember?" Suddenly a large, mean-looking dog began to growl. He was near the back of the yard, but turned toward the children as they walked by. Then, showing his teeth, he started in their direction.

"Run!" Shari yelled, and both children dashed down the street. And just as though the dog thought Shari was talking to him, he ran, too, right toward the children. He ran so hard that he slammed right into the chain-link fence that surrounded the yard. Then he stood there, fur raised, barking angrily. Shari and Rachel didn't slow down until they were several houses away. When they finally turned to look at the dog, he sat watching them, growling.

When they arrived, they told Aunt Lizzie about it. "Shari forgot all about how God was protecting her—you should have seen her run," Rachel teased her sister. "We didn't really have to be afraid, though. That fence kept the dog away from us."

"Yeah," Shari said, "but all I saw was the big dog." She laughed a little sheepishly. "I didn't even notice the fence."

Aunt Lizzie nodded. "Jesus has a 'fence of protection' around us all the time," she said, "but often the things that frighten us keep us from seeing that—and from remembering it. After this, every time you're afraid, think of the fence. Let it remind you that Jesus has promised to take care of you." *JAG*

HOW ABOUT YOU?

Did you know Jesus has a "fence of protection" around you? Fierce dogs, being alone, a hard math test, a raging thunderstorm, or giving an oral book report cannot tear down that fence of protection. This doesn't mean that you should go places that are dangerous or do risky things. But it does mean that God is in control and will take care of you when bad things happen. If you belong to Jesus, claim the promise that he will keep you in his care.

**Jesus' Care
Surrounds You**

MEMORIZE:
"But the Lord is faithful; he will make you strong and guard you from the evil one." 2 Thessalonians 3:3

July
24

Who Is Guilty?

Read Ephesians 5:6-16

Excitement filled the courtroom as one witness after another told about the defendant. All agreed that he was often fun to be with, he amused and entertained them, he told them of his travels, and he passed along a wide range of knowledge. But after he had established himself in their houses, many parents noticed that he often used very bad language, told dirty stories, displayed anger and violence, and was a bad influence for their children.

"Because of a story he told, I ran away from home," fifteen-year-old Sadie testified.

"He taught me that it's smart to drink," her brother, Josh, added. "I have problems with that now."

Another boy cried as he said, "He told me and my friend, Brett, that he had a foolproof plan for robbing a store. We tried it, but the store owner had a gun. Brett was killed."

"He told me that whatever I want to do is okay, and that others should accept me as I am," one girl stated.

And so it went all morning. Finally the defendant himself was called to the stand and asked to state his name. "I am Mr. T. Vee," he said. He went on to point out that the government allowed freedom of speech. "And I was only exercising my rights," he stated. "Besides, I was invited into each home by parents and children alike. They could have asked me to leave, but they never did."

When all testimony had been heard, the judge spoke. "Although I believe Mr. T. Vee is guilty of the charges brought against him, I cannot convict him," Judge Terrence stated. "He was an invited guest in each home, and the law does allow free exchange of ideas. It was the responsibility of those in the home to ask him to go. Since they did not, they are as guilty as he! Case dismissed!" *HCT*

HOW ABOUT YOU?

Is your TV on too much? Do you listen when God's name is used lightly? Do you listen to the dirty jokes? Immoral stories? Violence? These things will influence you. Turn off the TV set when this kind of programming is on. You're responsible before God for what you see and hear. (Note to parents: Do you know what your children are watching?)

MEMORIZE:

"Take no part in the worthless deeds of evil and darkness; instead, rebuke and expose them." Ephesians 5:11

Use the TV "Off" Switch

Kristi's Foolish Pride

Read Proverbs 16:16-20

"Has anyone seen my Sunday school book?" Kristi wailed one Sunday morning. "I can't find it anywhere." No one had seen it, and finally Kristi remembered she had left it at Peggy's house. Her perfect record would be spoiled! She had always had her lesson done, memorized her verse, and brought her Bible.

Kristi felt sick about ruining her record. *Maybe if I were sick, I could make up the lesson,* she thought. So back to bed she went, and there she stayed while her family went to church—except for Mom, who insisted on staying home with her.

When her brother returned, he brought her book. "Peggy sent this," he said. "Peggy wondered if you were still going to her house this afternoon, but Mom says you can't go," Carl continued. "And Carol said to try to come tonight. The Junior Choir sings, you know. She says if you can't come, she'll have to do that solo part, but she has a cold."

Oh no! I forgot all about those things, Kristi thought. *I really want to go, and I'm tired of lying in bed.* So Kristi announced that she felt better.

But Mom wasn't convinced. "If you were so sick that you had to miss Sunday school, you'd better stay home the rest of the day, too," she said. When Mom found Kristi sobbing into her pillow that evening, she was really concerned. "What's wrong, honey? Do you feel worse?" she asked.

Kristi shook her head. "I just wanted to go to church. I'm not sick. I wasn't sick this morning, either," she confessed.

"Kristi, Kristi!" Mom exclaimed when she learned what had happened. "Is that all your Sunday school lessons mean to you? How foolish to be so proud! Not only that, but you lied in the process. I'm afraid you were holding your head so high with pride that you couldn't see where you were going, and you tripped and fell."

"I sure did," Kristi agreed. "I got what I deserved. Next time I feel proud, I'll remember today." *AGL*

HOW ABOUT YOU?

Are you proud because you're the best at something? Best looking? Best dressed? Smartest? Most faithful? Do you feel that you deserve the praise of others? Be careful of that pride! Be sure God gets the glory for whatever he may accomplish through you.

MEMORIZE:
"Pride goes before destruction, and haughtiness before a fall."
Proverbs 16:18

Don't Be Too Proud

July
26

The Unseen Wind

Read 2 Kings 5:1-15

"Mom, why did God let me be crippled?" Karen asked one day. Shortly before her accident, Karen had dedicated her life to the Lord, and she had been quite sure he wanted her to be a missionary. But now the doctor said she'd never walk again!

"We don't know why God allowed this to happen, honey," Mom answered, "but we do know God has a perfect reason."

Karen sighed. "I just don't understand," she said. "I told God I was willing to go to the mission field in Africa. How can I do that here in a wheelchair?"

"I don't know, Karen, but if that's what God wants for you, he will make a way," Mom assured her.

A few days later, Karen read John 3:8—"The wind blows wherever it pleases." An idea came to her. *I could take cards, write Scripture on one side and my name and e-mail address on the other, attach a balloon to them, and then send them out on the wind,* she thought. *God could direct them to the people he wants them to go to.* So with her mother's help, she prepared the balloons. Then with prayers for God's guidance, Karen sent them off.

Karen was very excited when she received an e-mail one day. A man named Dr. Conrad wrote to tell her that he had found one of the balloons and had been unable to get the Bible verse out of his mind. He was a Christian and was now convinced God wanted him to be a missionary doctor to Africa! "Oh-h-h, I'm so glad," Karen sighed happily. "I'm going to pray for you every day," she wrote. And she did.

Before long, Dr. Conrad was serving God in Africa. Karen was thrilled when she received an e-mail telling of his first convert there. "God works in mysterious ways," he wrote. "Through me, he is using you to share Jesus' love in Africa even though you are in a wheelchair in the United States!"

Karen knew now that although her life would not be what she had planned, God was showing her his power in ways she had never expected. *HCT*

HOW ABOUT YOU?

Would you like to be a missionary to a foreign land? How about right where you are? Do you care about those who live in your neighborhood and those who go to your school? Pray for them. Tell your family, your friends, and your neighbors about God. Be faithful where you are. Only God knows how far-reaching your testimony will be.

MEMORIZE:

"Don't get tired of doing what is good. Don't get discouraged and give up, for we will reap a harvest of blessing at the appropriate time."
Galatians 6:9

**Witness Where
God Puts You**

A True Investment

Read Luke 12:15-21

On their birthday, twins Carmela and Sam visited their grandparents, and Grandpa gave them a personal tour of the bank where he worked. Just before leaving the bank, he took them into his office and gave each a personal savings account book. "I deposited some money into an account for each of you," he said. "Be sure to spend your money wisely—and I advise you not to spend all of it. Save some."

"I will," Sam stated firmly. "In fact, I'll save it all. Then it earns interest, doesn't it? I'll just sit back and relax, and pretty soon I'll have more and more and—"

"And you'll be a miser and an old man!" Carmela interrupted. "I'm going to save some of mine, but I'm going to use some to buy a piece of fake fur and eyes to make puppets. I'll sell them at Mom's yard sale next month. In a few weeks I'll probably have way more than you'll have in years!"

Grandpa chuckled. "Our family has always had bankers and businessmen," he said. "You have that heritage, and it sounds like you two fit right in. But our family has another heritage—a more important one. Can you guess what that is? It has nothing to do with money or investments."

"Oh, I know!" Carmela exclaimed, after thinking about it. "I've heard Dad say that we have a 'godly' heritage!"

"Oh, yeah," Sam agreed. "That's because Dad's a preacher, and Aunt Ellen's a missionary in Africa, and Uncle Ed's in seminary."

"And all our grandparents believe in Jesus, too," Carmela added.

Grandpa relaxed in his chair. "They've all invested their lives in serving God," he said. "I give you this money with my blessing, but remember that committing your life—including your money—to Jesus is the greatest and most satisfying investment any person can make." *RG*

HOW ABOUT YOU?

Does making a lot of money seem important to you? Never forget that money is only temporary. Unless you use your money for the Lord, it has no lasting value. Don't allow yourself to get all caught up in buying things. Invest your life in doing things that will last.

Money Doesn't Last

MEMORIZE:
"Be generous and willing to share."
1 Timothy 6:18, NIV

Spiritual Health

Read Psalm 27:11

"What do you have in your mouth, Annette?" Mom asked.

Annette quickly swallowed the half-eaten cookie. Its rough edges scraped down her throat. She was barely able to whisper, "Nothing." Chocolate crumbs spewed out in all directions.

"Nothing?" Mom shook her head. "What have I told you about telling me the truth?"

Annette hurriedly swallowed again, running her tongue over her teeth. "I didn't—"

Mom's voice sounded grieved. "Annette, we both know you're lying. Why?"

Annette kept her head down. "I didn't want you to know I took a cookie," she admitted.

"Look at me, Annette," Mom insisted. Reluctantly, Annette lifted her eyes. "We have two problems here," Mom continued. "You see, I love you very much, and I'm concerned about your health. I want you to eat the right foods. That's why I said you could have only two cookies when you came in. If you need more to eat, have a carrot or some celery."

"But I took only one extra," Annette murmured.

"Yes, but that brings us to the second and more serious problem—your spiritual health," Mom answered. "First you disobeyed, and then you lied. For good spiritual health you must learn not to lie, cheat, or steal. It fills you with guilt—you're guilty before God as well as before me."

"I'm sorry." Annette's eyes were filled with tears. "Will you forgive me? I really am sorry."

"Yes," Mom nodded. "I know God will forgive, too, but you must ask him."

"Okay." Annette nodded, slipping her hand into her mom's. "I will." *RG*

HOW ABOUT YOU?

Do you sneak things that have been forbidden to you? Do you sometimes lie to cover up your wrong actions? This habit will defeat you spiritually and get you into deeper trouble. Even if you succeed in fooling your parents, don't forget that God knows all about it. Ask him to forgive you and help you be honest.

MEMORIZE:

"Let us walk honestly." Romans 13:13, KJV

Be Honest

Like a Badger (Part 1)

Read Romans 12:9-18

"Hey, this animal is cool!" Caleb said, looking up from his magazine.

Angie peered over his shoulder. "Ooh! A badger! Isn't he cute?"

"You say 'cute' for everything!" protested Caleb. "When I say 'cool,' I mean it's interesting, not cute!"

Angie sniffed. "Well, I think that badger is cute," she insisted, "but what do you find so interesting about it?"

"Well, according to this article, badgers' homes are underground, and they're interconnected by a whole maze of burrows and passages," said Caleb.

"Hey, that is cool," Angie agreed. "That means they can visit each other."

Caleb nodded. "This says that badgers are nocturnal animals." He grinned. "That means . . . "

"I know what that means," said Angie. "It means they are awake at night and sleep during the day."

"You got it!" said Caleb. "Listen to this: 'If a badger is away from home when day breaks, he may stay and rest with another badger family for a while before heading for his own home.' "

Angie laughed. "Maybe the ones traveling are missionary badgers, and the ones they stay with are like our family," she joked. "Remember when those missionaries stayed with us not long ago?"

Caleb grinned. "There's more," he said. "It says here that sometimes the badgers even allow a fox to stay over! I haven't seen you entertain any foxes lately."

"Oh, I don't know," Angie said. "That's like . . . that's like . . . I can't think of anything that it's like."

"I can," said Caleb. "That might be like inviting someone you don't know very well—like those new kids who have started coming to Bible club—to come over and play."

"Better not let them hear you comparing them to foxes," said Angie, "but you're probably right. We'd be practicing hospitality, like our Bible club memory verse said we should." *MTF*

HOW ABOUT YOU?

Hospitality is one of the many virtues the Bible says you should have. Do you practice it both with friends and with kids you don't know well? Talk to the new girl in your class. Have lunch with the guy who always sits alone. Ask the lonely person to play with you at recess time. Make each one feel welcome and wanted.

MEMORIZE:
"Practice hospitality." Romans 12:13, NIV

Practice Hospitality

July

30

Like a Badger (Part 2)

Read Romans 12:4-8

"I found out more about badgers," Angie announced as the family sat down to dinner. "I checked out the encyclopedia."

"I can't imagine you bothering with heavy stuff like research," Caleb teased.

"I know I'm not as good as you at intellectual stuff, but I'm better at sports than you are," said Angie. "Anyway, have you ever heard of a ratel?"

Caleb, Mom, and Dad all shook their heads.

"It's a small animal, like a badger, and it's sometimes called the 'honey badger,' " Angie told them.

"Because it likes honey?" Caleb guessed.

"Right!" Angie said. "The honey badger has a bird friend called the 'honey guide.' When the honey guide discovers a beehive full of honey, it calls the honey badger and leads the way to the hive. Then the honey badger uses its claws to break open the hive, and it enjoys a treat of lovely, sticky honey while the honey guide patiently waits."

"Doesn't the honey guide get to eat some of the honey, too?" asked Caleb. Angie shook her head.

"Well, eating up all the honey isn't a friendly thing to do!" Caleb declared. "I don't think the honey badgers are very hospitable."

"The honey guide doesn't want the honey," said Angie. "It likes the beeswax and larvae, and that's what the honey badger leaves behind."

"Interesting," Mom said. "Each one helps the other."

Dad nodded. "It's another example of how the Lord has blessed each one with different gifts and talents," he said. "That seems to be true both in the animal kingdom and among humans. Some people are blessed with musical ability. Some are good at sports. Some have the gift of helping others. God wants us to use our gifts, not just for our own benefit, but also to serve one another." *MTF*

HOW ABOUT YOU?

What special talent, skill, or ability has God given you? Think about it. There is something you do well. Use that ability to help someone. Can you visit, share your things, give money, listen, pray, or lend a helping hand? Then do it today.

MEMORIZE:
"Do not neglect your gift." 1 Timothy 4:14, NIV

Use the Talent God Gave You

In the Way

Read Judges 6:12-17, 36-40

"Cat, you're driving me crazy!" Annika complained as she stepped over Mittens, the cat.

"What is Mittens doing?" Mom asked.

"Nothing. It's just that I've stepped on his tail so often," explained Annika. "I don't do it on purpose, but he's underfoot. Why does he just sit in the middle of the floor where we're likely to step on him?"

"I guess he trusts us to know he's there and to walk around him," Mom said.

"Well, he ought to watch out since we're so much bigger than he is," muttered Annika.

"I like to see how much he trusts us," Mom said. "If we were small and he were big, do you think we'd trust him not to hurt us?"

"Not me!" exclaimed Annika. "His claws are sharp. If he were any bigger, he'd be dangerous!"

"I can think of someone much bigger than we are who we can always trust," Mom said.

"You mean Dad?" asked Annika.

"Someone bigger than Dad," Mom replied.

"Who?" asked Annika. Then she answered her own question. "I know—God! He's so big he can take care of the whole world, and he never hurts us by mistake. Do you think we do things to get in God's way—like Mittens gets in our way?"

"I'll have to think about that," Mom said thoughtfully. After a moment, she said, "When Mr. Cardoso had a broken leg, it took me a long time to realize that taking dinner to him each day was a job God wanted me to do. I don't know why it took me so long—it's easy for me to do since we live right across the street. Maybe you could say that on every day I didn't do it, I was in the way—and God had to 'step over' me to find someone else to help." Mom grinned at Annika. "Whenever you have to step over Mittens, let it be a reminder not to make God 'step over' you and find someone else to do something he's asking you to do." *DMM*

HOW ABOUT YOU?

Are you sensitive to what God wants you to do to serve him? Are you willing to help your parents, a new kid at school, or a neighbor? Are you ready to go out of your way to be kind to someone? Don't get in the way of God's work. When he shows you what you can do for him, say, "I'll go! Send me."

MEMORIZE:

"I heard the Lord asking, 'Whom should I send as a messenger to my people? Who will go for us?' And I said, 'Lord, I'll go! Send me.'" Isaiah 6:8

Say Yes to Serving

Salted Leeches

Read Matthew 5:13-16

Jenny and Mark came laughing and splashing out of the water and onto the beach near their family cabin. The cool water felt wonderful on such a warm day, but as Jenny began toweling off, she stopped laughing. She shrieked in horror and pointed at her ankle.

Their mother came running from the cabin. "What's wrong? Are you hurt?" she asked.

Jenny pointed at her ankle and began to cry. "It's a leech! Get it off!" she exclaimed. "Get it off!"

"Calm down, honey," Mom said. "We'll take care of it. Mark, go into the cabin and get the salt shaker."

Mark ran for the salt while Jenny continued to moan and cry. Soon he was back and handed the salt shaker to Mom. "Watch," she said. Kneeling down, she poured salt on the leech. Immediately, the slimy little black blob curled up into a ball and fell to the sand. "There. All better," Mom said. "That wasn't so bad, was it?"

Jenny sniffed and tried to smile. "How did you know that salt would make it let go, Mom?"

Mom grinned. "It's an old trick I learned as a kid. When you live near a lake, you learn how to take care of leeches," she said. "My Sunday school teacher taught a lesson one day that has helped me to remember this little trick. She was explaining a verse in the Bible that talks about Christians being the salt of the earth, and I remembered how we used salt on leeches. I told my teacher about it, and she said we can think of sin as a slimy black leech clinging to people and sucking the life out of them. We Christians are the salt that will help release those people from the sin that is stuck to them."

"God has to do that, doesn't he?" Mark asked.

Mom nodded. "Yes, but God wants us to be like salt, helping people want to be free from their sin problem. We do that by living the way God wants us to and telling others what Jesus has done for them." *KMS*

HOW ABOUT YOU?

Do you know people who need to be set free from the grip of sin? Have you told them about Jesus and his gift of salvation? As the salt of the earth, Christians need to get out God's message—that Jesus sets sinners free.

Be a "Salty" Christian

August

2

Grounded in Love

Read Hebrews 12:5-11

Belinda was grounded for the day. She stared out the kitchen window and sighed. "Today's too beautiful to be stuck in here," she grumbled.

Mom handed her another dish to dry. "You should have thought of that yesterday when you decided to come home an hour late."

Belinda sulked. She dried the dish and continued to stare out the window. Her neighbors were tying up their Great Dane dog. "Poor Samson," she said. "He's being chained up. The Smiths aren't even letting him run around in the yard. He's a prisoner today, just like me."

They watched the big dog pull on his chain, trying to get loose. "He sure doesn't like those chains," Mom said.

Belinda put away the dry dish. "Why are the Smiths so mean to him?"

"Honey, they're not being mean," Mom replied. "Actually, they're showing him love."

Belinda raised her eyebrows. "Love!" she exclaimed. "I don't see how you can call that treatment showing love!"

Mom frowned. "Yesterday while I was pacing on the porch, waiting for you, Samson dashed into the street and almost got hit by a truck," she said. "The Smiths were terribly upset. They told me they were going to keep Samson chained up until new fencing is installed. They want him to be safe." Mom looked at Belinda solemnly. "Samson's freedom has been taken away because his owners care about him. In families, privileges are sometimes taken away out of love, too."

"You mean me, don't you?" asked Belinda.

Mom nodded. "You're grounded today because I love you," she said. "I want you to be healthy and safe."

Belinda gave her mother a little smile. "I'm glad you love me so much. I'm sorry I disobeyed," she said softly and grinned. "I'll have to thank Samson for teaching me a lesson today." *SML*

HOW ABOUT YOU?

Do you think your parents are mean when they punish you? Does it make you feel unloved? It shouldn't. God says that he disciplines his children out of love, the way earthly parents discipline their children. It's a sign that someone cares. Next time you're being punished, accept the correction as proof that you are loved.

MEMORIZE:

"A wise child accepts a parent's discipline." Proverbs 13:1

Accept Discipline

Really Forgiven

Read Psalm 103:8-14

CRASH! The sound shattered the afternoon quiet, and Julie stared in dismay at the pieces of blue glass on the floor. All summer she had been cleaning house for Mrs. Burns, an older woman from church. Now as Julie was dusting, she had accidentally knocked a beautiful vase from a dresser in the guest room. *Oh, no! What will I do?* she thought as her eyes filled with tears. *What will Mrs. Burns say when she gets back and finds out?*

Julie picked up the pieces of broken glass and put them in a bag, all the while struggling to stop the flow of tears. Before leaving, she wrote a note explaining what had happened and that she would pay for a new vase. *But what if this one was very expensive?* Julie's thoughts ran on.

At home, Julie told her mother about the vase. "Telling Mrs. Burns that you'll pay for a new one was the right thing to do," Mom said.

Mrs. Burns called that evening. "Thank you for leaving the note," she said, "but don't worry about paying for the vase. Just be more careful after this." Julie felt much better after the call. But even though Mrs. Burns had said not to worry about it, Julie couldn't stop thinking about the vase.

On Sunday, Julie approached Mrs. Burns. "You're sure I don't owe you anything?" she asked. Her voice trembled slightly.

The older woman's gaze rested on Julie's face for a few moments. "Owe me?" she asked uncertainly.

Julie nodded. "For the vase I broke," she said.

"Oh, yes—the vase," Mrs. Burns said. She shook her head. "I had forgotten about it, and I can't even remember what it was worth. It's forgiven, so you should forget about it, too, dear."

Later that day, Julie told her mother what Mrs. Burns had said. "I think she really had forgotten all about it."

Mom smiled. "That's a good example of the way God forgives our sin. Mrs. Burns forgave you and forgot about it. When we confess our sin, God forgives us, and he forgets it, too! He'll never bring it up again." *KRL*

HOW ABOUT YOU?

Do you continue to feel bad about something you did wrong, even after you have confessed it to God and asked him to forgive you? The Bible says that he removes our sins as far as the "east is from the west," and he "remembers them no more." Since he forgives you, you can forgive yourself.

God Forgives and Forgets Sin

4

Dustpan Needed

Read Romans 13:11-14

Mindy was helping by sweeping the kitchen at her grandma's house, where she was staying. She sighed as she leaned on her broom. "Why is it so hard to be a Christian?" she asked. "I mean . . . well, at camp last month, we had a speaker who talked about the influence of music, and I promised God that I'd be more careful about what I listen to. For a while I did okay. Then I started looking through my CDs one day, and I just couldn't stop myself from playing one of my old favorites. The lyrics weren't all that great. Afterwards, I told God I was sorry."

"Well, that's a start," Grandma encouraged.

"I don't know." Mindy sighed again as she swept all the dirt into a big pile. "My friends listen to everything, so when I'm with them, I'm listening to the same kind of garbage as before. It's just no use!" Before Grandma could comment, the phone rang, and Mindy went to answer it. Grandma took a load of laundry to the basement.

Some time later, Grandma returned to the kitchen. "Mindy! Come here!" she called.

When Mindy came in, she saw that the big pile of dirt she had carefully swept up was scattered all over the floor. "Oh, no!" she groaned. "I forgot to pick up the dirt. Looks like the dog has gotten into it."

Grandma nodded. "This reminds me of your problem with music," she said. Mindy looked at the dirty floor and back at Grandma. "The dirt got spread around again because you didn't do anything to get rid of it permanently," Grandma explained, "just as you didn't do anything to get rid of certain kinds of music permanently."

"How can I do that?" Mindy asked.

"Well, for one thing, you could throw away those CDs," Grandma suggested. "And you could spend less time with those friends who aren't the best influence on you."

Mindy looked shocked, but then she nodded slowly. "You're right, Grandma," she admitted. "I guess I need to do whatever it takes to avoid temptation." *SLK*

HOW ABOUT YOU?

Have you promised to give up some sin in your life? Are you finding it hard to live up to that promise? Maybe you need to make some permanent changes in order to get rid of your sin. Even if it means giving up a prized possession or one of your friends, decide now that you will live for Christ, no matter what. Get serious about dealing with sin!

MEMORIZE:
"Don't make plans to enjoy evil."
Romans 13:14, TLB

Avoid Temptation

Not Born Beautiful?

5

Read Psalm 139:13-16; Exodus 4:11

The minute Dad stopped the car, Kara sprang out and dashed straight to the willow tree in the backyard. The low-hanging boughs always made her feel like she was hidden in a special room. Here she could lie on the soft grass and, finally, cry. But soon Dad joined her there. "Mom and your new baby sister are doing just fine," he said as he patted her shoulder.

"Fine?" Kara exclaimed, shrugging off Dad's hand. She sat up to face him. "How can you say that? How can you act like there's nothing wrong when she's so . . . freaky?"

"Kara," Dad said sternly, "I don't want you to ever again say something like that about your sister!" More gently, he added, "Like I told you, a cleft lip, even a double one like Lindsey's, is nothing to get that upset about. It happens fairly often. You'll be surprised what surgery can do for her."

Kara couldn't hold back the tears. "She'll never look cute like Ashley's sister. It's just not fair!" she cried.

"The doctors can make her look good," Dad assured her, "but that's not the most important thing. What *is* important is that God can make her downright beautiful within. Even before she was born, we dedicated Lindsey to the Lord, and we're praying that she'll accept Jesus as Savior when she's old enough to understand. Physical looks change with time, but God's love within her will give her a beauty that won't wear out."

Kara remembered how her mother had looked when she smiled at the new baby. She also thought of her father's quiet, happy smile. Then she thought of her own attitude and knew there was nothing beautiful about it. She knew she needed to settle some things with God so she wouldn't be the only one in the family who wasn't beautiful. "I guess I do need to pray about my attitude, huh?"

Dad smiled and hugged her. *SCW*

HOW ABOUT YOU?

Do you know someone who was born with some kind of defect? Do you have such a defect yourself? Remember that physical perfection is not really important—in fact, everybody is less than perfect physically. However we are all born in God's image. What's important is that you reflect his love—an inner beauty that Christians can show. Let Jesus be seen in you.

MEMORIZE:

"Charm is deceptive, and beauty does not last; but a woman who fears the Lord will be greatly praised." Proverbs 31:30

Inner Beauty Is Important

6

The Brighter Side

Read Matthew 6:26; 10:29-31

"Ouch!" Alana yelled. She had tripped over one of the many boxes stacked up in the hallway. Moving day was only five days away, and the house was a mess. "Mom, why do we have to move?" she asked. "I don't want to leave my friends. And I don't want to go to another school!"

Mom sighed. "Honey," she said, "I know how difficult this is for you, but Dad's job requires him to make this move. Worrying about it and getting angry won't help."

"Well, what *will* help?" Alana wanted to know. She was close to tears.

Mom gave her a hug. "Trusting God even when you can't understand," she replied. "I know that's sometimes hard to do, but he loves you and he'll take care of you, even in a new school." She pointed out the window. "Do you see that sparrow on the feeder in the backyard, Alana?"

"Yes." Alana nodded.

"Look at it," Mom said. "It isn't considered a beautiful bird—not a bird of much worth. But God says he takes care of those little birds and gives them what they need. He also says he loves you and me much more than those little birds. That's one reason we know he'll take very good care of us."

Alana thought about what Mom had just said. "Do you think God will help me make new friends?" she asked.

"I'm sure he will," Mom replied. "He knows you need friends. Have you talked to him about it?"

Alana shook her head. "No, but I will," she said slowly.

Before leaving for school the next day, Alana showed her mother a little booklet she was taking to school with her. "It's an address book," she explained. "I'll have my friends write down their addresses, and then we'll write to each other. That way I'll keep my old friends, plus I'll be making new ones!"

"That's the spirit, Alana," Mom said. "Now you're looking on the brighter side of things. When we take our worries to God in prayer, he helps us see that everything has a good side, too." *TVA*

HOW ABOUT YOU?

Do you worry much? Sometimes it seems tough to stop worrying. When those times come, remember that God loves you and promises to take care of you. He cares about you. Tell him about your worries. Then trust him to work things out for the best.

MEMORIZE:

"Give all your worries and cares to God, for he cares about what happens to you." 1 Peter 5:7

Don't Worry

The Missionary Project (Part 1)

Read 1 Corinthians 3:8-11

"Thank you for your prayers and support." Haley was reading part of the Carlsons' prayer letter to her Sunday school class. "The Brazilian children love to hear the Bible stories. Please join us in prayer for money to buy a copy machine. Our old one is broken and can't be repaired. Thank you. In his service, the Carlsons."

When Haley finished, Danielle spoke up. "Isn't there some way we could help them buy a copy machine?" she asked.

"Be practical, Danielle," Shelly answered. "Those things cost a lot of money, and we don't have any. All we can do is pray."

"But why couldn't we have a class project to earn some money?" Danielle persisted. "After all, it's summer vacation. We have time."

Mrs. Adams, their teacher, thought it was a good idea and asked for some suggestions.

Trina raised her hand. "My neighbor is looking for strawberry pickers," she said.

The class agreed that picking strawberries would be a good project for earning money for the copy machine. All ten raised their hands to indicate that they would help.

Mrs. Adams was pleased. "You may be working in a strawberry patch, but you will be having a part in God's work of reaching people who have never heard about Jesus," she said. "Since I'm busy at my job during the week, I won't be able to help you, but I'll offer a reward for those who are faithful. All who pick berries every day this week are invited to my house on Saturday for a swim party and supper."

All the girls grinned and cheered at this suggestion.

"All right, ladies," Mrs. Adams laughed. "We'd better get busy with today's lesson." *JLH*

HOW ABOUT YOU?

Are you willing and available to serve the Lord? Do you sometimes excuse yourself from working for Jesus by saying, "All I can do is pray"? Prayer is important and necessary, but perhaps God wants to answer the prayer for workers by using you! Look around. There is plenty you can do!

MEMORIZE:

"We work together as partners who belong to God. You are God's field, God's building—not ours."

1 Corinthians 3:9

Serve the Lord

August
8

The Missionary Project (Part 2)

Read Luke 16:10-13

Early Monday morning, ten seventh-graders came to Mr. Barton's strawberry patch. Stacy wore light-colored jeans and a silky blouse, and she had a fancy braid in her hair. "You came to work, not to stand around looking good," Darla teased.

Stacy tossed her head. "I'll do more work than you'll ever think of doing," she shot back.

But before long, Stacy was in tears. Her jeans were smeared with berry stains, two of her nails were broken, and her hair dangled in her eyes. "Berry picking is hard and too dirty," she complained. "I've had enough!" She grabbed her things and walked away from the job.

On Tuesday, everyone was working hard when Mona and Mia began throwing berries at each other. Mr. Barton heard the commotion and came over to investigate. "What's going on here?" he asked gruffly. "I thought you came to work."

"We want to have some fun, too," Mia answered sarcastically. "But forget it—I'm going home!"

"Me, too," Mona added, and both walked off.

By Saturday, the number of workers had dwindled to three—Haley, Darla, and Trina. The others all had excuses to keep them from working. Some complained about the weather, the dirt, or the mosquitoes. Others decided that shopping, swimming, or playing soccer was more important to them than earning money for a missionary project.

Mrs. Adams was eager to hear about their week when the three arrived for the party. "Did you meet your goal?" she asked.

"No." Darla shook her head. "But Mr. Barton said we could pick again next week, so we figure we can earn the rest of the money we need then."

"Well, where's everybody else?" Mrs. Adams asked. "Aren't they coming?"

"They dropped out," Haley said. "At first everyone pitched in and helped, but then they started quitting. Darla and Trina and I were the only ones who worked every day."

"I'm sorry to hear that," Mrs. Adams replied, "but I'm glad the three of you were faithful in finishing the job. Now, what would you like first—some supper or a swim?" *JLH*

HOW ABOUT YOU?

Are you faithful in your youth group, your Sunday school class, the junior choir, or some other church activity in which you've become involved? Jesus is counting on you to do your part in his harvest field. Don't make excuses for not being there faithfully, and don't quit. Get the work done.

MEMORIZE:

"Be strong and steady, always enthusiastic about the Lord's work, for you know that nothing you do for the Lord is ever useless." 1 Corinthians 15:58

Don't Be a Quitter

Without Love

Read 1 Corinthians 13:1-3

"Oh, let me help you with that. It will earn me points!" Barbara exclaimed. She was working hard to win a week at camp by earning the most points in her Sunday school contest. Points were given for attendance, memory work, and carrying a Bible. Extra points were given for learning additional verses, good behavior in church, bringing friends to Sunday school, and good behavior at home. None of Barbara's family could believe how helpful she had suddenly become—she did dishes, made beds, offered to help with her sister's homework, baby-sat, and even carried out the trash!

But Barbara's sister, Jenni, refused to let her help. "Leave me and my things alone," Jenni said crossly.

Barbara did well, but another girl did even better and won the contest. "Oh, well," Barbara said with a sigh, "I learned a lot anyway." And to everyone's surprise, her helpful ways continued.

Even Jenni accepted Barbara's help now, and Barbara was puzzled over this. Finally she asked Jenni about it. "Why do you let me do things for you now?" she asked. "I mean, when we were having the contest, you wouldn't let me do anything for you."

"Well, now you really want to help me," Jenni answered. "Before, you just did it for points."

Barbara smiled. "That's true, Jenni," she said quietly, "but the last section of memory verses I learned for the contest was 1 Corinthians 13. When I recited it to Miss Wilson, she explained that no matter how much good we do, if we don't have love in our hearts, it isn't worth anything. God isn't pleased with us. I felt pretty silly when I thought of how I was just doing good things so I could win enough points for camp. I asked God to forgive me and to give me more love. I'm glad you could tell the difference!" *AGL*

HOW ABOUT YOU?

Do you do good deeds just to "win points" with others? Perhaps you feel that good works can even "win points" for you with God. But he says that without genuine love, all the good things you do are nothing. Such love can come only from God. You must first be born again by trusting Jesus as your Savior, and then let his love fill your heart and overflow to others.

MEMORIZE:
"Your love for one another will prove to the world that you are my disciples." John 13:35

Love One Another

10

The Wise Squirrel

Read Genesis 41:46-57

"Guess what Joseph is doing?" Bobbi exclaimed as she burst into the kitchen. "He's burying nuts near the apple tree."

"Who's Joseph?" Mom asked. "The new boy next door?"

"Oh, Mom! Joseph is the squirrel who visits our garden," Bobbi explained impatiently. "Why would he bury nuts instead of eating them?"

"He's storing them to eat next winter," her brother, Michael, told her.

Mom nodded. "While it's warm, squirrels collect nuts and grains and hide them," she said. "Then when winter comes and food is hard to find, they have their secret store to fall back on."

"That's like Joseph in the Bible," Michael pointed out. "He collected grain for seven years, so when the famine came, the people had plenty to eat. He was smart!"

"Hmmmm," murmured Mom. "We can learn something from both Josephs."

"We need to store up food in case there's a famine here?" Bobbi asked.

Mom smiled. "I was referring to a different kind of food—spiritual food," she explained. "I'm afraid that when things are going well for us—like now—we might be tempted to be lazy and neglect prayer and Bible reading and meeting with other Christians. We seem to realize that we need God's help when difficult times come, but we don't always remember that we should use the good times to store up spiritual food and strengthen our relationship with the Lord."

"I get it," said Bobbi. "If we store up that spiritual food, we can use it when hard times come. We can remember Bible verses and lessons we've learned in Sunday school and church."

Mom nodded. "Yes," she agreed. "We can draw spiritual strength from the many things we've previously learned from God's Word." *MTF*

HOW ABOUT YOU?

Is this time a good time in your life? Is God blessing you with happy times and pleasant circumstances? Then use this time to praise and thank him and to get to know him better. Is this a hard time in your life? Then draw upon the spiritual truth you've stored up.

MEMORIZE:
"I will delight in your principles and not forget your word." Psalm 119:16

Store Up Spiritual Truths for Future Needs

Dead Man's Reef

Read Psalm 119:129-135

"Uncle Milt said I could take his boat out all by myself!" Lisa's older sister, Stephanie, said proudly. "Want to come for a ride?"

Lisa nodded, and the girls jumped into the boat. Stephanie started the engine. Minutes later, they were laughing and shouting as the wind blew through their hair.

"Aren't you supposed to use this map?" Lisa asked, offering it to her sister. "I heard Uncle Milt explain it to you. And didn't he say not to go out this far?"

Stephanie shrugged. "Yeah . . . well, I'll just swing around and head back. I don't need the map."

Suddenly there was a jolt, followed by a crash! The engine sputtered and died. "We must be stuck on a reef," Lisa gasped.

"I didn't see it," Stephanie answered. "Let me look at that map." She studied it a moment. "Oh," she groaned, "here's where we are—at Dead Man's Reef. Why do you suppose they call it that? Hey! This thing is leaking!"

The girls looked at one another with despair in their eyes. "Oh, Stephanie," Lisa said in a worried tone. "What'll we do? We'll never be able to swim all the way to shore." But even as she spoke, they heard a sound—a motor! A Coast Guard launch was pulling up, and soon they were safely on board.

That evening they sat in their uncle's cottage with heads bowed and faces downcast. "I'm so sorry, Uncle Milt," Stephanie said. "I've wrecked your boat. I don't know how I'll ever pay for it."

"My insurance will cover a lot of it," Uncle Milt told them, "and your father says you'll have to cut your visit short and return home now, so you can work to pay for the rest. I'm sorry about that. But more important, you might have lost your lives! Why didn't you look at the map?"

"I thought I could get along without it," Stephanie admitted. "Now that it's too late, I see how wrong I was." *HCT*

HOW ABOUT YOU?

Do you realize that you need a "map" to guide you through life? God's Word, the Bible, serves as a map, or guidebook. Are you using it? Do you read it each day? First of all, it will point you to Jesus, the only way to heaven. It will also teach you to be honest, pure, loving, patient, and much more as it guides you in your Christian life.

MEMORIZE:
"Guide my steps by your word."
Psalm 119:133

Read the Bible Daily

August

12

Big Enough

Read Proverbs 3:5-7, 13

Della and Larissa were spending the summer with their dad in a desert area where he was working as an archaeologist. They could see the tall jagged pinnacles of rock from their camper, which was parked close to the place Dad worked. The pinnacles fascinated Della. "Never go out among those alone," Dad warned the kids. "You could get lost, or you might be bitten by a rattlesnake."

"I'm no baby," Della grumbled as she and Larissa played one day. "I'm old enough to look after myself, and I'm going to climb that tall pinnacle you can see in the distance over there. Come on."

Larissa knew better, but she went along with Della. When they reached the pinnacle, Della began to climb. It was quite a struggle, but she was nearing the top when suddenly a stone let loose. Down she fell, all the way to the bottom! "O-o-ohh," Della moaned when she tried to get up. "My leg! Oh, it hurts so bad!" She was unable to stand on it, and Larissa had to go back alone and get Dad to come and help.

Della was embarrassed and ashamed. "I . . . I'm really sorry I didn't obey you, Dad," she said when she was safely back home and resting on the couch. "I . . . I just thought I was old enough to do what I wanted. I should have listened to you."

"None of us ever gets big enough to disobey," Dad told her as he tightly wrapped her sprained ankle. "God gave you parents to guide you, and he expects you to obey me always. But even more than parents, you need to really make Jesus the Lord of your life. You not only need to trust Jesus as your Savior, but you need to let him control your life—then it will be easier to obey your parents, too. You'll never be big enough to get along without him." *HCT*

HOW ABOUT YOU?
Did you read today's Scripture passage? It contains good advice for anyone who thinks she's big enough to get along without the Lord. Allow him to direct your path. He is so much wiser than any person.

MEMORIZE:
"Don't be impressed with your own wisdom." Proverbs 3:7

You'll Always Need God

Hidden Sweetness

Read Colossians 3:12-16

Marcela cringed as she sipped her lemonade. Finally she pushed the glass away. "This isn't as good as usual," she complained. "It's awfully sour."

"That's odd," said Aunt Maddie. "It's the same brand we've always used. Maybe you didn't put enough sugar in it."

Marcela frowned and crossed her arms. "This lemonade is like Bianca," she said. "They're both sour."

"Bianca is sour?" asked Aunt Maddie. "You mean Bianca DeVries from church? She always seems like such a sweet Christian girl to me."

"She may be a Christian, but she's not sweet anymore," said Marcela. "Ever since she didn't make the cheerleading team, she's been really nasty."

"Really? Well, don't be too hard on her, honey," Aunt Maddie said. "Disappointment is painful; I'm sure she'll come around."

Marcela shrugged and again sipped the lemonade. She glanced at the pitcher standing on the table. Then she snapped her fingers. "I know why this lemonade is so sour," she said. "I put sugar in the pitcher, but I didn't stir it! Look! You can see the sugar in the bottom!" Marcela got out a long-handled spoon and stirred the lemonade. Then she tried it again. "That's much better!" she exclaimed.

Aunt Maddie smiled. "You were right when you compared Bianca to that lemonade," she said. "All the sugar was at the bottom of the pitcher, so the lemonade was sour—like Bianca—until you stirred the sweetness through it. I believe Bianca is a Christian, so the sweetness of God's love must be hidden at the bottom of her heart right now. It needs to be stirred up, too. Maybe the Lord can use you to bring some of her sweetness to the surface again."

"How would I do that?" asked Marcela.

"First, pray for her," Aunt Maddie suggested. "Be kind and understanding. Remind her that God loves her, and let her see that you're concerned about her, too." *SML*

HOW ABOUT YOU?

Do you know Christians who get upset or "sour" at times? Instead of reacting with indifference or anger, be kind and patient. Pray for them, and let them see that both you and God care for them.

MEMORIZE:

"Clothe yourselves with tenderhearted mercy, kindness, humility, gentleness, and patience." Colossians 3:12

Show Kindness and Patience

14

The Fireflies

Read Galatians 5:13-15

As their parents sat on the patio, Nadia and Zac ran across the dark lawn, trying to catch fireflies. Zac's voice rang out. "Leave that one alone! That's my firefly!"

Mom sighed. "There are a thousand fireflies out there, but they want the same one," she said. "They fuss so much lately—about everything."

Just then Nadia shouted, "Stop it, Zac! Don't put your firefly in my jar!"

Dad stood up. "Nadia! Zac!" he called. "Bring your firefly jars and come here." Still fussing, the children came to the patio.

"Do we have to come in already?" Nadia whined. "We're just starting to have fun."

Zac lifted his jar. "How many did you get, Nadia?"

Nadia held up her jar and started to count, "One, two, three . . . oh no! What is that firefly doing?"

Zac peered closely at Nadia's jar. "It looks like . . ." he paused. "Mom! Look, Dad!" Nadia held the jar so her parents could see. "It looks like one firefly is eating another one."

Dad nodded. "Fireflies do that," he said. "They eat one another."

"Wow!" Zac said.

"That's horrid," Nadia agreed.

"I don't know why that should bother you," Dad said. "You kids bite and devour each other, too."

"We what?" Nadia said.

"You bite and devour each other," Dad repeated. "That means you attack and tear each other to pieces."

Mom nodded and explained. "Just today, Nadia, you were crying because Zac said some ugly things about you to his friends—and Zac was hurt when you laughed at the birdhouse he was building."

"You're destroying each other's self-esteem and your love for one another," said Dad.

Nadia put her jar down. "I can't watch this," she said and turned to her brother. "Zac, I'm sorry."

"Me, too," mumbled Zac as he took the lid off his jar and released the fireflies.

Mom smiled. "I have a feeling that things are going to get better around here." *BJW*

HOW ABOUT YOU?

Do you show love to your brothers and sisters? That's what God says you should do—it's the opposite of "biting and devouring" one another. Don't constantly fuss and quarrel. Instead, love others as God says you should.

MEMORIZE:

Watch out! Beware of destroying one another." Galatians 5:15

Love One Another

Pulling Weeds

Read Mark 4:15-20

"Mom, do we have to pull the weeds again?" asked Monique. "It seems like we just got done pulling them."

"They keep growing back," Mom said. "We need to pull them if we want to enjoy lots of juicy red tomatoes and other vegetables."

"Why can't we just let the old weeds grow and still pick the vegetables when they're ready?" asked Monique. "What will it hurt if we just leave them there?"

"Well, for some reason weeds grow better than vegetables do," Mom replied. "If we leave them, they'll use lots of water and nutrients that the vegetables need—and their roots are liable to choke out good plants and cause them to die."

"Really?" asked Monique. "They'd really die?"

"Many probably would," said Mom. "The vegetables need the nutrients to live and grow. If they don't get enough, or if their roots are blocked or choked, they can't survive—or if they do, the harvest will be very small."

"Okay," said Monique, "let's go and get it over with."

That evening, Monique told her dad about her activities that day. "Mostly, I had fun today," she said. "The best part of the day was playing with my friends. The worst part was weeding the garden, but Mom says we need to or the weeds will choke out the vegetables."

"That's right," agreed Dad. "It's important to get rid of those nasty weeds." He smiled at Monique. "Did you know that things can come into our lives and choke out the good things God is doing in our hearts?"

Monique nodded. "Sin can choke out the good things like weeds choke out the vegetables, right?" she asked. "We talked about that in Sunday school. My teacher says we should grow to be like Jesus and that if the books we read or the shows we watch or the kids we play with interfere with that, they're wrong for us and we'd better get new books or friends."

"Exactly," said Dad. "We should not allow anything in our lives that chokes out the Word of God." *RT*

HOW ABOUT YOU?
Do you have any habits that hinder your spiritual growth? How about your choice of friends? TV shows? Music? Is it time to pull the "weeds" that may be growing in your heart?

Don't Let Weeds Grow in Your Heart

MEMORIZE:
"The worries of this life . . . and the desires for other things come in and choke the word." Mark 4:19, NIV

16

Do It Now

Read Proverbs 3:27-28; Galatians 6:9-10

As Jan and Chelsea were walking to a friend's house, they saw some yellow flowers by the side of the road. Jan stopped to smell them. "These look sort of like the flowers Mrs. Cranston used to have in her yard before she got too sick to take care of them," she said.

"Her yard's full of weeds now. I think she'd like to see some pretty flowers again. Let's take them to her," Chelsea suggested. "She probably doesn't get many visitors."

Jan frowned. "If we do, we won't have much time left to play with Melanie," she said. "Why don't we wait till next week to bring her the flowers?"

"I suppose we could." Chelsea looked thoughtful. "But remember the flowers we picked yesterday? They wilted before we got them home."

"I remember," Jan replied, "but if they do, we can find some others to take to Mrs. Cranston."

"I don't know, but I've often heard Mom talk about lost opportunities," Chelsea said. "Something might happen to keep us from doing it later. Let's do it now!"

So the girls gathered flowers and went to see Mrs. Cranston. They sang for her and told her about Kids' Club and the things they were learning there. "I can hardly believe you left your play to come visit an old person like me! Thank you, girls," Mrs. Cranston said. "I don't know much about God, but I'm sure he sent you here today. I was feeling lonely."

When the girls told their dad about their visit, he decided to go to see Mrs. Cranston, too. He was smiling broadly when he returned home. "Mrs. Cranston accepted the Lord," he told Chelsea and Jan, "and you two are responsible for starting her thinking about him. She was so impressed with your visit!"

The next day as Dad read the newspaper, he let out a gasp. "Mrs. Cranston!" he exclaimed. "A little item here says she died last night, apparently of a heart attack."

"Oh, I'm so glad we visited her when we did!" Jan exclaimed. "And that she accepted Jesus when Dad visited her."

Chelsea nodded. "From now on, when I think of something nice to do, I'll do it right away," she added. "Tomorrow may be too late!" *SLK*

HOW ABOUT YOU?

Is there something you've been meaning to do for someone? Perhaps there's someone you need to witness to, a kind deed you've thought of doing for your parents, or a friendly note you could write. If God has put a thought like this in your mind, put it into action. Do it now!

MEMORIZE:

"Remember, it is sin to know what you ought to do and then not do it."
James 4:17

Don't Waste Opportunities

A Cookbook and an Egg

Read John 1:1-4, 14

"Grandma," Nancy said as she helped her grandmother make a birthday cake for Dad, "in Vacation Bible School today, my teacher said that one can sometimes be three, and three can sometimes be one. That's crazy!"

"Oh, she must have been talking about the Trinity—God the Father, God the Son, and God the Holy Spirit," Grandma said. "They are three, and yet they are one."

"That's what she said," Nancy answered, nodding. "But it doesn't make sense to me. I thought those were just three different names for God—like some people call me 'Nancy,' and some call me 'Nan,' and Daddy calls me 'Sugar.' "

"Well, let's see if I can help you understand," Grandma responded thoughtfully. "Here . . . look at this cookbook. It's three in one. There's the cover, the pages, and the words. All three make one unit—this book. Right?"

"Yeah, I guess so," Nancy murmured doubtfully, as she broke an egg into a bowl.

"Take a look at that egg—it's another example," Grandma continued. "There's the yolk, the white, and the shell. Would you say they are three separate things?"

"Well, sure, but they're still one egg," Nancy replied slowly.

"That's right," Grandma agreed. "They're separate things, each with its own use. You couldn't use one in place of the other, yet they're dependent upon each other to make a single unit. It's like that with the Trinity. Each person of the Trinity has a special place and purpose in our lives, and yet they are one. They are God. Now . . . neither the book nor the egg is a perfect example of the Trinity, but I hope they'll help you get a little better idea of it."

Nancy nodded as she cracked another egg into the bowl. *AU*

HOW ABOUT YOU?

Some things in God's Word are hard to understand, aren't they? But you can believe what God says and trust him even if you don't fully understand. No one will understand the Trinity perfectly here on earth, but you can believe it because it's taught in the Bible, God's Word. Each person of the Trinity has a separate, important function in your life. Yet the three are one. What a great God!

MEMORIZE:

"There are three that bear record in heaven, the Father, the Word [Jesus], and the Holy Ghost: and these three are one." 1 John 5:7, KJV

God Is Three in One

August
18

Worm or Butterfly

Read John 3:3-8

"Look what I found, Grandpa!" Jamie exclaimed as she blew into her grand-father's kitchen like a gust of wind. "Can I please have a jar to put him in?" She held out the striped worm for Grandpa to see. It was anchored to a milkweed leaf and not about to interrupt its meal.

"Why, that's a monarch larva, Jamie," Grandpa said. "Are you going to keep it until it turns into a butterfly?"

"Do you think it will?" Jamie asked.

"Well, you'll have to feed it," Grandpa said, "until it builds a chrysalis."

"What's a chrysalis?" Jamie questioned.

"That's a sort of cocoon that monarch worms build around themselves while they turn into butterflies," Grandpa answered. Taking an empty jar from under the sink, Grandpa used a tool to poke several holes in the lid. "Now," he said, "Mr. Monarch will need something to fasten the chrysalis to."

Jamie was careful to bring the creature fresh, dewy milkweed leaves each morning, and each day the worm ate and grew, ate and grew. Then one morning Jamie didn't see Mr. Monarch in his jar. Instead, there was a small green thing hanging by a thread from the lid.

"Grandpa, come quick!" Jamie called. "Is this the chrysalis? Is Mr. Monarch really in there?"

"Oh, my," Grandpa said. "Yes, indeed, he's in there."

"What do I do now?" Jamie asked.

"Nothing. Just leave the jar alone," Grandpa said, "and one day soon the jar will hold a beautiful butterfly."

Jamie looked into the jar several times each day, but nothing was happening. She was growing impatient. At last the day came when Jamie found a beautiful orange-and-black butterfly slowly exercising its wings. "Grandpa!" Jamie called. "Come and see! Grandpa, how did he do that?"

"Only God knows," Grandpa answered, "but this butterfly reminds me of how we are changed when Jesus comes into our hearts. The Bible calls it being 'born again.' God changed your worm into a butterfly, and he changes us from sinners into 'born again' saints. He's full of miracles!" *JRL*

HOW ABOUT YOU?
Have you accepted Jesus as your Savior? If you have, you have been born again—changed from a sinner into a saint. If not, why not do it today? It's not something to delay!

MEMORIZE:
"Jesus replied, 'I assure you, unless you are born again, you can never see the Kingdom of God.' " John 3:3

You Must Be "Born Again"

Straight Paths

Read Psalm 25:4-5, 8, 12

"Dad, who marked the trees like that?" asked Lilia. She and her little brother, Alex, were hiking with their parents on a trail that went around a lake at their favorite state park.

"I'm not sure," said Dad. He examined colored markings on a tree along the path. "Someone probably cleared away the brush and marked this path many years ago. Then they could follow the markings and wouldn't have to find a new path every time they came here. Maybe it was an explorer."

"Wow!" exclaimed Lilia. "A trail made by some ancient explorer! Maybe like . . . fifty years ago?"

"Or even longer ago," replied Dad.

They walked along the trail, enjoying the colorful leaves and the sounds of birds and animals. As they wandered deeper into the woods, Lilia and Mom stopped to see some wild flowers. When Dad turned to speak to Alex, he discovered that the little boy was no longer right behind him. "Alex? Alex, where are you?" called Dad. Alex didn't answer.

Mom and Lilia also began calling. They retraced their steps, all the while trying to calm the heavy thumping of their hearts.

Suddenly, Alex burst out of the woods and jumped into Dad's arms. "I was so scared," sobbed Alex.

"Why didn't you stay with us?" asked Mom.

"I followed a pretty bird," said Alex, "but I got lost!"

As Mom and Dad comforted him, they also warned him and Lilia about the dangers of leaving the marked trail and not staying close to them.

"It's nice to have those marks on the trees, but they don't do us much good if we don't follow them," observed Lilia.

Dad nodded. "That's right," he said. After a moment, he added. "I'm glad we have trail markers for our lives as well as for the way around the lake. We need to be sure to follow them, too."

"Trail markers for our lives?" asked Lilia.

Dad nodded. "God gave us the Bible to guide us to him and away from danger. We need to read it regularly and obey it daily." *RT*

HOW ABOUT YOU?

Are you following the trail markers—the instructions—found in God's Word? The Bible shows the way to salvation in Jesus. For all who trust in him, there are instructions for Christian living. Follow them—it's the only way they'll do you any good.

Follow God's Trail Markers

MEMORIZE:
"Seek his will in all you do, and he will direct your paths." Proverbs 3:6

Little Lost Lamb

Read Matthew 18:10-14

"Mom!" Katarina called as she ran into the kitchen. "My lamb's gone! I'm sure I latched the door after I fed him, but it's broken now and Marshmallow is gone."

Mom sighed. "Well, we'd better go look for him," she said.

They started off, calling Marshmallow's name as they searched the ditch and fields along the road. When they reached the home of Grandpa and Grandma Heinz, they explained what they were doing. "Your lamb is lost?" asked Grandpa. "We'll help you look for him." So he and Grandma joined the search, leaving a half-mowed yard and weeds in the flower bed.

Grandpa Heinz was the one who finally found Marshmallow behind a neighbor's barn, and Katarina happily took her lamb home. After making sure he couldn't get out again, she went to thank her grandparents for their help. "I'm sorry I caused so much trouble," she told them, "especially since you had to leave your chores."

"That's okay," said Grandma. "We wanted to help."

"That's right, honey," Grandpa agreed. He smiled at Katarina. "Do you remember the parable Jesus told about the lost sheep?" he asked.

Katarina nodded. "The shepherd left all the sheep that were safe in the fold, and he went out to search for one little lamb," she said.

"That's right," said Grandpa. "People are like lost sheep, and Jesus—the Good Shepherd—left heaven and gave his life to find us and save us. I hope our search for Marshmallow will help us all remember that we should never be too busy to hunt other 'lost lambs'—other people, young or old, who don't know Jesus."

Katarina was thoughtful. "I'm pretty sure that my new friend, Marla, doesn't know Jesus," she said, "so she's just as lost as my lamb was, isn't she?" Grandpa nodded. "I'm going to ask God to help me tell her about Jesus," said Katarina. "I want her to be found—like Marshmallow—and not be lost anymore."

Grandpa and Grandma smiled. "Good for you," said Grandma. "We'll be praying for her, too—and for you." *NIM*

HOW ABOUT YOU?
Do you tell your friends about Jesus? Without him, they are lost in sin. Jesus came to find and save the lost, and each person is important to him. Do all you can to bring other "lost lambs" to Jesus.

MEMORIZE:
"It is not my heavenly Father's will that even one of these little ones should perish." Matthew 18:14

Tell Others about Jesus

Warning! Window Here!

Read Psalm 19:7-13

"Oh, no! That bird flew into the glass!" exclaimed Chris after hearing a thud at the window. She turned to her father. "I hope he's okay!"

Dad and Chris got up from the table and went over to the large plate glass window in the living room. "I don't see him," Dad said as they looked down at the ground. "I guess he must be okay—apparently okay enough to fly away, anyhow."

"Well, I think we should put up a poster or something to warn the birds that there's a window here," said Chris. "They can't see the clear glass."

Dad smiled. "What should it say?" he asked.

"Dad! You know they can't read," protested Chris. "It would just have to be something big and bright on the glass."

"Yes. Well, I'm afraid your mom would object to that kind of sign on her front window," Dad said.

Chris nodded. "I guess so," she agreed.

"You know, Chris, we're like that bird sometimes," Dad said thoughtfully.

"We are?" asked Chris. "How?"

"There are dangerous things in life that we don't see, either," Dad replied. "There's a difference, though—we don't know quite how to warn those birds, but someone does warn us of many dangers. God often warns us." Dad smiled at Chris. "Do you know how he does that?"

"Well . . . ah . . . my Sunday school teacher warned us about some bad shows on TV," said Chris. "In fact, she was pretty worked up about it. Is that how God warns us? Through our teachers?"

"That's one way," Dad replied. "What else?"

Chris was ready this time. "Last week, Pastor Grey preached about hell," she said. "He gave a strong warning."

"Right," Dad said. "Those were a couple of examples of what we might think of as 'big, bright' warnings. God often uses people to warn us, but he also speaks to us through his Word—the Bible. He quietly impresses something upon our hearts and minds as we think about what he has said. Always remember that when God warns you, you need to pay attention!" *KRL*

HOW ABOUT YOU?
Do you pay attention when God uses parents, teachers, or his Word to warn you about something? God sees dangers that you can't see. Avoid hurt and heartache by listening to his warnings and obeying him.

MEMORIZE:
"They are a warning to those who hear them; there is great reward for those who obey them." Psalm 19:11

Pay Attention to God's Warnings

August

22

Troublesome Melon (Part 1)

Read Psalm 32:1-5

Hearing her mom call, Eileen ran out to the backyard. Mom was standing behind the garage, looking at the ground. "Look at those melon plants," she said. There, almost hidden by tall grass, was a cluster of green vines. "The funny thing is," continued Mom, "I didn't plant any watermelons this year."

"Maybe they got planted accidentally," suggested Eileen. "Maybe a squirrel dropped some seeds there."

"Think so?" Mom asked. "I was thinking of something else. Remember when someone stole a watermelon from the front of Mr. Simkins' store last summer?"

"Yeah." Eileen shifted uncomfortably. "It was one of those big green ones with stripes, wasn't it?"

"You have a good memory—for a casual observer," Mom said. "I don't remember what kind it was, but I was wondering if maybe the person who stole the melon came here, ate it, and then buried the rinds and the seeds so no one would find out." Eileen's face was red as Mom looked closely at her. "Is there something you need to tell me?" she asked. Eileen refused to look her in the eye. "It was you, wasn't it, Eileen?" Mom asked softly. "I wondered about it last summer because of the way you reacted then."

"I . . . I . . . John and I did it," Eileen admitted, close to tears. "When we buried everything, I thought that would be the end of it. I didn't count on those little green plants coming right up out of the ground to tell on me!"

"No matter how you try to hide sin, it always comes back to tell on you," Mom said. "The Bible says your sins aren't hidden from God, and sooner or later the guilt catches up with you." *HCT*

HOW ABOUT YOU?

Do you try to hide things from others—and even from God? Trying to cover up sin causes trouble in the end. Instead of trying to hide sin, confess it! Let God's forgiveness make you clean, and let his strength give you victory over that wicked thing.

MEMORIZE:

"O God; my guilt is not hidden from you." Psalm 69:5, NIV

You Can't Hide Sin

Troublesome Melon (Part 2)

Read Luke 19:2-10

Eileen was horrified. She had confessed to her mom that she and a friend had stolen a melon from in front of a neighborhood grocery store the summer before, and now Mom said she had to go see Mr. Simkins, the owner, and tell him about it.

"But, Mom, that happened a long time ago," she protested. "I'll bet Mr. Simkins doesn't even remember it. Why can't I just be punished and then forget about it?"

"It happened long ago, but you did *steal* from Mr. Simkins, and you'll have to repay that debt," Mom replied sternly.

"Well . . . well . . . can't we just buy another melon and leave it at his door after dark tonight?" Eileen asked hopefully. "Then he'll have been paid back. And . . . and I'll ask God to forgive me, too. Isn't that enough?"

"Asking God to forgive you would be enough if you had sinned against God only," Mom replied, "but when you lie or steal or hurt someone, you need to also apologize to the person you've wronged. You must show you're really sorry you did wrong, not just sorry you got caught. In this case, you not only owe Mr. Simkins a watermelon, but you owe him an apology, too."

Ten minutes later, Eileen and her Mom arrived at Mr. Simkins' store, and Eileen haltingly confessed to the crime. Mr. Simkins agreed to forgive her and let her work off the debt by helping with some yard work.

"Well, Eileen, don't you feel better now that you've done the right thing?" Mom asked as they headed home.

Eileen nodded. "Yes," she said with a sigh, "but I sure hope I never have to do that again! I know I'm never going to steal another thing!" *HCT*

HOW ABOUT YOU?

Have you stolen, lied, disobeyed, or done some other thing that has hurt someone? Confess your sin to God, and be sure to also do what you can to make things right with the person you've hurt.

**Confess Sin
and Apologize**

MEMORIZE:
"If I have cheated anybody out of anything, I will pay back four times the amount." Luke 19:8, NIV

August

24

Gazelles and Thoughts

Read Psalm 18:28-36

Ella and her mom munched their popcorn as they stood in front of the gazelle exhibit at the zoo. The sleek and powerful animals stood quietly on the grass behind a chain-link fence. Ella guessed the fence was only about as tall as her dad. "Mom, can't those gazelles jump over the fence and get out?" she asked.

Mom smiled. "They probably could," she replied. "Can you guess why they don't try?"

"Not really," said Ella, shaking her head.

"Do you see how the top of the fence leans toward the gazelles?" Mom asked, and Ella nodded. "Well, an article I read says gazelles have poor eyesight and that when a fence leans into their area, it creates an illusion—a false idea—that the fence is much higher than it really is. According to the article, that's why they don't try to escape."

"Really? I guess they need glasses," joked Ella. She laughed as, in her mind, she pictured gazelles with glasses.

Mom smiled as they moved on toward the monkey exhibit. "The way the fence keeps the gazelles from running free is a little like the way our thoughts sometimes keep us from being free," she said.

Ella was curious. "What do you mean?" she asked.

"The way the fence is built gives the gazelles a false idea, and our thoughts can give us false ideas, too," Mom explained. "When we listen to thoughts that tell us we'll never be good students or that we're too clumsy to ever be good at sports, or when we think God doesn't love us, we get false ideas that keep us from being the best we can be."

"So . . . if the gazelles knew the truth, they could jump over the fence," Ella said thoughtfully, "and if we know the truth . . ." She paused. "What truth should we know?" she asked.

"God's truth—he says that we're special and that he'll help us do everything he wants us to do," Mom replied. "When we believe what he says, we can break free from false thoughts. With God's help, we can be and do whatever he asks of us." *RSM*

HOW ABOUT YOU?

Do thoughts that you are a failure or bad or not valuable to God create false ideas that keep you from being the person God wants you to be? Don't be trapped by illusions. Believe God and become the kind of person he wants you to be.

MEMORIZE:

"I can do everything with the help of Christ who gives me the strength I need." Philippians 4:13

Believe God

Call-Waiting

Read 1 Samuel 3:1-10

"Hold on, Mitch," Gracie spoke into the telephone receiver. "Something's wrong with our phone." She looked up and called, "Mom! The phone is beeping!"

Mom came into the kitchen. "Oh," she said, "I ordered call-waiting. Push the hang-up button and say hello."

Gracie did so and was surprised to hear Dad's voice. "Let me talk with Mom, please," Dad said.

Mom took the phone and pushed the button again. "Mitch, Gracie will call you back in a minute," she said. Once more she pushed the button. Then she began talking with Dad.

When she was finished, Gracie grinned. "Cool!" she exclaimed as she dialed Mitch's number.

Gracie was telling Mitch a joke when she heard the beeping tone again. *I'll get it after I finish this joke,* she thought, but before she was through, the beeping stopped.

That evening the phone rang again, and Mom answered it. She returned a few minutes later. "That was Grandpa," she told Gracie. "He called this morning to see if you wanted to go fishing today. Since nobody answered, he assumed no one was home."

Dad looked surprised. "That's odd," he said. "You were home all day, weren't you? And since we have call-waiting now, you should have gotten the call."

"I did hear a beep," admitted Gracie. "I guess I waited too long before I answered it, and Grandpa hung up." She sighed. "I wish I could have gone with Grandpa."

"It's too bad you didn't answer his call," Dad said. Then he added, "You know, my Bible reading this morning had a verse that discussed how when God tries to get our attention, we need to be careful to listen and not ignore him."

"He tries to get our attention? Like how?" asked Gracie.

"Sometimes through pastors or Sunday school teachers or parents," Dad said. "Other times he may speak to us through verses we read in his Word—or perhaps simply through the urging of the Holy Spirit in our hearts. If we don't respond, we miss a blessing."

Mom nodded. "It's always a shame to miss an important message," she added, "especially a message from God!" *SLK*

HOW ABOUT YOU?

Have there been times when you knew God was warning you about something or was urging you to do some work for him? Have you quickly responded and followed his leading? Always answer his "call" right away!

Answer God's "Call" Immediately

August
26

Flowerpot Lesson (Part 1)

Read Luke 8:5-8

Three flowerpots stood on a table in Erin's Sunday school room. One didn't seem to have anything in it; the second had a small, obviously struggling plant; the third displayed a beautiful, flowering plant. "I've brought these to help me teach the lesson," Miss Mendez said after the class studied the parable of the sower. "I hope these flowerpots will help us determine what stage we're at in our lives."

Erin asked the question that was on everyone's mind. "What do you mean by 'stage'?"

"See this pot?" Miss Mendez asked as she picked up the one that had only dirt in it. "I went through the motions of planting seeds in here, but I didn't bother to cover them with dirt or water them regularly." She put the flowerpot down on the table. "To me, this one represents people who say they accept Jesus when an invitation is given, but they aren't at all serious about what they're doing. They're just going through the motions. The seed in this pot didn't even get started. In the same way, the seed of God's Word doesn't take root in the hearts of those who aren't sincere."

"Do you mean like kids who pretend to be saved, and get baptized and join the church just because all their friends are doing it?" one girl asked.

"Or people who go forward in a service to accept Jesus as Savior, but then forget all about it the next day?" Erin chimed in.

Miss Mendez nodded. "People like that are just going through the motions, and their lives will still be as empty as this flowerpot. I want all of you to examine your hearts. It's my prayer that no one in this class will fit into that category." *RIJ*

HOW ABOUT YOU?

Have you gone through the motions of accepting Jesus as your Savior? If you were not sincere when you confessed your sin and asked Jesus to forgive you, you were not saved. You can receive God's gift of salvation only if you truly believe on Jesus. If you know that you are a sinner and you really believe that Jesus died and rose for you—if you sincerely want him to save you—bow your head right now and ask him to be your Lord. He will!

MEMORIZE:
"For the wages of sin is death, but the free gift of God is eternal life through Christ Jesus our Lord." Romans 6:23

Don't Pretend to Be a Christian

Flowerpot Lesson (Part 2)

Read 1 Peter 1:25; 2:1-5

The girls in Erin's Sunday school class looked solemn as they thought about the things Miss Mendez had just taught them. Then their attention was drawn to the second flowerpot on the classroom table.

Erin looked into it. "This one has a little plant," she said, "but it sure doesn't look very good."

"That's right," Miss Mendez agreed. "This one represents people who have given their hearts to Jesus. But they aren't regular in attending church or Sunday school, and they rarely read their Bibles. As a result, they don't seem to grow very much."

One of the girls pointed to the third flowerpot. "That one's beautiful!" she exclaimed. "Was it planted earlier than the others?"

"I did plant them at different times," Miss Mendez admitted, "but the one that's growing the best was planted last. So you see, age doesn't make much difference when the seed is planted right and the plant is cared for properly. We're like plants in many ways." Miss Mendez looked at Erin. "How long have you been a Christian?" she asked.

"Six years," Erin replied. "Since I was six."

"And how long have you been saved?" Miss Mendez asked Missy, who was seated next to her.

"Almost a year," Missy answered.

"Now," Miss Mendez said, "I'm older and have been a Christian a long time. Erin has been a Christian for six years now. But that doesn't necessarily mean we're more mature Christians than Missy. It isn't the length of time you've been saved that makes you a strong Christian—it's how you've used that time." She held up the third flowerpot again. "This was planted last," she said, "but fertilizer has been worked into the dirt, and the plant is on a regular watering schedule. It shows real growth. It's like those who truly accepted Jesus as Savior and want to live for him. They read their Bibles and attend church regularly so they can learn more about the Christian life. As they follow God's instructions and try to please him, they grow and mature in their Christian lives." *RIJ*

HOW ABOUT YOU?

Have you been a Christian a long time or a short time? The more important question is, are you growing spiritually? Make up your mind to learn all you can from God's Word so others can see Jesus in your life.

MEMORIZE:

"Crave pure spiritual milk so that you can grow into the fullness of your salvation." 1 Peter 2:2

Be a Growing Christian

August
28

No More Snarls

Read 1 John 1:7-9

Tricia peered into the mirror as she brushed her hair one Sunday morning. Finally, she brought the brush to her mom. "Would you do my hair?" she asked.

Mom smiled as she took the brush. "Are you sure you want me to?" she asked. "Usually, you complain if other people touch your hair. You always say you'd rather do it yourself."

"I know," Tricia sighed, "but it has more snarls than usual. Please brush it."

Tricia gritted her teeth as her mom began brushing out the snarls. Her eyes filled with tears a couple of times as the strokes of the brush pulled at her hair. Finally, Mom was finished. "I'm sorry, honey. I know that must have hurt," Mom said sympathetically. "You had a lot of tangles. You should brush your hair more often."

"I do brush it, but not as hard as you do," Tricia admitted. "I don't always get all of them out."

After church that morning, Dad commented on the pastor's sermon. "That was a good message today," he said. "We need to be reminded to get rid of sin in our lives."

"I guess so," Tricia shrugged, "but he makes it sound so easy. It seems like there are some sins I never can get rid of—no matter how hard I try."

Mom glanced at Tricia. "Pastor's main point was that we can't cleanse ourselves from sin—we have to let God do it." She smiled at Tricia. "Why did you ask me to brush your hair this morning?"

"Because there were so many snarls," Tricia replied, "and I couldn't get them out."

"In other words, you were really serious about getting the snarls out," Mom said. "It's that way with sin in our lives, too. We can't get rid of the snarls of sin by ourselves—but when we get serious about it and turn the sin over to God, we can be sure that he'll be able to get rid of it. It may hurt, but it's worth it!" *SLK*

HOW ABOUT YOU?
Have you tried to live a good life in your own power? Are you discouraged because you can't get rid of a sinful habit? Admit that you just can't do it yourself, and turn it over to God. Study the Bible and pray. Determine in your heart to obey God, and he will help you overcome that sin.

MEMORIZE:
"The blood of Jesus, his Son, cleanses us from every sin." 1 John 1:7

Let God Cleanse You

Try, Try Again

Read Psalm 37:27-31; 38:18

LeeAnn's best friend, Dawn, had been in a car accident when she was young, and now she needed crutches to help her walk. Although she couldn't run and play with LeeAnn, the two had a lot in common. Both were Christians, and the two talked about church, God, and salvation very naturally. Sometimes when one or the other had a special problem, they would even pray together.

"I'm a Christian, you know, but sometimes I do things that shouldn't be part of a Christian's life," LeeAnn confided one day. She waited for Dawn to say something, but her friend was quiet. "I told Mom a lie again yesterday," LeeAnn confessed. "Sometimes it seems useless to keep trying to do God's will."

"I know what you mean," Dawn said at last. "I sometimes feel that way about things, too. See these crutches? I keep thinking that someday I'll be able to walk without them, so I try every day."

LeeAnn was surprised. She thought Dawn had accepted being crippled for the rest of her life. "What happens when you try to walk?" LeeAnn asked, concern in her voice.

Dawn grinned. "I fall a lot."

"But doesn't that make you feel like never trying again?" LeeAnn asked.

Dawn nodded. "Sometimes," she said, "but I am doing better, and I'm going to keep trying. Since I still fall, I'll rely on my crutches to help me walk until I make it someday!"

Suddenly LeeAnn understood. "That's what I have to do, too, right?" she asked. "Since I'll have the problem of sin until I get to heaven, I have to confess to God and rely on him to forgive me—and go on from there, asking him to help me overcome."

Dawn smiled. "I think we all have to do that," she said. "We can't let Satan keep us down." *RIJ*

HOW ABOUT YOU?

Do you find yourself falling into sin more than you'd like? Maybe you've lied, cheated, stolen, or done something else that's wrong. Don't give up and give in to that sin. With God's help, you can overcome it. As often as you commit that sin, ask God's forgiveness. Ask him for will-power. He'll help you, but you must keep on trying.

Ask God for His Willpower

MEMORIZE:
"God is working in you, giving you the desire to obey him and the power to do what pleases him." Philippians 2:13

August

30

A Broken Plate

Read Ephesians 6:1-3, 10-11

Jean took her best friend into her bedroom to show off the plate rack Dad had made for her. Jean had collected china plates since she was five. Natalie looked at the rack and then down at the table where all the plates were. "I'll help you put them on the rack," she offered.

Jean shook her head. "Dad told me I should wait until tomorrow just to be sure all the glue is dry."

Natalie ran her fingers across the plate rack. "It looks dry to me. One little plate couldn't break anything."

Natalie's probably right, thought Jean. *Perhaps it's dry enough to put one up there.* "Which one shall we try?" she asked. She picked up one plate after another, holding each up to the rack where she could visualize it better.

Natalie did the same. "Here," she said. "This one."

Jean rested the plate on the middle of the rack. As she stepped aside, she bumped the table leg, knocking one of the other plates to the floor. The sound of breaking china brought her father into the room. "What happened?" he asked.

Jean whirled at the sound of his voice. "Oh, Dad! I broke the plate that Aunt Betty sent me from Canada." As she spoke, she knelt to pick up the broken pieces.

"How did it happen?" Dad asked, looking at the plate on the rack.

Jean rose to her feet. "Dad, I'm sorry. I know you said not to use it yet," she said, "but I wanted to show Natalie how nice it looked. I decided I'd put just one plate up there."

"Then she bumped into the table," Natalie added, "and a plate fell off."

"My favorite one," Jean said, with disappointment in her voice. "I should have obeyed you, Dad. It didn't hurt the rack, though, did it?"

"No, it probably didn't hurt the rack," Dad answered slowly, "but it hurt you. You broke your favorite plate, and you experienced guilt that comes from disobedience. God commands you to obey your parents. When you disobey, there's always a consequence." *RIJ*

HOW ABOUT YOU?

Are you influenced by friends—or by your own personal desire—to disobey your parents? Do you find that disobedience causes more problems than it's worth? Only as you obey God, and therefore your parents, can you expect his fullest blessing. Don't allow anything or anybody to persuade you otherwise.

MEMORIZE:

"You children must always obey your parents, for this is what pleases the Lord." Colossians 3:20

Obedience Is Always Best

Room to Grow

Read Acts 2:42-47

Lupe was feeding her fish when her mom came home. "Guess what?" Lupe called out. "Mrs. Jones is moving, and she doesn't want to take her fish tank with her. She gave me these Oscar fish."

"Aren't Oscars awfully big?" Mama asked skeptically, coming into the room.

"In the open lake they are, but if they grow up in a fish tank, they stay small," said Lupe. "They always grow in proportion to their surroundings."

"That's unusual," Mama said. "In fact," she added thoughtfully, "your fish might be something interesting to talk about on hobby night at youth group next week. In some ways, we're like those fish."

"We are?" asked Lupe. "Like fish? Well, fish don't go to youth group—and I don't think I should go, either. The kids in my grade have to move up to the older group this year. I wish we could just stay in our own small group!" Lupe stared at her peaceful fish. "Like these fish," she added.

Mama smiled. "Suppose fish did go to youth group," she said. "What if Mrs. Jones had sent those Oscars to a big fish youth group in the lake, instead of keeping them in a small tank? What would have happened to them?"

Lupe caught her idea. "They would have grown much bigger."

"Right," Mama said. "Now do you think that God would want us—his 'little fish'—to stay in a tiny cramped little tank, never growing the way we should? Or do you think he would want us to stretch and become 'big' Christians?"

Lupe knew the youth group often did things to help needy families. She remembered that they also had projects to help overseas missionaries. Her cousin had told her of the interesting Bible studies the youth group enjoyed. Lupe knew taking part in those activities would help her grow spiritually. "I guess God would want us to grow," she admitted. "Okay, I'll take my fish along on hobby night. Do you think they'll like going to youth group?" *HMT*

HOW ABOUT YOU?

Do you have a place where you can go to grow spiritually? Do you have Christian friends who help you? Don't keep yourself in a "small tank." God wants you to grow. Take advantage of opportunities to make new Christian friends and to serve God in new places.

Go Where You'll Grow Spiritually

Clumsy Clara

Read 1 Peter 3:8-11

As Kelsey turned away from the lunch counter at school, someone knocked her tray from her hands. Spattered with food, she looked angrily at the girl who had bumped into her. It was "Clumsy Clara." "Oh Kelsey, I'm so sorry. . . ." Clara began, blushing as the boys behind her teased and laughed. Kelsey stooped and began to pick up scattered silverware and broken glass as Clara tried to wipe up the food with a napkin.

"Don't bother." Kelsey stopped her. "I'll get a janitor."

"But I'm really sorry," the girl mumbled as Kelsey brushed by her. Clara took a seat in the far corner. She sat alone and picked at her food as big tears welled up in her eyes and threatened to splash down her cheeks.

Kelsey called home, and within a few minutes her mother arrived with a new outfit. "Poor Clara! She must be terribly embarrassed," Mom said when she heard the story. "Maybe you can help make her feel at ease."

Kelsey thought about that idea as she changed clothes. *Why should I make Clara feel at ease? I'm the one that was embarrassed!* Mom's words, however, kept returning to her mind. She also remembered her Sunday school verse—"Be kind to each other, tenderhearted, forgiving one another, just as God through Christ has forgiven you." Kelsey continued to think about Clara all afternoon.

As Kelsey got her lunch tray the next day, she glanced around the room. She knew Clara always sat alone and seldom talked with the other students. Making her way to the table in the far corner, Kelsey saw an uncomfortable blush creep up Clara's neck and into her face. "Hey—everything's all right now," Kelsey said with a smile.

"I'm sorry I bumped into you yesterday," Clara mumbled. "I didn't mean to."

"I know you didn't, Clara," Kelsey reassured her. "We all do things like that sometimes."

As the girls talked about some of their classes, Clara began to relax, and Kelsey felt better, too. *Dear Lord,* she prayed silently, *please help me be a friend to Clara—not just today, but every day. NKP*

HOW ABOUT YOU?

Do you know someone who is lonely? Someone who is clumsy? Someone who needs a friend? God wants you to show compassion to that person. Think about how that person feels. Then treat him or her with kindness.

MEMORIZE:
"If you give even a cup of cold water to one of the least of my followers, you will surely be rewarded."
Matthew 10:42

Be Kind

2

A Mighty Weapon

Read Psalm 119:1-8

"That was Janelle," Kayla told her sister, Alicia, as she hung up the phone. "She wants me to help her get even with that crabby lady who works in the school cafeteria. I told her I wouldn't. Remember Romans 13:10—the verse Grandpa Horne taught us? 'Love does no wrong to anyone.' "

Alicia nodded. "Let's go see Grandpa," she said. They rode their bikes to their grandfather's house.

But Grandpa didn't invite them in! "I can't visit with you today," Grandpa said slowly, "but I hope you've learned that verse—Psalm 22:11. Go on home and study it right now. That's Psalm 22:11. You can say it to me—soon!" He quickly closed the door.

"Grandpa seemed strange," remarked Alicia.

"Why does he want us to learn Psalm 22:11?" Kayla wondered aloud as the two sisters started off on their bikes.

"Let's look it up," said Alicia. "I still have my Bible in my bike bag." They stopped and looked up the verse. When they saw what it said, they gasped and hurried to tell their mom.

An hour later, they were back at Grandpa's—this time with their mother and a policeman. The officer explained that two thieves had a gun pointed at Grandpa when he answered the door. They had tied him up and were packing all the valuable things they could find when they were interrupted by the police. "How did you kids know there was trouble?" the policeman asked.

"Grandpa acted funny, and he sent us away with a Scripture reference," Alicia explained. "When we looked it up, we knew he was in trouble." She grinned.

"The verse said, 'Do not stay so far from me, for trouble is near, and no one else can help me,' " Kayla explained. "Grandpa, knowing Scripture has really come in handy today. A verse I learned helped me do the right thing this morning—and your verse helped stop a robbery!"

"The Bible is sharper than a two-edged sword," Grandpa agreed. "It's our weapon against sin—and a mighty weapon at that!" *JLH*

HOW ABOUT YOU?

Are you using your "weapon"—the Bible? Read it. Memorize it. Then apply the lessons you learn from it to your daily life.

MEMORIZE:

"For the word of God is living and active. Sharper than any double-edged sword." Hebrews 4:12, NIV

God's Word Will Help You Do Right

Under Construction

Read James 1:2-4

"Why are we slowing down?" asked Kaitlyn, as they stopped behind a line of cars.

Melissa poked her head out the window. "It's construction," she announced. "I can see a digging machine and a sign lady."

"Oh, no!" exclaimed Kaitlyn, "We'll be late! It's bad enough being new in school. But being late and having everyone stare at me will be the worst!"

"I'm afraid I'll be late for my job interview, too," said Mom, looking at her watch.

"I wish Daddy hadn't left. Then we'd still be living in our old house," said Melissa, "and we'd have all our old friends and be close enough to walk to school."

"I wish that, too," said Mom, "but we have to carry on."

Just then the line of cars began moving, and they followed the car in front of them onto a bumpy gravel path. They passed men working with loud jackhammers and a huge machine that was digging up great chunks of asphalt.

"Why do they have to wreck a perfectly good road?" Melissa wondered aloud.

"It reminds me of our family," Kaitlyn glumly said. "It was just fine. But then Dad left, and now everything's broken and torn up."

"It does feel like that," agreed Mom, "but think about this . . . the people in charge at city hall have planned for this to be a better road, and that's why they're allowing it to be broken up and worked on. They know that after the construction is finished, it will be better. As for us, God has plans. He's letting us go through a very difficult time, but he knows that as we learn to trust him and rely on him, we become stronger and better people." *VEN*

HOW ABOUT YOU?

Is it hard to believe that anything good can come from disappointment or pain? Road construction leads to a better road, and God will use hard times in your life to make you stronger, wiser, more patient, and compassionate—if you let him.

MEMORIZE:

"No discipline is enjoyable while it is happening . . . but afterward there will be a quiet harvest of right living."

Hebrews 12:11

Construction—God at Work in Your Life

September

4

The Promise in a Seed

Read Luke 8:11-15

"We can make applesauce, apple pies, apple strudel, apple butter, apple dumplings, baked apples. . . ." Heidi's voice trailed off as she ran out of suggestions.

"You've got grand plans for all these apples we picked," Aunt Sue said with a smile. She lugged a basket of apples into the kitchen. "Well, it's time we use some of these. We'll make a batch or two of applesauce and freeze some of it. Would you like to start peeling them?"

"Okay," Heidi agreed. She got out a knife and some pans and started working. After a while, she sighed. "How many do we need?" she asked. "It'll take forever to peel all these and take out the cores."

Aunt Sue laughed. "Oh, not quite that long. Have you ever wondered how many apples can come from just one of these seeds?" she asked.

Heidi shook her head. "Lots, I guess," she said.

"You're right," Aunt Sue agreed. "Lots and lots."

"Just think," Heidi said, "if one seed grows into a tree and produces a crop of apples, and if each seed from each of those apples grows into another tree, and each of those trees produces a crop of apples, and each seed from each of those apples grows into a tree, and . . ."

Aunt Sue rolled her eyes. "You're making me tired! That's an interesting thought, but that could go on for a very long time." Heidi laughed. "Here's another interesting thought," Aunt Sue continued. "If I plant just one seed for Jesus—if I witness for him by one word or deed—who knows what he can do with it? So often I forget that I just need to plant, but it's God who makes everything grow."

As she was speaking, Uncle Matt came in. "That's right," he said, grinning. "Now how about making me an apple pie?"

Heidi chuckled. "How about helping me peel more apples?" *KC*

HOW ABOUT YOU?

Do you plant seeds of God's Word, sharing with friends what you know about Jesus? God can use each truth you share from his Word to produce much fruit for him. He can also use each act of obedience to his Word—each act of helpfulness, courtesy, and honesty. People need to hear the gospel, and God is ready to work through you.

MEMORIZE:
"I planted the seed . . . but God made it grow." 1 Corinthians 3:6, NIV

Plant Seeds—Witness for Jesus

Special Gift (Part 1)

Read 1 John 5:13-15

Suzanne shook her piggy bank, and the coins bounced out and rolled across the table. She slowly counted the money. Then she counted it all over again, just in case she had made a mistake. But she hadn't. She had only a few dollars—what could she buy for Mom's birthday with that? Certainly not the beautiful blue blouse she had seen her mom admire. *I've just got to get that blouse,* Suzanne thought. *It's the perfect gift for Mom, and she deserves it. She's worked so hard to support us since Daddy died. What can I do? Mom's birthday is only three weeks away!*

Then Suzanne remembered what Mom had taught her—no problem is too big for God. So Suzanne prayed about it, telling God all about the blue blouse. "Dear Lord," she prayed, "please help me get the money for that blouse. Please help me give a special gift to Mom."

The very next day, Mrs. Porter, an older lady who lived next door, asked Suzanne to run a few errands for her. When Suzanne returned, Mrs. Porter insisted that she take a dollar for her work. As Suzanne thankfully put the money away, she had an idea. Maybe God would answer her prayer by giving her some more work to do.

She excitedly made a list of things she could do—watch children, walk dogs, run errands, clean house, and help with yard work. Then she went around the neighborhood letting people know she was available to work. "Thank you, Lord," she prayed, "for answering and showing me a way so quickly." *JLH*

HOW ABOUT YOU?

What do you do when you have a problem? Do you go to God in prayer? Nothing is too hard for God. Nothing is too small or too big. He is ready to help you, but you must ask for that help. Be sure to ask that his will be done, and then believe he will answer.

Give Your Problems to God

September

6

Special Gift (Part 2)

Read 1 Samuel 15:22; Colossians 3:20

Suzanne continued working to earn enough money to buy the beautiful blue blouse for Mom's birthday. She mailed a package for Mrs. Sisson and mowed the lawn for Mrs. Gates. When Mrs. Smith asked Suzanne to baby-sit after school, Suzanne was delighted! This would quickly add a lot to her account.

But Mom said, "I'm sorry, Suzanne. I wish I could let you take the job, but my boss promised me some overtime, and we need the extra money. I need you to watch Brad after school. Maybe you can baby-sit for the Smiths some other time."

Suzanne was disappointed. *I need to earn money now, not later,* she thought. *It doesn't seem right. After all, I don't want the money for myself; I want it for Mom! I thought God was answering my prayer by providing that job!* But Suzanne obeyed her mother and turned down the work.

That evening, Suzanne's friend Evie called to invite her to come over after school the next day to see some new puppies. "May I go?" Suzanne asked. "Brad can come, too."

"Oh, that sounds like fun," Mom replied, "but Aunt Joy may be calling tomorrow afternoon. I suppose she'll call back if nobody answers. I don't know— let me think about it. Ask me in the morning."

But the next morning they all overslept, and Suzanne forgot about the puppies until after school when Evie came by. "Suzanne, can you come with me?" Evie asked.

"No, I guess I can't," Suzanne replied. "Mom forgot to give me permission."

"Come anyway," Evie urged. "She won't care. She knows my mom."

Suzanne shook her head. "No," she said, "I can't go without Mom's permission."

Mom looked so tired when she got home from work that Suzanne decided not to mention the puppies, but Brad talked about his disappointment. "I'm so sorry, Suzanne! I forgot all about it," Mom apologized. She hugged Suzanne as she added, "I don't know what I'd do without you. I'm proud you obeyed me even in my absence. Come now, and we'll fix supper with a special dessert." *JLH*

HOW ABOUT YOU?

Do you obey your parents even when they aren't around to see you do it? Your obedience will earn their trust and praise. In obeying them, you are also obeying the Lord.

MEMORIZE:

"What is more pleasing to the Lord:
your burnt offerings and sacrifices or
your obedience to his voice?
Obedience is far better than sacrifice."
1 Samuel 15:22

**Obedience Is Better
than Gifts**

Special Gift (Part 3)

Read Matthew 22:35-40

Suzanne was discouraged! She had been so sure God had answered prayer by giving her jobs to do, but that hadn't worked out. Now something else came up. Suzanne played in the school band, and the rental fee for band instruments was due. Mom explained that she wouldn't have the money until the following week when she received her paycheck. She looked so concerned that Suzanne offered to use her savings to help out.

"Oh, Suzanne!" Mom exclaimed, relief in her voice. "That would be such a help! As soon as I get my check, I'll pay the money back!" So now Suzanne's money was gone, and she wondered what she would do for her mother's gift. She couldn't think of any way to get one—even a small one.

The day before Mom's birthday arrived, and Suzanne still had no gift! *Well, the least I can do is serve Mom breakfast in bed,* she thought with a sigh, so she set her alarm for early the next day. But the next thing she knew, her mother was saying, "Suzanne, breakfast is ready." Suzanne had overslept! She burst into tears.

"Suzanne! What's the matter?" Mom asked. "Don't you feel well?"

"Today's your birthday," Suzanne said between sobs, "and I love you so much, but I don't have a gift for you."

"Suzanne, you've already given me a gift," Mom declared as she sat on the edge of the bed and gathered Suzanne into her arms. "You've given me the best gift in all the world!"

"But, I haven't," Suzanne answered. "I tried. I wanted to get that beautiful blue blouse I saw you looking at, but I couldn't."

"Suzanne, you gave me the best gift—a gift you couldn't buy," Mom insisted. "You gave me your love, your obedience, and your service. All the money in the world couldn't buy those gifts! You have given me what I wanted most—yourself! What a special birthday gift that is!" *JLH*

HOW ABOUT YOU?
Do you know that the gift God wants most from you is your life? Give him the best gift—the gift of yourself, your love, your obedience, and your service. Have you done that? If not, do so today!

Give Yourself to Jesus

September
8

The New Student

Read Leviticus 19:16-18

After school, Lily and Mandy huddled together by the coat rack as Kim Lieu, a new student in their class, shyly walked by. "I heard she's from China," Mandy whispered, "and that her family eats strange food like dried fish eyes, and that they pray to a god in a little box of incense."

Lily looked a little frightened. "Oh, no!" she gasped. "She just moved into the house next to mine, and who knows what other strange things they might do!"

Lily could hardly wait to tell her mom what she had learned about their new neighbors, but Mom didn't seem impressed at all. "Sounds to me like someone's been gossiping," Mom said. "Remember—you can't believe everything you hear. Tell you what—I bought cookies today, and you can take them over to the Lieus. Why don't you invite Kim to go to Sunday school with you?"

"But, Mom!" Lily protested. "What about their strange religion?"

"Like I said, you can't believe everything you hear. Besides, Jesus died to save girls who were born in China as well as girls who were born in America, like you, Lily. Now run along," Mom insisted.

When Mrs. Lieu opened the door, Lily noticed that the house smelled deliciously like fried chicken. Mrs. Lieu thanked Lily for the cookies and invited her to have a snack with them. When Lily finally got up enough nerve to invite Kim to Sunday school, Mrs. Lieu smiled broadly. "Why, Lily," she exclaimed, "I'm sure our whole family would like to go with you next Sunday, if that's all right. You see, we're Christians, and we've been praying that God would lead us to a good Bible-believing church in this city."

Now Lily was anxious to get home and tell her mom some *real* news about their new neighbors—not just gossip! *PMR*

HOW ABOUT YOU?
Do you believe everything you hear? Does it please you to hear that a classmate failed a test, cheated, or perhaps that his parents are getting divorced? Is it exciting to hear that someone got caught stealing, lying, or saying bad words? Do you eagerly pass the news along? Very often gossip is not true, and it hurts others. Be careful neither to listen to nor pass on gossip.

MEMORIZE:
"They must not speak evil of anyone."
Titus 3:2

Don't Gossip

A Habit of My Own

Read Matthew 7:1-5

Callie was having a hard time adjusting to the small town to which her family had recently moved. She was lonesome and longed for a friend, but there was no one for her to hang around with—except Crystal. And Callie didn't care for Crystal. "She giggles all the time," Callie told her mom. "It drives me crazy!"

"Don't be too hard on her," Mom advised. "Maybe she's just nervous and needs a friend. The Bible teaches us to be careful about judging others—remember?"

Callie sighed. "Oh, you just don't understand," she said.

A few days later, Callie came bursting into the house after a Sunday school class party. "Crystal and her dad brought me home," she reported. "Is it all right if I go to the football game with her tomorrow night?"

Mom looked up in surprise. "That would be nice," she said. "Did you have a good time at the party?"

"Yes . . . but they laughed at me!" Callie reported. "We were all sitting in a circle playing a game I never heard of before, and I was so nervous that I cracked my knuckles. Nora Elmers made a big scene about it. She was so snobby and said loudly, 'Really, Callie, do you *always* have to crack your knuckles? We hate to hear it!' I was so embarrassed!"

"That wasn't very nice, but don't let it upset you. Just try to see it as a helpful hint," Mom suggested.

"But so many of the girls laughed about it!" Callie protested. She paused, then added, "Crystal didn't, though. She looked annoyed with Nora. Then I remembered how I criticized her for giggling, and I felt ashamed. So I rode home with her, and you know what? She's really nice!"

"Great," Mom approved. "It's good to remember that we all have some annoying habits. While we work on improving our own, we need to overlook them in others." *AU*

HOW ABOUT YOU?

Do you know someone who has a habit that you find irritating? It's easy to become annoyed with the habits of others and forget that we all probably have some strange little quirks. Don't let a small thing blind you to someone's good qualities. God wants you to do everything in love, not in a critical way.

Be Careful Not to Judge

September

10

Always Watching

Read Psalm 139:1-12

Ruthie sat on her bed and looked at her mother. "I wish I could just stay home," she said. "I'm still scared." There had been some violence at her school a few days before, and today was the first day back. Ruthie slowly got up and went to the window. Looking out, she noticed a little dove all alone on the grass, resting peacefully until two large pigeons landed nearby. The young dove began cooing loudly in alarm. Ruthie frowned. "If only that little dove had stayed in its nest, it would be safe," she said to her mom. But before Mom could answer, the mother dove appeared, and the curious pigeons flew away. "Wow! I'm glad the little dove wasn't left alone for long in this scary world," Ruthie said.

Mom gently turned Ruthie around. "Honey, that little dove was never really left alone," she said. "Its mother was always watching."

Ruthie sighed. "Well, I wish you or Dad could go wherever I go and watch and protect me all the time."

"We can't do that," Mom said, "but someone can—and does—watch over you all the time. You're God's child, and he's caring for you constantly. He loves you, and he'll protect you—and he'll do a much better job of it than Dad and I could do!"

"But we can't be sure he'll keep us safe, can we?" Ruthie asked. "I mean . . . sometimes Christians get hurt, too."

"That's true," Mom agreed, "but you can trust God to allow only what is good for you. No matter where you go, you're in God's sight. When you're in school, he sees you. When you play outside, he's with you there. Even when you sleep, God is watching over you, and nothing can happen that he does not permit."

Ruthie thought about Mom's words. "So since God is my Father and he's protecting me, I don't need to be afraid anymore, even though the world is such a scary place."

Mom nodded. "God is watching over you at every moment," she said. "Trust him, honey. He'll take care of you." *SML*

HOW ABOUT YOU?

Do you live in fear because of the terrible things that happen in the world? Are you afraid to leave your house? If you're a child of God, you don't need to live in fear and dread. You're never out of God's sight. Trust him with your life.

MEMORIZE:

"The eyes of the Lord watch over those who do right; his ears are open to their cries for help." Psalm 34:15

God Sees and Cares for You

The Default Setting

Read Romans 7:21-25

"Mom, how do I change this font?" Tracy called from the study, where she was working on homework at the computer.

"Here, I'll help you." Tracy's younger brother, Mark, jumped up from the floor where he was working on a puzzle. "What font do you want?" He showed Tracy the various ones she could use. After she chose one, Mark clicked the mouse a few times, and soon Tracy was finishing her homework.

When Tracy wanted to use the computer the next evening, there was the old font again. "Who changed this? Mark?" she called out. "Why did you change this back, you dummy? Now set it up again!"

"I didn't change anything," Mark said.

"Don't lie! You fix it right now, or I'll beat you up!" Tracy ordered.

"Not if you ask me like that," Mark replied. He let out a yell as Tracy jumped up and came after him.

"What's going on in here?" Mom demanded, entering the room.

"Mark changed the computer, and now he won't fix it," Tracy replied.

"I didn't touch it," Mark insisted.

"Why don't you learn to fix it yourself, Tracy?" Mom suggested, and she showed Tracy how to set it up. "But understand," Mom added, "that unless we change the default, the old font will come up again the next time we turn the computer on."

"The default?" Tracy asked. "What's that?"

"It's the way the computer is set to come on," Mom said. "Unless we make a permanent change, it will automatically come up with the old font."

"Let's change it then," Tracy said. Mom agreed, and soon it was done. "That takes care of one problem," Mom said, "but I'm afraid something else needs a change in its 'default setting.' Your angry reaction when things don't go your way indicates that a change is needed in your heart. You need to ask Jesus to help you make that change. And then you can start showing it by apologizing to your brother." *VEN*

HOW ABOUT YOU?

Do you often find yourself getting angry, telling lies, swearing, or doing other things you know are wrong? Maybe you're determined to change, but you keep reacting the same way. Only God has the power to change you. As he reveals to you various areas in your life that need to change, ask him to help you make the changes in your "heart's settings" to please him. You can have victory.

MEMORIZE:

"Thanks be to God! He gives us the victory through our Lord Jesus Christ."

1 Corinthians 15:57, NIV

Let Jesus Change You

September

12

The Rope

Read Psalm 119:9-16

"Peese come to school next Fwiday! Peese! Peese!" Aaron begged, wildly waving a printed reminder of the special Family Day at preschool.

"Of course I'll come," Mom answered, giving three-year-old Aaron a hug. "Janna can come, too. She doesn't have school next Friday."

"Yippee!" Aaron hollered as he went off to play with his toys.

Janna smiled. "It will be nice to see Mrs. King again," she said. "I still remember being in preschool. I had so much fun there."

When Mom and Janna visited Aaron's school, they watched as Aaron and his classmates colored a picture, listened to the story of *The Little Engine That Could*, and found things in the room that were blue.

After enjoying crackers and juice, Mrs. King clapped her hands for attention. "It's time to line up to go to the playground," she announced. She took two long ropes out of the closet. The boys lined up on one rope and the girls on the other. Each child held tightly to the rope. Mrs. King took a rope in each hand and led the way out. "Be sure to watch for cars," she reminded the children as they started across the parking lot. The three- and four-year-olds made their way past several parked cars and a big yellow school bus. Their feet kicked up small clouds of dust from the gravel, and they giggled as geese honked from above.

"I remember that rope," Janna told her mother as they followed the children. "I held on to it for dear life." Then she laughed and added, "The playground seemed much farther away then, and walking past all the cars scared me."

Mom smiled. "We may be older, but we still need to hang on to a rope," she replied. Janna looked puzzled, and Mom laughed. "Not a real rope," she said, "but in a way, God's Word is like a rope. We don't have to hold on to it to keep our salvation—we can't lose that. The Bible says we are 'kept by the power of God.' But the Bible also tells us to hold fast to what is good. We do this by reading, memorizing, and obeying what God says in his Word."

Janna nodded and smiled as she turned back to watch her little brother holding on to the rope. *LJR*

HOW ABOUT YOU?

First Thessalonians 5:21 says, "Hold on to what is good." Do you do that? Do you "hold tightly" to what God says? No one can plant God's words into your heart, except you. No one can make you memorize them. No one can force you to think about what God says in his Word and apply it to your heart and life. It's up to you to make the choice to do it. It takes time and effort, but you will be rewarded! Make Psalm 119:16 your promise to God.

MEMORIZE:

"I will not neglect your word." Psalm 119:16, NIV

Hold On to God's Word

Spread Too Thin

Read Colossians 3:17, 23-24

It was Saturday morning, and Katya hurriedly gobbled down a donut with a glass of milk. She had to hurry to school for a special band practice. Then she had to pick up materials to make signs for the baked goods sale her Girl Scout troop was having. "Oh . . . I invited some of the church kids over for lunch so we could talk about our retreat next month," she finally remembered to tell her mother as she was hurrying out the door.

"Oh Katya," Mom groaned, "I wish you would have asked me earlier. You'll have to fix lunch yourself, because I'll be running errands most of the day."

The morning went poorly for Katya. She hadn't had time to practice her clarinet for a week and didn't play well. She went to buy posterboard, but had to ride her bike to two stores before she found the right color. At lunchtime she searched the cupboards but found only a nearly empty jar of peanut butter. "Peanut butter sandwiches will have to do," she decided aloud. She spread it very thinly over the slices of bread, slapping the sandwiches together just as her friends arrived.

When the kids began to eat, Jack frowned. "What are these? Bread sandwiches?" he asked. The other kids laughed, and Katya felt terrible. What a flop her lunch was!

Later, when she told her mother about it, Mom shook her head. "I'm sorry, Katya," she said, "but you know, the peanut butter sandwiches remind me of you." Katya looked at Mom in surprise. "The peanut butter was spread too thin," Mom continued, "and you're spreading yourself too thin, too. By being involved in too many activities, you can't do a good job at any of them."

Katya sighed. "I guess you're right," she admitted.

"Why don't you write a list of all the things you want to do, and ask the Lord to help you decide which are the most important," Mom suggested. "Do those things first, and do them well. You'll be doing everyone a favor by not taking on more than you can handle." *SLK*

HOW ABOUT YOU?

Are you too busy? You shouldn't be so busy that you can't do a good job at each thing you do. Learn to say no if you don't have time to take on a new responsibility. Pray about it and then seek a parent's advice about which things you have time for. Make time to give your best effort.

MEMORIZE:
"Whatever your hand finds to do, do it with all your might." Ecclesiastes 9:10, NIV

Don't Get Too Busy

September

14

Bad Apples

Read 1 Corinthians 3:11-15

"Would you like to earn a few dollars?" Sophie's Uncle Roy asked. "I'll pay you for each bushel of apples you pick. Just get apples from the trees. Don't pick up 'drops'—apples that have fallen to the ground."

Sophie eagerly went to work. To pick apples from high branches, she used a ladder or a long pole picker. It was fun, but she couldn't fill bushels very quickly. *This takes too long,* thought Sophie. *The apples on the ground look just as good. I'll pick up some of those—just the good ones.* At first she was choosy about what she picked up. But the longer she worked, the less fussy she was.

Uncle Roy came back at lunchtime. "You sure are a fast worker!" he exclaimed. But when he began to load the apples onto his truck, he noticed what Sophie had done. "I'm sorry, honey. I can't pay you for picking up the drops," he told her.

"But they're almost spotless!" protested Sophie.

"Yes, but when they fell to the ground, they got bruised. Unless they're used right away, the bruised spots will begin to rot," he explained. "Then they'll cause the good apples to start rotting, too. It wouldn't be fair to sell them to my customers."

"And I thought I was making so much money," sighed Sophie. "All that work for nothing!"

In church the next day, Sophie was surprised to hear an illustration the pastor gave. "Last year my wife and I went out to an apple orchard and picked up some good 'drops,' " said Pastor Grey. "We got lots of them, and we enjoyed pie and applesauce, but we soon had rotten apples on our hands. Those drops didn't keep well—they didn't last. Many things in life are like that. People—even Christians—work so hard to gain many enjoyable earthly things. But earthly things don't keep. They last only a short time. God wants us to work for eternal, heavenly rewards. As a missionary named Jim Elliott once said, 'Only one life—'twill soon be past. Only what's done for Christ will last.' " *LAP*

HOW ABOUT YOU?

Are you working for what the world says is good—nice clothes, money, popularity, a good career some day? Those things are nice, but they last only a short time. To earn lasting treasure, make sure you do the things that please God. His rewards are eternal.

MEMORIZE:

"Let heaven fill your thoughts. Do not think only about things down here on earth." Colossians 3:2

Work for Eternal Rewards

To Speak or Not to Speak

Read Genesis 4:12; Joshua 1:5-9

Anne had made up her mind! *Now that we've moved to a new home, I'm going to be just like the other kids,* she decided. *I'm tired of being different. The kids at my old school called me a fanatic! The kids here don't have to know I'm a Christian. I'm not going to miss my chance to change things.*

Everything went fine until the day of Janey's party. "Okay, you guys," called Nisha when they were ready to play the first game, "Everybody has to draw a slip of paper from this basket. When your name is called, you have to perform the stunt written on the paper." She began to pass the basket. "There's a prize for the best performance," she added.

Anne eagerly looked at her slip of paper. "Oh, no!" she groaned. *Doing this would be mocking God, but if I don't do it, what will the kids say?* she wondered. *Oh, what am I going to do?* She tried to think of a way out. *Maybe I could trade with someone—but then I'd be asking someone else to mock God. Oh! Should I just do what this paper says, or should I say that I can't?* She hadn't made up her mind when she heard her name being called.

Slowly Anne stood up. She spoke hesitantly. "I—I'm supposed to bow in front of the fireplace with my forehead to the floor and recite the Lord's Prayer—but I can't do it," she said. The room became very quiet. "I'm a Christian, and I'd be mocking God if I did that. I'm sorry." She sat down.

After a moment, Nisha laughed. "That's okay," she said. "We'll skip you. Char, you're next." The party went on, but Anne hardly noticed. She didn't enjoy it anymore.

As Anne started home after the party, Paula caught up with her. "I'm glad for what you did," said Paula softly. "I'm a Christian, too, but I haven't been acting like one. I'm going to be a better witness for Jesus from now on." Anne was surprised and pleased. Together the girls went on down the street. *BP*

HOW ABOUT YOU?

Are you ashamed of Jesus? He was willing to die for you. By speaking up for him, you can be a witness to unsaved friends and also encourage other Christian kids.

MEMORIZE:
"I am not ashamed of this Good News about Christ. It is the power of God at work, saving everyone who believes."

Romans 1:16

Speak Up for Jesus

September

16

Lost Inheritance (Part 1)

Read Luke 17:26-30

Isabella came into the family room where her parents were watching the news. Together they listened to the report of a man trying to collect a large inheritance. "If that man's parents died, why can't he get the money that was left?" asked Isabella.

"He ran away from home when he was sixteen years old," Dad explained. "That was thirty years ago, and he never contacted his family again. Apparently his parents did discover what area of the country he had gone to, and they made repeated efforts throughout the years to contact him, but he wouldn't respond."

"But now that he's back, won't he get at least some of the money?" asked Isabella.

Dad shook his head. "It doesn't sound like it. I guess his parents gave up and decided not to leave him anything. They didn't put him in their wills. Now, after they've both died, he's finally shown up. He thinks he should have the inheritance, but now it's too late. He contested the will, but the courts upheld it. They said he was not entitled to any of the money."

"Wow!" exclaimed Isabella. "According to that news report, he claims that he always intended to come back sometime. I bet he's sorry now that he didn't come sooner."

"He's learned a hard lesson—and a very common one," Dad said. "Do you realize that something similar happens every day?"

"You mean there are lots of people who leave home and ignore their parents and aren't left any money?" asked Isabella.

"That happens often enough," Dad said, "but what I really meant is that God calls people to himself and many ignore him. They're too busy doing their own things. When the end of life comes, they're going to want a piece of the inheritance God had offered, but he's going to say, 'Sorry, I don't know you. Your name isn't in the "will"—the Book of Life.'" *HMT*

HOW ABOUT YOU?

Will you be able to claim the great inheritance God offers to all who trust in Jesus? He's offering something far better than money—salvation and a home in heaven for eternity. Receive Jesus as Savior today. Then he'll be able to say, "I know you! Welcome home!"

MEMORIZE:
"The Lord knows those who are his."
2 Timothy 2:19

Accept Jesus Today

Lost Inheritance (Part 2)

Read Romans 10:13-15

When Isabella came home from school, she had some exciting news. "Guess what happened at school today!" she said. "We got a new kid in our class, and you'll never guess where he came from!" Isabella paused and waited to see what her mom would say.

"Well, where?" Mom asked after a moment. "You said I'd never guess, and I believe you, so tell me."

"From Melville, Texas," said Isabella. She waited to hear exclamations of surprise from her mom, but none came. "You know," she prompted, "the city that guy lived in—the one who came back here hoping to get an inheritance, but his parents had left him out of their wills, and he couldn't get the money, so he protested and said that he should get it, and he . . ."

"Whoa! Slow down," Mom said. "I remember! Did the boy in your class know that man personally?"

Isabella shook her head. "No, but I thought it was interesting that he came from the same town."

Mom nodded. "Tell me," she said after a moment. "If you knew the man we heard about in the news, and if you had also known his parents when they were alive, what would you have done?"

"What would I have done?" repeated Isabella. "Well . . . I would have told him his parents were looking for him and that he'd better contact them. I would have warned him that he might be left out of their wills if he didn't go back and make up with them!"

"Good," Mom said. "Then it would have been up to him to decide what to do. Now, Isabella, I'd like you to tell me something else. Do you think there's anybody you know that your heavenly Father would like to have contact him?"

"Lots of people," admitted Isabella. "I guess I should do the same thing for them, shouldn't I? I should let them know that God wants them to trust in Jesus and warn them that someday it will be too late."

"It's something we all should do," Mom agreed. "In a way, they're runaways from God, and we should warn them to contact him right away." *HMT*

HOW ABOUT YOU?

Do you have friends who aren't Christians? Do you think of them as runaways from God? He wants them to come to him, and he may want you to be the one to tell them. Will you help bring them home before it's too late?

Tell Others about Jesus

MEMORIZE:
"I pray that you may be active in sharing your faith." Philemon 1:6, NIV

On Track

Read Deuteronomy 6:1-3

Jayden was working on her electric train set when she heard her father come home. Soon Dad joined her in the basement. "How's the train project coming along?" asked Dad.

"Good!" exclaimed Jayden. "It's almost ready to run."

"And how was school today?" Dad wanted to know.

Jayden frowned. "Okay, I guess," she said, "but I'm getting tired of all the rules we have. One of them says you have to stay in at recess if you're late more than three times. They just don't want kids to have any fun."

"I take it that you were late?" asked Dad.

"Only a couple of minutes!" said Jayden. "I don't see why it matters if I was a little late. At least I was there!" She reached over to hook a section of track in place.

"Hmmm," murmured Dad. "Well, Jayden, let's see how your train runs." He reached over, pressed the start lever, and the train began moving.

"Dad!" exclaimed Jayden. "What are you doing? I don't have all the tracks down yet. It's gonna wreck!" As she spoke, the train rounded the turn and rolled off the track, falling on its side. "I told you," said Jayden.

"So the train needs the tracks—they don't spoil things. Instead, they're helpful and allow the train to run smoothly, right?" asked Dad.

Jayden nodded. "Sure," she agreed.

"Well, rules are like those tracks," Dad said. "When you follow the rules, they allow your life to run smoothly and even allow you to have fun. When you choose to disobey rules, you get off track, and everything seems a mess. God wants us to follow the rules of those he puts over us—like parents and teachers."

"I get the point, Dad," admitted Jayden as she picked up the train. "Tracks are good for trains, and rules are good for kids."

"Right," Dad said, "and for grown-ups, too." *MRC*

HOW ABOUT YOU?

Do you get tired of rules? Do you wish you had no rules at all? Rules are made to help you enjoy life, not to keep you from having fun. Be careful to obey your parents and teachers—and most of all, God.

MEMORIZE:
"Everyone must submit himself to the governing authorities." Romans 13:1, NIV

Obey Rules

The Right Answer

19

Read Genesis 11:1-9

"In music class today, Miss Arguello taught us a silly song about a man who tried to go to heaven in a hot air balloon. When that didn't work, he tried a kite," Tori told her family one night. "I felt bad singing that song because it was making fun of the Bible."

"It doesn't sound like a very good song," Dad agreed.

"That's not all," Tori added. "After we were done singing, Angie raised her hand and asked Miss Arguello how people really get to heaven. Before Miss Arguello could answer, Johnny said you had to die first. Marsha said you had to do good deeds, and then Winona said her minister told her she had to be a member of their church to go to heaven.

"So I raised my hand, and I started to tell them that you have to believe Jesus died for your sins and that he rose again, and you have to accept him as your Savior."

"Good for you! What did Miss Arguello say then?" Mom asked.

"She said it was time to end the discussion because we weren't allowed to talk about religion in school!" Tori said. "She taught us that song, and she let the other kids talk, but when I wanted to tell what the Bible said, she changed the subject!"

"That's often the way things go." Dad shook his head. "People like to talk about heaven as if it's pretend, or they use the Bible as a good-luck charm, but they refuse to listen to the truth."

"People have always tried to get to heaven on their own," Mom said. "Think about the Tower of Babel. Way back then, people thought they could reach heaven through their own works."

"Well, I'm glad I know the Bible is true, and that I know the real way to get to heaven!" Tori exclaimed. "And you know what else? Tomorrow I'm going to talk to Angie and give her the right answer to her question." *LMW*

HOW ABOUT YOU?

Do you know the one true way to heaven? God's Word says that the only way is by accepting Jesus Christ as your personal Savior. If you haven't already done that, do it today.

MEMORIZE:

"God saved you by his special favor when you believed. And you can't take credit for this; it is a gift from God. Salvation is not a reward for the good things we have done, so none of us can boast about it." Ephesians 2:8-9

Jesus Is the Way to Heaven

September

20

Dayna's Mean Mom

Read Proverbs 6:20-23

"Mom! Something's wrong with Cassie!" Dayna cried. Hearing the anxiety in her daughter's voice, Mom dropped the dish towel and ran into the family room where Dayna's baby sister stood holding tightly to the playpen railing. She was trying to cry, but no sound came, and her usually pink lips had a dusky blue color. Her eyes were wide and frightened. "What's the matter with her, Mom?" Dayna asked anxiously.

Mom quickly lifted little Cassie and squeezed the baby's chest. After a moment, a bright green marble popped out of Cassie's mouth, and she burst into tears. Dayna began to cry, too. "You hurt her, Mom! It wasn't her fault. I gave her the marble."

While comforting the crying baby, Mom also drew Dayna into the circle of her arm. "Honey, how many times have I told you to keep your small toys picked up so Cassie doesn't get them?" she said. "She's not ready for some things yet. Do you understand that now? She was choking on that marble!"

When the children had calmed down, Mom said, "Last week some of the older kids wanted you to play down by the creek with them. Remember?" Dayna nodded, wiping away some leftover tears. "When I said no, you complained and told me I was a mean mom," Mom continued. "Just now you cried when I was getting the marble from Cassie. You thought that was mean, too, but it made her stop choking, didn't it?"

Dayna nodded solemnly. "But it looked like you were hurting her more," she said.

"It was something I had to do to help her. You see, Jesus has given you parents who love you very much, and we're doing what's best for you," Mom said tenderly. "Sometimes you may not understand, and it may even hurt you—but I want you to learn to trust us and obey us, just as we trust Jesus to help us do the right things."

Dayna looked into Cassie's rosy face and happy blue eyes. Then shyly she said, "I'm sorry for thinking you'd hurt Cassie. I know you'd never be mean to her." *PIK*

HOW ABOUT YOU?

Do you sometimes feel like calling your parents names and stamping your feet? God wants you to obey, honor, and respect them, even when you don't understand why they have had to do or say certain things. Ask him to give them—and you—wisdom and understanding in your relationship.

MEMORIZE:

"Obey your father's commands, and don't neglect your mother's teaching."
Proverbs 6:20

Honor and Obey Parents

No Fixed Stain

Read Psalm 4:4; Proverbs 15:18

Liz walked into the living room with her arms crossed and her jaw clenched. Mom looked at her and frowned. "Don't tell me you're still angry over what happened with Sonja," she said.

"Yes, I am!" replied Liz. "Sonja shouldn't have taken my seat on the bus. She knows I always sit with Janet."

"Maybe she does, but you shouldn't be mulling over it so long," said Mom as she knelt down to scrub the carpet.

Liz stared at the stain her mother was vigorously trying to get rid of. She saw that the stain made by spilled grape juice was becoming wider by the second. "That stain is getting worse instead of better," warned Liz. "Do you think it will ever come out?"

"I hope so," said Mom. "Of course, it would have come out a lot more easily if I had cleaned it right after the juice was spilled." Mom wiped the sweat from her brow and glanced up at Liz. "You should deal with your anger the way I should have dealt with this stain," she added.

Liz frowned. "What do you mean?" she asked.

Mom continued to rub the burgundy blotch. "Time has allowed this stain to penetrate into the carpet fibers," she explained. "Anger does something like that to your heart. If it's permitted to stay and saturate there, it becomes increasingly difficult to remove. Over time, it widens into bitterness and rage."

Liz looked at the stain on the carpet and sighed.

"Okay," she agreed. "I don't really see how I can help being angry with Sonja, but I'll try to get over it."

Mom smiled. "Right choice! Never let your anger turn into a fixed stain inside you," she said. "Start by talking to God about it. Pray for Sonja, too. It's hard to be angry with someone you're praying for. With God's help, you can let your anger go." *SML*

HOW ABOUT YOU?

Are you angry over something that happened a day ago, a week ago, or even a month or more ago? Has your anger spread into other areas of your life? God doesn't want anger to become a fixed stain on your heart. Ask him to help you release it. Don't wait—talk to him about it now.

Deal with Anger Now

September
22

The Oil and the Wick

Read Ephesians 5:15-20

Mom, can I make some colored water for the oil lamp?" asked little Susie. "It's almost empty."

"That lamp needs to be filled with oil, not water, silly," said Jenna, her older sister. She laughed. "Why do you think it's called an oil lamp? It burns oil."

"It does?" Susie asked, a puzzled tone in her voice. "It's the white thing that burns and makes the light."

Mom smiled. "The white thing is called the wick," she said, "and yes, it does have to burn. But Jenna is right—the pretty colored liquid is oil, not water. That wick soaks up the oil so it can burn. Without the oil, the wick wouldn't keep going at all."

Mother took a bottle of pretty green liquid from the cupboard. "This is oil for refilling the lamp," she told Susie. "You can help me with it." As Mom showed Susie what to do, she added, "You know, this reminds me of our life as Christians. I know you've learned the verse in the book of Matthew—where Jesus says, 'You are the light of the world.' Well, to be God's light, I need God's 'oil.' Just like this lamp wick needs oil, I need to be filled with the Holy Spirit."

"So we're like the wick, and the Holy Spirit is like oil," suggested Jenna.

Mom nodded. "As we soak up God's Word and spend time with God's people, and as we praise God and pray to him, we learn to yield to his Spirit," she said. "Then the Lord can shine through in our lives—and we can't take any credit for it because we don't do it; the Holy Spirit does." *LFW*

HOW ABOUT YOU?
Do you let the Holy Spirit shine through you? As you allow God's Spirit to fill you, you can do great things for him.

MEMORIZE:
"Be filled with the Spirit." Ephesians 5:18, NIV

Let God's Spirit Shine through You

Pickled Beets

Read 1 Samuel 16:6-13

"I can't believe it!" Maureen exclaimed as she kept an eye on the news channel while setting the table for dinner. "Jennifer Taylor has everything going for her. She's gorgeous, she's talented, she's rich, she's famous, and—"

"And she has spoiled her life by using drugs—and now she's been arrested," said Maureen's mother, shaking her head. "How sad!"

"If only I looked like that," Maureen said as she watched Jennifer Taylor being led away in handcuffs.

"Don't forget that looks can be deceiving," Mom said. She opened the refrigerator. "Oh, Maureen, please go down to the basement and get a jar of Grandma's pickled beets. We'll have some with our dinner."

"Okay," said Maureen, heading for the stairs. She soon returned with a jar of deep purple-red beets. "Just look at the color of these beets—especially the juice!" she exclaimed as she held the jar up to the light. "I wish I had a sweater this color."

Mom laughed. "They do look beautiful," she agreed.

Maureen handed the jar to her mother. "Oh, no," Mom said as she opened it. "This lid isn't sealed. We'd better not eat these beets. They may be spoiled!"

"But they look just fine," said Maureen.

"They may be okay, but when the lid isn't sealed, bacteria can get in. I'm not going to take a chance," Mom answered. She poured the contents down the garbage disposal. "If they are spoiled, they could cause serious food poisoning."

"Wow!" said Maureen. "I'm glad you noticed that the seal was broken."

"You know, honey, those beets remind me of Jennifer Taylor," Mom said. "She's beautiful and talented. To many people, her life looked perfect—but Satan was spreading his poison in her life."

Maureen sighed. "I guess you're right, Mom," she said.

"Appearances can deceive us," Mom said. "Things can look good to us when they're really not good at all—and people can, too. On the other hand, someone who is not attractive may be a fine person. We need to try to see what people are really like and not judge by appearance." *JRL*

HOW ABOUT YOU?

Are you careful not to judge kids by what they wear or how many things they have? By whether they're smart or good-looking? Get to know them—see if they're honest, if they're kind, and if they obey their parents. Find out if they love God. He doesn't judge by appearance, and he doesn't want you to do that, either.

Appearances Are Deceiving

MEMORIZE:
"Stop judging by mere appearances."
John 7:24, NIV

September

24

Beautiful Feet

Read 1 Peter 3:3-5; 1 Timothy 2:9-10

Annemarie took extra care getting ready for her Sunday school class party. She stood in front of the mirror and approved her appearance, admiring the way her bracelets jangled on her arm. She experimented with eye shadow and blush—until Mom made her scrub it off. Finally, she felt satisfied with her looks. *Not that it will be hard to outshine most of the girls in the class,* she thought smugly. *Especially that mousy Betty!*

In her mind, Annemarie liked to call her "Betty Beautiful Feet" because one Sunday morning, plain old Betty had read a scripture about "the feet of those who bring good news" being "beautiful" and how she wanted to have beautiful feet.

Hah!, thought Annemarie. *I'd rather look good all over!*

During the party, their class teacher, Mrs. Partridge, took time to hear people give a testimony of what God had done for them. Annemarie was inspecting her fingernails to make sure her nail polish hadn't chipped, when a new girl she didn't know spoke up. "I'm thankful for Betty, who brought me to Sunday school—but mostly for Jesus. I was saved last Sunday."

Annemarie glanced at Betty and saw that her face was positively glowing. *Why, she almost looks pretty,* thought Annemarie.

When Annemarie got home that evening, she told her mother about Betty's friend. "I sat with Betty during the refreshments," she said. "She's really nice. I guess I was always too busy looking at her face and ugly clothes to notice what she was really like. I guess looks aren't so important, are they?"

"They're certainly not the most important thing," Mom replied. "I'm sure God would like us to be neat and clean and look our best, but the latest clothes must never take first place in our lives. Read 1 Peter 3:3-4 before you get into bed tonight. It will help you put appearance in its proper place."

"I will," promised Annemarie, "and tomorrow I'm going to start working on beautiful feet." *HWM*

HOW ABOUT YOU?

What's important to you? Good looks and clothes? God says those things are secondary. Never let them become more important than pleasing God.

MEMORIZE:

"Be known for the beauty that comes from within, the unfading beauty of a gentle and quiet spirit, which is so precious to God." 1 Peter 3:4

Be Beautiful Inside

Out of Balance

Read Luke 2:42-62

"And Jesus increased in wisdom and stature, and in favor with God and man," read Dad during family devotions one evening. He closed the Bible.

"Jesus was well-balanced," observed Mom.

Luisa laughed. "I think you have balance on the brain," she teased. Due to an inner ear problem, Mom had been very dizzy and unable to keep her balance the day before.

Mom grinned. "I sure found out how important balance is," she agreed.

"And you think Jesus could walk without almost falling over?" asked Anita, but she knew that wasn't really what Mom meant.

Dad smiled. "Jesus was well-balanced in the way he was growing and developing," he said. "He 'increased in wisdom'—that's growing mentally."

"Brain power," said Luisa with a grin. "And growing in 'stature' means he grew physically, right?"

Dad nodded. "He was 'in favor with God,' and that tells of his good relationship with God. His growth 'in favor with man' shows that he developed socially and got along well with others."

"Right. He lived a well-balanced life. He's our perfect example," Mom said. "Too much of one thing and not enough of another will throw you off-balance and cause you to fail. For example, people may be very smart, but it will not make them happy if they can't get along with other people."

"Yeah—like you, 'Nita," said Luisa. Anita did very well in school, but she recently seemed to have problems with the other kids in her class.

"Look who's talking!" grumbled Anita. "All you ever do is aerobics workouts. You have strong muscles, but a weak brain."

"That will do," Dad said sternly. "Instead of criticizing one another, each of you should be thinking about how you can develop balance in your own life. And don't forget the spiritual side. Take time for God's Word and prayer. When you do that regularly, you may be surprised at how nicely the other areas develop." *BJW*

HOW ABOUT YOU?

Are you well-balanced? Do you eat well, get enough rest and exercise, enjoy and help people, and learn about and serve God? Check to see what you need to do to achieve a good balance to grow physically, socially, mentally, and spiritually.

MEMORIZE:
"Jesus increased in wisdom and stature, and in favour with God and man." Luke 2:52, KJV

Be Well-Balanced

September

26

Jump and Trust

Read Mark 10:13-16

Just as Mom and Chelsea sat down to eat lunch one day, the door opened and Dad walked in. His clothes and face were dirty, and his hand was bandaged. "What happened?" cried Mom.

"The apartment house near my factory burned, and I ran over there to help," Dad explained.

"You're injured!" Mom exclaimed, looking at his hand.

"Nothing serious—I'll be fine," Dad assured her, "but I'm home for the day. I'll go change, and then I'll tell you all about it while we eat."

Chelsea and Mom listened eagerly as Dad talked about the fire. "Smoke and flames were billowing from the house," he said, "and I saw a girl—about your age, Chelsea—at an open second-story window. I just held out my arms and called, 'Jump, honey! Jump! I'll catch you. I promise I will.' She was crying, but she hesitated only a moment before she jumped. Her clothes were on fire, but I caught her and got the flames out."

Chelsea was wide-eyed. "You're a hero, Daddy!" she exclaimed. "I'm so glad you caught her. You saved her life!" After a moment, Chelsea added, "She needed to be saved, and you . . . you just stood there and told her to come to you, didn't you?"

"Yes, honey, I did," Dad answered. "I'm glad she trusted me and jumped like I told her to."

"Me, too," said Chelsea. "It's kind of like the way we have to trust Jesus, isn't it? In Sunday school, my teacher said Jesus wants us to come to him. We need to be saved, and he loves us and wants to save us. I thought maybe I should wait until I was older—like you and Mom. But if that little girl was old enough to trust you and just go to you when you called her, Daddy, I guess I'm old enough to go to Jesus and trust him."

"Why, Chelsea!" Dad exclaimed. "Of course you can trust him. This is an answer to our prayers." *AGL*

HOW ABOUT YOU?
Do you know that you need to be saved from your sins? Jesus loves children—he loves you. He died for you. You, too, can go to him and give him your life and your love. Trust him to save you.

MEMORIZE:
"Let the children come to me. Don't stop them! For the Kingdom of God belongs to such as these." Mark 10:14

Give Your Life to Jesus

Correct Address

Read Acts 4:5-12

"Dad," called Chantal from the computer desk. "Can you help me with this e-mail? I sent it twice, but I don't think it went anywhere."

Dad put the newspaper aside, pushed himself out of the chair, and walked over to Chantal. "Are you sure you typed the address correctly?" he asked.

Chantal shrugged. "I guess so. Heather wrote it herself on this paper." She handed Dad a page from a notebook.

Dad pulled up a chair and sat beside Chantal. He looked at the paper and then at the computer screen. "I see the problem. You typed the letter *O* after Heather's name. It should be the number zero."

Chantal stared at the paper and then typed Heather's address again—this time with a zero. She clicked on the "send" key, and a moment later the screen showed that one message had been sent.

Chantal swung around in her chair. "Thanks, Dad," she said. "You were right. I had the wrong address."

That evening, Chantal and Dad shared some popcorn. "Guess what, Dad?" said Chantal. "I already got a reply from Heather." She grinned and added, "I'm glad you caught my mistake. That e-mail never would have gotten to Heather without the correct address."

Dad nodded. "You know, Chantal, the mistake you made with an e-mail address is a little like the mistake people make regarding salvation. They use the 'wrong address' to get to heaven."

Chantal stopped chewing. "Really?" she asked.

"Really," Dad said. "Many people think it doesn't matter if they believe in Jesus or Buddha or Muhammad or Moses—or even in their own good works. They think everyone ends up at the same place—heaven. That's not what the Bible says."

Chantal raised her eyebrows. "Wow, Dad! It's like they're using those people or things for the address to heaven, right?"

Dad nodded. "There's only one 'correct address,' and that's Jesus," he said. "If he's not the center of our faith, we won't reach heaven. Salvation is spelled J-E-S-U-S. No other name will get us to God." *RSM*

HOW ABOUT YOU?

Have you wondered if people who follow various religions will get to heaven? God says Jesus is the one and only name by which people can reach God. Do you trust only in him?

Jesus Is the "Correct Address" for Salvation

MEMORIZE:
"There is no other name in all of heaven for people to call on to save them." Acts 4:12

September
28

Marissa sighed and turned off the computer. She went to the kitchen, where her mother was working. "Mom, I'm tired of computer games. I want something different to do," said Marissa. "I wish I could take that photography class again."

"Well, that would be fine," Mom said, "but wouldn't you rather take a different class?"

Marissa shook her head. "I liked that class, and it would be like a refresher course if I took it again. Our teacher had so many ideas that I can't even remember them all." She sighed. "I'm bored, and it sounds like fun."

"Well, I guess you can repeat the class if you want to," Mom said, "but it's held on Saturday mornings. It won't help you now. How about your chores—are they all done?" Marissa nodded. "What about your Bible correspondence lessons?" Mom asked.

"Uh, I, I . . ." muttered Marissa, wondering just how to make her excuses sound good. "The lesson I'm up to is mostly Bible reading, and I've read those chapters so many times. I don't really think I need to read them again."

"Maybe you need a refresher course in Bible, too," Mom suggested.

Marissa sighed. "Can I bake some chocolate chip cookies now?" she asked. Mom agreed, so Marissa got out the recipe box and thumbed through it, looking for the one she needed. "Mom, the recipe isn't where it's supposed to be," she said.

"It isn't? Well, maybe you won't need it. You've made those cookies so often," Mom said. "Just make them from memory."

"From memory!" exclaimed Marissa. "I don't remember the recipe that well."

"You mean you don't remember cookie recipes as well as you remember Bible passages?" Mom asked as she helped search for the recipe. When she found it, Marissa accepted the card without comment, but she got the point—and while the cookies baked, she got out her Bible lessons and her Bible. She had quite a bit of catching up to do. *EMB*

HOW ABOUT YOU?
Do you feel like you know many Bible stories and are already familiar with the lessons they teach? When you read familiar passages, consider them to be a refresher course from God. When you read them again, ask him to teach you something new from them, and then put them into practice.

MEMORIZE:
"Your word is a lamp for my feet and a light for my path." Psalm 119:105

Read and Re-read the Bible

People and Cookies

Read 2 Thessalonians 3:3-5

With a big sigh, Vangie dropped her books on the table and flopped into the chair beside her mother.

"Something wrong, honey?" Mom asked.

Vangie nodded. "It's Marla," she said. "You know—that annoying girl in my class. I can't help it—I just don't like her at all, let alone love her. The best I've been able to do is to stop making fun of her."

"Well, I guess that's an improvement," Mom said.

"It's not enough," replied Vangie. "My Sunday school teacher says that Jesus expects us to love people—even those who hate us—and to do good to them. I don't think I'll ever be able to love people the way I'm supposed to!" She sighed. "God must be getting pretty annoyed with me," she added.

"Ask him to help you," Mom said. "Pray for Marla and keep working on your attitude toward her. Dad and I will pray about it, too."

"Okay," agreed Vangie. She stood up. "Can I bake something, Mom?" she asked.

"Sure," Mom said. "Need any help?"

"Nope! I can handle this," said Vangie. As she reached for the recipe book, her four-year-old brother burst into the kitchen. "Hey, buddy! Want to learn how to make cookies?" asked Vangie.

"Can I?" asked Jimmy eagerly.

Mom smiled. "Teaching Jimmy to make cookies will take some patience," she warned.

"That's okay," said Vangie. "I won't expect him to do them alone—I'll give him all the help he needs for as long as he needs it."

Mom nodded. "You know, from your comments about the problem you're having with Marla, I get the impression that you think God is less patient than we are," she said.

Vangie was silent. "I get it," she said after a moment. "It's taking time for me to learn to love Marla, but God will help me as long as I need him."

"Which is always," added Mom. *RB*

HOW ABOUT YOU?

Are you impatient with your spiritual progress? Don't give up. Jesus knows you have a lot to learn. He loves you, and he won't give up on you. Ask him to give you strength to keep on learning to do the things he wants you to do.

MEMORIZE:

"The Lord is faithful; he will make you strong and guard you from the evil one." 2 Thessalonians 3:3

Patiently Keep Growing Spiritually

September

30

Smiles

Read Romans 6:13-14

Elena was pouting when she and her mother returned home from shopping one day. "What's the matter, sourface?" asked her brother, Jack.

"Oh, shut up!" Elena growled. "Mom gets you everything you want, but she wouldn't buy a thing for me. All I wanted was a 'smile' shirt."

Jack howled with laughter. "A smile shirt on you?" he asked. "That would be a joke! Besides, who wears those things? But then, you never do know what's 'in' and what's not. Ow!" he yelled when his sister hit him. He promptly hit her back.

Dad stepped in. "Break it up," he said. "The place I'd like to see a smile is on your faces for a change."

The next Sunday, Jack and Elena got ready to go to Sunday school. They attended church regularly, and both had accepted Jesus as Savior, but their parents were not Christians. "Why don't you come to church with us today?" suggested Jack hopefully.

"Count me out!" exclaimed Dad. "You two fight constantly. If that's all the good your religion does you, I want nothing to do with it." Jack and Elena didn't know what to say.

"We've got to quit fighting," Elena told Jack later. "If we don't, Mom and Dad will never listen when we try to tell them how to be saved."

Jack nodded. "Let's try really hard," he said.

They did try hard, and they asked Jesus to help them. It wasn't long before their parents noticed the difference. A pitcher was broken one day, and instead of blaming each other, both Elena and Jack admitted that they were at fault. Dad was amazed. "I never thought I'd see the day!" he exclaimed.

The next Sunday, Dad surprised them all. "I don't suppose your mother and I are too old for church and Sunday school, are we?" he asked.

"You mean . . . you'll go?" Jack asked.

"If your mother would like to," Dad replied, and Mom nodded. Jack and Elena cheered. "Look!" Dad laughed. "That brought smiles to their faces!" *AGL*

HOW ABOUT YOU?

Do your actions and attitude show that you're a Christian? Each day ask Jesus to help you be cheerful and pleasant to those around you. Let others see that you no longer let Satan have his way in your life.

MEMORIZE:

"Those who become Christians become new persons. They are not the same anymore, for the old life is gone. A new life has begun!"
2 Corinthians 5:17

Actions Speak Louder than Words

What Do You See?

Read Ephesians 4:23

After supper, Grandpa asked Holly to come out and sit on the porch swing with him. Things were pretty quiet as they watched a squirrel bury a nut. "Grandpa, how does that squirrel remember where he buries all those nuts?" Holly asked.

"Well," Grandpa replied, "a magazine article I read the other day said God gave the squirrel such a good sense of smell that his nose tells him where he buried the nuts. The article also said that he can smell which ones are good and which ones are bad—so he stores away only good ones for the winter." Grandpa turned and looked at Holly and asked, "Are you happy, sweetheart? I've been wondering about that."

"No, not really," Holly answered, lowering her head. "Nothing seems to go right, and I hate school."

"You know, Holly, there are good and bad things in every situation. We choose which we'll store up—the good or the bad. Our choice will affect our hearts and our lives."

"But our noses can't tell us what's good and what's bad," Holly said, looking at the squirrel.

Grandpa grinned. "No," he replied, "but God gives us the ability to see the positive and the negative in every situation."

"What do you mean?" Holly asked.

"Let me give you an example," Grandpa answered. "You said you hate school, and I'm sure some things there are hard for you. But try not to dwell on the negatives. Instead, think positively—remembering that some children will never have an education. You can do it with God's help, and you'll be a much happier girl. And it will show in what you do and say."

Holly sighed, then smiled. "I'll work on that, Grandpa."

Grandpa gave Holly a big hug. "In any situation, look for things you can be thankful for. Store up the good!" *SKV*

HOW ABOUT YOU?
Do you try to see the good in your life, or do you always see only the bad? How you look at things that happen each day will affect your heart and life. God loves you, and he's given you much to be thankful for. Each day ask him to help you focus on the positive things in your life and not the negative.

Store "Good" in Your Heart

MEMORIZE:
"The good man brings good things out of the good stored up in his heart." Luke 6:45, NIV

October

2

Who's George Conway?

Read Romans 13:1-7

Betsie was raking leaves one day when a car pulled into the driveway. The driver rolled down his window. "Is this the Peterson house?" he asked.

"Yes, it is," Betsie answered.

"Good." The man smiled. "Would you please tell your parents that George Conway and one of the men from his campaign committee are here?" He and another man got out of the car.

Betsie had no idea what the man was talking about, but she ran inside to tell her mother about them.

"Oh, I've been expecting them," Mom said as she stood up from her desk.

"Who's George Conway?" Betsie asked.

"We met Mr. Conway at the school board meeting the other night," Mom answered. "We told him he could put a campaign sign in our yard."

"Why?" Betsie asked as she followed her mother back outside. The men were pounding a post into the Petersons' front yard. On the post was a sign that read "Reelect George Conway."

"Mr. Conway is a Christian," Mom explained as they watched. "He's done a good job on the school board this last term, and he wants to be reelected. It's important that we support him, because some of the people who are seeking election don't care about the Lord's standards."

"Do you think he'll win, Mom?" Betsie wondered aloud.

"I don't know," Mom answered, "but we can pray for Mr. Conway and support him by encouraging others to vote for him. It's good for Christians to have positions of leadership in the community."

"Why does it matter so much?" Betsie continued her questions.

"Well," Mom patiently responded, "our leaders—whether they're leading the school board, the church, or the government—make decisions that affect us. Their values—whether pleasing to God or not—influence our lives."

Smiling, Mom went forward to greet Mr. Conway, and Betsie decided to start praying for the election. *LMW*

HOW ABOUT YOU?

Do you know a Christian who has campaigned for an elected office in your city or town? It's good to have qualified Christian leadership. You might think that because you're too young to vote, you're too young to help. That isn't true. You can help by praying for your Christian leaders.

MEMORIZE:

"I urge . . . that requests, prayers, intercession and thanksgiving be made for everyone—for kings and all those in authority." 1 Timothy 2:1-2, NIV

Pray for Your Leaders

The Winner

Read Galatians 5:22-25

Belinda desperately wanted to win the expensive camera being offered as a prize in a wildlife photo contest sponsored by a local photography shop. "But I haven't got a chance," she moaned. "My old camera has no adjustments for speed or distance, and I'll never get close enough to a wild animal to take a good picture."

"No problem!" her brother, Troy, said. "Just snap a picture at the zoo."

"That would be cheating," Belinda protested. And though Troy urged her to do it, she refused. But when the contest was over, Belinda was notified that she had won! She was surprised and so excited!

Troy went to the store with her to pick up her prize. But when Belinda saw the winning picture, she knew there had been a mistake. It was a wonderful picture of a fox—a picture *she* had not taken. Troy nudged her. "I took it and entered it for you," he whispered. "I took it at the zoo."

Belinda's thoughts ran wild. *After all, I didn't do anything dishonest, and it isn't like the picture belongs to anyone else—and o-o-oh! That new camera is so beautiful! But, no! To keep it would be dishonest, and I'm a Christian.*

Reluctantly, Belinda explained the situation to the man at the store, and the rightful winner was awarded the prize.

On the way home, Troy was very quiet. At last he told Belinda what he was thinking. "I wanted to help, and it didn't seem so terrible to me if I cheated just a little," he said. "But you've shown me something. I always thought I was just as good as any Christian, but now I know differently. I know I wouldn't have done what you just did. I . . . I guess maybe I do need to ask Jesus to help me work on being more honest." *BP*

HOW ABOUT YOU?

If you're a Christian, do your actions show it? Are you kind? Helpful? Obedient? Slow to get angry? Honest? Cheerful? Today's Scripture lists "fruit," or characteristics, that should be seen in the life of a Christian. Others are watching you. The things you do and the way you act are a testimony to them. By your life, point others to Jesus.

Your Life Is a Testimony

MEMORIZE:
"By their fruit you will recognize them." Matthew 7:20, NIV

October

4

First Things First

Read Matthew 6:19-21, 28-29

Alonya was excited. She had been asked to sing for a school program. Since she and her family had lived in America only a short time, she was also asked to tell how she liked her new country. "I'm going to sing 'I'd Rather Have Jesus,' " she told her mother, "and I'll say that even though this country means so much to me, if I had to make a choice, I really would rather have Jesus."

Alonya's family was pleased. Though they were very poor, they decided that Alonya should have a new dress for the program. Together they worked and scrimped and saved. "I think we've finally got enough," Mama announced one Saturday evening. "We'll go shopping next week and see what we can find." Alonya was thrilled.

But on Sunday, something changed their plans. A special offering had been taken to buy a much-needed vehicle for one of the church missionaries, and the Sunday school announced that not enough money was received. Back home, Alonya's family talked about it. Alonya was rather quiet at first, and then she said, "I thought of something—I don't really need that dress. Let's give the money for the car."

"But, Alonya," Mama protested, "I want you to have something special to wear when you sing."

"That won't matter," Alonya assured her. "Honest!"

After discussing the matter some more, Alonya's parents and brothers and sisters could see that she really wanted to give away the money. "Okay," they agreed at last, "we'll do it."

On the day of the school program, Alonya wore her old dress. But her family thought she never looked better as she sang, "I'd rather have Jesus than anything this world affords today." All who knew the story knew that she really meant what she sang. *BP*

HOW ABOUT YOU?

Are clothes one of the most important things in the world to you? Are you unhappy unless you can get the latest fashions and brand names? God says such things are really not important. The important thing is to put him first in your life. Then he'll take care of your needs—and guess what? He'll give you joy and peace besides—you'll be happier than any brand-name clothing could make you.

MEMORIZE:
"Seek first his kingdom and his righteousness." Matthew 6:33, NIV

Put Jesus First

The Turnabout (Part 1)

Read 1 Corinthians 3:5-9

"But, Dad, why do we have to leave?' Sarah asked tearfully. "We like it here."

Dad nodded understandingly. "I know, honey," he said sadly, "but the government has ordered all missionaries out of the country in eight months. That includes us. We'll have to return to the States."

"I don't see why," Sarah wailed. "The people here need us."

"I don't understand why, either, honey," Dad replied. "The government says we're pushing our beliefs on the people and destroying their culture. It isn't true, of course, but that's their excuse."

"But our friends are here," Ben protested. "Besides, what about the Bible translation? The New Testament is almost finished!"

"I know," Dad said, "but this is God's work. We'll trust it to his care. He wants his work to go on even more than we do! We may have only eight months, but we can make each day count. We'll cancel all trips, and everyone will be assigned extra duties. We'll work even harder to get the translation completed. The government may force us to leave the country, but it can't stop us from leaving God's Word behind when we go."

Sarah clapped her hands. "What can Ben and I do?" she asked eagerly.

Mom smiled. "You children can work on the prayer letters I'll be sending all over the world," she said. "You can also help more at home, so I'll be free to help Dad."

Ben jumped up. "Let's get started," he urged. "We won't give up!" He grinned. "I'm glad they can't make God leave!" *JLH*

HOW ABOUT YOU?

Do you give up when things get tough? Jesus wants dependable workers—people who will trust him, keep at the job, and leave the results to him. Can he count on you to keep working with him?

MEMORIZE:

"We work together as partners who belong to God. You are God's field, God's building—not ours."

1 Corinthians 3:9

Keep Working with Jesus

October

6

The Turnabout (Part 2)

Read Philippians 1:12-18

The Watson family and the other missionaries worked hard to preach and publish the gospel before they had to leave the country. They trained national people to take over the work when they left. They were encouraged as people all over the world prayed about the situation and sent extra gifts of money to buy more equipment and paper to speed up the publishing of the newly translated Bible.

Election time brought a wonderful surprise as several new leaders took office. "I've heard that the new government officials are going to investigate our work again," Dad said one day. "I think they'll be surprised and pleased at the great amount of good the mission does by building hospitals and schools throughout the country."

Dad was right. The new officials decided they wouldn't make the missionaries leave! How Ben and Sarah and their parents praised God when they learned that they could stay! "Our enemy became our friend," Dad said. "Those who tried to stop our work made it grow."

"They did?" Ben asked. "How?"

"The possibility of having to leave made us work harder, pray more, and train others to get involved," Dad explained. "The news reports made more people aware of our work. Christians prayed and gave."

Ben was beginning to understand. "And so more Scriptures are being printed and passed out than would have been otherwise," he said thoughtfully.

"Yes." Dad nodded. "God took the problem and turned it around. He had everything under control." *JLH*

HOW ABOUT YOU?

Do things sometimes seem to get out of control in your life? Do you wonder where God is, or what he's doing? Don't be discouraged. God is greater than anything or anybody. Nothing comes as a surprise to him. In his time he will work out all things for good.

MEMORIZE:
"The one who is in you is greater than the one who is in the world." 1 John 4:4, NIV

God Is in Control

A Protecting Shield

Read Psalm 3

Mom was working on the computer as Savannah opened the door. "Hi, honey," Mom greeted Savannah. "How was your day at school?"

"Oh, Mom, it was just rotten," came the answer. "You know what happened?"

Mom set a plate of cookies on the table. "Let's sit down and have a snack while you tell me," she suggested.

As soon as they sat down at the table, Savannah started talking again. "You know Ryan? Well, I had my spelling test ready to hand in, and just as I was getting out of my seat, he turned around and scribbled on it and ripped it!"

"What did your teacher say?" Mom asked. "Did he see what happened?"

Savannah nodded. "He called Ryan up to the desk, and now Ryan has to write the spelling words fifty times each. Mom, why is he always so mean to me? Why does he always try to get me in trouble? I wish I could just stay away from him, but he sits in front of me." Savannah sighed deeply.

Mom smiled and reached for her Bible. "I was reading Psalm 3 this morning, and I think it has a verse for you," she said. "Let's see—here it is . . . verse three. It says, 'You, O Lord, are a shield around me, my glory, and the one who lifts my head high.' That would be a good verse for you to learn."

Savannah repeated it slowly. "But what does it mean?" she asked.

"It means that the Lord protects us," Mom explained. "King David wrote it when he was running for his life because his own son was going to hurt him. Even with all his problems, David said the Lord was his shield. A couple of verses later David says he even went to sleep in a time of trouble, and God watched over him. He knew he could trust the Lord."

"And you're saying that if David could trust the Lord in his problem, I can trust him in mine, right?" Savannah asked. She smiled and added, "Okay. I guess he protected me today by letting my teacher see what happened." *BR*

HOW ABOUT YOU?

Are you having trouble getting along with someone at school or in your neighborhood? Is there someone who always seems to be mean to you? Don't be mean in return. Instead, trust the Lord to protect you.

The Lord Will Help You

MEMORIZE:
"You, O Lord, are a shield around me, my glory, and the one who lifts my head high." Psalm 3:3

8

Angela's Anger

Read Ephesians 4:26-27; James 1:19-20

Angela threw down the magazine she was reading and gave a long sigh. "I'm bored," she said to her mother. "It's Saturday afternoon, and all my friends are either busy or gone. There's no one to play with."

"Why don't you invite Felicia over?" Mom asked. "I saw her out in her back-yard a few minutes ago."

"Last time she came, she got into my rock collection," Angela said. "She never even asked! I had them sorted just the way I wanted them, and she messed them all up."

"Perhaps she didn't realize how important they were to you," Mom suggested. "Did you tell her how you felt?"

"Nah," Angela mumbled. "I figured she'd just get mad if I said anything about it. Besides, she should know how I feel without my having to tell her!"

Mom frowned. "So instead of telling her how angry you were, you just decided not to play with her anymore. Do you realize that you're disobeying a command-ment in the Bible?"

"I . . . I guess we're not supposed to get angry," Angela admitted.

"Well, in this case, I'm not sure you should have," Mom said smiling, "but actually, the verse I'm thinking of says, 'In your anger do not sin.' Then it goes on to say, 'Do not let the sun go down while you are still angry.' "

"What does it mean to not let the sun go down on your anger?" Angela asked.

"It means you should try to make up with the one you're mad at as soon as possible," Mom said. "If you let anger stay inside of you, it will soon damage your relationship with your friend—and with God. Even when there's good reason for us to be angry, we need to handle it God's way."

Angela was silent as she thought about it. Then she sighed. "I know you're right," she said. "I think I'll give Felicia a call. I really have missed playing with her." *SLK*

HOW ABOUT YOU?

Has someone made you angry or hurt your feelings? Think about what happened. Make sure that you're not just being too sensitive. If you still feel you have a reason to be angry, talk to the person about it. Don't let anger eat away at you inside. Handle it the right way—God's way!

MEMORIZE:

"In your anger do not sin: Do not let the sun go down while you are still angry." Ephesians 4:26, NIV

Handle Anger God's Way

A Bright Greeting

Read 1 Corinthians 13:4-7

As Carrie walked into her house after school one day, her mother noticed that she looked a little glum. "Something wrong, Carrie?" she asked. Carrie shook her head. "Really?" Mom asked. "Are you sure there isn't something you'd like to tell me about?"

"Well . . ." Carrie hesitated. Then the story tumbled out. "At school today, I saw Tammi waving and smiling really big at me. I was so glad, because she usually doesn't even talk to me, and she always plays with other girls. I waved and smiled back, but she frowned and looked funny at me. Then she smiled again, and this time she said, 'Hey Robin! Let's play together at recess time.' So she wasn't waving and smiling at me at all, only at Robin who was right behind me." Tears filled Carrie's eyes.

"I'm sorry, honey. I know that hurts—I've had the same sort of thing happen to me," Mom comforted, putting her arms around Carrie. "But we learn from those experiences, too. Think for a minute about the kids at school and at church. Are you always friendly to each one of them? Do you greet each and every one with a smile?"

Carrie was thoughtful. "I will from now on," she said with determination.

"Good," Mom said. "The very next time you're tempted to snub somebody, remember how much it hurt to have someone treat you that way. And keep on being friendly to Tammi, too. Who knows? Someday she may respond. I remember that Grandmother Hearne used to tell us to always be generous with smiles. That was good advice. You never know what an impact they might have on someone's life." *SD*

HOW ABOUT YOU?
Do you smile at and greet only those you like best? Jesus teaches you to love everybody—even your enemies. Isn't offering a friendly smile to others the least you can do? Will you do that for God?

Be Generous with Smiles

MEMORIZE:
"Greet each other in Christian love."
1 Peter 5:14

October

10

Checks and Promises

Read Hebrews 10:22-23; 2 Peter 1:4

As Patti started home from school, a car pulled up to the curb. "Anybody need a ride?" her father called.

Patti ran to the car, opened the door, and hopped inside. "Oh, Dad, I'm glad to see you!" she exclaimed. "I hate walking home past Mr. Lott's old tumbledown house. He's so strange, and his dog is so scary. I wish I could go home a different way."

"He is different," Dad agreed as he started up the car, "but we've checked him out. He's harmless, and the dog—well, as they say, 'his bark is worse than his bite.' I think you know that. We want you to walk home on Pearl Street, because it's the shortest and safest way home." He looked at his daughter. "Don't you know the Lord will take care of you, honey?" he asked.

Patti hesitated. "I . . . I know the Bible says he will," she replied, "but I just can't help being scared."

Dad stopped the car in their driveway. "Do you remember the check I gave you for your birthday, Patti?"

"Sure!" she replied. "That was great."

"What did you do with the check?" Dad asked. "Did you frame it and put it on your wall?"

Patti laughed. "Of course not," she said. "I cashed it at the bank."

Dad nodded. "And that's when it did you some good. God's promises are like checks he's written to us. They're in the Bible, waiting for us to cash them in."

Patti looked puzzled. "But how do I do that?" she asked.

"Learn what they are by reading the Bible," Dad replied. "Right now you need freedom from fear. You might claim this promise from Psalm 27:1: 'The Lord protects me from danger—so why should I tremble?' Pray, believe God, and walk home unafraid."

The next afternoon, Patti came home from school with a big grin on her face. "I cashed in on God's promise," she said. "I prayed for God to protect me, I believed him, and I walked past Mr. Lott's house and his dog. And I wasn't afraid." *MRP*

HOW ABOUT YOU?
Do you have needs in your life? God has promised to take care of you. As you read your Bible, watch for specific promises, and claim them—"cash in" on them by really believing them. Pray for the Lord's will to be done. Sometimes you may have to wait for an answer, but God will do what he promised. Act on your belief in him.

MEMORIZE:
"Let us hold tightly to . . . hope . . . for God can be trusted to keep his promise." Hebrews 10:23

Claim God's Promises

The Bat (Part 1)

Read Hebrews 11:1-3; 1 John 5:4-5

"Look out!" yelled Cody as his sister stumbled over a chair. "You're as blind as a bat, Sierra!"

Sierra tossed her head. "Bats aren't blind," she said.

Cody started to argue, but Dad interrupted him. "Sierra's right," Dad said. " 'Blind as a bat' is an expression people use, but bats really aren't blind."

"They don't see very well, though, do they?" asked Cody. "In science class we learned that they find their way around by listening to sound waves instead of by seeing things with their eyes."

"That's true," Sierra agreed. "We studied bats last year, and I remember that my teacher said they fly at night and make squeaky, high-pitched sounds and then listen for the echoes. When sound waves bounce off something and the echo comes back quickly, the bat knows there's something close by. If the echo takes a long time, he knows the thing is far away."

"Very good!" applauded Dad. After a moment, he asked, "Did you know that, like the bats, you should depend on something other than just the things you can see and understand?"

"We should?" asked Sierra. "Like what?"

"I know," said Cody. "The bats use their ears, and we should use our ears, too. A train whistle warns us that we'd better stop because a train is nearby. Traffic sounds warn us to be careful crossing the street. Right?"

"That's right," Dad agreed, "but there's something even more important than either eyes or ears. What you need is faith in Jesus and in what the Bible says. The bat's wonderful sense of hearing helps him get around safely at night. A strong faith helps you to walk safely through life. It helps to keep you from stumbling into sin in times of difficulty and temptation." *MTF*

HOW ABOUT YOU?

When bad things happen, do you continue to trust God? For example, if you're treated unfairly, a loved one is sick, or you're having trouble with schoolwork, do you see beyond the problems and remember that God cares about you and is in control? Christians must walk by faith in Jesus—not just by sight.

Live by Faith

MEMORIZE:
"We live by believing and not by seeing." 2 Corinthians 5:7

October

12

The Bat (Part 2)

Read 1 Peter 5:8-11

"At school today, we learned more about bats," Cody announced. "We learned that there are different kinds, and one kind is the fruit bat. Fruit bats are . . ."

"That's easy!" Sierra interrupted him. "They're bats that eat fruit—that's why they're called fruit bats. Even I knew that, Mr. Smarty!" She grinned at her brother.

Cody grinned back. "Right," he agreed, "so farmers who grow fruit have to find ways to protect their crops."

"How about putting up a notice that says, 'Bats that eat this fruit will be prosecuted'?" suggested Sierra, giggling.

"Genius!" Cody said. "Got any other good ideas?"

"What do the farmers really do?" Sierra asked.

"They harvest their crops early, before the fruit bats attack," Cody replied, "or they use nets to protect their crops."

Dad, who was listening to the conversation, smiled. "We learned a lesson from the bats yesterday," he said, "and today the fruit farmers have something to teach us. From them, we learn that we need to protect our fruit."

Cody and Sierra stared at him. "What fruit?" Sierra asked. "We don't grow any fruit."

"I'm thinking of a different kind of fruit," Dad replied. "The Bible says the fruit of the Spirit is . . ."

"Love, joy, peace, patience, kindness, goodness . . ." chanted Sierra.

"Faithfulness, gentleness, and self-control," finished Cody.

"I'm glad you know your fruit," Dad said, "but don't forget—just like the hungry fruit bat is waiting to gobble up that freshly-ripened fruit, Satan is always on the lookout for ways to attack your fruit. He's a powerful enemy, but God is much more powerful. Use a net of prayer and obedience to God to protect your fruit before Satan strikes. Ask God to help you guard against allowing Satan to destroy the fruit God wants to see in your life." *MTF*

HOW ABOUT YOU?

Is Satan trying to destroy the fruit of the Spirit in your life? He is always waiting to attack, but he's not as powerful as the Holy Spirit, who lives in each Christian. Ask God to help you guard against Satan's attempts to pull you into sin and away from him. Pray each day for God's protection.

MEMORIZE:

"Be careful! Watch out for attacks from the Devil, your great enemy. He prowls around like a roaring lion, looking for some victim to devour."

1 Peter 5:8

Guard against Sin

Minced Words

Read Matthew 5:33-37

One evening Janis and her friend Carmen were at their school football game. "Oh, no!" Carmen groaned, adding a curse word and using God's name in vain. "Look at that hairdo on the head cheerleader! Isn't it hideous?"

Janis cringed when Carmen swore this way, but she didn't say anything about it. Just then the cheerleader moved to where Janis could see her. "Oh, my gosh!" Janis exclaimed. "It *is* horrible, isn't it?"

The girls didn't pay much attention to the game, but they did realize their school was losing badly. When the opposing team made another touchdown, Carmen said the name "Jesus" in a disgusted tone. "Our team is no good!"

Janis cringed again, but still she didn't mention the swearing to Carmen. When Carmen used "God Almighty" a little later, however, Janis had to speak up. "Gee, Carmen," she said, taking a deep breath, "do you have to swear so darn much?"

Carmen stared at Janis in surprise. "Well," she said indignantly, "why should it bother you? You do it, too!"

Now Janis was upset. "I do not!" she protested.

"You just did," Carmen answered with a laugh. "Oh, I know I say God's name and Jesus' name, but you say 'my gosh' or 'gee' just as often. And, what's so much better about saying 'darn' and 'heck'? What's the difference, Janis? You just change a couple of letters. You remind me of my mom and onions!"

"Your mom and onions!" Janis exclaimed. "What are you talking about?"

"Well, my mom hates to peel onions because they hurt her eyes, so in recipes that call for a lot of onions, Mom uses 'minced' ones,'" Carmen explained. "They're dried onions, and they come in a box and taste the same, but they don't hurt her eyes. You can't use regular swear words, Janis, because they hurt your ears, so you use 'minced' swear words. They mean the same thing as the words I use, but it's easier on your ears. If what I say is wrong, then so are the words you use!"

Janis couldn't argue. What could she say? Carmen was right. *AU*

HOW ABOUT YOU?

Are you careful not to swear at all? Or are you guilty of "minced" swearing? Today's Scripture warns against swearing in any way. Ask the Lord to help you be a better testimony by using only language that will honor him.

Don't Use "Minced" Swear Words

MEMORIZE:
"Do not swear—not by heaven or by earth or by anything else."
James 5:12, NIV

October

14

Squabbles

Read Psalm 133

"You chose last time!" Deb yelled.

"I did not!" argued Jill. "You did!"

"I guess I remember better than you," stormed Deb.

Jill scowled as she turned and walked to the house. She and Deb were cousins, and they lived next door to each other, but they didn't always get along very well.

Jill's brother, Tom, met her just outside the door. "What's going on?" he asked, looking at her stormy eyes. "Another argument?"

"Deb always wants to decide what we play," Jill grumbled. She and Tom both looked up as a line of wild geese, honking loudly, flew high overhead.

"I wonder what their problem is. They sound terrible," said Tom. "Maybe one of them wanted to be the boss and butted into the front of the line."

"Don't they take turns being leader?" asked Jill.

"I suppose they do," said Tom. "Maybe one of them was counting the number of times he had been the leader, and decided he wasn't getting his fair share of turns." He grinned at his sister. "I guess that's what happens when you act like a silly goose," he added.

They watched as the long line separated into four lines, and then merged into two. The honking became a bit more quiet, and finally the two lines merged into one long V. "I wonder which one decided what should be done," said Tom. "It takes a real leader to be able to accomplish that." The geese were honking more quietly now.

"A real leader," Jill said quietly. She looked over to where Deb was standing. *That's what I want to be—a leader, not a silly goose,* she thought. "Okay, Deb," she called. "You can decide this time."

She looked at Tom. He nodded approval. "Keep your feathers calm," he said. Tom heard no further squabbling that afternoon. *LAW*

HOW ABOUT YOU?

Do you always want to be the leader—or the boss—when you play games? God is pleased when you put others ahead of yourself. Make sure they have as many, or more, chances to be first or to choose games.

MEMORIZE:

"How wonderful it is, how pleasant, when brothers live together in harmony!" Psalm 133:1

Learn to Get Along with Others

Give Me

Read Luke 15:11-24

"I'm working on your dress for the youth banquet," Mom said when Annette came in after school. "Maybe you could sew the buttons on when it's ready for them."

"I suppose," grumbled Annette, "but you could do it so much faster." She put down her books. "Can I have some money?" she begged. "I'll need it tomorrow for a school sweatshirt. And can I go over to Jill's for a while?"

"Not right now," Mom said. "You need to clean your room today."

"Can't you do it for me for once?" asked Annette with a pout. But Mom was firm, and Annette plodded off, still grumbling.

After supper that evening, Mom asked Annette to clear the table. "Oh, Mom, do I have to?" Annette groaned. "I told Pam I'd come over this evening. Can you take me over there?"

"You'll have to change your plans," Dad told her. "You know you need to take care of your little brother tonight. Mom and I have Bible study."

Annette spoke angrily. "Why can't you take him with you for once?"

"It seems to me, young lady, that you want all the blessings of being our child, but none of the responsibilities," Dad said.

Mom nodded. "You want us to provide you with money, clothes, and transportation, as well as many other things," she said, "but when it comes to chores—like washing dishes, baby-sitting, or cleaning your room—you don't want to be part of the family."

"It's easy to fall into a 'give me' rut," added Dad. "We all have trouble with those words sometimes. We do that with our heavenly Father, too. We ask him to give us things, and then we forget to thank him and to give of ourselves to him."

Annette knew her parents were right. "I'm sorry," she said after a moment. "I'll do better. I'll start now by calling Pam to tell her I can't come." She got up. "And, Mom," she added on her way to the telephone, "thanks for making my dress. I really love it, and I can do the buttons—no problem." *BJW*

HOW ABOUT YOU?

Listen to yourself—do you often say "Give me"? Like the younger son in today's Scripture, you may need to go to your parents, as well as to your heavenly Father, and make things right by saying "I'm sorry" and "thank you," and by doing your share to help.

MEMORIZE:
"I will go home to my father and say, 'Father, I have sinned against both heaven and you.'" Luke 15:18

Don't Be Greedy

October

16

The Slumber Party

Read Ephesians 5:15-17; 6:1-3

Lourdes smiled as she came into the kitchen after school. "Oh, good, Dad! You're baking cookies! I need some for a party at Lacey's Friday night," she said. "We're all bringing something. The other girls are bringing pizza, pop, chips and dip, and pickles."

"Yikes!" Dad said. "I'll send along something to settle your stomachs before you sleep—not that you will. You'll probably just eat, play games, listen to CDs, and talk all night, right?" Dad teased. "Lacey's parents are brave to be willing to put up with all that noise."

Lourdes took a bite of a chocolate chip cookie. "Oh, they won't be home till around three in the morning—when they're sure we'll be asleep," she said.

"They won't?" Dad frowned. Lourdes shook her head. "Well, I'm sorry," Dad said, "but if Lacey's parents aren't going to be there, I can't let you go."

"You can't not let me go!" cried Lourdes, but Dad remained firm.

"You don't trust me," Lourdes protested.

"I trust you, but I don't trust the circumstances," Dad explained. "Just because I know you're a good swimmer doesn't mean I'd let you try to swim Niagara Falls. I'm sorry, but my answer is no."

Lourdes moped around the rest of the week—but on the day after the party, Lacey phoned. "Oh, Lourdes," she said, "the most awful thing happened! The party was going fine, but then two of the girls started calling up boys. They found out where we were, and came and forced their way in. They ate our food and made a mess of the house."

"Wow—that's awful!" said Lourdes.

"And now the neighbors think we invited the boys over, and lots of people are saying bad things about us," continued Lacey. "I sure wish my parents had been here!"

After she hung up the phone, Lourdes ran to give her Dad a big hug. "What's that for?" he asked.

"For loving me enough to be strict with me!" Lourdes replied. *AGL*

HOW ABOUT YOU?

Do you realize that you can't always see the dangers in a situation? If your parents are being strict with you, thank God that you have someone to look out for your welfare. Thank your parents, too. That will please—and perhaps surprise—them.

MEMORIZE:

"So be careful how you live, not as fools but as those who are wise."
Ephesians 5:15

Trust the Judgment of Your Parents

Accidents Do Happen

17

Read Matthew 18:21-22

Tessa stomped into the house. "Who trampled on my pumpkin vines?" she grumbled.

"Gabe and Eric were playing basketball, and the ball landed in your pumpkin patch," Mom explained.

"They ruined my two best plants!" Tessa's dark eyes were snapping. "I've worked on them for weeks. I planned to enter my pumpkins in the school fair."

"I know. It's a shame," Mom comforted, "but it was an accident, Tessa. The boys were very sorry. They said they were going to call later to apologize to you."

"Apologize! What good is that? My best pumpkin vines are ruined!" Tessa's anger was about to dissolve into tears. Choking back a sob, she left, slamming the door.

Soon Mom heard the rumble of the lawn mower. Tessa had mowed only a couple of rounds when the motor stopped. After several moments of silence, Mom went out to see what was wrong. She found Tessa with a sick look on her face, holding a small branch. "What happened?" she asked.

"Oh Mom!" she exclaimed. "Your lilac bush! I . . . ran over it!" Mom took the branch from her hand. She had been working so hard to get it to grow. In less than thirty seconds, Tessa had destroyed it. "I . . . I'm so sorry, Mom," Tessa apologized. "It was an accident."

Mom sighed. "Accidents do happen, Tessa—to lilac bushes and to pumpkin vines."

Tessa's lips quivered. "I guess they do. Will you forgive me?" she asked.

"Of course," Mom said. At that moment they heard the faint ring of the telephone. "You run ahead and answer it, Tessa," Mom said. "It's probably for you."

As Mom stepped into the hall a little later, Tessa glanced up and smiled at her while speaking into the phone receiver. "Oh, don't worry about it, Gabe. It was just a couple of pumpkin vines. I have lots of others. Accidents happen." As she hung up the phone, Tessa turned to Mom, who gave her a big hug. *BJW*

HOW ABOUT YOU?

Do you find it hard to say, "I'm sorry"? Sometimes it's even harder to say, "You're forgiven." Is there someone you need to forgive? If so, why not do it now? You'll feel much better when you do.

MEMORIZE:

"Forgive us our sins—just as we forgive those who have sinned against us." Luke 11:4

Forgive As God Does

October

18

One of the Flock

Read Ecclesiastes 4:9-12

"I wonder why geese always fly in a V-formation," said Corinne as she and her dad trudged through the tall grass around Grandpa's pond. Overhead, a flock of geese honked their way southward in the cloudless fall sky.

"When I was a boy out here on the farm, I used to wonder about that, too," Dad replied. "Do you see how closely they fly together? I've read that as each bird flaps its wings, it creates an uplift for the bird following it, and that by flying in this V-formation, the whole flock has about a 70 percent greater flying range than if each one flew alone."

"Hey, that's cool!" exclaimed Corinne. "Smart birds!"

The next evening, there was a special meeting at church for the young people in Corinne's age group. "Are you ready to go to your meeting?" Mom asked.

"Oh, no! I forgot all about it," said Corinne. "Jill and I planned to work with her new chemistry set tonight."

"I think," Mom said, "that you'll have to call Jill and tell her you can't come."

Corinne groaned. "Do I have to?" she asked. "Our church group is going to finish plans for our next service project, and I already know what I'm supposed to do for that."

Dad put down the newspaper. "Corinne, remember the geese we saw yesterday—and how they cooperated with one another by flying in formation?" Corinne nodded. "Their cooperation helped all of them," continued Dad. "We need that kind of cooperation in Christian circles, too. You're one of the 'flock' that makes up your youth group, so even if you don't need the group tonight, they need you." He paused, then added, "But actually, you need each other."

"Well, I suppose I better go then," said Corinne with a sigh. A moment later, she grinned as she added, "Each of us birds has to do her part." *RCW*

HOW ABOUT YOU?

Do you realize that regular attendance at church activities is very important? Your commitment to "the flock" could very well inspire others to learn and work better and accomplish more than if each one tries to work alone.

MEMORIZE:

"Two people can accomplish more than twice as much as one; they get a better return for their labor."
Ecclesiastes 4:9

Cooperate with Other Christians

Shoes and Salvation

Read Acts 4:8-12; John 14:6

"Mom, I've got a question," said Alexis as she climbed into the passenger seat of her mom's car. "Some of the kids in my class say it doesn't make any difference who you believe in to get to heaven—Muhammad or Buddha or . . . or whoever! Even my teacher says all religions lead to heaven." Alexis sighed. "How can anybody ever convince them that they're wrong?" she asked.

"That's something only the Holy Spirit can do," Mom said. "The Bible is very clear that Jesus is the only way to heaven. It's our duty to point that out to people and to pray for them, but only God can work in their hearts and convince them of the truth of his Word."

Alexis nodded, then changed the subject, "We're going to stop and look for new shoes for me, aren't we?"

"We'll stop," Mom assured her.

When they arrived at the shoe store, Alexis headed toward the display of the most expensive brand of shoes, while her Mom went to the lesser-known brands. "How about these, Mom?" Alexis held up a pair of shoes. "I need this brand."

"Those are awfully expensive," objected Mom. She held up another, less expensive pair. "These are almost the same, except for the name and the price." Alexis frowned, but when they left the store, she was carrying the less costly shoes.

On the way home, she sighed. "I still wish I could have gotten those other shoes," she said. "That brand name would have impressed my friends."

"You need to impress your feet," Mom said with a grin, "not your friends." After a moment, she added. "I know what you can tell the kids when you wear those shoes tomorrow. Tell them that when it comes to shoes, they're impressed only when kids wear a certain brand name, so they should be able to understand that when it comes to getting into heaven, God is impressed only with a certain name."

"Hey, that's right!" exclaimed Alexis. "The name that will impress God is the name of Jesus."

Mom nodded. "The Bible says his name is the only name 'by which we must be saved.'" *JCP*

HOW ABOUT YOU?

Have you trusted in the only name that will get you to heaven—the name of Jesus? There is no other way into heaven. The Bible is clear about that. Trust Jesus as Savior today.

Jesus Is the Only Way to Heaven

MEMORIZE:
"There is no other name under heaven given to men by which we must be saved." Acts 4:12, NIV

20

Remembered No More

Read Psalm 103:1-4, 10-12

Lara's Sunday school class was having a skating party, and she would be skating for the first time! She was so excited she could hardly get her skates on.

Skating looked so easy, but Lara found it to be harder than it looked. She clung to the handrail at first, finally easing out onto the floor. She was doing quite well, when suddenly her feet seemed to roll right out from under her, and she fell! "Whoops!" she exclaimed. She got up slowly, went back to the handrail, and hung on once again like she had done in the beginning. After a while, she ventured out onto the floor again. As kids went whizzing past her, she lost her balance and fell again. She got up slowly, skated a short distance, and then— oops! She fell again . . . and again . . . and again!

Lara sat down on a bench—and stayed there.

"Need some help?" her teacher, Mrs. Bell, asked when she came by.

Lara shook her head. "I can't skate," she said with a sigh. "I just keep falling."

"It takes practice," her teacher said. "Forget about falling, and keep trying. I'm sure you can learn to do it." Lara wasn't so sure, but she agreed to try again, and by the time the party was over, she was skating much better.

In Sunday school the next day, the lesson was about victory over sin. Mrs. Bell smiled at Lara. "As I watched you skate yesterday, it made me think of conquering sin in our lives," she said. "When you learn to skate, you can't let falling defeat you. You have to forget about it and try again and again. It's like that when we sin. We need to confess it, and then we need to forget it and go on living for God. He forgives us—and he forgets it! We must, too. We shouldn't let sin defeat us."

Lara nodded. She knew just what her teacher meant. *BJT*

HOW ABOUT YOU?

Do you feel you must ask God's forgiveness several times before you are really forgiven? God promises to forgive confessed sin. Believe that he has forgiven you just as he said he would. Don't go back and dwell on your sins. Forget them and go on to serve the Lord.

MEMORIZE:

"Forgetting the past and looking forward to what lies ahead, I strain to reach the end of the race and receive the prize for which God, through Christ Jesus, is calling us up to heaven." Philippians 3:13-14

Don't Let Sin Defeat You

Spider Web

Read Romans 6:16-22

Susan sat in her room admiring a beautiful gold locket. *This would look so pretty with my blue sweater,* she thought, *but if I keep wearing it, Mom will ask more questions about it.* And Susan had stolen it. She had slipped it into her pocket at the store. How guilty she felt as she hid it in the bottom of a drawer!

The one day Susan wore it, her mother asked where it came from. Susan lied and said it was a gift from a friend.

Then she felt so guilty for lying that she became grumpy and cross with her family.

Susan's Sunday school lesson about choosing to live in the new nature God gives to Christians, instead of giving in to the old nature of sin, didn't make her feel any better either.

Susan's thoughts returned to the locket. "When you yield to Satan, one sin leads to another," her teacher had explained. "Look out the window, girls—that spider web we've been watching is bigger than ever. The web was small at first, but the spider keeps making it bigger and bigger. Satan tries to work in your life like that. He wants to make his control over you bigger and bigger."

As Susan listened, she remembered the effect her sin had made in her life. Stealing the locket had led to telling lies and to being crabby and very unhappy. Back home, she took the locket from the drawer and went to find her parents. "I . . . I have to tell you something," she said and told the whole story. "What can I do?" she asked with a sob.

"I think you know what to do, Susan," her father answered gravely. "First, you need to ask God to forgive you. Then you'll have to take the locket back to the store. The manager will decide whether to let you return it or not. If not, you must make arrangements to pay for it."

Susan nodded. "It will be hard to do," she said, "but at least it will be better than giving in to sin!" *JLH*

HOW ABOUT YOU?

Is there something you need to confess? Have you disobeyed, stolen, cheated, or lied? Has it led to further sin? The only way back to happiness is to confess to those you have wronged and to God. Then yield to him each time you are tempted.

MEMORIZE:

"Don't you realize that whatever you choose to obey becomes your master? You can choose sin, which leads to death, or you can choose to obey God and receive his approval." Romans 6:16

Yield to God

October
22

The Election

Read 1 Corinthians 12:14, 20-22, 25

Elections for the church youth group officers were coming up, and Kathleen wanted to be president. "I'm sick of our dull meetings," she told her brother, Curt. "If *I* were president, we'd have better meetings." So she did everything she could think of to make herself noticed.

To Kathleen's dismay, the youth group did not elect her to be president. They chose Denny Sparks, and Kathleen was elected secretary. She was upset! *Why should Denny be president? He's so bashful he can hardly look at people,* Kathleen thought. She shared her complaints at home. "Now I won't get to try out any of my ideas," she grumbled. "Denny just doesn't have it."

"But he must have some good qualities, or he wouldn't have been elected," Dad said gently.

Curt spoke up for Denny, too. "He's so nice to everyone, and he's always willing to help and to let others help him," he said.

"Oh, he's nice enough, but still . . ." Kathleen got up to answer the phone. It was Denny, and as Kathleen hung up, she looked ashamed. "Denny wants all the officers to bring ideas for programs and projects to the next meeting," she said.

"That sounds like a good start," Dad said. "Apparently Denny wants you to have a part in planning the programs. He seems to recognize that all of you are important." Dad smiled. "It reminds me of what the apostle Paul wrote to the people of Corinth," he added. "Paul said that Christians are all members of the 'body of Christ.' Just as our eyes, ears, hands, and feet are important parts of our physical bodies, so every Christian is important to Christ. No one should be over-looked or looked down upon."

Kathleen nodded thoughtfully. "I guess I can see now why it's good that Denny was elected president. If I were in charge, I'd have run everything my own way," she admitted. "I guess that's something for me to work on, huh?" *AGL*

HOW ABOUT YOU?

Do you always want everything your way, or are you willing to cooperate with others and let them develop their talents for God, too? God has a place for every Christian to serve him. Each one is important and needed.

MEMORIZE:

"Some of the parts that seem weakest and least important are really the most necessary." 1 Corinthians 12:22

Each Person Is Important

Disposable Friends

Read John 15:13-15

Clarissa carried a handful of cookies and a glass of milk into the laundry room where Dad was folding towels. "Dad, can I call Amber and invite her over?"

Dad added a washcloth to the stack on the dryer. "Who is Amber?"

"She's my new friend." Clarissa dunked a cookie into her milk.

"Are you going to call Robyn, too?" Dad asked.

Clarissa shook her head. "No. She's not my friend anymore. We had a fight. Anyway, Amber is more popular."

"Oh?" Dad said thoughtfully. "Would you take these towels into the guest bathroom?"

As Clarissa set her milk on the dryer, Dad asked, "What about Staci and Madison? Are they still your friends?"

"Not really," Clarissa shrugged, reaching for the towels. "They were my friends, but Amber's more fun. May I—oops!" Milk poured down the side of the dryer. "Sorry!" Clarissa reached for a towel.

"No! Don't use that clean towel!" Dad said. He quickly pulled paper towels from the roll on the wall. "Here! Use these!"

Clarissa sopped up the milk and then threw the paper towels into the trash. Dad watched thoughtfully. "Paper towels are pretty handy. Just use them and toss them."

Clarissa shrugged.

"You've been treating your friends like paper towels," Dad said. "You seem to want to use them and then throw them away. But friends are not disposable. Friends are valuable." He pointed at a lovely yellow towel on top of the stack. "When a friendship gets smudged, clean it. You need more than one friend, just like our family needs more than one towel."

Clarissa held the stack of clean-smelling, fluffy towels to her cheek. She smiled. "Can I call Amber and Robyn and Staci and Madison and invite them over?"

"All of them?" Dad laughed. "You got me that time. Call them. The more the merrier." *BJW*

HOW ABOUT YOU?
Do you value your friends? Are you willing to spend time working on friendships? Or do you jump from friend to friend? Making new friends is wonderful, but follow God's advice and don't toss the old ones in the process.

MEMORIZE:
"Never abandon a friend." Proverbs 27:10

Be True to Your Friends

October

Not a Kid Anymore

Read Proverbs 1:5-9

Mary and Ginny were friends as well as sisters, and they agreed on almost everything—that is, until Mary began to go out with Drew. "You never do anything with me anymore," Ginny complained one day to her older sister. "You've let Drew spoil everything. Besides, you know that if they knew, Mom and Dad would think you're too young to date."

"I'm not a kid anymore," Mary retorted, "and I can make my own decisions." She glared at her sister. "And you just keep quiet about it," she added.

The next day as Dad washed the breakfast dishes, he cut his hand on a sharp knife. Mary quickly offered to bandage it. When she was finished, she was rather pleased with herself. She had always said she wanted to be a nurse. Mary was quiet the rest of the day. That night she had a talk with her mother. "Why can't I go out on dates yet?" she asked.

"You're growing up fast, honey," Mom replied, "but you're still too young for that."

"Drew Bates is a boy I like," Mary said, "and he wants me to join the Photography Club and quit the Future Nurses Club. But when Dad cut his hand, I couldn't wait to bandage it. That helped me decide that I shouldn't change clubs."

Mom looked thoughtful for a moment. "Well, then I guess I'm glad for that cut, even though of course I didn't want Dad to be hurt," she said with a smile. "I guess God is using the cut to help you know his directions for your life."

Mary laughed, but then she became solemn. "I . . . I've been hanging around with Drew quite a lot even though I knew you wouldn't like it," she confessed. "I see now that by disobeying you and Dad—and God—I was going in the wrong direction for my life. I'm sorry, Mom."

Mom put an arm around Mary. "Thanks for telling me, honey. I'll be praying that you'll always be sensitive to God's leading and follow his direction." *AGL*

HOW ABOUT YOU?

Do you feel you're too grown up to listen to your parents anymore? Do you find their ideas old-fashioned? Remember that they have years of maturity and experience that influence them in the rules they make. They make rules because they love you. You are not so grown up that you may disobey the parents God gave you.

MEMORIZE:

"Listen, my child, to what your father teaches you. Don't neglect your mother's teaching." Proverbs 1:8

Listen to Parents

Sally's Solution

Read Romans 6:11-12

Sally cringed as she listened to her Sunday school teacher. "It's often easy for us to see that alcohol, drugs, or smoking are harmful to us," Mrs. Snow said. "We know that it's wrong to let such things control us. But whenever anything besides the Holy Spirit controls us, then that, too, leads to sin. It can be harmful. Take food, for instance. Bad habits of overeating or undereating can be very dangerous."

Sally knew she was very much overweight. She decided to talk with Mrs. Snow about it. "I've tried lots of times to diet," Sally said, "but then I seem to think about food more than ever."

Mrs. Snow nodded. "Sally, I think learning the principle of replacement would help you," she said. "When you're tempted to eat too much, don't just sit and try to *think* the food out of your mind. Get rid of the thought of food by replacing it with Scripture thoughts. For example, it would be good to memorize Romans 6:11-14." Mrs. Snow turned to those verses in her Bible and read them. "When you're tempted to eat too much, say these verses to yourself and substitute the word 'overeat' for 'sin,'" she suggested. "Or even get out your Bible and read the verses. You can also replace food thoughts by doing something for Jesus. Walk quickly to the nursing home to visit your grandma, or run an errand for somebody. The Lord will give you other ideas. Just remember to replace your thoughts of food with thoughts or actions that please God."

Sally listened thoughtfully. *I'm going to try it,* she decided. The battle with her weight was about to begin.

Mrs. Snow was holding out a picture—a picture of the heaviest lady Sally had ever seen. "Wow!" Sally exclaimed. "That lady must weigh five hundred pounds! Too bad she doesn't have someone like you to help her. Who is it?"

Mrs. Snow blushed. "That's a picture of me," she said. "It was taken several years ago. Then someone shared these verses with me, and you can see that this system of replacement really does work. It's not easy. It's slow, and you sometimes get discouraged, but Jesus is right there to help you. Remember your goal is to let God, not food, rule over you." *REP*

HOW ABOUT YOU?

Do you abuse your body—maybe by overeating or by not getting enough sleep? Whatever your bad habit is, use the method of replacement to overcome it. Remember, if you allow something that harms your body to control you, that thing is sin. Yield yourself to God rather than to sin.

MEMORIZE:
"Do not let sin control the way you live; do not give in to its lustful desires." Romans 6:12

Replace Wrong with Right

October 26

Interesting Genealogy

Read Genesis 5:18-27

Barbie just couldn't get as excited about family history as her mom did, but when Mom asked her to help with a genealogy project, Barbie reluctantly agreed to go along to the library. What a surprise awaited her!

Mom requested microfilms. "First we'll look at the census record of 1870. We'll see if we can find anything about your great-great-great-grandfather, Elias Conrad," Mom said as she showed Barbie how to thread the microfilms through a machine called a reader. As the machine magnified the tiny film, Mom moved it along quite rapidly.

"Wait, Mom!" Barbie whispered excitedly. "Back it up! I thought I saw the name Conrad over here in this column."

Mom moved the film back. Sure enough! There was the name they were looking for. They found that Elias Conrad worked as a sharecropper. Barbie became more and more interested as they continued the search.

At supper that evening, Barbie told Dad all about it. "We found out that Great-great-great-grandpa Conrad's farm was burned by the Yankees on their way to Atlanta in 1864, so he had to be a sharecropper after the Civil War!" she said. She eagerly talked on and on until it was time for devotions.

The family had agreed to read all the way through the Bible, one chapter a day, and it was Barbie's turn to read aloud. When she saw the chapter she was to read, she turned to her father. "Can we skip this chapter?" she pleaded. "It's all that genealogy—about whose son was whose, and how long people lived."

"Barbie, you weren't interested in our family genealogy until you studied it," Dad reminded her. "Now you think you aren't interested in this Scripture, but how do you know until you study it? All of the Bible is important. So, like an old commercial says, 'Try it—maybe you'll like it!' "

So Barbie read the passage, and again she was surprised! "Hey! In the middle of all those names is the story of Enoch!" she exclaimed. "He went to heaven without dying." She grinned at Dad. "I guess the whole Bible can be interesting and worthwhile after all," she admitted. *REP*

HOW ABOUT YOU?
Do you read all of God's Word? Or are there portions of the Bible that seem boring to you, so you don't read them? Don't ignore them. Why don't you try them—you just might like them! (Did you notice that today's reading not only told about Enoch, but also about the man who lived longer than anyone? Do you know his name?)

MEMORIZE:
"For everything that was written in the past was written to teach us."
Romans 15:4, NIV

Study All of the Bible

The Toaster and the Bible

Read James 1:21-25

"Mom, I can't get the toaster to work," called Nadine. "Mom!" she called again. Receiving no answer, she went to the laundry room where her Mom was working. "I want to make some toast, but I can't get the toaster to work," Nadine explained. "It doesn't heat up at all."

"Is it plugged in?" Mom asked.

"Plugged in?" repeated Nadine. "I guess so—it always is, but I'll go check." Nadine went back to the kitchen. *Oops!* she thought. *No wonder it didn't work.* She plugged in the toaster, put two pieces of raisin bread into it, and soon was enjoying perfectly browned, buttered toast.

In Sunday school class the next morning, Nadine's teacher held up her Bible. "I'm sure you've all learned that you should read your Bible every day, right?" asked Mrs. Scott. Heads nodded. "Good," she said. "I hope you do that, but are you aware that just reading the Bible isn't enough? What you read there needs to be plugged in to your life."

"What do you mean by that?" asked Samantha.

Nadine raised her hand. "I have an example of something that needed to be plugged in," she said. "I was trying to make toast yesterday, but the toaster wouldn't work. When I checked, I found out that it wasn't plugged in."

"I know about plugging in toasters," said Samantha, "but I still don't get how we plug the Bible into our lives." She grinned. "The Bible doesn't have a cord."

Mrs. Scott smiled. " 'Plugging it in' means doing what it says," she replied. "God's Word was meant to change us. For instance, if you read 'Obey your parents,' but then you try to get out of doing your chores, you're not letting the Bible change you. You haven't plugged it into your life."

"But if we read 'Forgive one another,' and then we do forgive somebody who treated us badly, we've plugged in what we read," suggested Nadine.

"You've got it!" agreed Mrs. Scott. "This week, let's not just read the Bible. Let's 'plug it in' by allowing it to change our lives as we obey it." *JMJ*

HOW ABOUT YOU?

Do you read your Bible each day? Is it plugged in to your life—does it change your behavior? It should. Let it bring you comfort and blessing, and be sure to put into practice what you read.

Put Bible Truths into Practice

MEMORIZE:
"Anyone who listens to my teaching and obeys me is wise." Matthew 7:24

28

The Things I Remember

Read Psalm 119:9-16

Mara looked up when she heard Grandpa Burns' question. "Ma, do you know where I left my glasses?" asked Grandpa as he reached for his Bible. Mara was spending the weekend with her great-grandparents.

"Now, Pa, did you lose those glasses again?" scolded Grandma. "You had them on when you paid the paperboy."

"That wasn't today. I paid him yesterday," Grandpa said. "Now . . ." He stopped a moment to cough.

"Your cough doesn't seem to be clearing up," murmured Grandma. "You'd better order more medicine."

"I just got some," Grandpa said. "That's who came today—Leo!" Grandpa turned to Mara. "Leo lives next door, and he went and picked up medicine for me."

Just then Mara spied Grandpa's glasses lying on the table. "Here are your glasses, Grandpa," she said. She laughed when Grandma asked for help in finding hers. "They're on your head," she said.

Grandma laughed, too. "I declare!" she exclaimed. "I clean forgot putting them on."

Grandpa opened his Bible. "Do you memorize many verses, Mara?" he asked. "We used to memorize whole chapters when we were kids."

Grandma nodded. "For example, we both learned Psalm 91 and Psalm 103," she said. "And John 14." She smiled. "Such beautiful verses," she added.

"That's right." Grandpa rocked back and forth. "Sometimes when our eyes are tired, we just say some of them together," he said.

"There's something I can't understand," Mara said with a puzzled look. "You can't remember things that happened just today—even just a little while ago—so how do you remember things from so long ago?"

Grandpa smiled. "The fact is that most of the things you'll remember are things you learn and do as a child," he said. "They might be good, or they might be bad. That's up to you, but you'll remember them."

"That's right," Grandma agreed.

Mara grinned. "Well, I have to learn lots of verses for my Bible club," she said. "It seems like a lot of work now, but I guess I'll be glad someday." *HCT*

HOW ABOUT YOU?

Are you hiding God's Word in your heart? Did you learn some verses this past week? Today? To truly learn them—to really have them in your heart—you need to obey them as well as memorize them. Do that. Some day you'll be glad you did.

MEMORIZE:

"I have hidden your word in my heart,
that I might not sin against you."
Psalm 119:11

Memorize Bible Verses

The Way to Grow

Read Matthew 5:14-16

"That's not fair! You've got your shoes on, Elisa. That makes you a little taller," wailed Adrienne. "Take them off!"

"All right," came the answer from Elisa.

Adrienne and Elisa were measuring each other's height against the door post. "See there! I'm still taller than you!" boasted Elisa. "And I'm a year younger!"

The children turned as Mom came into the room. "We wanted to see how much we had grown," Elisa told her. "And I'm taller than Adrienne! See!" She pointed to the mark on the door post.

"That may be true," Mom said, "but you never know—in another year Adrienne may pass you again. And don't forget, there are more important things to be concerned about than just growing physically. I was pleased to see from your last report cards that both of you are growing in knowledge."

The girls grinned, and Mom spoke again, "There's another way in which I hope you two are growing. Both of you have received Jesus as your Savior. You know him, but are you growing spiritually—growing in the 'special favor and knowledge' of Jesus, as the Bible says?" Mom asked.

"I probably should do better," confessed Elisa.

"Me, too." Adrienne admitted.

"Do you know what makes you grow taller and stronger?" Mom asked.

"Eating good food and exercising," replied Elisa.

"And I know I grow in knowledge by studying hard," added Adrienne.

"Right," Mom agreed, "and you grow 'in grace and in the knowledge of Jesus' by studying God's Word and obeying it."

"So we need to know and grow," said Adrienne.

"Yes. Two little words that rhyme, and we can add a third—glow!" Mom said. "When you know Jesus, and grow in him, you will glow. Others will see Jesus in you, and your life will glorify him." *HMP*

HOW ABOUT YOU?

Do you know Jesus as your Savior? Do you grow spiritually by studying his Word and obeying him? Does your life glow for him by the things you do and say?

MEMORIZE:
"Grow in the special favor and knowledge of our Lord and Savior Jesus Christ." 2 Peter 3:18

Know, Grow, and Glow!

October

30

Stop Signs and Christians

Read Ephesians 4:17-24

"Look!" exclaimed Keely as she pointed toward the ditch. "Someone knocked the stop sign down again."

Dad nodded and stopped the car. "I wish," he said as he got out, "that people would learn to slow down when they come around this corner."

Keely and Brandon got out of the car, too. "What are you going to do?" asked Keely.

"We'll see if we can put the sign back where it belongs," Dad replied. "If drivers don't stop at this corner, there could be a serious accident." He walked down into the ditch. "Help me carry it back to the road."

"We're right behind you," said Brandon.

Together the three of them lifted the sign and carried it to the corner. They tried to stand it up against the jagged pole still sticking out of the ground, but it kept falling over. Dad frowned. "We'll lay it down against the pole," he said. "That will have to do until the Highway Department fixes it properly."

"But when we put it down like this, the sign lays sideways," said Keely. "Won't it be hard to read?"

"Yes," Dad said, "but drivers can recognize it by its shape and color, not just by what it says."

"That's something like what Mr. Paul told us in Sunday school last week," said Brandon. "He says there are ways people can recognize us as Christians— sort of like the way people will recognize this sign."

"They'll recognize us by our shape and color?" asked Keely with a grin. She knew that wasn't right.

Brandon laughed. "No, but people can recognize Christians by what they do as well as by what they say—or sometimes by what they don't do or say. Mr. Paul says we can't expect others to know we're Christians if we swear or lie or cheat like lots of kids do."

"Mr. Paul is right," Dad agreed. "People should know we're Christians by our words. But more than that, our attitude and actions should show that we belong to God." *ECM*

HOW ABOUT YOU?

Can you be recognized as a Christian by the way you live? It's great to tell others that you belong to Jesus—but make sure they can also tell that you're a Christian by your attitude and by the way you act.

MEMORIZE:
"I will show you my faith by what I do." James 2:18, NIV

Let Others See Jesus in You

Really Saved

Read Romans 8:31-39

"You're ugly!" Cassie shouted at Nancy, who lived next door. "I'm going home!" But as she ran home, she felt terrible. Just the day before, she had accepted Jesus as Savior. *I shouldn't have gotten into a fight with Nancy,* she thought. *I wish I hadn't said those things.* She knew she had sinned, and it bothered her the rest of the week.

At the end of the morning service the next Sunday, Pastor Eubanks gave an invitation for those who wanted to be saved to come forward. Cassie was the first to go! "Didn't you come last week, too?" Mrs. Davis, the counselor, asked. Cassie nodded. "Well, let me explain this again," Mrs. Davis said. She showed Cassie some Bible verses about God's forgiveness and prayed with her. Then Cassie felt much better.

That evening, Mom asked Cassie to do the dishes. "You know I hate to do dishes," Cassie grumbled. But Mom didn't let her off, and Cassie was very annoyed. "Oh, I hate you!" she mumbled—under her breath, of course. Again she felt awful. *I don't deserve to go to heaven!* she thought. She could hardly wait for Sunday to come along so she could "get saved" again.

When Cassie again went to the front of the church the next week, Mrs. Davis again talked with her. "I need to get saved again!" Cassie said. "I did some bad things."

"I see," Mrs. Davis replied. "But, Cassie, if you really meant it when you said you were sorry for your sin and asked Jesus into your heart, you were born into God's family—and now you're his child forever."

"Really?" Cassie asked. She was beginning to understand.

Mrs. Davis nodded. "It's just like when you were born into your parents' family," she said. "They don't disown you every time you do something wrong, and neither will your heavenly Father disown you every time you sin. When you sin, you should pray right away and confess the sin and ask for strength not to repeat it. But you remain a part of God's family."

Cassie breathed a sigh of relief. *REP*

HOW ABOUT YOU?

When you sin, do you wonder if you're really saved? Do you ever feel unsure of your salvation? God promises eternal life. He promises that when Christians confess their sins, they are forgiven. His promises never fail. If you believe in Jesus, take God at his word and know that you are saved. You are a part of God's family.

MEMORIZE:

"I am convinced that neither death nor life . . . nor anything else in all creation, will be able to separate us from the love of God that is in Christ Jesus our Lord." Romans 8:38-39, NIV

Salvation Is Forever

Change Needed

Read Psalm 19:12-14

"I'm glad you're letting me help repair this horse stall," said Elizabeth as she joined her father in their small barn. Just then a large striped cat jumped from a hay loft to Elizabeth's shoulder. "Hey, cat," Elizabeth exclaimed, "do you want to help us fix this stall?" Laughing, she picked up the hammer. "Tell me what to do, Dad," she said.

After getting her instructions and working several minutes, Elizabeth missed the nail she was using and hit her thumb instead. Without thinking, she muttered a swear word—one often used by kids at school.

"Elizabeth," Dad said sternly. "You know better than to talk like that."

"Uh . . . Dad . . . I . . . I don't usually say those words," Elizabeth muttered. "I bet you've never heard me say them before!"

"*I* may not have heard them," admitted Dad, "but how about the kids you play with at school? Have they heard you use words like that?"

Elizabeth looked down without speaking. She knew she did carelessly use the same kind of language she often heard other kids use. "I'll do better," she mumbled.

"Good," Dad said, "but think about the cat we saw a little while ago. It has stripes, right? And it can't change that. There's a Bible verse that reminds us that just like we can't change the color of our skin, and an animal—a leopard, in the verse—can't change its markings, we can't do good when we're used to doing evil. I think that principle applies to the language we use. When you're in the habit of using bad words, they sometimes slip out when you don't intend for them to do so. I'm glad you want to repair that bad habit, but you need God's help with that. Ask him to help you control your language at school and other places, and then you won't have a problem with it at home, either." *AJS*

HOW ABOUT YOU?

What words do you use? Be honest! If you swear or use bad language, confess it to God. Ask him to help you change that bad habit. You can't change yourself, but he can change you.

MEMORIZE:

"Can the Ethiopian change his skin or the leopard its spots? Neither can you do good who are accustomed to doing evil." Jeremiah 13:23, NIV

Never Use Swear Words

2

Important Rules

Read Psalm 119:165-174

"Guess what, Mom!" Hillary exclaimed as she dropped her books on the table. "We're having a poster context. The winner gets fifty dollars, and I'm going to use it to buy . . ."

Mom laughed. "Better not spend it until you win it," she warned. "What kind of poster do you have to make?"

"It has to be about conservation—saving our natural resources such as water, trees, and wildlife. I got an idea before Mrs. Larson even finished reading the rules. My slogan is 'Here today—Gone tomorrow.' " Hillary jumped up on a kitchen stool as she continued. "On half of the poster I'll put some blackened tree stumps. In the middle I'll draw a lighted match."

"Not bad," Mom agreed. "You just might have a winner."

"Sure I do!" exclaimed Hillary. "Now can I have some money to buy poster board?"

"What size does it have to be?" Mom asked as she handed Hillary some bills.

"Uhhhhh . . ." Hillary scratched her head. "I think it has to be half of a regular poster board."

For the next two weeks, Hillary worked untiringly on her poster. On the last day, just before the final bell, she handed it in. "Very neat, and a good idea, too," said Mrs. Lawson with a smile. But she frowned as she studied it. "Hillary, didn't you read the rules?" she asked.

"Well . . . well . . . ah, you read them to us," stammered Hillary.

"Rule number four says there must be a one-inch margin on all sides," reminded Mrs. Lawson. "The branches of your trees go all the way to the edge." Hillary could have cried! "I'll give this to the judges, but I'm afraid it isn't eligible to win," Mrs. Lawson continued. "No matter how good a poster is, I'm sure they'll insist that it meet the rules. Too bad, Hillary. It might have been a winner." *BJW*

HOW ABOUT YOU?

Have you been reading God's rule book—the Bible? It's important to know and obey the rules God has given for your life so you won't miss out on things far greater even than a fifty-dollar prize.

MEMORIZE:

"I obey your commandments and decrees, because you know everything I do." Psalm 119:168

Keep God's Rules

The Magnet

Read Isaiah 40:28-31

"I hate homework," Lisette complained as she and her brother sat at the kitchen table. She jabbed the sharp tip of her pencil at a division problem.

Jonah lifted his nose out of his science book. "I don't mind doing science homework," he said. "These magnets are interesting. Watch this." He picked up a nail and rubbed it across a magnet several times. Then he held the nail close to a straight pin.

"Wow!" Lisette exclaimed. "That nail picked up the pin just as if it were a real magnet. Why does it do that?"

"Some magnetism gets rubbed off onto the nail," Jonah explained.

"Can I try it?" Lisette asked. She took the nail and held it over a few paper clips. She giggled as they sprang up toward the nail.

"My book says the nail will soon lose its power to attract things if it isn't rubbed against the magnet again," Jonah said. "You have to do that quite often."

Lisette reluctantly turned back to her math paper while Jonah continued to tinker with the magnet. A few minutes later, he broke the silence. "This nail is just like a Christian," he said.

"What are you talking about?" Lisette asked.

"My Bible teacher used a magnet like this for an object lesson," Jonah answered. "Look—this magnet is like God, and the nail is like us. When we get saved we get close to God." Jonah illustrated by rubbing the nail against the magnet as he continued. "We receive power from God to act like Jesus, and that attracts other people to him."

Lisette listened closely, then suggested, "And if we don't stay close to the Lord by obeying him and reading the Bible and praying, we begin to lose our power to attract others to Jesus."

Jonah nodded. "Then we're more like a plain old nail. I'd rather be like a magnet."

"Me, too," Lisette agreed. "Now, back to math!" *ECO*

HOW ABOUT YOU?

Will you be like a magnet today, attracting people to Jesus with your words and behavior? To do that, you need to receive power from God. Read your Bible; think about what it says; obey it; talk to God in thanksgiving and prayer. Don't be a "nail" that has lost the ability to attract. Be a magnetic Christian.

MEMORIZE:

"When the Holy Spirit has come upon you, you will receive power and will tell people about me everywhere."

Acts 1:8

Be a Magnetic Christian— Attract Others to Jesus

November

4

A Matter of Honor

Read Ephesians 6:1-4

Gail scuffed her shoe in the dirt beneath the swing as Olivia, one of her classmates, sat down beside her. "Would you like to jump rope with me?" Olivia asked.

"No, thanks," Gail responded gruffly.

"Is something wrong?" Olivia asked.

"I just don't like it here. All my friends are at my old school," Gail answered as she began to swing.

Olivia joined her, keeping her swing even with the back-and-forth motion of Gail's. "Why don't you still go there?" Olivia continued.

"We moved because our family got too big for our house," Gail answered. "My parents keep telling me things will get better, but I still don't like it."

"Well, it sounds like your parents really care about you," Olivia said.

"I suppose," Gail grudgingly agreed. "But right now I just don't like the *way* they care about me. And I really don't like their decision to move."

"Do you go to church?" Olivia asked. "My Sunday school teacher made a big deal of having us learn the fifth commandment. She says a lot of kids act like they don't know it."

Gail nodded as she dragged her feet to stop her swing. "We learned the Ten Commandments, too," she said. "That's the one about parents, right? Well, I do obey my parents. I'm here, aren't I?"

Olivia fingered her braid. "Yes, but that commandment says to honor, or respect, our parents," she said. "My teacher says that includes more than just obedience. It includes accepting their rules and discipline without getting all mad about it or holding a grudge against them. Last summer my dad and mom grounded me for a month for talking back to them. Boy, did I feel the same way you do now!"

Gail drew a pattern in the dust with her shoe. She felt guilty—she knew her attitude was wrong. Finally, she looked up. "I guess I should be glad my parents watch out for me," she admitted. Then she smiled at Olivia. "I could always make some new friends," she added. "Do you still want to jump rope with me?" *VCM*

HOW ABOUT YOU?

Do you honor your parents in addition to obeying them? Or do you obey them just so you won't get in trouble? Do you grumble and complain when they tell you to do something? God gave you parents to guide you and care for you. Thank God for them. And thank them for caring for you.

MEMORIZE:
"Honor your father and mother."
Exodus 20:12

Honor Your Parents

A Walrus Family (Part 1)

Read John 16:7-15

"Listen to this, Adele," Seth said. "My book says a walrus calf is fed by its mother. When it grows older, the mother walrus pushes her calf into the freezing water to make it learn how to search for its own food."

Adele shivered. "Br-r-r-r! I'm glad I'm not a walrus," she said.

Just then Mom appeared in the doorway of the family room. "It's time to leave for the nursing home, Adele," she said.

Adele frowned. "I decided that I don't want to go," she said.

"I need your help," Mom said. "You promised to pass the cookies."

"But I don't like the way the nursing home smells," Adele complained.

"Life isn't all pleasant things," Mom told her. "This is one way we can bring a little joy to the people there. God is pleased when we serve others."

"Why doesn't Seth have to go?" Adele asked.

"He'll be going another time," Mom explained patiently. "Come along now."

Adele was in good spirits when she and her mother returned home later that afternoon. "You should have come, Seth," she said. "You missed some great stories. There's a man there that everyone calls Gramps, and he told one funny story after another!" Adele turned to her mother. "When can we go back, Mom?" she asked.

"How about next Tuesday, after school?" Mom suggested. "You could go then too, Seth."

"No, thanks," he answered. He looked up when Adele gave him a sharp shove. "What did you do that for?" he asked angrily.

"Remember the mother walrus in your report?" Adele asked, grinning. "Mom knew it would be good for me to go to the nursing home, so she gave me a shove— like that mother walrus. Now I'm giving you a shove."

Mom smiled. "The Holy Spirit gives us nudges, too," she told them. "He never forces us to do things, but he finds ways to encourage us." *LJR*

HOW ABOUT YOU?

Have you ever felt that you should tell someone about Jesus? Did you notice God's Holy Spirit nudging you to speak up? Maybe he has also nudged you to do other things, like putting a generous part of your allowance into the missionary offering or helping around the house. Don't be afraid of God's nudges—even if they seem to be difficult or uncomfortable things to do. When you obey him, he will reward you.

Obey God's Nudges

MEMORIZE:
"When the Spirit of truth comes, he will guide you into all truth." John 16:13

November

6

A Walrus Family (Part 2)

Read Proverbs 11:24-28

"I knew you'd be surprised at how much fun you had!" Adele remarked to her brother, Seth, as they helped their parents prepare supper.

Seth nodded. "I actually liked going to the nursing home, and I'm thinking about helping at the city mission, too."

"Me too," Adele said. "Pastor Jim says a lot of the people who go in there are homeless and don't have warm clothes. Our youth group is already collecting coats and thermal underwear to give them."

"That's great," Mom said. "I think you'll both enjoy that."

"I hope so," Adele replied. She grinned. "Thanks, Mom, for forcing us to get started by making us go to the nursing home."

"I think I'm getting credit for something the Holy Spirit did," Mom said. "I think he has been working on you two."

"Well, maybe," Seth agreed.

Mom gave Seth a hug. "Like I said, I think you'll enjoy the mission work," she told him, "and I *know* you'll be blessed. The Bible says we'll be rewarded when we help the poor."

"Rewarded with blubber, I guess," Dad added, laughing.

"Blubber?" Adele exclaimed in horror. "That sounds gross. I don't think I'll help with anything like that anymore." She looked at her father. "What did you mean?" she asked.

"Well, it sounded like this was a walrus family, and God gave walruses lots of blubber—or fat—to protect them from the freezing cold," Dad told her. Adele groaned and Dad laughed, then continued more seriously, "When we help the poor, God gives us what we need to protect us from the cold hardships of life."

Mom laughed, too. "Service for God never goes unrewarded," she said. *LJR*

HOW ABOUT YOU?

Do you know any poor people? If you share, you will be blessed. How can you help? Could you go without a few candy bars or sodas to buy gloves and hats to send to a mission? Could you collect canned goods and give them to a community pantry? However you choose to help the poor and homeless in your community, you will be blessed.

MEMORIZE:
"If you help the poor, you are lending to the Lord—and he will repay you!"
Proverbs 19:17

Help the Poor

Face the Music (Part 1)

Read 2 Timothy 2:1-7

Missy and her friend Dolly settled into their seats at the concert hall. "These things are boring," Dolly complained. "I wouldn't even come if it wasn't for the Gold Cup." Both girls were piano students, and a Gold Cup Trophy was something each was hoping to win. To be eligible, they had to play in the fall competition and attend three concerts. Anyone who earned a superior rating would be awarded the Gold Cup.

Missy sighed. "I don't mind the concerts," she said, "but I already attended three, and I can think of things I'd rather do today. I forgot to sign in at one of them, so I have to attend this one, too." She leaned back and yawned.

"Hey, I've got an idea," Dolly said suddenly. "We're signed in, so why don't we just leave? Lots of kids do it! We can go out to the bathroom and just not come back. The monitors will never notice." She stood up. "C'mon," she urged as she saw Missy hesitate. "After all, you've already attended three concerts. You just forgot to sign in once, so it's not like you're cheating."

The concert hadn't started yet, and Dolly's argument sounded convincing. So in spite of her doubts, Missy walked out with Dolly. No one challenged them or even seemed to notice them go. "That proves it's okay," Missy said, trying to convince herself. "But my mom and dad won't be convinced, so what do we do now? It's too early to go home."

"We go window-shopping," Dolly said. "Let's find ourselves a new outfit. Then if we can persuade our moms to buy them for us we'll already have them picked out!" Missy couldn't think of a better plan, so the girls went window-shopping for a while, arriving home just in time for supper. *REP*

HOW ABOUT YOU?

Have you ever been in a situation where something seemed sort of all right, yet deep down you knew it was wrong? Today's Scripture tells you to "follow the Lord's rules." In other words, don't take shortcuts to reach your goal. Don't cheat along the way. Do what's honest and right. Ask yourself, "In this situation, what would Jesus do?"

MEMORIZE:

"Follow the Lord's rules for doing his work, just as an athlete either follows the rules or is disqualified and wins no prize." 2 Timothy 2:5

Compete Fairly

Face the Music (Part 2)

Read Psalm 34:11-18

Dad had just answered the phone, and all Mom and Missy could hear was Dad's side of the conversation. "Yes, this is Mr. Martin. . . . Yes, she did. . . . Why, yes, I believe so. . . . Is that right? Well, I'm surprised to hear that. I'll certainly check it out. . . . Of course. I understand. . . . Yes, I'll get back to you. . . . Good-bye."

"What was that all about?" Mom asked. Missy was afraid to ask, but she waited anxiously for Dad's reply.

"That was Missy's piano teacher," Dad replied. "She said the names of those who attended the concert today were entered in a drawing for free tickets to a play." He paused and looked questioningly at his daughter. "Missy, your name was drawn," Dad continued. "You didn't claim your prize, so they thought they'd better investigate. It seems there were a few people who said they saw you and Dolly leave before the concert even started. Is this true?"

"Why, I . . . I . . ." Missy stammered. "Dolly wanted to leave, and she said I wouldn't be cheating since I had already attended three concerts. I agreed. It wasn't fair to make me go to four!"

"We've been through all that before," Dad replied. "You clearly understood that you were required to attend another concert." He shook his head. "Your teacher said she's sorry, but you won't be able to compete for a Gold Cup this fall."

"A whole year of practice and no Gold Cup!" Missy wailed as tears came into her eyes. She was deeply disappointed and angry with herself for not doing what she knew in her heart she should have done. *REP*

HOW ABOUT YOU?

Have you ever had to learn a hard lesson because of something wrong you did? It leaves you feeling depressed and angry, doesn't it? Confess your sin to the Lord, and let him give back your joy. Then the next time you're tempted to think you can get away with doing something wrong, remember that you can't hide sin. Don't learn the same lesson all over again!

MEMORIZE:
"Be sure that your sin will find you out." Numbers 32:23

You Pay for Sin

Written Down

Read Exodus 2:1-10

Jayla listened closely to the instructions when she went to baby-sit for the Randall boys. "Specific directions and phone numbers are written down on the notepad," Mrs. Randall said. "I shouldn't be gone long."

Later that evening, Jeff begged for ice cream and Jerry wanted cookies. Jayla checked Mrs. Randall's notes. "Sorry, Jeff, but your mom says you can't have ice cream," she said. "How about some popcorn? You may both have that." They agreed.

After a snack and story, it was bedtime. "Jeff, you've got to take your medicine now," Jayla reminded the little boy.

"I don't want to," he grumbled. "I'll wait for Mama. We can stay up till she gets home. It's not a school night."

"Your mom said you had to be in bed by nine," Jayla patiently explained. "Jeff, if you take your medicine right away, I'll give you both a piggyback ride upstairs."

"Okay," Jeff agreed.

The boys were sleeping when Mrs. Randall came home. "My, it looks nice in here, Jayla. Thanks for doing the dishes and picking up the toys. Did you have any trouble?" she asked.

"No, I just followed your instructions and everything went fine," Jayla answered. "Jeff wanted to skip his medicine, but I insisted he take it."

"Good." Mrs. Randall smiled. "I'm pleased with the job you've done. Would you like to baby-sit again next week?" she asked. "My husband and I have to go to a banquet, so we may be out rather late. But I'm sure you can handle it."

"Sure," Jayla agreed, "but I'll have to check it out with my mother first."

"Fine. Let me pay you now," Mrs. Randall said as she reached for her purse. *JLH*

HOW ABOUT YOU?

Are you a good worker? Maybe you think you're too young to be expected to stick to your work when there's a job to be done. Not so! Today's Scripture is just one of several examples in the Bible of a child (Moses' sister) who accepted responsibility. People should be able to depend on you to do a good job. Little jobs can lead to greater jobs if you can be counted on to do your best.

MEMORIZE:
"Even children are known by the way they act, whether their conduct is pure and right." Proverbs 20:11

Be Responsible

10

The Missionary Party

Read 2 Corinthians 9:12-15

As Anya lay in her clean, cool bed, scenes from the missionary movie she had seen that evening flashed through her mind. She could not forget the skinny, ragged children playing with tin cans in the dirt in front of tiny huts.

The next afternoon, Mom looked up from the desk as Anya entered the room. "I'm inviting all of your cousins to come and help celebrate your twelfth birthday," Mom said as she flexed her fingers. "What would you like for your birthday?"

"A keyboard," Anya answered immediately.

Mom frowned. "But, honey, we can't afford that," she said with a sigh.

Anya nodded. "I figured you'd say that." She thought about her room filled with games and toys, and about her closet full of clothes. Then another picture flashed through her mind—ragged boys and girls playing with tin cans in front of little huts. She had an idea. "Mom, could we have a missionary party?" she asked eagerly. "Could I give my birthday presents to children like the ones we saw in the video last night?"

Mom thought a moment. "It might be difficult to send packages," she replied, "but maybe we could ask your cousins to give an offering instead of a gift."

Anya put her chin in her hand. "Could we ask the mission to use it for the children?" she asked.

"Why not?" Mom said with a smile. "It's a wonderful idea, Anya. I'm proud of you."

On the day of Anya's missionary party, there were no wrapped presents—not even from her parents and grandparents—only envelopes. When Anya counted the money, she was amazed. "One hundred and ten dollars!" she squealed. "Just think how much this will buy for those poor children." Anya hugged her mom tightly. *BJW*

HOW ABOUT YOU?

Have you ever thought of sharing with missionaries or poor children on your birthday? Maybe you could have a missionary party, too. If you'll try it, you may find that it's the best party you've ever had.

MEMORIZE:
"Whoever gives to the poor will lack nothing." Proverbs 28:27

Share Your Blessings

The Neatest Job

Read Ephesians 6:5-9

Kendall sat at the piano to practice her lesson. "I wish I could stay home from school for the next two weeks," she muttered as she opened her music book.

Mom smiled. "Does this wish have anything to do with the two-week responsibility Mrs. Murphy assigned you?" she asked.

Kendall sighed. "It would be neat to have a job for that long if it were a good job," she said. "But who wants to pick up all the scraps of paper and other stuff that fall under our desks?" Kendall placed her hands on her hips. "Marty gets to wash the chalkboard; Robin gets to clap the erasers—but me, I have a dumb job. It's so embarrassing, crawling around with the waste can."

"When I was young, my dad had a truck that he used for picking up old furniture," Mom said thoughtfully. "He fixed up and sold some pieces, and he chopped up others for firewood. Our backyard was piled full of old desks and chests of drawers and upright pianos from other people's houses. Talk about an embarrassing sight!" She shook her head.

"Sounds like you had a messy yard," Kendall gasped.

Mom nodded. "My mom reminded me that the old furniture provided a living for us," she continued, "and in addition, my dad served God by giving wood to people who didn't have any. Sometimes he also gave the mended furniture to people who needed it."

"I'd say that Granddad had a neat job," Kendall said.

"He made it neat by choosing to be happy, and he served God with a task that others saw as lowly," Mom said. "He knew that being able to serve God was the most valuable part of it."

Kendall began to practice her scales. "I suppose my job could help make the janitor's work easier," she said.

"Then does this mean you'll be going back to school tomorrow?" Mom asked, and they both laughed. *NEK*

HOW ABOUT YOU?

Do you ever think that some of your chores are dumb? Are you embarrassed doing jobs you feel too grown up to do or that don't look important? Decide right now to be willing to serve God in ways people consider lowly. Ask him to help you.

MEMORIZE:
"Work with enthusiasm, as though you were working for the Lord rather than for people." Ephesians 6:7

Serve God in All You Do

12

A Feast of the Heart

Read Psalm 33:20-22

Maybe my stomach will feel better if I lay on my side, Rosa thought as she carefully rolled over.

"Do you think you could handle a little soup?" her father asked.

Rosa shook her head. She closed her eyes and tried again to get comfortable on the couch.

"I'm sorry you have to miss Eva's party," said Dad.

"Me, too," murmured Rosa, "but I told Eva she could come over here next weekend. We could have a late birthday celebration—just the two of us." Rosa rolled over onto her back. "Dad, could you get me another blanket?" she asked. "I'm cold."

"Sure, honey," replied Dad. "Got one right here."

Rosa smiled as her dad covered her all the way to her chin. "It's nice having you take care of me while Mom is gone to her meeting. When I feel better, can we play a game?"

"Now, that's a good idea." Dad sat on the end of the couch and rubbed Rosa's feet gently. "Know what, honey? I appreciate the fact that you're not fussing about missing Eva's party. Her mom always fixes a big feast for you kids, and you always enjoy it."

"Yeah," said Rosa, "but food doesn't sound good today."

"Well, you and I are having a feast right here at home," said Dad.

Rosa opened her eyes in surprise. "Not me," she said, "and all you had was soup. That's no feast."

"When we have a cheerful heart, Rosa, we have a continual feast," responded Dad.

"Did you make that up to make me feel better?" asked Rosa.

Dad shook his head. "That's from God's Word," he said. "I said that because you have a good attitude about getting sick and missing the party."

"And that's a feast?" asked Rosa.

"A feast for our spirits," said Dad. He covered Rosa's toes and turned out the light. "Now rest. Before you know it, you'll be able to give your stomach a feast, too." *MFW*

HOW ABOUT YOU?

Do you trust God even in times of disappointment? Or are you quick to complain and fuss when things don't go as you want? If you're truly trusting God, you can have a cheerful and hopeful attitude.

MEMORIZE:
"For the happy heart, life is a continual feast." Proverbs 15:15

Maintain a Cheerful Attitude

The Whining Sister

13

Read James 4:1-3

As Leticia took out a pile of homework, she heard her three-year-old sister, Tamara, loudly complaining about something. She began to work, but the noise Tamara was making distracted her. "Mom, what's wrong with Tamara?" Leticia asked impatiently. "Her whining is driving me crazy; I have more homework than anyone should be expected to do, and she's not making it any easier." Tamara made a face and threw a sock at Leticia.

"She wants someone to put her socks on for her," Mom answered calmly.

"But she knows how to put her socks on," said Leticia. "Oh, well . . . I'll do it, just to quiet her down!"

"Just a minute," Mom said. "Tamara also knows how to ask nicely for things. So far, all she's done is whine and throw her socks."

"Yeah," muttered Leticia, "but I don't know if I can stand that noise much longer."

"I wonder if God ever feels that way when we complain and get angry instead of asking him for what we need," Mom said thoughtfully. "We often complain about things instead of praying about them."

Leticia frowned. "You mean like just now when I complained about my homework and Tamara's noise?" she asked. "Does God even want me to pray about those kinds of things?"

Mom smiled. "I wasn't thinking of that," she said, "but, yes, God wants us to pray about everything." She smiled. "Why don't we pray now?" Mom and Leticia bowed their heads. "Dear Father, Thank you for caring about all the details of our lives. We recognize that you know what's best for all of us," prayed Mom. "Right now we ask you to help Leticia with her homework and to help Tamara learn to ask instead of whine. Please help us to do that, too, and thank you for hearing us."

As Mom finished praying, Tamara walked up to her and held up her socks. "Will you put my socks on, Mommy?" she asked sweetly. As Mom hugged Tamara and helped her, Leticia silently thanked God for helping her and then got busy with her homework. *DY*

HOW ABOUT YOU?

Do you pray only at mealtimes and bedtime, or do you pray about things all through the day? God cares about everything you care about, and he wants you to ask for his help. He is pleased to give it.

MEMORIZE:
"Keep on praying. No matter what happens, always be thankful."
1 Thessalonians 5:17-18

Pray Continually

November

The Right Size (Part 1)

Read 1 Peter 2:21-23

Kylie waited until the last minute to get out of bed, and then she poked at her breakfast. "Hurry, Kylie—the bus will soon be here," Mom said. "You wouldn't want to miss school today."

"Yes, I would," said Kylie.

"You would? Why?" Mom asked. "Don't you feel well?"

"Yes . . . I mean, no," Kylie stammered.

"Whatever is the matter?" Mom wanted to know.

"It's the kids at school . . . they tease me because I'm so small. They call me 'Stubby.' " Tears shone in Kylie's eyes.

"Don't let their words bother you, Kylie. Ignore the unkind words, and the kids will probably leave you alone," advised Mom. "Be friendly to them. Your attitude and actions are more important than your appearance."

"But today we're playing basketball in gym, and no one will want me on her team. I'm the wrong size," Kylie protested.

Mom gently put her arm around her daughter's shoulder. "Kylie, you may be smaller than you want to be, but God made you just as you are. He doesn't make mistakes. Maybe you'll grow faster when you're older, and catch up," she encouraged, "but even if you don't, God has a plan for you. He knows what is best. Trust him. Now here comes the bus. You do your best in gym—I'll pray for you today."

As Kylie expected, she heard some groans when the gym teacher assigned her to a team. Some of the kids teased her, but when she didn't get angry about it, she found they usually stopped. The day wasn't quite as bad as she expected, but she still wished that just once she could be the right size! *JLH*

HOW ABOUT YOU?

Are you teased about your size? Skin or hair color or freckles? Are you called names? Teasing sometimes hurts, but don't strike back. Learn from Jesus. People were unkind to him, too. He'll help you to ignore teasing and to get along with others.

MEMORIZE:

"He did not retaliate when he was insulted." 1 Peter 2:23

Get Along with Others

The Right Size (Part 2)

Read Psalm 139:14-17

When school was over for the day, Kylie inched her way through the crowded bus and wearily plopped down in a back seat. It would be good to get home to a warm house and a hot supper. It was getting colder outside and raining hard.

As the bus started out, Kylie closed her eyes. She was sleepy, for she hadn't slept much the night before—she'd been too worried about the basketball teams. The next thing she knew, she was suddenly shoved across the seat and thrown onto the floor. The bus had hit a slippery spot as it went down a country road. It had skidded and landed on its side in a ditch. Glass broke, metal crunched, and children screamed. The door would not open, and they could not get out.

"We'll have to wait for help," said the driver. He did his best to calm the children and make them comfortable. But the passing minutes seemed like years, and no help came. "Hey, let's go out a window," suggested one of the kids. Several tried it, but they were too big. Then they thought of Kylie. "Kylie, you try it! You're little," they said.

Kylie wiggled. She squirmed and twisted. Suddenly she was out the window. She climbed up the bank to the road, but nothing was in sight. Limping along, cold and bruised, she finally made it to the nearest house, and soon help was on the way.

Several days later, Kylie received a citizen's award. She was credited for her part in the rescue. "Wow! I guess God made me the right size after all," she marveled.

Mom nodded. "You were just the right size for the job you had to do," she said. "God never makes mistakes." *JLH*

HOW ABOUT YOU?

No matter how you feel about your looks or your personality, God thinks you're great! You're a special person, made by God for a specific purpose. He has a plan for your life. Be content with the way he made you, and trust him to guide you.

You Are God's Special Creation

MEMORIZE:
"I have made them for my glory. It was I who created them." Isaiah 43:7

November

16

Braces for Marcy

Read Psalm 100

Marcy and her mother sat in Dr. Thompson's office and listened to the dentist outline the details of straightening Marcy's teeth. *This sure doesn't sound very pleasant,* Marcy thought. *It's so expensive, too! No wonder Mom has to wait to get new carpet in the living room!*

That afternoon, Marcy went to a neighborhood Bible club. Mrs. Garcia, her teacher, began the lesson by asking the children to think of something that happened that day for which they were thankful.

Marcy tried to think of other things she'd done that day, but the trip to the dentist's office filled her mind—mostly with dread! When it was Marcy's turn to share an idea, she shrugged. "I went to the dentist today," she said glumly. "I have to get braces, and it's going to cost a bunch! I can't find anything to be thankful about when it comes to having braces!"

"Let's think about that," Mrs. Garcia said. "Do you know what people did before we had dentists and modern medicine?"

"Their teeth rotted?" Carlos asked, who was sitting behind Marcy. All the kids laughed.

"Well, it's true that many people lost their teeth or had serious problems with pain," Mrs. Garcia agreed. "Who gave the scientists the intelligence to straighten teeth and to correct mouth problems?"

"God did," Marcy said.

Mrs. Garcia nodded. "Right. So don't you think we should be thankful to God for the new techniques?"

"I never thought about it like that," Marcy admitted.

"I can think of another reason to be thankful," Mrs. Garcia added. "Be thankful that your parents can afford the braces. Many parents would like to get dental work for their children but don't have the money."

"Hmmmm." Marcy smiled. "I guess the Lord really has given me a lot to be thankful for," she admitted. *LMW*

HOW ABOUT YOU?

Have you been complaining because you have to wear braces or glasses? Do you grumble because you have to take special medicine for allergies? Instead of complaining about these circumstances, thank the Lord for giving doctors the intelligence to provide answers to your problems. In whatever circumstances you find yourself, find ways to thank the Lord for his goodness.

MEMORIZE:

"Always give thanks for everything to God the Father in the name of our Lord Jesus Christ." Ephesians 5:20

Be Thankful for Doctors

A Measure of Faith

Read 2 Peter 1:2-4

Lucy and Julia leaned back against the car seat. A vacation to Philadelphia had sounded like fun, but getting there seemed to take forever. They were tired of looking at scenery, counting cars, and watching license plates.

Finally they arrived, and they soon forgot all about the struggles of the trip. They toured Independence Hall, and Lucy was fascinated by the Liberty Bell. "It would've been neat to hear that bell ring every day!" she exclaimed.

"That peal of freedom was dear to the hearts of many," Dad agreed. "We owe a lot to our founding fathers. They had the faith and the vision to fight for our freedom. It didn't come easily, but they never gave up. They knew the importance of fighting for what they believed in."

Julia pointed to a plaque on the wall. "Philadelphia, the city of brotherly love," she read. "I wonder why it's called that."

"William Penn founded the city," Dad explained. "History books tell us that the settlement in this area was kind of an experiment in holy living. Under William Penn's plan, peace, goodwill, and brotherly love were to be extended to all, including the Indians."

"We studied that in school," Lucy chimed in with enthusiasm. "William Penn treated the Indians fairly, and they trusted him. He trusted them, too."

Dad nodded. "He took them at their word and acted upon it," he said. "They had faith in one another."

"Mr. Penn must have been a smart man," Julia decided.

"Yes, he was," Dad agreed. "He realized the importance of trust between people—and we all can learn from his example. But you know . . . there are promises more dependable than those of either Mr. Penn or the Indians. God has given us all kinds of promises, and we need to have faith in him. Mr. Penn had faith in the Indians and acted upon their promises. We must have faith in God and act upon his promises—we must put them into practice if we want to reap the benefits. It takes faith and trust in God to be victorious Christians." *JLH*

HOW ABOUT YOU?

Are you claiming God's promises by faith? God says, "I will supply all your needs." Do you trust him to do that? When you are in doubt, do you pray for the wisdom he promises to give you? When you are afraid, do you remember his promise that he will never leave you? Jesus said that faith as tiny as a grain of mustard seed could move a mountain (Matthew 17:20). Will you, by faith, claim God's promises?

Claim God's Promises

MEMORIZE:
"He has given us all of his rich and wonderful promises." 2 Peter 1:4

November

18

Spilled Milk

Read Luke 17:1-5

Hannah was furious with her little brother, Jonathan. "How could he be so careless?" she cried. "This is my brand-new sweater, and now it has milk all over it. Leave it to my clumsy brother to spill his cereal on everything!"

Jonathan was tearful. "I really am sorry, Hannah," he whimpered. "I didn't mean to get your sweater dirty."

Hannah scowled and turned away.

"Hannah, don't you think you're being a bit harsh with Jonathan?" Mom asked. "He did apologize. How about trying a little bit of forgiveness?"

But Hannah stormed out of the kitchen and up to her room. "Being sorry doesn't make my sweater clean," she muttered.

Hannah had a hard time keeping her mind on her schoolwork that day. She was glad when it was time for art—her favorite class. Maybe it would help her forget the upsetting morning. On her way to the art table, Hannah stopped to admire a painting her friend Lana was working on.

"Wow, Lana, you sure are talented! You're probably the best artist in school."

Lana smiled. "Thanks, Hannah, I really do enjoy painting. Oh! Look out, Hannah! Watch your paintbrush!"

Accidentally, Hannah had swept her paintbrush across the corner of Lana's picture. "Oh, Lana, I'm so sorry! I've ruined your beautiful painting."

Lana looked sadly at her picture. "I know you didn't mean to do it," she said. Then her face lit up. "I think if I paint over it with another color, it will cover it right up."

That evening, Hannah told her mother how Lana had covered the smudge on the picture.

Mom nodded. "You know," she said, "there's a verse that I'm reminded of—one I learned when I was about your age. It's Proverbs 10:12: 'Hatred stirs up quarrels, but love covers all offenses.' Lana showed love when she covered the smudge you made—and I think it would have been good if you had done that this morning when Jonathan spilled his milk." Soberly, Hannah nodded, then went to apologize to her litte brother. *DLR*

HOW ABOUT YOU?

Do you find it difficult to forgive others? If you're a Christian, the Bible says your sins are covered by the blood of Jesus. He does not hold one thing against you! And the Bible teaches that Christians are to practice that same kind of love and forgiveness.

MEMORIZE:

"Be kind to each other, tenderhearted, forgiving one another, just as God through Christ has forgiven you." Ephesians 4:32

Forgive Others

Show Me the Way

Read John 14:1-6

I will not cry! I will not cry! I have to keep calm, Elise told herself. *They were here just a minute ago.* While waiting in line with her sister and cousins for a ride on the roller coaster, Elise had turned away for a moment. When she looked back, they were gone! Elise's first idea was to walk along the line looking for them. So she walked up and down the entire line four times, but they were not there! "Where can they be?" Elise muttered, choking back a sob. She quickly backtracked to the merry-go-round, but the others weren't there. Elise checked out the lunch counter where they had eaten—but her family was nowhere in sight. *What am I going to do?* she wondered.

Suddenly, Elise remembered something. Her oldest cousin, Peter, had said that if they got separated, they should all meet by the big double ferris wheel. Peter had said the ferris wheel was so big, you could see it from anywhere in the park. Elise looked around. Sure enough! There was the ferris wheel—way over on the other side of the park. She hurried in that direction.

In just a few minutes, Elise was hugging her sister and laughing again with her cousins. Soon she felt better, and they all enjoyed the rest of the day at the park.

On the way home, they talked about their day. "It was scary being lost," Elise said. "I should have thought of the ferris wheel sooner. It was there all the time, but I didn't pay any attention because I forgot it could help."

"Being lost is scary, and just think—a lot of people in the world are lost spiritually," Peter declared. "I'm glad Jesus is there all the time—they can look to him to save them. They don't have to be lost. It's sad that so many keep trying to find the way to heaven by themselves and refuse to follow him." *REP*

HOW ABOUT YOU?

Do you know the way to heaven? You may try lots of ways—like doing good deeds, going to Sunday school, giving money, or making sacrifices. But unless you know Jesus, you will not reach heaven. He's been there all the time, waiting for you to come. Accept him as your Savior today.

Jesus Is Waiting to Save You

MEMORIZE:

"Jesus told him, 'I am the way, the truth, and the life. No one can come to the Father except through me.' "

John 14:6

November

20

The social studies class was buzzing with excitement. "Class, I'd like to hear your opinions of last night's program," said Mr. Pike after calling the group to order.

"I'm still shaking!" Alexis exclaimed. "I didn't sleep all night." There was a murmur of agreement.

Ron raised his hand. "I don't think such a war will ever happen," he said bravely.

"They're just trying to scare us. No one would be crazy enough to push a button that would destroy the world."

"Oh, yeah?" Tony said. "I wouldn't be so sure. I think we oughta build more weapons. We don't want to give some other country the chance to blow us to bits."

In the discussion that followed, there were various opinions about what should be done, but everyone agreed that it was a most frightening problem. A few students seemed quite alarmed.

Near the end of class, Mr. Pike called on Marianne. "You seem quite calm about all this," he said. "Tell us what you're thinking."

Marianne blushed. "It scares me, too," she said nervously, "but I'm a Christian, so I know that God is in charge. Even if I do die, I'll go to heaven because I asked Jesus to be my Savior."

The class had become quiet. "Interesting," Mr. Pike murmured. "Well, I see it's time to go home. Tomorrow please turn in your reports on this TV special."

Vanessa approached Marianne after class. "Do you really believe what you said?" Vanessa asked. "I mean, about going to heaven."

Marianne nodded. "That's what the Bible says."

"Ever since I saw that program, I've been scared about dying," Vanessa admitted. "And I don't know what to do."

"You need to trust Jesus as your Savior," Marianne said. "Then you won't need to be scared anymore."

"Sounds good," Vanessa said, "but I don't know anything about stuff like that, Marianne. Can you tell me more about it?" Happily, Marianne nodded. *JLH*

HOW ABOUT YOU?

Do you use opportunities in school to share your faith? Could you tell someone else how to be saved by showing them verses in the Bible? God says it's your responsibility to warn the lost. Are you doing it?

MEMORIZE:

"It is destined that each person dies only once and after that comes judgment." Hebrews 9:27

Warn the Unsaved

Persistence Pays

Read Romans 5:3-4; 1 Timothy 6:11

"This stupid map will never look like the United States!" Jessica exclaimed, pushing her half-completed project aside.

"What seems to be the problem?" her dad asked.

"I just can't draw very well!" Jessica whined. "I'm supposed to have this map done by tomorrow, and I'm not even half through yet. I might as well quit!"

"Come now, Jessica. Is that what they teach you at school—to quit when things get difficult?" Dad asked.

"No, but there's just no sense in trying to finish this map," Jessica answered. "There wouldn't be enough time before I'm supposed to be in bed, so why bother at all?"

"Well, I think you should get to bed right now then," Dad said, "and you can get up early tomorrow and finish the map when you're rested."

"Oh, Dad," Jessica whined, "I just don't like making maps. Can't I tell Mrs. Payne I didn't have time to do it?"

"That wouldn't be true, would it?" Dad asked. "Besides, I seem to remember that you learned a verse for Sunday school last week that would apply in this situation. Did you forget it already?"

Jessica thought for a moment. "You mean Galatians 6:9?" she asked. "The one that says, 'Don't get tired of doing what is good. Don't get discouraged and give up, for we will reap a harvest of blessing at the appropriate time.' "

"Yes," Dad said. "I think it can apply to this situation. It seems to be saying, 'Don't be a quitter.' That could include drawing maps, don't you think?"

"Well . . . I suppose," Jessica reluctantly agreed.

Dad smiled. "You know, Jesus wasn't a quitter, so if you want to be like him, you can't be a quitter, either. Persistence pays—you'll see." *JK*

HOW ABOUT YOU?

Do you feel it's no use trying to learn that long list of spelling words? Do you want to quit when you've tried and failed to make a math problem come out right? Are you sure you may as well give up playing in the band because you're obviously not a musician? Whatever task God has given you at this point in your life, it deserves your careful, persistent effort. Don't quit. Pray about it, and with God's help, do your very best.

MEMORIZE:

"So don't get tired of doing what is good. Don't get discouraged and give up, for we will reap a harvest of blessing at the appropriate time."

Galatians 6:9

Don't Be a Quitter

November

22

Spiritual Snobs

Read Galatians 3:26-28

When Stephanie, Barry, and Sharon missed Sunday school three weeks in a row, Miss Pulanski visited their homes. All three complained about the way the other kids treated them.

"Some of the kids think they're hot stuff because they go to the Christian school," Stephanie said. "Some of the girls won't even sit with me in church. Once I heard Susie say, 'Stephanie probably uses bad words and believes in evolution. They learn those things in public schools.' "

Barry was honest, too. "The last time I was in Sunday school, Jeremy made fun of me. He found a verse in the Bible real fast, and then he said, 'I'll help Barry. He goes to the public school, so he doesn't know his Bible.' "

Sharon was near tears as she voiced an opposite complaint. "The kids who go to public school say I'm stuck up because I go to a Christian school," she said. "They say I'm not a good witness because I don't know as many unsaved kids. I think they're the ones who are stuck up."

On the next Sunday morning, Miss Pulanski asked the class to open their Bibles to Galatians, chapter three. Together they read verses 26-28 (see today's Scripture). "If Paul were writing to our class," she said, "I have a feeling he would have added the words 'There is neither Christian school student nor public school student nor homeschool student' to the list we read here." The children looked at Miss Pulanski in surprise. "Many of you go to a Christian school," she continued, "and others go to the public school. And plenty of you have become spiritual snobs!" She explained how bad attitudes had caused some kids to quit coming.

Many in the class felt ashamed. After the lesson and prayer, they got phone numbers so they could call Stephanie, Barry, and Sharon to convince them to return to Sunday school. *REP*

HOW ABOUT YOU?

Do you go to a Christian school? Or do you and your parents feel your place is in public school? Don't look down on kids who don't do things exactly as you do. If you're getting Christian training at home or in a Christian school, thank God for that and remember that when much spiritual truth is taught to you, much will be required of you. If you go to a public school, you may be blessed with special opportunities to witness, so ask God to help you use them! Serve the Lord and support one another, no matter where you go to school.

MEMORIZE:

"For you are all Christians—you are one in Christ Jesus." Galatians 3:28

Don't Be a Snob!

The Persecuted

Read 1 Peter 3:13-17

Bethany and Grandpa had been reading the Bible together and came across a verse about Christians being mistreated, or *persecuted*. "I know how this verse about persecution fits into your story of Germany. I hope I never have to face persecution like some Christians have had to." Bethany shuddered. "I'd be so scared!"

"It is scary," Grandpa agreed, "but many verses in the Bible promise special blessing to those who are persecuted for Jesus' sake. Christians are still being persecuted in some countries. I can testify to the fact that Jesus is with us in times of trial."

After studying the verse for a while, Bethany grew restless and ran outside to play. About an hour later, she returned. Grandpa was surprised to see her crying. "What's wrong, little one?" he asked.

"Oh, Johnny Burnett is picking on me again," Bethany said with a sob. "He threw a stone, and it hit my leg." Then her face brightened. "But maybe I'll get blessed by God for being persecuted!"

"Wait a minute!" The old man chuckled. "We need to decide if your persecution was for righteousness' sake. Did Johnny throw the stone because you were witnessing for Jesus or doing some good deed for Jesus' sake?"

"Um, well, no," Bethany stammered. "He threw it because I, um, kind of threw a stick at him first."

Grandpa tried to hide his smile. "Ach, Bethany. You cannot claim God's blessing for bad things you bring on yourself. The 'blessing' mentioned in this last beatitude comes only if you suffer for being a Christian!"

"Oh, I see," Bethany said solemnly as she got a cold cloth to put on her leg. "I'll remember that." Then she gave Grandpa Hohenberger a big smile. "Thank you, Grandpa," she said, "for helping me to see who Jesus promised to bless, and why!" *REP*

HOW ABOUT YOU?

Do you think you're suffering persecution every time someone is nasty to you? It's one thing if kids at school are mean to you because you're mean to them. But on the other hand, if they are mean because you're a Christian, you should rejoice. Jesus promises to bless you if people persecute you or lie about you for his sake.

MEMORIZE:
"God blesses those who are persecuted because they live for God, for the Kingdom of Heaven is theirs."
Matthew 5:10

Trials Can Bring Blessing

November

24

Her Sister's Shadow

Read Romans 12:6-10

Shelly felt that she was often compared with Carly, her older sister. Carly was a straight-A student. Not Shelly. Carly was a master at the piano. But not Shelly. Carly kept her room neat. Shelly's room was messy. The only thing Shelly could do better than Carly was artwork. She received an A+ in art class!

"Carly's going to play 'The Lighthouse' on the piano at the youth talent contest," Grandma said one day when the girls were visiting. "What are you going to do, Shelly?"

"Nothing," Shelly grumbled. "Everything I do, Carly can do better! I'm sick of being her shadow."

Grandma raised her eyebrows. "Maybe you walk in Carly's shadow because you want to," she said. "Maybe you lag behind her because it's easier than taking on the responsibility of learning for yourself. It's easier to drift than to work—but privileges and honors come after you take on responsibilities! Now, back to the talent contest—I saw the beautiful lighthouse picture you brought home yesterday. Couldn't you do a chalk drawing of a lighthouse while Carly plays?"

Shelly hesitated. "I guess so," she mumbled.

"Yeah, Shelly!" Carly exclaimed. "We could enter as a team! That's a neat idea, Grandma!"

So the girls began practicing together. By the day of the contest, each girl's talent complemented the other's, and they won first place! After the program, they looked for their parents and their grandma. "There they are!" Carly pointed across the crowded room. "Grab my hand, Shelly, and we'll squeeze through the crowd."

As the two reached their family, Grandma stepped forward and hugged them. She spoke warmly. "I'm so proud of you!" she said, as the girls' parents nodded and smiled in agreement. "And look at you! You're holding hands! No longer is Shelly 'Carly's little shadow.' You're side by side, and you can see that God has given each of you a special ability. You've learned to work together."

The girls grinned at each other, and Shelly reached over and gave Carly a big hug. *BJW*

HOW ABOUT YOU?

Are you jealous of your brothers and sisters? Does it seem as though they are talented but you aren't? That isn't true. God has given certain abilities to each person. It's up to you to do what God enables you to do. Be thankful for your differences, and work together.

MEMORIZE:

"Work hard and cheerfully at whatever you do, as though you were working for the Lord rather than for people."
Colossians 3:23

Use the Abilities God Gave You

Something Better

Read Genesis 13:7-18

Chloe and Kadie were sisters, and they really did love each other. However, there were times when Kadie said, "Why can't Chloe do it?" or Chloe whined, "If Kadie can, why can't I?" Often envy and competition crept in, but more often than not Kadie gave in to Chloe.

One day Mom said she needed one of them to baby-sit their little brother, Nicholas, while she ran to the store. "Not me! I'm going to Mary Beth's house," Chloe quickly spoke up.

"I stayed home the last time Mom went shopping," Kadie protested, "but I guess I can do it for you this time." So Kadie stayed home.

Soon after Mom had gone to the store and Chloe had left for Mary Beth's house, the phone rang. It was a neighbor, Mrs. Ryan, and she needed someone for a regular baby-sitting job. Since Kadie was home, Mrs. Ryan asked Kadie to do it.

Kadie was thrilled about her new job, but when Chloe heard about it, she pouted. "I wish I had a chance like that," she grumbled.

"Well, this all came about because Kadie chose to stay home and help me," Mom reminded her. "It seemed as though she made the lesser choice, but she really got something better." She paused, and after a moment she added, "Reminds you of Abraham and Lot, doesn't it?"

"Abraham and Lot?" Chloe repeated.

Mom nodded. "God gave all of the land of Canaan to Abraham," she said, "and Lot was there with him, too. But when the two men couldn't stay together, Abraham let Lot choose the land he wanted. Abraham took what was left, and things turned out better for him than they did for Lot. Remember, girls—what looks best *to* you, isn't always best *for* you." *AGL*

HOW ABOUT YOU?
Do you insist on having things your own way? Or are you willing to give in to others and put their interests ahead of your own? By doing so, you please God, and he will bless you for it.

Don't Be Selfish

November
26

Right Side Up

Read Matthew 6:25-34

Chandra took a bite of chicken. "How come there are so many unhappy Christians in this world?" she asked. "You should have seen the scowl Mrs. Ford gave me today, and I hadn't done a thing. And Mr. Preston always looks so sad."

"You're right," Dad agreed. "It's too bad Christians so often don't enjoy the peace and joy available to them."

"But don't pick on just adults," Mom advised. "Many boys and girls who are saved have problems, too. Maybe they worry about tests, or get angry quickly, or cheat."

"Wadah!" two-year-old Ethan demanded. He wasn't at all interested in this discussion. "Wadah! Wadah!" He pounded his cup on his high chair tray.

"Be patient there, little brother," Chandra said, picking up the water pitcher to pour water into the cup he was holding. Just as the water began streaming out of the pitcher, Ethan heard a fire truck outside. As he turned to look out the window, he tipped the cup upside down. Instead of going into the cup, the water poured onto the floor. "Ethan!" Chandra exclaimed. "Look what you've done!"

As Dad mopped up the water, he turned to Chandra. "When Ethan was interested in something else, his cup was turned away from the pitcher so no water could get into it," he said. "And when Christians get too interested in the things of this world, they tend to turn away from God. They live as though they've forgotten all about him. They aren't in a position to receive his blessings."

Chandra was thoughtful. "But we can't sit around just thinking about God all day long," she protested. "We need to go to school, for example. And is there anything wrong with playing with friends or reading a book?"

"No," Dad answered, "but when such things become more important than spending time with the Lord, we're like the upside-down cup. He can't fill us with his blessings."

"When we spend time with God, trying to live as he wants us to and thinking of him often throughout the day, then we're turned toward him," Mom added. "Then we can expect to be filled with his joy and peace, no matter what our circumstances." *HWM*

HOW ABOUT YOU?

Are you "turned toward God"? There's nothing wrong with riding your bike or enjoying your toys. It's okay to wear nice clothes and live in a nice home. But none of the things you have are as important as your relationship with the Lord. Take care of that first, and then everything else will fall in place.

MEMORIZE:

"Your unfailing love is better to me than life itself; how I praise you!" Psalm 63:3

Put God First in Your Life

Paid in Advance

Read 1 Peter 1:17-21

"Oh, no! We're out of stamps!" Mia moaned. "Now I can't mail this birthday card until Monday."

"Why not?" asked Mia's little sister. "The mailman didn't come yet. I'll go put it in the mailbox for you."

Mia shook her head. "Without a stamp on the envelope, this won't go anywhere, Joy."

Joy looked thoughtful for a moment and then bounded off to her bedroom. She soon returned with her hands behind her back and a grin on her face.

"What are you hiding?" asked Mia.

Joy's face beamed with pride as she held out a roll of dinosaur stickers. "You can use one of my stamps to mail your letter," she offered.

Mia smiled at her sister. "Thanks, honey, but I can't use your stickers," she said. "They aren't real postage stamps. Letters have to have real stamps on them or they won't get delivered."

Joy looked a little hurt, so Mia tried to explain. "Postage stamps are special kinds of stickers, Joy. You buy them at the post office. When you stick one on a letter, it shows the mailman that you've paid in advance for the letter to be delivered. Then he takes it to the post office, and they make sure it goes on its way." Joy frowned and looked at her stickers. "Sorry, honey," added Mia, giving her sister a hug.

Joy grinned and peeled off one of her dinosaur stickers. She stuck it on the back of Mia's hand. "You can have a sticker anyway," she said, "even if it doesn't get you delivered anywhere."

Mom, who was standing nearby, smiled as Joy skipped away. "You know, Mia," she said, "your explanation of how letter delivery has to be paid for in advance reminds me of salvation. Jesus died on the cross to pay for our salvation—he paid our way to heaven in advance. Sometimes people try to pay their own way by doing good deeds, but that's like using a dinosaur sticker on a letter. To get to heaven you need the real thing—the blood of Jesus." *KMS*

HOW ABOUT YOU?

Have you accepted Jesus as your Savior? He gave his life to pay the price for your salvation. Accept him today and know you'll be "delivered" to heaven some day.

MEMORIZE:

"Since we have been made right in God's sight by the blood of Christ, he will certainly save us from God's judgment." Romans 5:9

Accept Christ's Payment for Your Sin

November

28

Tidal Wave

Read Matthew 7:24-29

The kitchen door slammed shut behind Brenna. After greeting her mom, she poured milk into a glass and plopped down in a chair. "You won't believe what happened to my project today," she said. Brenna had worked for two weeks creating an ancient Mayan city that included a temple, palace, and several small buildings.

"Tell me about it," Mom said.

"After you dropped me off at school, Mike came over and started asking questions about the project," said Brenna. "Well, he was carrying a bowl of water to use on his own project. Before I had two words out of my mouth, someone else bumped Mike, and my Mayan city was hit by a tidal wave."

"Oh, dear!" exclaimed Mom.

"It washed the ground right out from under the main temple," continued Brenna. She frowned. "When I was working on it, somebody suggested that I should use plaster for the ground instead of sand. I should have listened."

"Well, I'm sorry your project was messed up," sympathized Mom.

"Me, too," said Brenna. She laughed. "But my teacher said it was the most realistic disaster project she'd seen. And she said I should always remember that sand doesn't make a firm foundation, and things don't last unless they stand on a strong foundation."

Mom nodded. "Your story reminds me of the Bible passage that talks about the importance of building our lives on the right foundation," she said. "If we trust in anything or anybody other than Jesus, it's as though we're building on sand. The only lasting foundation is the Lord Jesus Christ."

"Yeah." Brenna nodded. Then she grinned. "Well," she said, "I chose the wrong foundation for my project, but I have the right one for my life, and that's more important!" *JW2*

HOW ABOUT YOU?

Do you have the right foundation for your life? Have you trusted Jesus as your Savior? Any other foundation—things you may trust in like being kind, doing good—will be swept away some day. Accept Jesus now.

MEMORIZE:

"No one can lay any other foundation than the one we already have—Jesus Christ." 1 Corinthians 3:11

Build Your Life on Jesus

Big Sister

Read Acts 16:19-25

"Get married?" exploded Jordan. "You're going to get *married?* To Jim Ford? How can you? He's got two kids already. He doesn't want us. Why don't you marry Dad again?"

"Jordan, you know that after your dad left us, he married someone else. He won't be back," Mom said quietly. "I thought you liked Jim."

"Not for a father!" Jordan exclaimed. Without grabbing a coat, she turned and ran out the door and into her neighbor's backyard. "Mom's marrying a man with two little boys!" Jordan told Mr. Callahan angrily. "I don't want someone else's dad! I've got to get away. I'm leaving too—for good! I'd never be happy here." She sank down onto a porch step.

"And do you think you'll find happiness someplace else?" asked Mr. Callahan. Jordan shrugged, starting to shiver. "I sure won't find it here!"

"You know, Jordan," said Mr. Callahan, "happiness isn't something you *find*. It's something you *make* by trusting God. The Bible tells us that Paul and Silas sang even though they were in prison. Learn from their example. Realize that you can be happy, too, even when things aren't particularly pleasant. Won't you trust God to help you?" he asked.

"But I . . . but he . . ." Jordan began to protest.

"I know this is difficult for you, but what about your little brother and sister?" Mr. Callahan asked. "They'll need their big sister. Your new brothers will need help, too—it'll be difficult for them too. You can be a witness for the Lord to all of them."

Jordan hesitated. "Well, maybe," she said hesitantly. Then she sighed. "I'll stay," she decided at last.

"Good," encouraged Mr. Callahan. "I think your new stepfather deserves a chance to be a good dad, don't you?"

Again Jordan hesitated. "Everyone deserves a chance, I guess," she admitted reluctantly.

Mr. Callahan nodded. "Let's both pray that God will help you make happiness for all of you." *AGL*

HOW ABOUT YOU?

Does something in your life make you unhappy? Do you wish you could leave it and go your own way? Happiness comes from trusting God, even in difficult times, not from running away from problems. Ask God to help you accept things you cannot change. Work hard to make life happy for those around you.

Face Your Problems and Trust God

MEMORIZE:
"Those who trust the Lord will be happy." Proverbs 16:20

Puzzles and Lives

Read Psalm 37:23-28

Alexandra shuffled through the pieces of the jigsaw puzzle. "Wow! I've never tried to work a puzzle with so many pieces before!" she exclaimed.

"I know it looks hard, but I'm sure you can do it," replied her mom. "Want some help? I could turn the pieces right side up for you."

"Okay," agreed Alexandra. "I'll work on the barn." She started to sift through the jumbled pile, looking for the red pieces.

"Alexandra, do you know what this jigsaw puzzle reminds me of?" Mom asked as she turned pieces.

"Ahhh . . . my room, I guess. A big mess," answered Alexandra with a laugh.

Mom chuckled. "It does look a lot like the clutter under your bed," she said, "but what I had in mind was something else—our lives. Sometimes life seems to be filled with overwhelming problems. We can't see how the pieces of our lives can possibly fit together, but God knows how they will fit perfectly. Isn't it wonderful that he has a plan and purpose for everything that happens in our lives, even when we can't see what it is?"

"Do you mean like the time I didn't make the Parkside soccer team?" asked Alexandra.

Mom nodded. "Yes," she said. "You were so disappointed. You didn't see how that 'piece' of your life fit at all—you said you thought you might as well give up playing soccer. Then Mr. Kendall called and asked if you'd like to play the goalie position on the Greenwood team that he was coaching. You found that you really liked playing with that team."

"Yeah, that was pretty awesome," agreed Alexandra.

"I think God wanted you on Mr. Kendall's team so we could get to know their whole family," Mom said. "They accepted our invitation to come to church and heard about Jesus." She glanced at the pieces Alexandra was putting together. "You have that barn almost finished already!" she exclaimed. "Always remember that just like the pieces are fitting together to make a barn, God fits all the 'pieces' of our lives together to make something wonderful." *ASB*

HOW ABOUT YOU?

Are you a Christian who is in the midst of disappointment? Does your life seem to be a jumbled mess that will never fit together? Trust God. He has a plan and purpose for all things in your life, and he will work them together for your good.

MEMORIZE:

"We know that God causes everything to work together for the good of those who love God." Romans 8:28

God Has a Purpose for Everything

Fit for Heaven

Read Revelation 21:1-4, 18, 23-27; 22:1-5

Shaniqua listened closely as her Bible club teacher described heaven. Mrs. Braun told of a beautiful city with gates made of pearl. She told of a pure river—clear as crystal—and of a special "tree of life." Best of all, she said there would be no pain in heaven and no crying. Shaniqua thought it must be wonderful not to be sad. She was often sad. Both her grandpa and grandma had died recently, and now her mother and father were getting a divorce.

"Heaven is so wonderful that God cannot allow any sin to spoil it," Mrs. Braun was saying. "He wants us to live in that beautiful place someday, but no sin may enter there." *Oh, no,* Shaniqua thought, *then I won't be allowed to enter.* She thought of the mean things she had said that very day, and she knew she was a sinner even before Mrs. Braun said so.

"The Bible tells us that all have sinned," her teacher explained. "Sin is lying, stealing, disobeying parents and teachers, being mean to others, and even thinking in a mean way about others. It's all the wrong things you do." Mrs. Braun smiled as she went on, "God sent Jesus to pay for your sins. When Jesus died on the cross, he took the punishment for every bad thing that you've ever done. Then he rose from the grave, and now he lives in heaven. He can take away your sin and make it possible for you to go to heaven, too."

Shaniqua leaned forward and listened eagerly. "If you'll receive Jesus into your life, he'll record your name in the Book of Life so that you may live in heaven some day."

Mrs. Braun asked the girls to bow their heads. "If you believe that Jesus paid for your sins, ask him to save you right now," she said. "Tell him that you know you're a sinner and that you want to receive him into your life," Mrs. Braun urged. "Would you like to do that?"

Oh, yes, Shaniqua thought. And she began to pray. *CEY*

HOW ABOUT YOU?

Do you want to live in heaven someday? Do you know you are a sinner? Only Jesus can remove your sin and make you fit for heaven. Will you ask him right now to do that?

MEMORIZE:
"But to all who believed him and accepted him, he gave the right to become children of God." John 1:12

Sin Can't Enter Heaven

December

2

"You don't really believe what that preacher said, do you, Linda?" In the backseat of the car, Gina listened closely as Uncle Larry talked with her mom. Uncle Larry had gone to church with them, and it was the first time Gina could remember her uncle going to church.

"Yes, I do believe what Pastor Grange said, Larry," Gina's mother answered.

"Ahhhh now, Linda," Uncle Larry protested, "Granddad Casey used to preach about the end of the world when we were kids. Nothing's happened yet."

"A lot has happened," Mom countered. "A great deal of prophecy has been fulfilled."

"Like the prophecy of Ezekiel and Daniel?" Gina joined the conversation.

Her mother looked surprised. "What do you know about Ezekiel and Daniel?"

"Quite a lot," Gina answered with a smile. "We've been studying the major prophets in Sunday school."

Uncle Larry grinned. "Tell me about it, kid." Gina knew her uncle was making fun of her, but she didn't care. People had made fun of Isaiah, Jeremiah, Ezekiel, and Daniel—and Jesus, too.

"People laughed at Jeremiah," Gina said. "They called him the weeping prophet. Guess they were the ones weeping when his messages came true."

Uncle Larry blinked, and Gina's mother nodded. "If you'll read the newspaper, Larry, along with some Bible prophecies, you'll find God's Word is still being fulfilled."

"I'd rather not think about it." Uncle Larry shivered. "It sounds spooky to me."

Gina started to tell her uncle about the way the people had treated Jeremiah and Ezekiel, but when Uncle Larry refused to talk about it any more, Gina decided she'd said enough. She would just pray for Uncle Larry. God would take care of him. All Gina could do was deliver God's message. *BJW*

HOW ABOUT YOU?

Do you get discouraged because people don't like hearing about what the Bible says? Maybe you feel like you might as well forget witnessing to them and leave it to someone older. Don't give up. Continue to give them God's message.

MEMORIZE:

"You must go wherever I send you and say whatever I tell you." Jeremiah 1:7

Share God's Message

The Shared Birthday

Read 2 Corinthians 9:6-11

"For the next two weeks we'll be gathering Christmas gifts for the children's home in Mexico," announced Miss Lillian, the fifth-grade Sunday school teacher. "We need to send them soon so they will arrive by Christmas. The items you bring must be new or in like-new condition, and they should be lightweight. The cost of postage is very high, and we can't afford to send a lot of heavy things."

Robin told her parents about their class project. "I have five dollars," she said. "Maybe I could send a game."

"Talking about buying gifts reminds me that someone in this family is having a birthday in a couple of weeks." Dad winked at Robin. "What do you want for your birthday?"

"And what kind of a party do you want?" Mom asked.

Robin thought for a moment. When she spoke, her eyes were shining. "I want to have a Mexican party, and I want all the gifts to go to the children's home."

"Why, Robin, what a beautiful idea!" Mom smiled. "We'll get some books from the library to find out how to have a Mexican party."

"And on all the invitations put a note saying that the gifts are for the children's home," Robin said.

Twelve of Robin's friends came to her party. After they played Mexican games, Robin opened the gifts. Then her friends helped her rewrap them in Christmas paper. "This was the best birthday party I have ever had!" Robin told her dad after the party. "We had so much fun, and I feel so good inside."

On Sunday, Robin beamed as she took, not one gift, but thirteen to Sunday school. "Your birthday party was like Jesus' birthday celebration," Miss Lillian said. "On his birthday, most of the presents are for others, too. Sharing pleases him, and it makes you feel good, too, doesn't it?" *BJW*

HOW ABOUT YOU?

Have you ever thought about sharing your birthday with others who have less than you? Think about it. Jesus shares his birthday every year. Wouldn't you like to do it once and experience the blessing of giving?

MEMORIZE:
"Give generously, for your gifts will return to you later." Ecclesiastes 11:1

Share with Others

December

4

Needed: The Key

Read Romans 13:1-7; Hebrews 13:17

Colleen walked over to the car a neighbor boy had driven to town. She was surprised to see him standing beside it, a forlorn look on his face. He kicked a tire. "I lost my car keys today," he told her. "Now I can't drive until I get another set."

As Colleen reported the incident at home that evening, the phone interrupted her. When she hung up, she didn't look very happy. "That was Gail," she said. "She wanted me to try again to get permission to come to her party next weekend. I told her that never worked—that the answer is no."

"Did you tell her why you can't come?" Mom asked.

Colleen nodded. "Yes, but Gail can't see why having beer at the party means I have to stay home. No one's going to force me to drink, so she thinks it's a silly rule."

"What about you? Do you think it's silly" Dad asked.

"Well, yes, to be honest," Colleen replied. "After all, you know I wouldn't drink. I thought you'd trust me."

"Why, honey! This isn't about trust," her father said in surprise. "Gail's parents are breaking the law by allowing a group of young people to drink at their house. Would you like to be there if a neighbor called the police? Or what if things got out of hand and something dangerous happened? God gave us the responsibility of caring for you, and we made that rule for your safety and to protect your reputation, not because we don't trust you."

Colleen was silent for a moment. "I guess I didn't think of that, Dad," she said. "It helps to know the reason for that rule."

Mom smiled. "You didn't whine and beg to go to the party even before you knew the reason," she said, "and we appreciate that. The Lord is pleased with your attitude, too."

"You were just telling us about that boy," Dad reminded Colleen. "He needs his car keys in order to go anywhere. And we need 'keys' for our lives—rules we all have to live with. I think one of those keys is an attitude of acceptance and obedience." *CR*

HOW ABOUT YOU?

Do some of the rules you have to follow seem foolish to you? Everyone has to live by rules—at work, at school, on the highway, and in the home. If a rule is hard for you, ask the reason for it. But remember that the key to a truly happy life is obedience and a proper attitude. God expects those things of you.

MEMORIZE:

"Obey your spiritual leaders and do what they say. Their work is to watch over your souls, and they know they are accountable to God. Give them reason to do this joyfully." Hebrews 13:17

Rules Are Needed

Pretty Presents

Read Matthew 22:37-40

"Oh, Mom, those packages are so pretty!" Faith exclaimed as she walked into the kitchen. She glanced at the pile of toys on the floor beside Mom. "Who are all of these for?"

Mom grinned. "Lots of people," she said, "but none of them are for you, so it's okay for you to see them."

Faith sat on the floor beside her mother. "Can I help?" she asked. "You still have lots to do."

"Sure," Mom replied.

Faith picked up a roll of bright red paper. From the pile of gifts, she chose a doll dressed in a pink sleeper. "Is this one for Felicity?" she asked, and Mom nodded. When the doll was wrapped, Faith tied a gold ribbon around the package. "Do you know what I like most about presents?" she asked.

Mom laughed. "I think you're about to tell me," she said.

"It's what's inside them," said Faith. "That's the best part of a present."

"I agree," said Mom, and a thoughtful expression crossed her face. "P-r-e-s-e-n-t spells an interesting word. It can be pronounced pre'sent, meaning a gift—or it can be present', meaning to give."

Faith laughed. "So when I give a gift, I present' a pre'sent," she said.

Mom nodded. "As we prepare and present all these presents," she said, "it makes me think of a Bible verse—the one that tells us to present ourselves to God."

Faith reached for a piece of wrapping paper. "When we do that, we should make sure our lives are like a present—filled with good stuff, right?" she asked. "We shouldn't look really nice on the outside but be messed up on the inside."

Mom nodded. "If we love God and obey his Word, the best part of the present we give him will be what's on the inside," she said. *ECM*

HOW ABOUT YOU?
Have you thought about your life as being a present? Are you filled with good things—like loving God and being kind and helpful? Jesus looks on the inside. Make sure he finds only good things there.

Let God's Love Control You

MEMORIZE:
"Give your bodies to God. Let them be a living and holy sacrifice—the kind he will accept." Romans 12:1

December

6

Horn Honkers

Read Psalm 75:4-7

Patricia clapped her hands over her ears. "Todd, you're hurting my ears with all that horn honking!" she exclaimed. "Mom, make him stop!"

Mom grimaced. "Todd, let Patricia help you take your tricycle to the playroom in the basement."

"But I wanna ride up here," wailed three-year-old Todd. "I like my new horn." He reached for the squeeze bulb on the handlebars.

Patricia grabbed his hand. "Stop that! You're bursting my eardrums!" She picked up the tricycle and started for the stairs, with her little brother following and wailing loudly.

When Patricia returned to the kitchen, she said, "Now I can tell you my news, Mom. I've been promoted to the advanced class. Only 5 percent of the kids make that class." Her chin went up.

Mom turned off the water and gave her a hug. "Congratulations, honey!" she said.

Patricia beamed, "I've got to call and tell Granddad and Aunt Mary and Stephanie and some others." She picked up the portable phone and dialed. For fifteen minutes, Patricia paced the floor and talked on the phone. The more she talked, the more serious Mom looked.

When Patricia hung up after the sixth call and started dialing another number, Mom said, "That's enough, Patricia. You're hurting my ears!"

"Hurting your ears!" Patricia exclaimed. "But, Mom, I'm not screaming."

"Not in volume," Mom responded, "but you're blowing your own horn, and it is not pleasant to hear."

"What do you mean, Mom? I just—" Patricia began.

Mom held up her hand. "You've been telling people how wonderful you are—and how smart. Bragging is 'blowing your own horn,' and no one likes to hear it. God has blessed you with a sharp mind. You have much to be thankful for—but remember that all you have comes from the Lord." Honk-honk-honk! The faint sound of a tricycle horn drifted up the stairs. Mom smiled, "If you're going to honk your own horn, honey, do it in the basement." *BJW*

HOW ABOUT YOU?

Do you enjoy hearing people brag? Maybe you catch yourself bragging at times. When you do something well or receive a special honor, don't brag about yourself. It's much more pleasant to the ear when others praise you. Never forget that your abilities and talents come from God.

MEMORIZE:
"Don't praise yourself; let others do it!" Proverbs 27:2

Don't Blow Your Own Horn

To Fight or Do Right

Read Romans 12:17-21

"How did you get that bruise on your cheek?" Dad asked Linette as they made the salad for supper.

"This? Just a little present from Faye Boudreau in third period science," Linette answered. "She always sits right behind me when we're placed alphabetically. Is there some way I can change my last name?"

"You could get married," Linette's brother, Joe, suggested with a grin. He laughed at the face his sister made.

"Faye tripped me, and I fell flat on my face," Linette continued. "But don't worry, I'll get her back tomorrow. I'll make her sorry she was born!"

"What do you have in mind?" Dad asked sternly.

Linette realized she'd already said far too much. She knew her dad would never approve of what she intended to do with superglue and Faye's pile of spiral-bound notebooks. "Nothing," she said quickly. Her face reddened a little. Lying had never come naturally to her.

"Do you think getting even would be God's way to handle this?" Dad asked, obviously not convinced.

Linette shrugged. "If I don't do something, she'll think she can walk all over me!"

"I recently learned a few things about Faye and her family," Dad said. "I think you should know them, too." He then explained that Faye's learning disabilities had caused her to be held back twice, her father had recently left the family and moved to Nevada, her mom worked two jobs, and her older brother had joined the Marines and so was seldom home. Dad was quiet a moment, then said thoughtfully, "Faye spends most of her time after school alone. Perhaps she plays tricks on people to get attention."

Linette was very quiet when Dad had finished. "I'll try to be nice to her instead of fighting back," Linette finally replied. "Should I invite her for dinner sometime?"

"Certainly!" Dad said with a smile. *LBM*

HOW ABOUT YOU?

Do you try to "get even" when someone hurts you or embarrasses you? Instead, try to put yourself in the other person's place and see if you can understand her actions. Pray and ask God to help you find ways to make peace rather than try to get revenge. Perhaps you'll even be able to turn an enemy into a friend!

MEMORIZE:

"Never avenge yourselves. Leave that to God. For it is written, 'I will take vengeance; I will repay those who deserve it,' says the Lord."

Romans 12:19

Don't Try to Get Even

Check It Out

Read 1 John 4:1-6

"Mom, I met a new girl in school today," Jackie said. "Her name is Sharon Willard, and her dad is a pastor."

"That's nice. What church are they from?" Mom asked.

"That big brick one downtown—the one on the corner of State and Park Streets," Jackie said. "Can I go there with Sharon some Sunday?"

Mom looked concerned. "I don't think so, honey. From what I've heard of that church, its teaching is quite different from what is found in the Bible. Not every church preaches the truth, you know."

"Oh, Mom, sometimes you're so narrow-minded!" Jackie protested with a scowl. "Sharon's really nice, and I'm sure her church is okay, too. I don't see why you won't let me go."

Several weeks later, Jackie and Sharon got into a discussion about the things they would like to do someday. "I can't wait till I'm old enough to drink and smoke and stuff," Sharon said. "I might even try marijuana sometime."

Jackie frowned. "My folks say it's wrong for Christians to hurt their bodies that way," she murmured.

Sharon shrugged. "Well, my dad says Christians have a right to do anything they want, as long as it doesn't hurt anybody else," she informed Jackie.

"That doesn't sound like something the Bible would say," Jackie replied, "or like something Jesus would do."

"The Bible? Oh, who believes that old book anymore?" Sharon laughed. "My dad says Jesus was just a good man, like anyone else, and the Bible is full of mistakes."

Jackie was quiet when she came home that night. "You were right, Mom," she said. "Since Sharon's dad is a pastor, I figured he must be a Christian. But even though the whole family is nice, they sure don't know Jesus." *AU*

HOW ABOUT YOU?

Have you ever thought a church or religious group was all right because its members seemed friendly and sincere? Don't be fooled by outward appearances. Find out if the group believes in the Bible as the true Word of God, in Jesus Christ as God the Son, and in salvation through faith in Christ, not by good works.

MEMORIZE:

"Dear friends, do not believe everyone who claims to speak by the Spirit. You must test them to see if the spirit they have comes from God. For there are many false prophets in the world."
1 John 4:1

Check Beliefs against God's Word

The Gang (Part 1)

Read Matthew 9:10-13

"You know what's happening at school?" Courtney asked in Sunday school one day. "A new boy, Jerry Stone, is trying to form a gang. He's always causing trouble." Mr. Carr, the Sunday school teacher, looked thoughtful as some of the other kids made comments about the new gang Jerry was trying to get together. "What can we do about it?" they wanted to know.

"Well, let's talk this over a bit more," Mr. Carr suggested. "Give me your ideas—what do you think you can do to keep this gang from causing trouble? Any ideas?"

"Well, there couldn't be a gang if nobody would hang around with Jerry," Bob suggested.

Mr. Carr smiled. "True," he agreed, "but even if all the kids in this class refuse to hang around with him, there are others who would. Any more suggestions?"

Sarah raised her hand. "Couldn't we get Jerry sent to another school?" she asked.

Mr. Carr shook his head. "No," he said, "but even if you could, would it really help to send your problem to another school? No, I believe you can lick this problem here."

Courtney spoke up. "Since the kids who join this gang are those who need friends, maybe we should include them more in our friendships," she suggested. "We could walk along to class with them and even invite them to parties and stuff. We should do that with Jerry, too. I guess he's just so different that we're afraid of him. Maybe he's forming this gang in self-defense."

That was the kind of answer Mr. Carr was looking for. "You have the right idea, Courtney," he said. "I'm not suggesting that you become best friends with them, but it is important to make others feel needed and wanted." *AU*

HOW ABOUT YOU?

Has it occurred to you that the kids you would normally avoid may be just the ones Jesus wants you to witness to? The Bible says Jesus ate with sinners, but he did not participate in any of the sinful things they did. Perhaps you should be friendly to them. But make sure you don't join them in wrong activities. Pray about it, and see what God would have you do.

Reach Out to Others

MEMORIZE:
"I came to invite sinners."
Matthew 9:13, ICB

December
10

The Gang (Part 2)

Read 1 Corinthians 9:19-23

"Our Sunday school class is going to try to win the kids in the new gang at school to Jesus," Courtney told her father. "I'm going to see if I can get Jerry to come to church—he's the gang leader."

"Good." Dad nodded. "I'll be praying with you, honey. It may not be easy, and you need to be very careful. Jerry may laugh at you and even avoid you. Be sure you depend on the Holy Spirit to win him."

Dad was right—Jerry was hostile. Courtney began by offering to study with him for a history test. Jerry eyed her suspiciously and snarled, "When I want your help, I'll ask for it!" Next, Courtney walked to class with Jerry a few times. She thought he was beginning to act more friendly, so Courtney invited him to Sunday school. "Go to church? Oh, sure. That's just what I was hoping to do," Jerry mocked. Courtney was getting discouraged.

One day when Dad came home from work, Courtney was waiting impatiently. "Can you teach me all about your stamp collection right away, Dad?" she asked.

"Well, now, hold on a minute," Dad said in surprise. "I'll be glad to get it out right after supper, but why this sudden interest? You never cared about stamps before."

"Well, see . . . I was trying to think how I could make friends with Jerry," Courtney explained, "and I remembered a sermon that told how the apostle Paul tried to 'find common ground with everyone' in order to bring them to Jesus. I heard Jerry talk about his stamp collection, and I figure if learning about stamps will help win Jerry to Jesus, that's the least I can do. I told him about your collection, and he wants to see it. I'll study up on it a little and then ask him over . . . if that's okay with you, Dad."

Dad smiled. "It's perfectly okay," he agreed. "I believe this will be your first step in winning Jerry to Christ." *AU*

HOW ABOUT YOU?

Are you having trouble making friends with someone? Is there something that person especially enjoys, such as a collection or a certain game or activity? Even if that's not your special interest, would you be willing to spend time at it, and do it cheerfully? It could be the first step in winning that person to Jesus.

MEMORIZE:

"I try to find common ground with everyone so that I might bring them to Christ." 1 Corinthians 9:22

Witness through Friendship

The Hypocrite

Read Jeremiah 17:9-14

"But, honey, I don't understand why you don't want to be an angel in the Christmas program." Marilyn's mom smiled proudly at her daughter as she continued, "I think you'd make a perfect angel. Just last week your Sunday-school teacher told me what a good class member you are. Your lesson is always done, your verse is always learned, and you have a perfect attendance record. You've been such a help to me lately, too. The Lord must be pleased with you!"

Marilyn cringed at her mom's words. *Mom doesn't know that I do my Sunday school lesson to earn awards. As for helping Mom lately, that was easy with Christmas just around the corner and gifts starting to pile up under the tree.* Marilyn was silent, but her thoughts were loud and clear in her mind. *Another thing Mom doesn't know is that I've pretended to be a Christian, but I know I'm not. It's easy to fool people, but surely God knows what a hypocrite I am! I'm sick of pretending!*

As Marilyn watched her mom put an angel at the top of the Christmas tree, she decided she had to speak. "I . . . I'm no angel," she faltered, "and I'm not even a Christian!"

"But, Marilyn . . . I remember the day when you asked Jesus to come into your heart," Mom protested.

"But I didn't mean it," Marilyn confessed. "I just did it because I knew you wanted me to, and because . . . because it was just before my birthday. I wanted you to be so pleased with me that you'd get me a bike." Mom was speechless, and Marilyn hid her face in her hands. "I'm so ashamed and miserable," she cried. "I wish I could really be saved. Do you think Jesus would still save me, Mom?"

"Of course he will," Mom answered. "Let's talk to him about it now." *AU*

HOW ABOUT YOU?

Does everyone think you're a fine Christian? Are you really one, or have you perhaps gone through all the motions just to make an impression on others? You may fool people, but remember that God sees your heart. If you have never asked Jesus to save you—and really meant it—won't you ask him today?

MEMORIZE:
"I, the Lord, search all hearts and examine secret motives."
Jeremiah 17:10

Be Sure You're Saved

12

The Prescription

Read John 14:27-31

"Why does God allow war?" Melanie asked after hearing a news report on TV.

"That's a hard question—it's one men have been asking for centuries," said Dad. "It's hard to . . ." He paused as the door opened and Mom came in carrying Penny. Dad jumped up, took the whimpering little girl, and laid her on the couch. "What did the doctor say?"

"She has strep throat," said Mom. "Dr. Thom gave her a shot and this prescription." She handed Dad a slip of paper. "Could you get this filled while I fix dinner?"

Melanie reached for her coat. "I'll go with you," she said.

When they returned, Dad smiled at Penny, who was very fretful. "I'll give her a dose," Dad told Mom.

"I don't want it!" Penny wailed. "My throat hurts!"

"This will make your throat feel better," Dad said gently. He held a spoonful of medicine toward her.

Penny hid her face in the pillow. "No! I don't want it. It'll make my throat hurt worse."

"It will make it feel better," Dad again said patiently.

"I can't swallow," Penny wailed.

"If you can scream and cry like that, you can swallow," Dad said firmly. "Now take this."

The little girl recognized the do-what-I-say-or-else tone. She took the medicine and soon was sleeping soundly.

Later that evening, Melanie returned to her question. "Why does God allow war?"

"I think I have an answer now," said Dad. "Think of war as a sickness caused by sin. When Jesus died on Calvary, he gave this world the prescription to cure sin. God invites all of mankind to trust in Jesus as Savior. The doctor's prescription wouldn't have done Penny any good if she hadn't taken it, and the prescription God offers doesn't help people when they don't take it by trusting in Jesus. I made Penny take her medicine, but the Lord Jesus does not force anyone to accept his prescription."

Melanie nodded. "I get it," she said. "Because people refuse to follow Jesus' prescription, people get into conflicts and war." *BJW*

HOW ABOUT YOU?

Have you wondered why there is always war in this world? You cannot stop war in the world, but you can follow Jesus' prescription and have peace in your heart. If everyone had the peace of God, the world would be a much happier place. Peace starts with you.

MEMORIZE:

"I am leaving you with a gift—peace of mind and heart." John 14:27

Peace Comes from God

Different, but Alike

Read 1 John 4:7-11

"I love being out in the snow," said Jocelyn, catching a snowflake on her tongue.

"I can tell," said her dad. "You're never ready to come in, but Mom sent me out to tell you dinner is hot and ready to eat."

Jocelyn and Dad went in and washed up for dinner. "Did you have a good time playing with our new neighbor?" asked Mom as they sat down to eat.

"Not really," said Jocelyn. "We played for a while before she went in, but she's hard to understand. Her accent is too strong. I don't think I'll play with her very much."

"Give her a chance," encouraged Mom. "After all, you don't know her very well yet."

Jocelyn shrugged. "I don't care if I never know her very well. She's too different," she said as she glanced out the window. "Oh, look! It's snowing again—big snowflakes! They're so pretty!"

"Yes, they are," agreed Mom, "and scientists tell us they're all different—like people."

Dad nodded. "Did you know that even though each snowflake is different from all the others, all of them have something in common?" he asked. "Each one has six points. That's like people, too."

Jocelyn laughed. "You mean people have six points?" She knew that wasn't what Dad meant.

Dad laughed, too. "We generally think about the fact that no two people are exactly the same or have the very same experiences," he said, "but we often forget that they're also alike in some ways."

"I guess they are," said Jocelyn.

"Each country and nationality has its own language and customs, but some things are still the same," insisted Dad. "Prejudice and selfishness are the same in any country and in any language. So are kindness and acceptance and love. Which of those traits do you think God wants us to display?"

"The last ones," murmured Jocelyn.

Dad nodded. "All people were created by God," he said, "and he loves each one. He asks us, as his children, to share his love—even with those who seem very different." *JMJ*

HOW ABOUT YOU?

How do you treat a new classmate? Do you include everyone—even kids you think are different—in your fun and games? Ask God to help you be kind and thoughtful. Ask him to help you be friendly toward all your classmates and neighbors.

MEMORIZE:

"Since God loved us that much, we surely ought to love each other."

1 John 4:11

Be Friendly and Kind

December

14

"Let's stop at the bookstore," Dad said as he and Diana walked through the mall. "I want to find a new travel guide."

"Okay," Diana quickly agreed. She loved reading, and when they reached the bookstore, she decided to find a book for herself. Soon she was back at her father's side. "Can I get this book, Dad?" she asked. "I have enough money for it."

Dad took the book, read the back cover, and then opened it and leafed through the pages. "Honey," he said, "I've heard that this series deals with things that aren't honoring to God, and I saw several swear words. I'm sorry, but no—you can't buy it."

"Please, Dad," Diana begged. But her dad shook his head. "Oh, all right," Diana grumbled angrily. She frowned but took the book back.

Diana was quiet as they left the bookstore, and she was still pouting when they sat down in the mall's food court. Dad looked at her thoughtfully for a moment. "Watch our stuff, Diana," he said, "while I go over to the trash can and get some food."

Diana looked up in surprise. "What are you talking about?"

"I saw some people dump leftover pizza in that trash can," Dad said. "I'm sure there's other food in there, too. I thought I'd get some for you." Dad smiled as he spoke.

"Dad, that's sick!" Diana exclaimed, a bit of a smile coming to her face, too. "You've got to be kidding, but what's your point?"

"You don't want to feed garbage to your body, do you?" Dad asked. When Diana shook her head, he continued, "So why do you want to feed garbage to your mind by reading things that are filled with bad language and wrong values? We're responsible to God for the things we put into our minds. That's why I didn't let you get that book. I want you to give your mind good things to chew on. Now let's get some real food—I'm hungry!" *KMS*

HOW ABOUT YOU?

Do your parents set rules regarding what you may watch, listen to, and read? Do you wish you could choose for yourself? Healthy minds need healthy food. Whether it's TV, music, or books, don't put garbage into your mind.

MEMORIZE:
"I will refuse to look at anything vile and vulgar." Psalm 101:3

**Feed Your Mind
Wholesome Food**

A Delightful Fragrance

Read Genesis 8:18-22

"Yvonne?" Upon hearing her name, Yvonne looked up. "Will you come up here a minute, please?" said her teacher.

Mrs. Hollis handed Yvonne a sealed envelope. "Please take this to your parents for me," she said with a smile. "I want them to know how pleased I am with your attitude here at school."

When Yvonne got home, she sniffed as she opened the door to the back porch. *What do I smell?* she wondered. *I know—apple pie! Yum! Maybe Mom will let me have a piece for supper.* Her stomach growled as she went into the kitchen. No Mom. No apple pies, either.

Yvonne found her mother sorting magazines. "I have a note for you from Mrs. Hollis, Mom," she said with a grin. "I think it's good."

Mom read the note aloud. "Mr. and Mrs. Bradley, what a delight it is to have Yvonne in my class. Several times she has given up her free time to help her classmates. She has befriended the new girl from Indonesia. She is like a breath of fresh air in our class. Yvonne has invited me to try your church sometime, and I'm going to do that."

Mom beamed and gave Yvonne a big hug. "I am so proud of you, honey."

Yvonne looked pleased. "Now, where's the apple pie?" she asked. "I know you made one—I can smell it. Can I have a piece?"

Mom wrinkled her brow. "Apple pie? I didn't make any . . . oh, it's the candle." She pointed to the candle burning on the mantle. "It's an apple pie spice candle."

"Oh." Yvonne was disappointed. "It makes me hungry for apple pie," she said.

Mom smiled. "Your life is like that candle," she said. "The candle makes you hungry for apple pie; your actions and attitudes made your teacher hungry for what you have—I think that's why she wants to come to church sometime. She just doesn't realize yet that what she's really hungry for is a relationship with Jesus." Mom looked at the clock. "Come on—we'll make an apple pie before dinner." *BJW*

HOW ABOUT YOU?

Do your actions and attitudes send out a fragrance that makes people want to be around you? Would your behavior cause anyone to want to know Jesus? Your life should be a testimony for him.

MEMORIZE:

"Wherever we go he uses us to tell others about the Lord and to spread the Good News like a sweet perfume."

2 Corinthians 2:14

Be a Sweet Fragrance

December

16

Canning the Word

Read 2 Timothy 2:15; 3:14-17

"What a vacation this has turned out to be!" Danielle moaned. "When we moved to the country, I thought I would ride the horse, wade in the creek, and have fun. Instead I've been snapping beans, husking corn, shelling peas, and now peeling peaches for canning."

Mom smiled. "Fall will come soon, and then you can relax," she said. "And when winter comes, you'll be glad we canned all this food."

"I doubt it," Danielle replied. "We'll never eat all this."

Fall came, and Danielle returned to school. In November the snow came. Then, after Christmas, a real blizzard began, and soon Danielle and her family were snowed in.

"Oh, Mom, what are we gonna do?" Danielle wailed as she stared through the window a few days later. "It may be days before we can get out!"

Mom nodded her head toward the fireplace and then the pantry. "Well, we've got lots of wood for the fire," she said, "and plenty of good, home-canned food to eat."

"That's true!" Danielle agreed. "I sure am glad we did all that canning last summer." Then she sighed. "But I'm so bored. Isn't there anything interesting we can do?"

"You could work on your memory verses," her mom suggested.

"Yeah—but I don't see why we have to learn so many verses," Danielle said. "We've got lots of Bibles around. Anytime we need a verse, we can just look it up."

"Remember last summer, when you grumbled about all that canning?" Mom asked. "Now that we're snowed in and can't get to the store, we're glad we have lots of food stored up. It's the same way with the Word of God. You never know when hard times will come, or a temptation, or an opportunity to witness. At those times, you'll be glad to have those precious verses stored up in your heart." *BJW*

HOW ABOUT YOU?

How many Bible verses do you know by heart? Could you learn more? Hiding God's Word in your heart will bring many rewards. Don't just memorize the words, but think about the meaning, and ask God to make the verses real in your own life.

MEMORIZE:

"The word of God is full of living power. It is sharper than the sharpest knife, cutting deep into our innermost thoughts and desires." Hebrews 4:12

Memorize God's Word

A Worthy Gift

Read Deuteronomy 10:12-14

Kyra's Sunday school teacher asked the class some questions. "What is the most precious thing you own?" asked Mrs. Raye. "Is it your bicycle? Some jewelry? Money? A pet? I'm going to read a story to you. See if your ideas change as you listen."

Mrs. Raye began to read.

"Queen Helena ruled a tiny kingdom. She was the last of her family and had no heir to her throne, so she decided to search for a child who loved and served God as she did. 'I am looking to God to help me choose the next ruler of this land,' she told her people. 'Any child who wishes to become the next ruler must bring to me his most precious possession—a gift worthy to be given to your queen, and also to God himself! The child who brings such a gift will be the next ruler.'

"When the appointed day came, hundreds of children waited with their gifts. One by one, they presented them to the queen. She was offered money, power, land—all kinds of things—but all were turned away. 'They are not worthy,' said Queen Helena. 'It is getting late. I will see one more child today.'

"A young girl came slowly into the room. 'Your Majesty,' she murmured, 'I didn't plan to come today, because I am very poor and thought I couldn't possibly offer a gift you would accept. But as I sat praying, it seemed that God told me I should offer to you what I have already given him.' The girl knelt before the queen. 'I lay at the feet of my queen a heart of love and devotion and a life of service.'

" 'Rise to your feet,' said Queen Helena. 'A heart of devotion and love, a life of service—these are the qualities that can rightly rule a nation. God accepts them, and so do I. You will be the queen; your gift alone is worthy!' "

As Mrs. Raye closed the book, she smiled. "Search your own hearts," she said. "Give God the things that please him—your love, devotion, and service." *HCT*

HOW ABOUT YOU?

Do you live for yourself, or have you fully given your heart and life to God? He wants you to love him and faithfully serve him each day.

MEMORIZE:

"What does the Lord your God require of you? He requires you to fear him, to live according to his will, to love and worship him with all your heart and soul." Deuteronomy 10:12

Love and Serve God

December

18

Cold Hot Chocolate

Read 1 Timothy 4:11-16

Adele stirred her cup of hot chocolate. "Why the sad face?" she asked when her little sister came in.

"No reason," Alexa replied. She looked at the floor.

"Want some hot chocolate?" asked Adele.

"No thanks," Alexa murmured. She fidgeted uneasily on her chair. "We cut across Mr. Jordan's lawn on the way home from school," she blurted out at last.

Adele set her cup down. "You did!" she exclaimed. "You know that makes him angry. Why did you do that?"

"Well, the kids say there isn't anything wrong with taking a shortcut and that Mr. Jordan has to learn not to be so cross," said Alexa, her eyes downcast. She paused, then added, "So it must be okay."

"Now how do you figure that?" Adele asked gently.

"They're older than me," replied Alexa.

"And that means they know more and are always right?" asked Adele. Alexa's shoulders drooped lower, but she nodded her head. Adele looked thoughtful. "Are you sure you don't want some hot chocolate?" she asked. "The water's finally cold enough."

Alexa wrinkled her brow. "You mean the water's hot enough," she corrected her sister.

"No. It's cold enough," said Adele. "I'll get it." Alexa followed Adele into the kitchen and watched her take a pitcher of ice water out of the fridge.

"Adele, it's supposed to be hot chocolate," protested Alexa. "The water has to be hot!"

"Really, Alexa, you should listen to me," scolded Adele. "I'm older. That means I'm right!" For the first time since coming in, Alexa smiled. Adele smiled, too, as she sat down across from Alexa. "Can you see that 'older' doesn't always mean right?" asked Adele. "Do you remember what Pastor said Sunday?"

Alexa's brow furrowed. "He said that no matter how old or young we are, we can know and do what God says is right."

"Yes, and that includes you, Lexie," replied Adele. She smiled as she hugged Alexa. "Now, how about some hot chocolate? Or would you prefer to apologize to Mr. Jordan first?" *MJM*

HOW ABOUT YOU?

Are you tempted to do wrong things because older friends say they aren't wrong? If the Bible says it's wrong, don't do it, no matter what others say. Do what's right.

MEMORIZE:

"Don't let anyone think less of you because you are young. Be an example to all believers." 1 Timothy 4:12

Do the Right Thing

No Room

Read Luke 2:1-7

"Pam, how would you like to have a roommate for a few days?" Mom asked when Pam came in after school. "Pastor Rollins is looking for places for the Jones children to stay while their mother is in the hospital. I thought maybe we could take Hannah."

"Oh, no!" Pam groaned. "I suppose she'll have to tag along everywhere I go. Maybe if she were my age it would be different, but as it is, she'll spoil everything!" Grumbling, Pam went to her room.

That evening, Pam's family read part of the Christmas story during family devotions. Pam thought about it when she went to bed. In her mind, she could almost see Joseph's disappointment when he asked for a room and the innkeeper turned him away. She imagined the innkeeper saying, "Sorry. We have no room," and she wondered if it was the innkeeper who suggested they stay in the stable.

As Pam turned over to go to sleep, she seemed to continue to hear, "No room! No room for the Son of God!" And some words from a recent memory verse echoed through her mind—"Whatever you did for one of the least of these . . . you did for me." She tried to forget those words, but she could not.

When Pam entered the kitchen the next morning, she smiled at her mother. "I hope you're going to tell Pastor Rollins to send Hannah to us," she said.

Mom smiled back. "Well, I'm certainly glad you've decided that," she said, "but what brought about the change in you?"

"I thought a lot about the innkeeper last night," Pam said, "and I don't want to make the same mistake he did."

"Innkeeper?" Mom asked. "Oh, you mean the one who didn't have room for Jesus."

Pam nodded. "I know Jesus isn't coming here—just Hannah," she said, "but I remembered, too, that Jesus said, 'Whatever you did for one of the least of these . . . you did for me.' That means Hannah, too, so I want to make room for her in my life this Christmas." *BJW*

HOW ABOUT YOU?

Have you made room in your heart for Jesus? Don't let the "busy-ness" of the season take too much space. Make room for others, too—your neighbor, a member of your class, an older person who is lonely, or someone who has less fun than you do. By taking time to help them, you are pleasing Jesus.

MEMORIZE:
"Whatever you did for one of the least of these . . . you did for me."
Matthew 25:40, NIV

Show Love to Others

December

20

White Christmas

Read Psalm 51:1-7

Christmas had always been one of Delia's favorite family times, but this year she was feeling blue. As she dragged her feet into the living room, the rest of the family heard her mutter, "I just can't get into the Christmas spirit. How can anyone celebrate Christmas in eighty-degree weather? I wish we had never moved to Florida in the first place!"

Mom put an arm around Delia. "I know it's not the same here as in Vermont," she said understandingly, "but it's beautiful here, too—just in a different way. Besides, honey, for Christians the Christmas spirit doesn't depend on the weather, but on truths that never change."

"That's right," Dad agreed, "and in a certain sense we actually are going to have a white Christmas."

"White Christmas?" Delia asked, imagining a crazy scene of Florida palm trees covered in heavy Vermont snow. "What do you mean?"

"The prophet Isaiah wrote about God's forgiveness and what it means to those who trust him," Dad explained. He picked up a Bible from the table and turned to Isaiah. "Here, Delia, read chapter one, verse eighteen."

Taking the Bible in her hands, Delia read, " 'Come now, and let us argue this out,' says the Lord. 'No matter how deep the stain of your sins, I can remove it. I can make you as clean as freshly fallen snow.' " She looked up.

"You see, Delia," Dad said, "those of us who have asked Jesus to save us and forgive our sins have a heart that God has made as white as snow." He smiled. "And that's more important than having a white Christmas outside, don't you agree?"

Delia sighed, but she nodded as she took a box of decorations from her dad. "Well, I still miss the snow," she said, "but I am glad that Jesus came!" And in her heart Delia thanked Jesus for reminding her that she would have the best kind of white Christmas. *DLR*

HOW ABOUT YOU?

Where does your Christmas "spirit" come from? Do you think more about what the weather will be like, what clothes you will wear, or what presents you will get than you do about the real meaning of Christmas? If you have accepted Jesus as Savior, let the real joy of Christmas come from knowing him. He has made your heart as white as snow!

MEMORIZE:

"No matter how deep the stain of your sins, I can remove it. I can make you as clean as freshly fallen snow." Isaiah 1:18

Christmas Celebrates Jesus

A Shared Gift

Read Deuteronomy 15:7-11

Misty and Dave knew they wouldn't get everything they wanted for Christmas, but they also knew their parents were generous. Many items would appear under the Christmas tree. But as Misty looked forward to receiving lots of nice things, she began to worry about the little girl who lived next door. "Lynne will be lucky if she gets anything," she told Dave one day. "Don't you think we should do something for her this Christmas? Her dad's been out of work for over six months."

"Well, that's their problem," Dave reasoned. "We can't help it. We can't give her dad a job!"

Misty just couldn't give up that easily. "But she's our friend!" she protested. "We go to church and Sunday school with her. I still think we should do something for her."

As Christmas came closer and the pile of presents under the tree grew, Misty felt more concern for Lynne. Finally she went to her parents and asked if she could give some of her presents to Lynne. "Then she'll have some things to open Christmas morning, too," she explained.

Mom and Dad were surprised—but pleased—at Misty's request. Still, they were cautious. "Misty, you know you won't get as much as Dave if you do this," Mom reminded her. "Will you feel bad when he has more presents to open than you do?"

"I don't know," Misty replied honestly. "I might, but it's something I think Jesus wants me to do." So, with her parents' guidance, Misty picked out a few presents and delivered them to the house next door.

On Christmas, Misty's best present came when Lynne stopped in. She was wearing a dress that could have been Misty's. It had hurt Misty a little to see Dave get more presents than she did, but now the smile on Lynne's face made it worth it all. Deep inside she felt good. She had learned the joy of sharing—that it really is more blessed to give than to receive! *REP*

HOW ABOUT YOU?

Have you been more interested in getting gifts this Christmas than giving them? Have you ever noticed that the more you get, the more you want? Receiving gifts can never give as much satisfaction as giving gifts. Look for someone with whom you can share.

MEMORIZE:
"It is more blessed to give than to receive." Acts 20:35

Share with Others

December

22

Worth the Wait

Read Luke 2:25-33

"Oh, Dad! I don't think I can wait another day! How much longer is it till Christmas?" Jessica asked the same question for the third time that Saturday.

"Jessica," Dad said firmly, "it's still three more days, just like it was the last two times you asked me!"

"But Dad! I just can't wait!" Jessica exclaimed. "It's been a whole year since we saw Uncle Jim and Aunt Midge. And Grandma and Grandpa Turner haven't been here since summer!"

"Well, I'm glad to hear that your excitement over Christmas isn't only due to the gifts you'll get," Dad said. "But how about helping me make cookies? That will make one day go more quickly anyway."

The next afternoon Jessica was again getting impatient. Mom sighed. "Go get your Bible and look for the word 'wait' in the concordance," she suggested. "Pick out three verses about waiting and memorize them, Jessica. One verse for each day until Christmas!" This kept Jessica busy quite a while. She was surprised to see how many times the word "wait" was used in the Bible.

That evening at family devotions Mom suggested reading a passage of Scripture about a man who was waiting for Jesus to be born (see today's reading). And Dad explained that it was important to learn to wait patiently. He also talked about Old Testament Jews who had waited hundreds of years for Jesus, their Messiah, to be born.

The next day, Grandma and Grandpa Turner arrived. "Oh, having you here two days early will make it much easier to wait for Christmas Day!" Jessica said excitedly.

Finally Christmas Day came and went. As Mom tucked Jessica into bed that night, Jessica yawned, "Oh, Mom! Today has been perfect!" she said sleepily. "Christmas was worth all the waiting."

Mom smiled. "Good," she said. "Let's thank Jesus for coming to earth that first Christmas—and also that this Christmas he taught you something about waiting!" *REP*

HOW ABOUT YOU?

Do you ever find it hard to wait? Sometimes the Lord just wants you to wait patiently and quietly for him to act in your life. Learning to wait patiently for Christmas can help you learn to wait patiently in all areas of your life.

MEMORIZE:

"Be still before the Lord and wait patiently for him." Psalm 37:7, NIV

Learn Patience

Security

Read Psalm 125:1-2; Proverbs 3:24

"Maya, I'd like you to put Matt down for his nap today, please," Mom said. "I need to make an important phone call."

"Okay," agreed Maya. "Nap time!" she announced to the energetic toddler. Laughing, Matt toddled away, wanting his sister to chase him. Maya caught him quickly. She took him to his crib, set him down, and raised the side. Little Matt scrambled around on the mattress, ignoring soft toys and stuffed animals. "Sweet dreams," Maya whispered, backing out of his room.

"Blankee!" Matt protested. "Blankee!"

As Maya peeked in, Matt pulled himself up and began to shake the rail. Maya frowned and shook her head. *Where did he leave his blanket?* She wondered. She checked the TV room. She dug through the toy box. She searched the hall closet. She looked under the dining room table and on the chair seats. Finally, she found the blanket in a lower cupboard in the kitchen.

As soon as Matt saw his "blankee," his crying stopped. He dropped to the mattress, clutching the blanket in his arms. After a few shaky breaths, he smiled contentedly at Maya. "Sweet dreams," Maya said again as she left.

"Matt had to have his blankee before he settled down," Maya told her mother later. "Good thing I found it, or he never would have gone to sleep."

Mom nodded. "That blanket is his security," she said. "I guess we all need security—even grown-ups! What's your security, Maya?"

Maya shrugged. "You, I guess," she said. "I know you're here to help me if I need you." She grinned and added, "You're my 'blankee,' I guess. What's yours?"

Mom smiled. "Well, we all find some security in family and friends—but a Christian's real security is in God and in his love and forgiveness," she said. "He's always available." She ruffled Maya's hair. "Quite frankly, I don't know how I'd manage without him!" *MMI*

HOW ABOUT YOU?

Even parents can't be with you all the time, but God can. He's with you twenty-four hours a day, seven days a week! Depend on his unfailing love and presence in your life.

God's Love Is Always Available

December

24

Choice of a Lifetime

Read Psalm 90:4-6, 10-12

"You always do that, Mom," Claire moaned.

"Do what?" Mom asked, waiting for traffic to pass.

"You drive up to the road where you need to turn," replied Claire, "and then you wait for the traffic to go by even if you could go before it gets here!"

Mom made the turn onto the street. "Well, maybe I could have gone ahead of those cars," she said, "but I didn't want to take a chance on having an accident."

"But we always wait forever!" Claire protested.

Mom laughed. "I know you're eager to get to Kara's party, honey, but we waited only a minute—an important minute."

Claire frowned. "What do you mean?"

"Imagine what could have happened if I chose to do the wrong thing during that minute," Mom said. "We could have been in an accident and been hurt—or worse! Then you'd have missed Kara's party completely. Instead, here we are, driving up Kara's street, and you'll enjoy the party!"

Claire laughed. "I suppose you're right," she said.

That evening Claire and her brother joined Mom and Dad for their family Bible study. They read from Psalm 90 (see today's Scripture reading). "You know, Mom," said Claire, "that's like the important minute when we waited for traffic today!"

Rob shook his head. "Claire's a little weird," he teased. He looked at his sister. "What are you talking about?" he asked.

Claire laughed and told Dad and Rob about the conversation she'd had with Mom. "The verses we just read say that our lifetime on earth is really short—like that minute when we waited for traffic," Claire explained. "It was important for Mom to make the right decision in that minute, and it's important to make the right decision in the short time we live on earth, too. We need to accept Jesus while we're here. That decision makes all the difference in how we'll spend life here—and especially how we'll spend eternity."

"You're right, Claire," Dad said. "Good thinking!" *PAP*

HOW ABOUT YOU?

Do you think you've got lots of time to decide to become a Christian? Life on earth is very short compared to eternity, and you can't even be sure you'll get to be very old. You don't know how long you'll live. Now is the time to trust Jesus.

MEMORIZE:
"Now is the day of salvation."
2 Corinthians 6:2, NIV

Choose Jesus Today

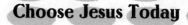

Home at Last

Read 2 Corinthians 4:6-9, 14; 5:1

"It's snowing," Terri exclaimed. She and her parents were traveling to spend Christmas Day with her grandparents. "I hope Grandpa takes us on a sleigh ride."

They arrived at their destination a few hours later. The day was bursting with good things, just like the Christmas stockings hanging on the fireplace mantle. Delicious food, plenty of company, wonderful presents, a special time of devotions—and the sleigh ride Terri had hoped for—all added to the fun of the day. They all had a great time, and at the end of the day, they hated to leave.

Several inches of snow blanketed the highway, and Dad told them he wished they had started home sooner. The snow swirled around, making visibility poor. Traffic crawled, and one time the car almost slid into the ditch before Dad got it under control. Tension mounted, and everyone was praying that they would get home safely.

"Let's sing to keep our minds on the Lord instead of the weather," Mom suggested. As they sang, they were surprised to find how much it helped. It was early the next morning before Dad wearily pulled into the driveway.

"Home at last!" Terri exclaimed. "I never thought home would look so good."

"It sure is good to be here," Dad agreed.

Mom smiled. "You know the songs we sang about heaven?" she began. "I think this is how we'll feel when we get there. There are many problems and stresses here on earth, but they will be behind us when we get to heaven. We'll never feel helpless or afraid again."

"Right," Dad agreed. "We'll really be 'home at last.' How awesome will that be!" *JLH*

HOW ABOUT YOU?

Do you ever have bad times that seem unending? Don't get discouraged by problems on earth. If you've accepted Jesus as your Savior, learn to keep your mind on him and your future in heaven instead of on the problems you're facing. Trust him, and take courage and look forward to the day you'll go "home" to heaven.

Look Forward to Being in Heaven

MEMORIZE:

"Our present troubles are quite small and won't last very long. Yet they produce for us an immeasurably great glory that will last forever!"

2 Corinthians 4:17

December

26

Read 2 Timothy 2:24-26

Snowball

Kristin was thrilled! For Christmas, she had been given a puppy! She'd named the tiny ball of white fur Snowball. She decided to start training Snowball immediately so that she'd become the best-behaved puppy in the whole neighborhood.

"Come, Snowball. Come here!" Kristin said it over and over, but the dog just looked at her with shy, blue eyes. Kristin was getting impatient! "Snowball, come here!" She thundered the words so loudly that Snowball let out a screech and went flying to another room.

Kristin's father came in from the kitchen. "Kristin, if you're going to act that way we'll have to take the puppy away from you," Dad said sternly. "Snowball doesn't understand you. You can't speak to her gently ten times and then suddenly scream at her! You need to have patience."

Kristin sighed. "I'm sorry," she said. "I just wish I could get Snowball to obey me."

"Well, honey," Dad said with a smile, "the proper way to train the dog is to show her a piece of food. Then say the same words of instruction over and over. Be sure your tone is always the same, too. When the puppy responds and does what you say, encourage her by saying 'Good, Snowball,' and give her the food. But she isn't going to learn everything right away. It will take time and patience!"

Kristin did what her father suggested. After a long time, Snowball did learn to obey.

"You know, Kristin," Dad said as he watched one day, "watching you work with Snowball reminds me of how the Lord Jesus has to work with us. It's a good thing he has patience, because we are often slow in doing what he wants us to do. When we do obey, it pleases him, just as Snowball pleases you when she obeys you."

Kristin grinned. "Hey, that's neat," she said with a smile. "And since God is patient with us, I guess we should be patient with each other, too, shouldn't we? I'll ask him to help me be patient with Snowball—and with people." *JLH*

HOW ABOUT YOU?

Are you impatient? Do you always have to have everything right now? If someone is slower than you, do you get upset with that person? Work on your attitude, and ask the Lord to help you learn to be patient. It's a quality that pleases him—one he wants you to develop.

MEMORIZE:
"Be patient with everyone."
1 Thessalonians 5:14

Learn to Be Patient

Focus Trouble

Read James 4:7-8

April loved basketball! She loved to play it, she loved to read stories about it, and she loved to watch it on TV. Basketball was always on her mind. When she was supposed to be doing science questions at school, she would be working on basketball plays. And she heard very little of the sermon at church because she was thinking about basketball.

April's eyes recently had been bothering her, so Mom made an appointment with Dr. Jackson, an eye doctor who was also April's Sunday school teacher. Dr. Jackson chatted with April as he slipped different lenses in front of her eyes. "Are you still crazy about basketball, April?" he asked.

"Sure am, Doc," April replied. "I love it more than anything else in the world."

"More than you love God?" asked Dr. Jackson.

"Naw," murmured April, but she looked down at the floor. She was embarrassed because she knew she wasn't telling the truth.

"Hey, let's do an experiment, April," the doctor suggested. "I want you to focus your eyes intently on the big *E* on my chart while you read my diploma to me."

April looked around. "But Dr. Jackson, I can't!" she said. "Your diploma is hanging on the back wall. You can't focus your eyes on two things at the same time. Even I know that!"

Dr. Jackson chuckled. "You're right, April," he said. "It is impossible to focus your eyes on two things at once. It's also impossible for a person to please God if she tries to focus her heart on two things at the same time. God tells us to focus our hearts and minds on him, and not to be double-minded."

April looked confused for a minute. Then she realized what Dr. Jackson meant. "I think I get the point," April replied. "You're saying that if I love basketball with all my heart, and still try to love God with all my heart, I'll be double-minded—right?"

"Right," replied Dr. Jackson. "I'll be praying that God will help you keep your mind on him more than on basketball. Okay?"

With a grin, April nodded. *REP*

HOW ABOUT YOU?

Are you double-minded? In other words, is it hard for you to concentrate on God because your mind wanders to something else? Obey the commands given in today's Scripture reading, and God will help you to be single-minded for him.

Focus on God

MEMORIZE:
"A double minded man is unstable in all his ways." James 1:8, KJV

December
28

Not Impossible

Read Luke 18:27-30

Even though her parents were not Christians, Eleanor had dedicated her life to the Lord. Now fourteen years old, she felt sure he wanted her to serve him on the mission field. *I'm going to save my baby-sitting money for my education,* she thought. *I know Mom and Dad won't help.* But the money Eleanor saved soon disappeared—her father found out about it and took it! He not only used his own salary for alcohol, but also took the grocery money and any other money he could get his hands on to support his drinking habit. *I'll never get to be a missionary!* Eleanor thought sadly. She was very discouraged.

Her Sunday school teacher knew about Eleanor's problems at home. "I'd like to give you a book to read," she said one day.

Eleanor took the book and began reading that very day. It was the story of a missionary, Mary Slessor. How familiar the story sounded! Mary's father had been an alcoholic, too. He had used his own earnings, plus any other money he found in the house, to buy liquor for himself and his friends. Sometimes he was very cruel, beating his own wife and children.

Eleanor sighed. *At least Dad doesn't beat anyone,* she thought. She was thankful for that. As Eleanor continued to read the book, her own determination to keep her missionary goal began to grow. *If God could help Mary Slessor to become a missionary when her problems seemed bigger than she could handle, then he certainly can help me, too,* she thought.

Eleanor began again to save her baby-sitting earnings to use for her education some day. She didn't know how she would ever get enough money to go to Bible college, but she knew that if God wanted her to go, he would somehow supply her needs. And that was all she needed to know. *RIJ*

HOW ABOUT YOU?

Have you read about some of the old-time missionaries? There are many good lessons to be learned from their lives. Eleanor needed to learn to trust God, rather than herself. Have you learned this lesson? You may never become a missionary, but learning to trust Christ is an important step in the life of every Christian.

MEMORIZE:

"What is impossible from a human perspective is possible with God."
Luke 18:27

Give God Your Future

Hidden Inside

Read Ephesians 2:4-10

"Hi, Mom. What's for supper?" Casey chirped as she came into the kitchen. Mom grinned. The first thing Casey asked when she got home from school was the same every day. "I'm so-o-o hungry when I get off the bus," added Casey. Walking to the stove she started lifting lids off the pots and peering inside. "Wow, is this what I think it is? Are we having tacos?" At Mom's nod, Casey let out a whoop.

"Now, young lady, how about scooting upstairs and getting changed?" Mom said. "Then come down and help me cut up the rest of the stuff."

Casey grinned, grabbed her books, and bounded up the steps. "Well, what should I do first?" she asked when she reappeared.

Mom pointed toward the tomatoes. "You may cut those up into that blue bowl," she said. "They're already washed."

Picking up a shiny red tomato, Casey began to slice it. "Ugh, Mom! It's all rotten in the middle!" she exclaimed.

Mom came over to see. "Hmmmm, that's funny," she said. "It looks perfect on the outside—there isn't even a bruise. But on the inside, it's rotten. Well, we can't use that one."

Later, as Mom added tomatoes to her taco, she said, "You know, Casey, people are often kind of like that rotten tomato."

Casey gave her mother a puzzled glance. "I hope you're not talking about me!"

Mom laughed. "A lot of times people put on a good show. They do good works, and they look fine on the outside," she explained. "But God sees their hearts. He knows that on the inside they really are rotten. He says that even the good things we do in our own strength are like filthy rags."

"So they're useless—like that rotten tomato," Casey said.

"Right," Mom said. "We can't fix the tomato and make it good, so we just dump it. But God can fix people. When they trust him, he gives them his goodness and they are whole and useful again. Isn't that great?" *CPH*

HOW ABOUT YOU?

Do you look good to yourself and other people because you do a lot of good things? Do you expect God to allow you into heaven for that reason? It doesn't work that way. He sees your heart—he knows you're a sinner. You need Jesus. Confess your sin to him and ask him to forgive you and help you become more like him. He wants to do that.

MEMORIZE:

"We are all infected and impure with sin. When we proudly display our righteous deeds, we find they are but filthy rags." Isaiah 64:6

**Good Works
Can't Save You**

December

30

Not Greek to God

Read Acts 17:24-27

"Yesu yana kaunar yara," sang Rochelle.

"What language is that anyway?" asked her friend Geri. "Like my grandma always says when she doesn't understand something . . . 'It's Greek to me!' "

Rochelle laughed. "It's not Greek," she corrected. "It's Hausa. I learned the song from my Aunt Mary and Uncle Steve, who are missionaries in Nigeria."

"What does it mean?" Geri wanted to know.

Rochelle smiled. "It means, 'Jesus, he loves the children,' " she explained.

"Oh, that's almost the same as one of our songs!" exclaimed Geri. "The tune sounded familiar, too."

Rochelle nodded. "Aunt Mary teaches a class of Nigerian girls who are the same age as we are. She says one girl reminds her of me, because we act so much alike—and the neatest part is that both of us love the Lord. We're going to write to each other, and Aunt Mary will translate for us. It'll be fun having a Nigerian pen pal."

"I guess maybe we're not really so different from kids in other countries as we think we are," observed Geri.

Rochelle shook her head. "Aunt Mary always reminds me that we're all the same to the Lord," she said. "He loves Nigerian children, and all the children in the world, just like he loves us."

"Right," agreed Geri. "Just like your song said. How did that go again?" Rochelle sang the strange words again, and she laughed as Geri tried it, too.

"That's okay. You can laugh at me," said Geri. She grinned and added, "I bet the Nigerians would laugh at you!"

"Probably," agreed Rochelle. "But who cares? God understands—even when we mispronounce all those words. It's not Greek to him."

"Let's make it a duet," suggested Geri. And they did. *LMW*

HOW ABOUT YOU?

Have you ever really thought about children all over the world who love the Lord? They're like you in many ways. They memorize the same verses and even sing some of the same songs, but in a different language. Always remember that Jesus loves you—and everyone else.

MEMORIZE:
"For God so loved the world that he gave his only Son." John 3:16

God Loves You—and Everyone Else

Show It

Read Philippians 2:13-16

"There's a parking space," Morgan said. She pointed. "Right there by the door."

"Great!" said Maria. Mom had allowed her to take the car to school, and she had to stop for some groceries before heading home. But as Maria drove toward the empty spot, she saw a blue and white sign. "We're not allowed to use a handi-capped space," she said.

"Oh, come on!" Morgan whined. "We're in a hurry." Just then another car pulled into the space. "That guy doesn't look handicapped," exclaimed Morgan as they saw a man get out of the car and walk toward the store. "We could just as well have parked there!"

"You can't always see a person's handicap," said Maria, "and he does have a sticker." She drove on and soon found another place to park.

When they reached home, Morgan told Mom about the parking spaces. "I don't see why we couldn't park there," Morgan grumbled. "That man didn't look any more handicapped than I do. He didn't have a cane or a walker or anything!"

"Oh, Morgan! You've been grumbling all afternoon," said Maria. "Like I told you, some handicaps don't show—like heart or breathing problems."

"That's true," Mom said as she saw Morgan make a face at her big sister. "There are also handicaps such as bad attitudes."

"Bad attitudes?" Morgan asked. "I don't get it."

"When Christians display bad attitudes and actions, they're handicapped in their testimony for the Lord," Mom explained. "It makes it hard for others to tell that they know the Lord. It's too bad when that happens."

Morgan felt sure Mom was talking about her, so she tried to make a joke of it. "Maybe they should have handicap stickers and special parking places, too," she mumbled.

"I don't think so," Maria said dryly.

Mom shook her head. "It certainly wouldn't be a sticker to be proud of," she said. "We need to tell people we're Christians, and we also need to show it by our actions." *SN*

HOW ABOUT YOU?

Do your actions and attitudes show that you love Jesus? Do you cheerfully put others before yourself and act unselfishly? When you show others you love Jesus by the way you treat them, it makes your witness more credible.

Tell—and Show—That You Love God

MEMORIZE:

"For God is working in you, giving you the desire to obey him and the power to do what pleases him."

Philippians 2:13

Index of Topics

Index of Scripture Readings

Index of Memory Verses

Acts 20:35 *December 21*
Romans 1:16 *April 26, September 15*
Romans 3:23 *February 17*
Romans 5:1 *May 31*
Romans 5:9 *November 27*
Romans 6:11 *May 11*
Romans 6:12 *October 25*
Romans 6:13 *February 5*
Romans 6:16 *October 21*
Romans 6:23 *August 26*
Romans 8:2 *July 9*
Romans 8:16 *March 1*
Romans 8:17 *May 8*
Romans 8:26 *January 8*
Romans 8:28 *November 30*
Romans 8:38-39 *October 31*
Romans 10:13 *January 25*
Romans 12:1 *December 5*
Romans 12:10 *November 25*
Romans 12:13 *July 29*
Romans 12:17 *April 15*
Romans 12:19 *December 7*
Romans 12:20 *May 20*
Romans 13:1 *September 18*
Romans 13:13 *July 28*
Romans 13:14 *August 4*
Romans 14:7 *May 7*
Romans 14:13 *May 28*
Romans 15:2 *June 15*
Romans 15:4 *October 26*
1 Corinthians 3:5-6 *February 23*
1 Corinthians 3:6 *September 4*
1 Corinthians 3:9 *August 7, October 5*
1 Corinthians 3:11 *November 28*
1 Corinthians 4:14 *March 23*
1 Corinthians 6:20 *July 14*
1 Corinthians 9:22 *December 10*
1 Corinthians 10:31 *February 8*
1 Corinthians 12:22 *October 22*
1 Corinthians 13:12 *June 1*
1 Corinthians 15:57 *April 25, September 11*

1 Corinthians 15:58 *August 8*
1 Corinthians 16:13 *March 14*
2 Corinthians 2:14 *December 15*
2 Corinthians 2:15 *January 11*
2 Corinthians 4:5 *February 2*
2 Corinthians 4:16 *May 17*
2 Corinthians 4:17 *December 25*
2 Corinthians 5:7 *October 11*
2 Corinthians 5:8 *April 19*
2 Corinthians 5:17 *May 19, September 30*
2 Corinthians 6:2 *December 24*
2 Corinthians 6:14 *June 18*
2 Corinthians 8:12 *June 10*
2 Corinthians 8:14 *March 30*
2 Corinthians 12:9 *June 12*
Galatians 3:26 *January 20*
Galatians 3:28 *November 22*
Galatians 4:4-5 *June 9*
Galatians 5:15 *August 14*
Galatians 5:22-23 *February 3*
Galatians 6:7 *April 2, July 6*
Galatians 6:9 *July 26, November 21*
Galatians 6:10 *June 26*
Ephesians 2:8 *April 29*
Ephesians 2:8-9 *September 19*
Ephesians 4:11-12 *March 2*
Ephesians 4:15 *January 2*
Ephesians 4:26 *January 23, October 8*
Ephesians 4:29 *April 14*
Ephesians 4:31 *February 18*
Ephesians 4:32 *June 11, November 18*
Ephesians 5:1 *March 19*
Ephesians 5:2 *February 19*
Ephesians 5:6 *April 1*
Ephesians 5:11 *July 24*
Ephesians 5:15 *October 16*
Ephesians 5:18 *September 22*
Ephesians 5:20 *November 16*
Ephesians 6:1 *July 8*
Ephesians 6:7 *November 11*
Philippians 2:3 *July 15*

Philippians 2:13 *August 29,*
December 31
Philippians 2:14 *January 30, April 23*
Philippians 2:15 *March 22*
Philippians 3:10 *June 20*
Philippians 3:13-14 *October 20*
Philippians 4:11 *March 9*
Philippians 4:13 *August 24*
Colossians 2:3 *June 23*
Colossians 3:2 *September 14*
Colossians 3:12 *August 13*
Colossians 3:13 *February 6, June 17*
Colossians 3:15 *July 16*
Colossians 3:20 *February 9, August 30*
Colossians 3:23 *July 1, November 24*
1 Thessalonians 4:13 *June 5*
1 Thessalonians 5:6 *June 6*
1 Thessalonians 5:14 *December 26*
1 Thessalonians 5:17-18 *November 13*
2 Thessalonians 3:3 *July 23,*
September 29
1 Timothy 2:1-2 *October 2*
1 Timothy 4:12 *June 4, December 18*
1 Timothy 4:14 *July 30*
1 Timothy 6:6 *July 12*
1 Timothy 6:8 *May 6*
1 Timothy 6:18 *July 27*
2 Timothy 1:7 *January 29*
2 Timothy 1:8 *January 17*
2 Timothy 2:5 *November 7*
2 Timothy 2:19 *September 16*
2 Timothy 2:24 *July 21*
2 Timothy 3:16 *April 17*
Titus 2:12 *January 28*
Titus 3:2 *September 8*
Titus 3:5 *May 21*
Philemon 1:6 *September 17*
Hebrews 4:12 *September 2,*
December 16
Hebrews 6:10 *March 7*
Hebrews 8:12 *August 3*
Hebrews 9:27 *November 20*

Hebrews 10:23 *October 10*
Hebrews 10:25 *August 31*
Hebrews 12:1 *March 24*
Hebrews 12:7 *April 28*
Hebrews 12:11 *September 3*
Hebrews 13:5 *April 6*
Hebrews 13:17 *December 4*
James 1:8 *December 27*
James 1:19 *June 29*
James 2:18 *October 30*
James 4:7 *May 12*
James 4:8 *May 13*
James 4:17 *August 16*
James 5:12 *October 13*
James 5:16 *February 20, May 27*
1 Peter 2:2 *August 27*
1 Peter 2:23 *November 14*
1 Peter 3:4 *January 18, September 24*
1 Peter 3:8 *May 10*
1 Peter 4:10 *June 8*
1 Peter 5:7 *February 10, August 6*
1 Peter 5:8 *October 12*
1 Peter 5:14 *October 9*
2 Peter 1:4 *November 17*
2 Peter 1:6 *May 22*
2 Peter 3:18 *October 29*
1 John 1:3 *April 20*
1 John 1:5 *March 21*
1 John 1:6 *March 10*
1 John 1:7 *August 28*
1 John 1:9 *April 8*
1 John 3:18 *July 3*
1 John 4:1 *December 8*
1 John 4:4 *October 6*
1 John 4:10 *February 14*
1 John 4:11 *December 13*
1 John 5:7 *August 17*
Jude 21 *July 2*
Revelation 2:10 *June 28*
Revelation 21:4 *March 17*
Revelation 22:12 *June 19*